TALKING WITH STUDENTS IN CONFLICT

LIFE SPACE CRISIS INTERVENTION

Third Edition

Nicholas J. Long

Mary M. Wood

Frank A. Fecser

Signe Whitson

© 2021, 2001, 1991 by PRO-ED, Inc.
1301 W. 25th St., Suite 300
Austin, TX 78705-4248
800-897-3202 Fax 800-397-7633
www.proedinc.com

LIBRARY OF CONGRESS CATALOGING-IN-PUBLICATION DATA

Names: Long, Nicholas James, 1929- author. | Wood, Mary M., author. | Fecser, Frank A., author. | Whitson, Signe, author.
Title: Talking with students in conflict : life space crisis intervention / Nicholas J. Long, Mary M. Wood, Frank A. Fecser, Signe Whitson.
Other titles: Life space crisis intervention
Description: Third edition. | Austin, Texas : PRO-ED, Inc., [2021] | "Revised edition of: Life space crisis intervention: talking with students in conflict, c2001." | Includes bibliographical references and index.
Identifiers: LCCN 2021006569 (print) | LCCN 2021006570 (ebook) | ISBN 9781416411901 (paperback) | ISBN 9781416411918 (ebook)
Subjects: LCSH: Educational counseling. | Crisis intervention (Mental health services) | Oral communication.
Classification: LCC LB1027.5 .W59 2021 (print) | LCC LB1027.5 (ebook) | DDC 371.4--dc23
LC record available at https://lccn.loc.gov/2021006569
LC ebook record available at https://lccn.loc.gov/2021006570

Art Director: Jason Crosier
Designer: Bookbright Media
This book is designed in ITC Berkeley Oldstyle and Franklin Gothic

Printed in the United States of America
2 3 4 5 6 7 8 9 10 11   31 30 29 28 27 26 25 24 23 22

CONTENTS

PREFACE

ecause you have chosen to read this book, we assume that you are working in a professional capacity with children and youth. We offer our sincere and profound gratitude for your efforts and your expertise! To work with young people in today's complex world is one of the toughest challenges. There are plenty of problems facing all of us! How to guide young people through stressful situations and traumatic experiences, how to help them make sense out of perceived injustices and inequities around them, how to help them deal with conflict, social isolation, failure, and rejection, how to overcome obstacles to learning and mental health, how to manage pain, loss, anger, and anxiety, and how to make the most of themselves—these are our shared concerns.

Adults who can do these things have something significant to contribute. We focus on Life Space Crisis Intervention (LSCI) in this book because it is a way to accomplish these goals. We use LSCI skills every day in our work because we believe that adults have a responsibility to look beyond the surface behavior of young people and to understand what is really going on in their brains, their bodies, and their lives. We understand that young people inherently want to do well and that one of the most fundamental duties of adults is to teach them the skills they need to constructively manage stress and crisis. This book is our dialogue with you about how we do it.

LSCI is a brain-based, trauma-informed, relationship-building verbal strategy that helps adults turn problem situations into learning opportunities for young people who exhibit challenging behaviors in schools, communities, and in the home. Based on the belief that young people need to feel heard and understood, along with the knowledge that relationships heal, LSCI's six-stage verbal framework provides professionals and parents with a consistent way to build healthy relationships, de-escalate crisis situations, foster self-awareness and insight, develop new social-emotional skills, and bring about long-term behavioral change.

The results are stronger adult-child connections, better emotional regulation, improved peer relationships, lower suspension rates, fewer juvenile justice system referrals, and improvement in an adult's preparedness to use de-escalate crisis situations.

We look forward to sharing our knowledge and experiences applying LSCI with children, youth, and families in schools, communities, and homes over the last seven decades.

AUTHORS' NOTES

Nicholas J. Long

LSCI is a revolutionary idea. More than just a list of psychological concepts and skills, LSCI is a particular way of perceiving, thinking, feeling, and behaving toward others while also being aware of one's feelings.

It all started in 1951, when Fritz Redl and David Wineman reported the findings of their residential treatment program for aggressive students, *Children Who Hate*. They challenged the traditional way of treating aggressive students. The 50-minute therapy "hour" was replaced by Milieu Therapy and Life Space Intervention. The professional interest in these two concepts was so great, Redl replicated his residential treatment program by studying the six most aggressive students east of the Mississippi. I served on his staff as the house father to these boys. In the last two years, we emphasized the importance of the other 23 hours of the day.

In 1959, Redl published a 16-page article defining the structure of LSCI for the very first time. The importance of this paper was similar to the Wright Brothers' first successful flight. The article provided us with the structure to develop the concepts of (a) de-escalation skills; (b) emotional first aid; (c) clinical exploration of a student's life event. Over the next years, Doctors Wood and Fecser and I wrote the first book on LSCI in 1991. We took Redl's 16-page theory and demonstrated how it can be used in a crisis. We also developed a video program which showed how crises can be managed. Much to our surprise, LSCI was so successful that it became an international program. We now know that LSCI is here to stay as a major crisis intervention program.

Personally, there is no end to experiencing the excitement of talking with a student in a crisis. Every student has a story to tell and LSCI provides us with the skills of hearing it. I wish I could be alive to witness how LSCI will grow to become the number one mental health resource for schools in the future. LSCI's time has come and I am pleased to be part of it.

Mary M. Wood

In 1963, I had a post-doctoral fellowship with Dr. Nicholas Long at the Hillcrest Children's Treatment Center in Washington D.C. Dr. Long was expanding Dr. Fritz Redl's original concepts about crisis intervention (see Chapter 1). It was as if the intervention road map to responsible behavior opened up a whole new vista for me. More than that, LSCI was a perfect fit with a new developmentally focused approach to educating children with social, emotional, or behavioral challenges. In the ensuing years as director of the Rutland Center, the Developmental Therapy Institute, and a University of Georgia graduate program for teachers, it became increasingly evident to me that LSCI was a perfect tool for guiding young people through crisis situations to resolution. In this process, LSCI engages a young person and the supporting adult in interactive learning that results in expanded social, emotional, and behavioral competencies at any age or stage of development. By blending the best of clinical psychology and social learning theory into educational practices for "thinking developmentally," LSCI has grown to worldwide recognition as the "go to" practice with youth in stressful situations.

Frank A. Fecser

One of the highlights of my career has been working with talented young people who choose the difficult path of helping challenging children and youth. They arrive on the scene with lots of energy and enthusiasm, compassion, and bright-eyed hope to do their part to improve lives. Often relying on little more than their own instincts, they quickly learn that they need far more than desire to help. They cannot understand why their efforts are often rejected, sometimes violently, and they are surprised by their own angry response to rejection. Nothing they learned in their education or social work courses prepared them for this!

That's why the skills of LSCI are so important. LSCI helps practitioners and caregivers understand the dynamics of conflict and how to avoid getting caught up in a young person's struggles. LSCI offers specific strategies that empower helpers to see beyond behavior and into the undercurrents that drive it. LSCI provides a roadmap to insight into self-defeating patterns of behavior while strengthening the relationship between worker and student that is the foundation for trust and change. Adults who are trained in LSCI not only help children build more satisfying ways of living, but themselves enjoy the satisfaction that comes with professional competence.

Signe Whitson

I was first certified in LSCI in the year 2000. Fresh out of a clinically focused master's program, I attended LSCI as a young professional with a ton of idealism for improving the lives of kids, a graduate degree's worth of book knowledge, and about two years of real-world experience working with children and adolescents in school and residential treatment settings. What I thought I would get out of LSCI training was an interesting professional development experience and perhaps another proverbial "tool for my toolbox." What I got instead, in under a week of training, was an advanced set of clinical skills that rivaled anything I learned in graduate school, along with a paradigm for understanding the dynamics of conflict that profoundly impacts all of my interactions with students and clients—and even my own children! I am not exaggerating when I say that I use elements of LSCI *every. single. day.* in my professional work as a school counselor and child and adolescent therapist. My hope is that you will find LSCI as instrumental in your career as I have in mine.

ACKNOWLEDGMENTS

LSCI Certified Senior and Master Trainers

One of the most wonderful things about the LSCI Institute is the network of intelligent, compassionate, creative, committed professionals that it brings together. We are tremendously grateful to our certified Master and Senior Trainers around the world who not only teach LSCI skills to others but who also contribute to our knowledge base through research, practice, and the development of tools to enhance the use of LSCI in schools and organizations.

Below, we offer our sincere gratitude and appreciation to specific individuals and groups whose contributions to this book have been immeasurable.

Intervention Examples

Each of the vignettes offered in this book are snapshots of real-life encounters with young people. They are written by the authors and shared with us by LSCI trainees and practitioners, all based on actual experiences. We are thankful for all those who allow us to tell us their LSCI stories.

We are especially grateful to the LSCI Trainers who share their stage-by-stage use of LSCI, including the writers of these featured interventions:

The Red Flag intervention (Brandon) in Chapter 10, and The Double Struggle intervention (Mrs. Borland, "The Big, Fat, Know-It-All!") in Chapter 16 were conducted and shared by LSCI Master Trainer, Mark Freado.

The New Tools intervention (Sophia) in Chapter 12 was conducted and shared by LSCI Master Trainer James Freeman.

The Regulate and Restore intervention (Assad) in Chapter 14 was conducted and shared by LSCI Emeritus Trainer Mary Beth Hewitt.

The Peer Manipulation Set Up intervention (Carlos and Khalil) in Chapter 15 was conducted and shared by LSCI Emeritus Trainer Dr. Mitchell Beck.

Activity Ideas and LSCI Tools

LSCI Training is ever-evolving due to the creative, innovative minds of our Trainers and practitioners. We are grateful to all those who contribute ideas for new ways to teach our concepts, to engage our learners, and to make documentation and data collection more accessible in programs and schools. We want to give special recognition to:

Dr. Carol Dawson (Emeritus LSCI Trainer) and her team at the New York City Department of Education for their significant contributions to LSCI training activities and training materials. In particular, thank you for sharing the *Consider This* activity (Chapter 4, Self-Concept and Beliefs), *Personal Plan for Button Pushing* (Chapter 6), *Pre/Post Survey* (Appendix), and the *Life Space Crisis Intervention Interviewing Skills Checklist* (Appendix).

Eric Mann (LSCI Master Trainer) for his development of the *LSCI Reentry Checklist* (Appendix) that helps schools and organizations effectively implement Stages 5 and 6 of LSCI.

Eric Mann and Howard Muscott (Retired LSCI Trainer) for their development and contributions to the *Life Space Crisis Intervention Interviewing Skills Checklist* (Appendix).

Alex Cameron and James Natural (LSCI Master Trainers) for their development of the *LSCI Tracking and Fidelity Form* (Appendix).

Early Readers

We are grateful for the perceptive minds and discerning eyes of our early readers who were instrumental in suggesting important ideas, clarifying concepts, and getting all of the details right. Our thanks go especially to LSCI Master Trainers Dr. Bridget Walker, Alex Cameron, and James Natural.

LSCI Training Participants

Since the founding of the LSCI Institute in 1997, we have trained tens of thousands of professionals, whose work positively impacts millions of young people around the world. We feel tremendous admiration and gratitude for those of you who share our commitment to reaching and teaching our most vulnerable young people. Thank you for all that you do on a daily basis to connect with, calm, and show care for the stories of our youth.

We all do better when we all do better. (Senator Paul Wellstone, 1998).

PART 1

THE FOUNDATIONS OF LSCI

In Part 1 of this book, we present the full range of foundational skills needed to carry out a comprehensive and complete Life Space Crisis Intervention. The first nine chapters include theory and research that back the evidence-based practices on which LSCI is built.

Chapter 1 introduces readers to LSCI, explaining it as a brain-based, trauma-informed, relationship-building verbal strategy that has been effectively utilized in school, inpatient, therapeutic residential, and family settings since the 1950s. Then, in Chapter 2, we explain why our unique approach works, detailing how the brain and body respond to stress and how both neuroscience and trauma-informed practices support the six-stage process of LSCI. In Chapter 3, we explore the fundamental role that positive relationships and genuine connections play in helping young people cope with stressful events, heal from trauma, and use problem situations as learning opportunities.

In Chapters 4 to 6, we take a deep dive into the psychological worlds of young people during difficult situations. First, we trace the impact of stress on the development of a young person's self-concept, belief systems, perceptions, thoughts, feelings, and, ultimately, behaviors. Next, we study how the reactions of adults and peers to a young person's behaviors can escalate the dynamics of conflict and cause problem situations to spiral into crisis. Then, we look at the adult's role in breaking Conflict Cycles™, identifying six core listening skills that are critical to carrying out the LSCI process.

Chapter 7 breaks down the six stages of LSCI, identifying the core objectives, roles, skills, and tasks of each one. This chapter also provides insight into using LSCI with groups of young people and concludes with a comprehensive list of the do's and don'ts of implementing LSCI. In Chapter 8, we study typical developmental anxieties of youth and look at three universal questions that need to be considered before beginning an LSCI. Finally, in Part 1, we highlight 15 core strategies of the helping process along with 12 potential pitfalls of using LSCI that all practitioners should know.

"I hate this school!"

"I hate reading!"

"I hate staff!"

"I hate you!"

INTRODUCTION TO LSCI

When young people say things like the feelings expressed in quotations on the previous page, the next move is yours. You are part of their daily experience, their "life space." Those who work with challenging children and youth frequently face incidents that require thoughtful responses and skilled interventions. Sometimes, incidents may seem trivial or insignificant; other times, problems are of such magnitude as to be overwhelming, with no apparent resolutions. In any event, what is needed is a reliable, consistent, and effective way to help young people assume responsibility for changing their behavior in ways that produce constructive, long-term results.

Life Space Crisis Intervention (LSCI) is a brain-based, trauma-informed, relationship-building set of skills that helps adults turn problem situations into learning opportunities for young people who exhibit challenging behaviors. The process uses a young person's reactions to stress to bring about genuine and lasting changes in their perceptions, thoughts, feelings, and behaviors. Based on the belief that young people need to feel heard and understood, along with the knowledge that relationships are the agents of change (Perry & Szalavitz, 2017), the LSCI process cultivates growth, insight, and long-term change into the lives of children, adolescents, and families.

> *Life Space Crisis Intervention* (LSCI) is a brain-based, trauma-informed, relationship-building set of skills that helps adults turn problem situations into learning opportunities for young people who exhibit challenging behaviors.

How Does LSCI Work?

Conflicts and crises do not happen by appointment. Kids don't plan or schedule emotional meltdowns according to "convenient" times of day when a certified counselor is available or when a favorite teacher has a free period. The skills of LSCI are important because they enable any caring adult to step into a young person's *life space*—the heat of a stressful moment—and be able to intervene effectively. The six-stage LSCI process helps adults de-escalate the emotional intensity of a crisis, gain an understanding of the conflict from the young person's point of view, offer new ways to think about the incident, and ultimately promote the youth's personal responsibility for behavior.

> The skills of LSCI are important because they enable any caring adult to step into a young person's *life space*—the heat of a stressful moment—and be able to intervene effectively.

One of the most important parts of the LSCI process involves helping young people acknowledge and understand the pain-based beliefs, perceptions, thoughts, and feelings that drive their negative behaviors. Through LSCI, young people learn to say "yes" to their anger and other uncomfortable feelings but "no" to expressing their pain through problematic behaviors. LSCI promotes self-awareness, personal responsibility, and behavioral change. Unlike psychotherapy, LSCI is not an open and permissive process; yet, unlike strict behavioral programs, LSCI does not deny the power of personal feelings.

> Through LSCI, young people learn to say "yes" to their anger and other uncomfortable feelings but "no" to expressing their pain through problematic behaviors.

The subject of this book is how to talk effectively with young people during and after problem situations. The goal of LSCI is to foster self-regulated, pro-social behavior. We offer a consistent framework and set of skills to achieve this goal. Talking creates conditions in which young people feel heard and understood. The logical, problem-solving part of their brain is engaged as they learn to put language to their emotions (more about this in Chapter 2). Kids' motivation to change behaviors increases as their trust in adults grows (more about this in Chapter 3). With sensitivity to a young person's feelings and consideration of the circumstances surrounding stressful incidents, adults can provide the emotional support kids need while teaching them lifelong problem-solving and coping skills. If adults are effective, young people will develop beyond the need to rely on adult authority for behavior control. They will learn to manage their own behavior, control their impulses, tolerate painful feelings, live by rules and values, make constructive decisions, and interact with others in positive ways.

How Does LSCI Fit With Existing Programs in Schools and Treatment Settings?

LSCI integrates evidence-based practices such as social-emotional learning (SEL) instruction, cognitive behavioral therapy (CBT), and trauma-informed practices to create a consistent framework that guides adults in helping young people find solutions for challenging problems.

LSCI in Educational Settings

LSCI is used in both general and special education programs around the world. It provides a conceptual framework for teachers and staff to understand, prevent, and respond effectively to emerging behavior issues. Throughout the United States, LSCI supports multitiered systems of supports (MTSS) such as school-wide positive behavior interventions and supports (SWPBIS) and Response to Intervention (RTI) behavior initiatives in a number of ways, including:

1. Provides a systematic, comprehensive approach to addressing escalating behavior that can be used for students in preschool through high school across all three tiers of the MTSS model as well as in special education settings
2. Systematically integrates evidence-based practices into tiered instruction, including:

   - Trauma-informed crisis prevention and intervention
   - Cognitive behavioral approaches
   - Social-emotional learning strategies
   - Behavior management systems and supports

3. Provides school staff with proactive, consistent strategies for de-escalating crisis situations that can reduce rates of suspensions and expulsions (Dawson, 2001), as well as the use of restraint and seclusion
4. Uses problem incidents to identify the self-defeating patterns of behavior and reteach appropriate replacement behaviors while promoting the development of positive, supportive relationships with school staff
5. Is designed to give school staff and students an increased understanding of the function of problem behavior, improving the effectiveness of function-based behavior support plans

While LSCI was developed to meet the needs of the 20% of young persons in the top two tiers in the PBIS model, we know that this relatively small percentage of young

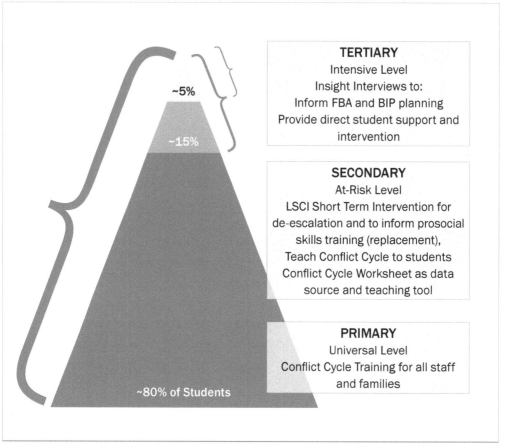

Figure 1.1. LSCI across the multitiered model. *Note.* From "How Features of LSCI Fit Within the Multitiered Model," by B. Walker and H. Muscott, 2020 (https://www.lsci.org/learn-more/pbis-lsci/). Copyright 2011 by Bridget Walker and Howard Muscott. Reprinted with permission.

people can consume up to 90% of the time and attention of adults. *For this reason, LSCI skills are needed by all adults in educational, therapeutic, and trauma-informed programs.* LSCI is applicable well beyond "crisis" situations, providing the foundation for positive relationships and de-escalation skills that prevent problem situations from exploding into crises.

> LSCI is applicable well beyond "crisis" situations, providing the foundation for positive relationships and de-escalation skills that prevent problem situations from exploding into crises.

LSCI in Residential and Group Care Settings

James Freeman, director of training at Casa Pacifica Centers for Children and Families in California, says that those who work alongside young people in residential or group care settings can see the benefit of both the conceptual and practical elements of LSCI on a daily basis (personal communication, March 19, 2020). He explains that "since most youth are placed in a residential or group care setting to get more help than is available at home, the conceptual elements of LSCI can get the adults (and even peers) aligned with understanding the dynamics of conflict and importance of being heard. The practical elements, most notably the language of insight questions, and social-emotional skills training allows for repeated experience and practice with new ways of thinking and interacting."

Freeman also notes that the intensity of residential care, in which multiple adults and youth live out their days together, provides daily (if not hourly or minute-by-minute) opportunities for adults to learn more about a young person's perspective and to be present with them in trying out a new skill in a safe and supported way.

Lastly, Freeman points out that LSCI supports new workers with tangible "steps" of the conflict cycle and a consistent framework for responding to certain behaviors as they focus (rightly so) on the foundation of safety and establishing relationships. At the same time, it allows more experienced workers opportunity to lean more into their relational skills as they trust the skills they have gained to navigate conflict and look beyond surface behaviors.

LSCI in Therapeutic Practice

In the classic book *When We Deal with Children* (Redl, 1966), LSCI is described as "the clinical exploitation of life events." Fritz Redl and David Wineman (learn about their significant role in the development of LSCI on pages 10–12) go on to describe the purpose of LSCI as "making use of momentary life experiences in order to draw out of [youth] something that might be of use for long-range therapeutic goals." Mark Freado, director of Growing Edge Training and co-author of *The Art of Kid Whispering: Reaching the Inside Kid*, calls LSCI "a very versatile application that can be adapted to a variety of therapeutic settings and circumstances with young people in need of adults who can be present, attentive, and understanding" (personal communication, July 20, 2020). Freado explains that LSCI is an excellent process for engaging in a reciprocal dialogue that helps a young person understand and work through problems. Effective LSCI interventions not only address immediate challenges in a youth's life but also reveal chronic patterns of self-defeating behaviors. Freado says that it is the recognition of these patterns that sets the stage for positive therapeutic engagement during counseling sessions. Such counseling can take place in the day-to-day functioning of a school or in residential or other program settings, as well as through more formal counseling settings.

> LSCI is an excellent process for engaging in a reciprocal dialogue that helps a young person understand and work through problems.

LSCI and Trauma-Informed Practice

One of the most prominent and promising models for helping children whose brains are affected by stress and trauma is Dr. Bruce Perry's Neurosequential Model of Therapeutics, also known as NMT (Perry & Szalavitz, 2017). As its name indicates, Perry's model teaches us that the stressed brain has specific needs that must be met in proper sequence in order to be effective. *Regulating, Relating, and Reasoning* are the three essential (and sequential) steps for assessing and addressing the challenging behaviors of young people. We summarize the 3 R's as follows:

Regulate

Based on knowledge of the limbic system's dominance of a young person's brain (see Chapter 2 for further explanation), we know that before we can be of any real help to a child, we must make them feel safe both physically and emotionally. *Regulation* is a process that involves calming—or in LSCI terms, *draining off*—the intense emotions triggered in the brain by a stressful event or memory. Adults help kids become more regulated when we do things like providing a space for them to calm down; encouraging deep, rhythmic breathing; giving opportunities for movement to burn off the neurochemicals associated with the fight/flight/freeze response; offering a drink of water; and reassuring them that they are safe. Similarly, *co-regulation* is a process through which adults purposefully and skillfully use their own calm demeanor as a tool to create feelings of calm in a child. Regulation and co-regulation skills (further explored in Chapter 3) are standard practice in the LSCI process.

- *Every LSCI intervention begins with providing the time, space, and place for a young person to become physically and emotionally regulated. In LSCI, we call these practices Surface Management and Drain Off.*

Relate

Until a child's brain is regulated, he/she is unable to relate in any meaningful way to a helping adult. Perry's model and the LSCI approach share the practice that after regulating/draining off a child's intense emotions, the next priority is connection and *relationship*. Adults effectively relate to kids when we listen to them, validate their feelings, decode the meaning behind their behaviors, and affirm that we care about their well-being.

- *In the LSCI model, you will recognize Regulate and Relate skills in what we call Stage 1: Drain Off.*

Reason

Usually when kids are experiencing stress, we observe a high intensity of emotion along with perhaps loud talking, pacing, crying, defiance, aggressive behavior, self-harm, or other expressions of their feelings. Too often when we see a child seething with emotion after a conflict, we also observe a well-intentioned adult asking them things like, *"Why did you do that? What were you thinking? How are you going to fix this? What's your plan?"*

We recognize that the adult is trying to be helpful by employing *reason* with the child. The problem is, of course, that the child cannot process reason, language, and logic at this time because his limbic brain is engaged but his neocortex is not. (This triune brain model is explained in Chapter 2.)

Both Dr. Perry and the LSCI approach recognize that real, effective *reasoning* can only take place after the child is *regulated* and has established the basis of a trusting *relationship* with an adult. Once these prerequisites are in place, the child can engage in the higher-level, thinking brain functions of perspective-taking, reflection, and problem-solving.

- *Stage 2 of the LSCI process, called the Timeline, is a systematic process of helping kids reason by putting language to emotion, telling their stories, and feeling heard and understood. The subsequent LSCI stages extend the reasoning process by fostering insight into troubling patterns of behavior, building pro-social skills, and setting the conditions for long-term behavioral change.*

LSCI and Restorative Practices

The fundamental hypothesis of restorative practices is that human beings are happier, more cooperative and productive, and more likely to make positive changes in their behavior when those in positions of authority do things *with* them, rather than *to* them or *for* them (Wachtel & McCold, 2004).

LSCI and restorative practices share the custom of joining *with* a young person to allow their unique set of perceptions, thoughts, and feelings to be voiced. Both LSCI and restorative practices rely on affective statements and open-ended questions that engage a child's brain. The LSCI processes extend the restorative questions in addressing proactive and responsive levels within adult-wary youth.

> LSCI and restorative practices share the custom of joining *with* a young person to allow their unique set of perceptions, thoughts, and feelings to be voiced.

Through both approaches, a young person's behavior that is often subconscious in nature becomes more conscious, allowing for new insights and long-term change. Dr. Frida Rundell, professor and founding member of the International Institute for Restorative Practices (IIRP), says that "the combination between the two practices is a unique and beneficial win-win for professionals and the adult-wary youth" (personal communication, June 18, 2020).

Another way that LSCI and restorative practices align is in their commitment to helping a young person better understand how their behaviors impact others. In

Chapter 7, The Structure of LSCI, you will learn how the Timeline and Insight stages of the LSCI process focus on cultivating interpersonal understanding. Likewise, LSCI and restorative practices share a focus on restoring and rebuilding relationships where harm or difficulty has been experienced. The idea of repairing relationships and taking responsibility for behavior is the deep learning that takes place in the final two stages of the LSCI process (see Chapter 7 for further detail) that helps young people learn to build trusting relationships and self-regulate their own behavior.

A BRIEF HISTORY OF LSCI

In a world of "new" and "fast-acting" approaches to timeless, persistent problems, we are proud of LSCI's deep roots and vetted use with young people. In this section, we share with you a bit of the history and evolution of Life Space Crisis Intervention skills, beginning all the way back to Sigmund Freud!

LSCI is a psychoeducational strategy, meaning that we recognize that there is an unconscious part of the mind that is beyond our immediate recognition and cognition. The unconscious mind drives perceptions, thoughts, and feelings. In turn, feelings can be expressed as specific behaviors. When we use LSCI, we look beyond the surface of a child's behavior to find out what unconscious forces are driving it.

Sigmund Freud's daughter Anna Freud was very well known for her work in child psychology. She introduced the concept of *defense mechanisms* (see Chapter 4). Anna Freud also discovered that there are ways that people unconsciously deal with stress and that if these ways become repetitive patterns, they can become destructive.

Fritz Redl was born in Austria and trained as an analyst by Anna Freud. Redl immigrated to New York City in 1936 and moved to Detroit, Michigan, in 1940. With social worker David Wineman, he co-authored groundbreaking books including *Children Who Hate* (1951), *Controls from Within* (1952), and *The Aggressive Child* (1957).

Redl and Wineman believed that adults who work directly with students during a crisis have the greatest opportunity to intervene in therapeutic ways and to make lasting change. They developed the "marginal interview" for use by direct care staff. The "marginal interview" became the "life space interview," indicating that the intervention took place in the *here and now*, the real-life setting, rather than in a therapist's office during a planned session.

In 1952, while Redl and Wineman were working in Detroit, William Morse established the University of Michigan's Fresh Air Camp, which became a renowned interdisciplinary training center for psychiatry, psychology, social work, and special education. Redl and Wineman served as teaching consultants at the Fresh Air Camp and proposed LSI as a major therapeutic strategy. Nicholas Long, a graduate student of Morse, received his initial LSI training at the Fresh Air Camp.

In 1956, Redl solicited the most severely aggressive cases from 200 hospitals along the Eastern Seaboard and selected six of the most difficult cases to become part of the Aggressive Child Project. Nicholas Long served as the director of the Children's Treatment Center, the residential component of Redl's research project.

Further development of LSI occurred under the direction of Morse and Long to extend its use beyond the clinical setting and into the educational environment where it could be used by teachers. Among many publications resulting from this project was *Conflict in the Classroom* (1965), now in its seventh edition.

In 1971, while at American University, Nicholas Long founded the Rose School in Washington D.C. The Rose School was a community-based psychoeducational program that combined special education and mental health, serving some of the most troubled children in the city. The Rose School served as a training site for special educators, psychologists, and psychiatrists during its 20-year history. During that period, Long trained hundreds of clinicians and educators in LSI through modeling and coaching. He began to identify the core components of LSI and to organize them into teachable concepts that could be learned outside of the direct service environment.

With Mary Wood, founder of the Developmental Therapy Center in Athens, Georgia, Long co-authored the original LSCI textbook, *Life Space Intervention: Talking with Children and Youth in Crisis* (1991). The *Life Space Interview* became *Life Space Intervention* to more clearly identify the technique as a tool of change rather than a clinical assessment. LSI uses the crisis as an opportunity to convey the adult as mediator among the stress, the youth's behavior, the reactions of others, and the private world of feelings that young people are sometimes unable to handle without help.

During the early 1990s, Long began developing a model for LSI training. With Frank Fecser, CEO of the Positive Education Program (PEP) in Cleveland, Ohio, he designed and piloted several versions of five- and six-day training programs leading to a certificate of competency in LSI. With the increasing intensity of problems played out in today's schools, *Life Space Intervention* became *Life Space Crisis Intervention* to reflect its application in school and treatment settings as used by professionals nationwide.

By 1997, the demand for training in the skills of LSCI was significant. Long and Fecser founded the LSCI Institute to train and certify Senior and Master Trainers who maintain the standard of quality of LSCI training. LSCI training is now conducted across North America, Europe, Asia, and Australia. As more and more helping adults around the globe seek to effectively meet the needs of young people, LSCI will provide its comprehensive, field-tested, trauma-informed approach. *More information about LSCI training and certification opportunities can be found in Part 3 of this book.*

What Does LSCI Sound Like?
Listen in on an LSCI Intervention Example

Before going into the next chapters, we want to offer you a preview of what the LSCI approach can sound like when used in conversation with a young person. Below, we present a real-life example of LSCI as a basic illustration; the crisis is neither so complex that it might obscure the LSCI process nor so simple that it might mislead you into concluding that LSCI is a simple procedure. "The Math Problem Crisis" is typical of daily life for many students. For instructional purposes, the example takes you through the six LSCI stages in a straightforward sequence; in practice, there is often some back and forth between stages in order to calm intense emotions, review statements, summarize, etc. For your benefit, in the example below we note when each new stage begins and provide brief commentary on key decision points in each stage. We hope to show how effectively LSCI skills can be learned step by step.

It is not necessary to know how to apply everything in this book before you begin using LSCI. Gradually, however, as you use LSCI, you will find yourself becoming increasingly insightful and skilled in talking with young people in crisis.

The Math Problem Crisis

The setting is Nathaniel Hawthorne High School in a working-class neighborhood of Cleveland, Ohio. Dane is an eleventh grade student with a history of challenging behaviors. He was diagnosed with a behavioral disability when he was in middle school, following a series of incidents involving lying and extorting younger students. For the past two years, Dane has been assigned to an emotional support classroom from which he is mainstreamed as often as possible. He is well known for loud, explosive displays when things do not go his way. Dane's long-standing beliefs about himself center around his idea that adults are not to be trusted and that they go out of their way to make life difficult for kids. He blames adults for his problems and accepts little responsibility himself.

Dane takes math in the emotional support classroom led by Ms. Westerman, the lead teacher, and Mr. Randall, the instructional assistant. One reason Dane is not mainstreamed for math is that he dislikes the subject so much that it is often a source of stress for him, triggering feelings of failure, frustration, and anger that he finds difficult to contain. On this day, Dane rushes through the assignment and turns in his paper. Ms. Westerman looks it over and realizes what has happened. She returns the paper to Dane and tells him that she will help him get through the first couple of problems but that he will have to correct the other six before he can go to the extra gym class in the next period. Dane is not pleased with this situation, but because he values the extra gym period, he makes an effort as Ms. Westerman walks him through the first two problems. Just as the one-to-one instruction is concluding, Ms. Westerman is summoned to the office. Dane drifts from his task and does not correct the other problems. When the bell rings, Mr. Randall says to the group, "OK, turn in your math and let's go to the gym." Dane turns in his uncorrected paper and goes to the gym with Mr. Randall and the rest of the group. When Ms. Westerman returns, she finds Dane's uncorrected paper and goes to the gym to bring Dane back to the classroom to finish the assignment. We begin the incident as Ms. Westerman (T) calls Dane (D) off the basketball court.

Stage 1: Drain Off

T: Dane, would you come here please?

D: (*Angrily*) Talk to me later.

T: Dane, I need to see you right now. Step out in the hall, please.

D: Later!

T: Dane, I know you like the privilege of having an extra gym period, but I need to speak with you now.

D: (*Slamming the ball on the floor and approaching Ms. Westerman with an angry scowl*) What do you want?!

T: Dane, please, let's step into the hall so we can talk privately.

D: (*Steps into the hallway, crosses his arms. and leans back against the wall*)

T: Thank you for coming out here. I know that wasn't easy for you to do. I have to tell you something that won't be easy for you to hear. When I left the classroom, I told you to correct your math sheet before going to the gym. Your math sheet is not corrected.

D: (*Loudly*) Mr. Randall said I didn't have to! He told me to turn in my paper and come down here!

T: Dane, what exactly did you hear Mr. Randall say?

D: He said, "Everybody, turn in your math and go to the gym!" Go ahead and ask him—ask anybody. That's what he said! You people are really messed up! Now I'm getting into trouble because I'm following the g-damned directions!

Ms. Westerman knows Dane well and understands what is probably going on. Because she had to leave the room unexpectedly, she did not communicate to Mr. Randall that Dane was to correct his math sheet before going to gym. Therefore, when he told the group to turn in their assignments and go to gym, Dane took advantage of the adults' lack of communication. Rather than accept responsibility for his expectation, Dane uses this as an example of how adults "wrong" students and blame them for their mistakes. Ms. Westerman will check out this hypothesis in the Timeline stage.

Stage 2: Timeline

T: Something went wrong here, and we need to figure out what. Let's start from the beginning. You turned in your math sheet with a lot of mistakes on it. That tells me you were having a hard time right from the start.

D: You know I can't do math! I hate it!

T: Math is tough for you, I know.

D: I want to go back to the gym!

T: Dane, let's work this out. You're showing a lot of self-control and patience right now—this isn't easy, but you're handling it. Let's go on. Do you remember that I brought the paper back to you?

D: (*Impatiently*) Yeah, yeah, I remember.

T: Can you tell me what you thought when that happened?

D: I was thinking, I want to get out of here.

T: Sure, you wanted math to be over and you were looking forward to going to gym. What happened next?

D: You made me do the first two problems.

T: Right. And even though math is tough for you, you worked on those two until you got them right. Somehow you controlled your feelings and made the choice to work on the problems. Then what happened?

D: Somebody came to the door and you left the room.

T: True, but do you remember what I said before I left about your finishing the other problems before going to the gym?

D: Yeah, I remember.

T: What did I say?

D: You said finish them, then go to gym.

T: That's right. How did you feel just then?

D: I was sick of that stuff!

T: So, you were already feeling frustrated by the assignment and one thing you did to relieve that stress was to hurry through the work and turn it in with wrong answers. You were feeling sick of math; you wanted to get it over with. Then, when I brought the paper back to you, you were even more frustrated, but you managed to work through the first two problems with me. You were handling the situation pretty well at that point. What happened next?

D: Mr. Randall said for everybody—got that—EVERYBODY—to turn in the sheets and go to gym. So, I followed directions like you guys always tell me to do and I went to gym and now I'm missing it because you two can't get your acts together!

Dane has just dropped a clue. He knows there's been a miscommunication between the staff. Ms. Westerman will use this to move Dane toward seeing the role he played in the problem.

Stage 3: Central Issue

T: What you're saying is important; let's see if I have it straight. You and I were correcting the first two problems, and even though you were feeling frustrated, you managed your feelings and focused on the task. Then I was interrupted and had to leave the room, but as I left, I told you to complete the corrections before going to gym. That was not good news because you were struggling trying to get through the first two.

D: Yeah, so?

T: Then when the bell rang, Mr. Randall told everyone to turn in their assignments and get ready for gym. You had not corrected your problems, but you turned in your sheet anyway and went to gym.

D: Yeah, that's right. I did as I was told.

T: Well, now I'm not sure I understand that because it seems that if you had done as you were told you would have corrected the problems first.

D: Hey, I got another direction after that, so I followed it!

T: That's true—there was a miscommunication between Mr. Randall and me. I didn't tell him that you were supposed to finish the problems first.

D: And now, because you're not doing your job, you're giving me a hard time! What am I supposed to do when a teacher says to do something? If I don't do it, I get in trouble and if I do it, I get in trouble. Don't even talk to me! You don't know how to run this classroom! You think you're helping kids but you're messing them up!

Stage 4: Insight

T: Dane, listen, you're a bright kid. You understand people, and you're good with words. There was a miscommunication between Mr. Randall and me—no question about it. I accept responsibility for that. But clearly, there was no miscommunication between you and me. You and I both knew the expectation I left you with. You verified that yourself. So, I have to ask you a question. When Mr. Randall said for everyone to turn in the assignments and go to gym, you knew I hadn't told him about our arrangement. What went through your mind?

D: I guess I thought, "Cool, they screwed up so I can go!"

T: So, suddenly, there was a way out of doing the math, a way to instantly relieve your frustration. You decided to take a gamble on not getting caught and turned in the incomplete paper and went to gym.

D: You try sitting there for an hour with a bunch of boring bull! I couldn't take it anymore! Don't you understand that?

T: Dane, I really appreciate your honesty. You're not telling me that you were confused or that you didn't understand. You're telling me the truth. You're saying, look, "I was feeling overwhelmed. I took a gamble—I lost." You're owning up to that. That's really impressive, Dane; that's progress. A couple of months ago, you wouldn't have been able to take that kind of responsibility, and here you are, talking about it, managing to keep your cool.

D: You don't know how much I need to get a break from that room. I hate that math mess.

T: No question about it, you've got some strong feelings about math—it's been a tough subject for you and I'm not saying those feelings are wrong. But you had a choice to make, and this time, you let your strong dislike for math get in the way of making a good choice.

Stage 5: New Skills

D: So now what; what are you going to do?

T: What do you think would be a good solution?

D: I knew it! You're going to make me miss gym and go back and do that crap!

T: I asked what *you* thought would be a good solution—is that it?

D: (*Walking toward the room*) This place sucks!

T: It would be easy for you to argue and refuse, but you're making the responsible choice to finish the work. No kidding, Dane, that's really progress. I'm there if you need help.

D: All right—let's get it over with so I can get back to my game.

T: (*Walking back to the classroom*) You know, Dane, in a way, I'm kind of glad this happened, because I think we learned something here. We learned that even under pressure you can own responsibility for choices you make. You're just a short step from being able to independently make choices that will work out best for you, even though it's tough to do. You're getting to the point where you will no longer need adults to check up on you. That's independence, and you're on your way. Just to finish this up, can you think of some other ways to deal with your frustration about math? What other choices do you have in a situation like this?

D: I don't know, I guess I could ask to do it later, or ask for some help or something.

T: You mean you could tell Mr. Randall or me that you're having trouble and need help? That alone could relieve some of the pressure. How are you going to remember to do that?

D: I don't want to miss gym. I'll remember.

Stage 6: Transfer of Learning

T: OK, I'll try to remind you. Now, just one more thing. What are you going to tell the other kids when they ask you where you were?

D: I'll just tell them I had to take care of something.

T: What if they pressure you or laugh or try to put you on the spot?

D: I'll just blow it off. I'll say it's personal.

T: OK—I'll back you up. Let's get that math done.

Intervention Discussion

In this LSCI, in addition to supporting the student for taking personal responsibility for resolving the immediate issue, progress has been made toward long-term goals. Dane has:

1. Used rational control for directing behavior
2. Shown insight into how he contributes to problems and how this pattern of responding makes his life more difficult
3. Suggested new ways to behave
4. Conveyed attitudes of responsibility and self-esteem
5. Seen the adult as a helper rather than an adversary

It may be worth noting that Ms. Westerman accepted some strong language from Dane, and some might say it bordered on disrespect. Ms. Westerman was very much aware of Dane's choice of words and made a clear choice not to address that issue. At stake was the greater goal—for Dane to accept responsibility for his failure to complete the corrections. Dane was already prepared to draw Ms. Westerman into a Conflict Cycle and tried to do it by blaming the situation on poor communication between the adults. Had Ms. Westerman focused on Dane's choice of words, Dane most probably would have used that as an opportunity to divert attention from the real issue. One of the strongest features of LSCI is that it provides the adult with a road map to reach desired outcome goals and to avoid the "side trips" often suggested by young people.

> LSCI is a unique set of skills that involves not just a focus on the child's behavior but also a weighty responsibility on adults to understand and skillfully manage their responses to young people.

About This Book

In this introductory chapter, you learned about LSCI as a brain-based, trauma-informed, relationship-building verbal strategy that enables adults to turn problem situations with young people into lasting learning opportunities. LSCI is a unique set of skills that involves not just a focus on the child's behavior but also a weighty responsibility on adults to understand and skillfully manage their responses to young people.

The skills of LSCI are rooted in decades of field-testing and practice with some of the most challenging children and adolescents in schools and treatment organizations around the world. Compatible with all the prevailing evidence-based, child-centered models, LSCI blends psychodynamic, therapeutic, trauma-informed, and restorative practice elements into a comprehensive, consistent, goal-oriented approach to reaching and teaching young people.

In Chapter 2, we provide you with information about how recent advances in the fields of neuroscience and trauma have affirmed and validated the LSCI skills that practitioners have been using since the 1940s. Chapters 3 through 9 teach the foundational skills that will help you effectively conduct LSCI interventions with young people. In Part 2 of this book, you will learn each of the LSCI interventions, which address the most common patterns of self-defeating behavior exhibited by kids. In Part 3, you will learn about additional applications of LSCI as a model for group work with kids, for parenting interactions, for changing passive-aggressive behaviors, for work with very young or developmentally delayed children, and for managing the complex thoughts and feelings that professionals experience when working with challenging children and youth of all ages.

About LSCI Training

Since its founding in 1997, the LSCI Institute has offered training to professionals and parents working and living with young people who exhibit challenging behaviors. From brief workshops that provide a comprehensive overview of LSCI to our full certification course that teaches participants how to fully and effectively carry out each of the six LSCI interventions, we offer live and online training programs to meet a wide range of learning needs. LSCI training is conducted throughout North America, Europe, South Africa, New Zealand, Australia—and wherever you are! Through our network of certified Senior and Master Trainers, the LSCI Institute can bring our training programs to your schools or organizations anywhere in the world. To learn about our various training programs and see our full list of international training sites, please visit us at www.lsci.org.

"LSCI is trauma-informed care in action."

WHY LSCI WORKS
Alignment With Neuroscience and Trauma-Informed Practice

t is not uncommon for untrained observers of the LSCI process to be curious about this unique way of reaching and teaching young people. Indeed, colleagues tend to take note when an LSCI-certified professional begins doing things a bit differently than they used to and getting better responses from kids! Common questions of LSCI practitioners include things like:

- How do you manage to stay so calm when interacting with a child who is so worked up?
- Why did you ask Josh to tell you what happened in his own words, when Mr. Shaw had already filled you in?
- I notice that you ask a lot of questions and always try to put events in a logical sequence when you talk to kids. What's that all about?
- How did you know to ask Bella about her thoughts?
- Why did you spend so much time listening to Malik's point of view when you know he exaggerates everything? He was probably just trying to get out of going to class.
- Why did you spend so much time asking Juan questions when you already know what happened? Aren't you just giving him attention for doing the wrong thing?

These are all great questions about LSCI. And they get to the very heart of how—and more importantly *why*—LSCI works.

Truth be told, it has only been in our more recent years that LSCI-trained professionals have known how to answer the question of "why" LSCI works. Before that, we just knew from field-validated experience after experience after experience that it did. In the last two decades, as the world has seen incredible advances in our knowledge of how the brain reacts to stress and the body heals from trauma, the *why* of LSCI's effectiveness has become more easily explainable.

LSCI works because its comprehensive, six-stage process of helping kids navigate problem situations is extraordinarily well-aligned with what we now know the human brain needs for regulation, connection, problem-solving and lasting behavioral change. As Alex Cameron (personal communication, May 27, 2020), Senior Director of Clinical Services for Pressley Ridge notes, "*LSCI is trauma-informed care in action.*" In the pages that follow, we'll offer an overview of adverse childhood experiences and traumatic stressors, explain how traumatic stress affects the brain and show you how trauma-informed practices like LSCI can promote healing.

> LSCI works because its comprehensive, six-stage process of helping kids navigate problem situations is extraordinarily well-aligned with what we now know the human brain needs for regulation, connection, problem-solving and lasting behavioral change.

Adverse Childhood Experiences (ACEs) and Traumatic Stress

Trauma and Traumatic Events

> "LSCI is trauma-informed care in action."

Traumatic events are defined as incidents that expose a person to death, serious injury, or violence. The essence of trauma is that it is overwhelming, unbelievable, and unbearable (van der Kolk, 2014). Events that are commonly experienced as traumatic for a young person include:

- The death of a family member
- Separation from loved ones
- Natural disaster
- School shooting
- Physical or sexual abuse
- Domestic violence
- Community violence
- Systemic racism
- Displacement from the home
- Illness (or fear of illness)
- Sudden or chronic loss of stability, routines, and sense of safety

Distinct from the event(s) itself, *trauma* has to do with an individual's experience and response to the event. Short-term reactions to traumatic events typically include shock and denial while longer-term experiences of trauma are characterized by emotional dysregulation, impaired interpersonal relationships, difficulty focusing and sustaining attention, anxiety, distrust, flashbacks, and various physical symptoms such as headaches and nausea.

In *The Body Keeps the Score: Brain, Mind, and Body in the Healing of Trauma*, Dr. Bessel van der Kolk (2014) summarizes the significant and widespread impact of trauma throughout the body:

> Research . . . has revealed that trauma produces actual physiological changes, including a recalibration of the brain's alarm system, an increase in stress hormone activity, and alterations in the system that filters relevant information from irrelevant. We now know that trauma compromises the brain area that communicates the physical, embodied feeling of being alive. These changes explain why traumatized individuals become hypervigilant to threat at the expense of spontaneously engaging in their day-to-day lives. They also help us understand why traumatized people so often keep repeating the same problems and have such trouble learning from experience. We now know that their behaviors are not the result of moral failings or signs of lack of willpower or bad character—they are caused by actual changes in the brain (pp. 2–3).

The emotional and physical toll of trauma can impact both those who live through a traumatic event in person as well as those who experience it vicariously by witnessing it, watching it replay over and over again via media, or even learning that it happened to someone with whom they feel a close connection. It is important to note that trauma is an individualized experience and that an event that might be traumatic for one person might not create the same powerful reaction in another. For example, after living through a natural disaster, one child might be fully recovered several months later, while her friend may still be struggling for months or years to come. That's because trauma depends on many factors beyond the event itself, including a person's perception of the event, their proximity to it, their previous experiences of trauma, their experiences of support—or lack thereof—after the event, their sense of helplessness, and more (Ehmke, 2020).

Trauma is typically classified in these three categories:

1. Acute trauma: Trauma that results from a single incident, such as a school shooting.

2. Chronic trauma: Trauma that is chronic and prolonged, such as abuse or systemic racism.

3. Complex trauma: Complex trauma occurs when a person experiences multiple traumatic events, often interpersonal in nature.

Throughout this book, we will be talking about how LSCI skills can be applied to help alleviate the impact of trauma on young people.

Adverse Childhood Experiences

Adverse childhood experiences, commonly referred to as ACEs, are traumatic events that occur in a person's life before the age of 18. According to the US Department of Health and Human Services (2020), ACEs include all types of abuse and neglect as well as parental mental illness, substance use, divorce, incarceration, and domestic violence. We identify ACEs as *traumatic stressors* because (1) they are beyond the realm of expected stressors of growing up and (2) young people are typically unable to manage this kind of stress by themselves.

A landmark study of 17,000 people, conducted by the Centers for Disease Control and Prevention (CDC) over a ten-year period of time, established a significant relationship between the number of ACEs a person experienced and a variety of negative outcomes including anxiety, depression, antisocial behaviors, risk-taking, and substance abuse (Felitti et al., 1998). Multi-problem young adults suffering from an accumulation of psychological problems/disorders and substance abuse and experiencing court involvement are likely to have experienced one or more ACEs during childhood (Thompson et al., 2015).

The more ACEs experienced, the greater the risk for these outcomes. According to the World Health Organization (WHO) World Mental Health Surveys, ACEs account for 29.8% of all psychiatric disorders (Kessler et al., 2010). When working with young people who have experienced trauma, understanding the impact of ACEs on their psychological world can lead to more appropriate interventions. In the last section of this chapter, we will talk more about how to apply an understanding of ACEs and traumatic stress to your work with young people.

How the Brain and Body Respond to Stress

In order to effectively guide young people through problem situations, it is essential to have a basic understanding of how the human brain and body respond to stress and trauma. Having an awareness of the sequential development of the brain assists us in understanding how best to implement an LSCI Intervention.

It goes without saying that the human brain is incredibly complex; models are a simplified means to help us identify and work with the complexity through which

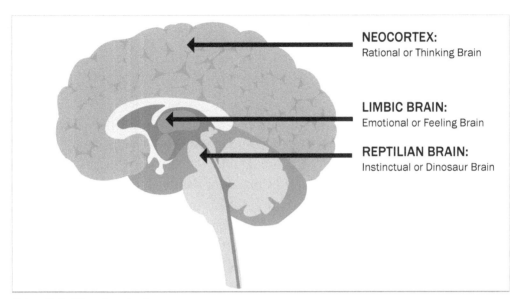

Figure 2.1. The triune brain.

the brain processes and becomes sensitized to internal and external information. In the pages below, we explain the fundamentals of the Paul MacLean's triune brain model, Dr. Bruce Perry's state-dependent functioning, and Dr. Stephen Porges' polyvagal theory.

The Triune Brain

In the 1960s, the neuroscientist Paul MacLean introduced the concept of the *triune brain*, a simplified but helpful model that focuses on the interaction of three specific regions of the human brain during stressful events. For our purposes, we summarize MacLean's model as follows.

The Brainstem (Reptilian Brain)

From an evolutionary perspective, the oldest part of the human brain is called the *brainstem*. Also known as the *reptilian brain*, this part of the brain (which still dominates the overall behavior of creatures like snakes and lizards) controls human survival functions such as breathing, heart rate, blood pressure, and balance. A key feature of the brainstem is that it does not learn well from experience but rather repeats instinctual behaviors over and over in a fixed way (Baars & Gage, 2010).

Applying knowledge of the brainstem to our interactions with kids helps us understand that when the brainstem is activated, a child's heart may automatically race, their breathing may instinctively quicken, cortisol and adrenaline may be released causing their bodies to feel uncomfortable, their hands may ball into fists, and/or their blood pressure may suddenly rise, causing their face to flush. All of these physical responses are automatic and beyond a child's active control. They are the brain's natural way of preparing the body to protect itself from danger—which is essential for survival.

The Limbic Brain

Housed deep within the human brain is the *limbic system* or, in simplest terms, the *emotional brain*. The limbic system directs the human body's emotional responses. Developmentally, young people's brains tend to be dominated by the limbic system. When adults casually remark that a child seems to be driven by their emotions, they are usually quite correct.

> Developmentally, young people's brains tend to be dominated by the limbic system.

The limbic system, which includes the hippocampus, thalamus, and amygdala, is the part of the brain most directly involved in regulating emotions and memories. Together, these structures contribute to the body's *fight, flight, or freeze* response. In practical terms, when the limbic brain perceives any kind of danger, it directs the body to either fight the threat (e.g., through yelling, physical aggression), flee the situation (e.g., by running away, withdrawal), or freeze up (e.g., by shutting down emotionally). The limbic brain works in tandem with the reptilian brain to power large muscles, divert blood blow, and enable other bodily responses that make fight, flight, and freeze reactions possible. Bottom line: the human body's responses to perceived threats are brain-directed and instinctual, rather than purposeful, willful, or intentionally defiant acts. This is a critical fact to be aware of when working with young people through stressful situations.

In his book *Social: Why Our Brains Are Wired to Connect,* renowned psychologist Matthew Lieberman (2014) shows that human beings are hard-wired to seek out and maintain social connections and that the limbic brain reacts to social pain—such as perceived rejection or feeling disrespected—in much the same way as it does to physical pain. In school and treatment settings, professionals often marvel at how a dirty look, a barely audible insult, or a "mere" tweet can trigger such extreme emotional reactions from young people. Awareness that social *connection is a* primary driver of human behavior affords us an entirely new understanding of the powerful behavioral impact of events that make young people feel socially disconnected or alienated.

Lastly, it is critical to understand that the limbic system *does not have access to words and language.* When activated by a real or perceived threat, this part of the brain is not able to communicate with the parts of the brain responsible for language or logic. In the next section, we explain why this separation of feelings from language is so significant and explain how the LSCI approach helps bridge this critical gap.

> The limbic system does not have access to words and language.

The Neocortex

The *neocortex*, or the *thinking brain*, as it is commonly called, is involved in "higher" brain functions such as evaluating, problem-solving, reasoning, planning, logical thought, and language. High stress diminishes the neocortex's ability to carry out these functions. Developmentally, the neocortex is not fully mature until a person is in their mid-twenties. It is not surprising then—nor should it be the mark of a "problem" child—that kids need consistent adult intervention and guidance to be able to fully access the logical, rational, thinking part of their brain.

It is also worth noting that while adult brains typically are dominated by the neocortex, we, too, in times of stress can revert to behaviors that are driven by our limbic brains. An essential feature of the LSCI approach is the management of our own responses to a young person's troubling behaviors and making sure that we, as adults, control our reactions in a thoughtful way, rather than in a limbic-driven, emotional, conflict-fueling one. The conflict-fueling reactions of adults are often referred to in this text as *counter-aggression*.

State-Dependent Functioning

State-dependent functioning, a core concept of Dr. Bruce Perry's Neurosequential Model of Therapeutics (NMT), suggests that people process and store information in different ways depending on their current internal state (Perry, 2020). Threat and fear shift a person's internal state dramatically, influencing the way they perceive, think, feel, and behave. The more threatened a person feels, the less access they have to the higher-level processing abilities of their cortex and the more reactive their limbic brain becomes. This is very important to keep in mind when working with a young trauma survivor who, because of their history of ACEs, has a limbic brain that is chronically hypervigilant for danger and threat in their environment.

> The more threatened a person feels, the less access they have to the higher-level processing abilities of their cortex and the more reactive their limbic brain becomes.

According to Perry, when kids are in an alarm state, they *functionally regress*, moving from the more complex part of their brain where speech and language occurs (the neocortex) to the more reactive parts (the limbic brain) where fight/flight/freeze instincts dominate (2020). Knowing this is critical because it helps us understand why young people in stressful situations can become more emotional and why their behaviors can become less rational.

Polyvagal Theory

Dr. Stephen Porges' polyvagal theory centers on the brain-body connection, including a person's physiological response to a (perceived) threatening situation. It posits that for many people who have been traumatized, the event is bad enough but the long-term consequences of that event on their brain and nervous system are what profoundly change their ability to adapt in the world (2015). Porges focuses on the body's physical responses to stress and trauma, including sensations of immobilization, dissociation, fear, and rage.

For example, polyvagal theory suggests that under threat, the nervous system impacts muscle tension in the middle ear, loosening tension of the inner drum so that lower frequencies are more likely to be detected. Lower frequencies increase a human's perception of danger. Imagine, if you will, the low sound of a lion's roar and the instantaneous fear that "travels" through your body when this sound is perceived. As helping adults, when we apply this specific insight about how the brain responds to stress and trauma, we can make a conscious choice to use a calm, soft, higher-frequency voice with a young person during a stressful situation, to help convey safety at an unconscious, physiological level. Also, in the Timeline stage of LSCI (see Chapter 7), we make sure to ask the youth questions such as, "What do you notice in your body right now?" in order to acknowledge and build awareness of their physiological responses to stress. While looking at the many complexities of polyvagal theory are beyond the scope of this book, it is helpful for LSCI practitioners to have a working knowledge of the fact that that the way we interact with young people in crisis can significantly impact their brain and body's responses to stress.

Types of Memory

We know that memories and thoughts are stored in different parts of the brain. Let's distinguish between two types of memory: implicit memory and explicit memory.

Implicit Memory

Implicit memory uses past experiences to remember and recall things without consciously thinking about them. For example, when you tie your shoes in the morning or make your daily drive home from work in the evening, you aren't consciously aware that you are thinking about "how to" do either one; these memory processes are occurring below or outside of your conscious awareness. Implicit memory is both unconscious and unintentional, though it directly affects both our thoughts and our behaviors. This type of memory is sometimes referred to as non-declarative memory since you are not able to consciously bring it into awareness (Cherry, 2019). Implicit memories are stored in the limbic brain and are sensory, rather than language-based.

> Implicit memory is both unconscious and unintentional, though it directly affects both our thoughts and our behaviors.

It is important to note that when traumatic experiences occur, they "land" in the implicit memory and because they are associated with bodily sensations and emotions rather than with words, they are experienced much differently than ordinary memories. Specifically, implicit memories return not as neatly sequenced narratives that can be easily verbalized, but rather as intense emotional reactions, nightmares, horrifying images, aggressive behavior, physical pain, and bodily states (van der Kolk, 2002). For this reason, traumatic memories are far more difficult to process and much more likely to lead to spontaneous behaviors when triggered. Likewise, memories of trauma can become "stuck" in the limbic brain, replaying over and over and triggering sensory-based, behavioral responses during times of stress.

> Traumatic memories are far more difficult to process and much more likely to lead to spontaneous behaviors when triggered.

Explicit Memory

Explicit memory is conscious and involves information that is easily recalled and recited. When you are intentionally trying to remember something, such as an appointment date or a person's name, this information is stored in your explicit memory. In contrast to implicit memory, explicit memory is language-based and therefore easier to process. When we can process perceptions, thoughts, and feelings effectively (e.g., through talking, journaling, lyrics), we are less likely to spontaneously act them out through behaviors.

With LSCI, our objective is to move kids' raw memories from the part of the brain that doesn't have language to the part of the brain that does. We do so first by helping kids become more emotionally regulated and then by using the Timeline skills to sequence events and put language to emotion. You will learn more about how to carry out these two key components of the LSCI process in Chapter 8.

> With LSCI, our objective is to move kids' raw memories from the part of the brain that doesn't have language to the part of the brain that does.

Neuroscience, Trauma, and the LSCI Approach

Having a sequential model of how the brain develops, processes, and stores information is extremely helpful in understanding both "how" and "why" LSCI works. With this awareness, we recognize that a dysregulated individual (child, youth, or adult) will have a difficult time benefiting from educational and therapeutic efforts targeted at, or requiring, "higher" cortical networks. This knowledge helps us understand why (rather than assign blame to) a dysregulated individual will be inefficient in mastering any task that requires relational abilities (limbic) and will have a difficult time engaging in more verbal/insight-oriented (cortical) therapeutic and educational efforts.

Essential Ways to Apply This Information

1. It is important to know that traumatic stress creates chronic activation of the limbic brain and is often reflected in a young person's unwanted behaviors. In some youth, traumatic stress appears as an inability to focus, difficulty managing impulses, poor emotional regulation, anxiety, or aggressive behavior. These characteristic signs of trauma can mimic symptoms of ADHD, ODD, and/or conduct disorder. It is not uncommon for a young person who has experienced trauma to be improperly diagnosed and even prescribed psychotropic medications, with treatment focused entirely on the symptoms rather than their cause. For others, trauma mimics dissociative symptoms. A child can appear to have difficulty sustaining attention, poor motivation, social withdrawal, zoning out, numbness, self-harm, or avoidance. In school and treatment settings, it is important to understand the full context of a child's life space, including the impact of traumatic experiences, in order to effectively reach and teach them. Appendix A of this book includes *A Comparison of Traditional Accommodations and Accommodations Using the Lens for ACEs*, which provides a list of supports and resources for young people who carry in pain-based behaviors and need accommodations that address their attachment and regulation needs.

2. The more active the lower parts of the brain (reptilian brain and limbic system), the less access we have to our logic, our reason, and our intellect. In short, the more activated by stress we are, the less rational we become.

   As we work with young people, it is critical to keep in mind the range of events that can activate a prolonged stress response. While the traumatic impact of abuse or the death of a loved one tends to linger in the forefront of an adult's mind when they interact with an affected child, many of us are less proficient at holding "everyday" systemic traumas, such as racism, sexism, homophobia, and poverty, in our consciousness. These pervasive, painful, powerful forces can too easily be overlooked because of their daily presence in a young person's life, but it is up to all of us who work with young people not to discount their deep and significant impact.

3. A working knowledge of the reptilian brain, limbic brain, and neocortex can help us understand and identify signs of regulation and dysregulation in young people. When we understand dysregulation as a brain-based state that can be mitigated through specific strategies (see Drain Off, Chapter 7)—rather than

seeing it as intentional misbehavior deserving of punishment—we improve the way we interact with stressed-out kids. When we are able to recognize the signs of a well-regulated brain, we can shift to more cortex-based strategies (see Timeline, Chapter 7). See Table 2.1 for common signs of regulation vs. dysregulation as reflected in a young person's mind, mood, and body.

4. Remember that *the limbic brain does not have access to language or logic.* It is critical to be aware that when a young person's body is instinctively gearing up to deal with a stressful situation, it is physically unable to put words to all of this emotion. As adults, we want (and often demand) kids to "use their words" to tell us why they are upset. Having an understanding of the limbic system's dominance over a young person's brain during a stressful situation helps us understand why, in the heat of the moment, kids *lack the ability*—not

TABLE 2.1 SIGNS OF WELL-REGULATED AND DYSREGULATED THOUGHTS, FEELINGS, AND BEHAVIORS IN YOUTH		
	Signs of Regulation	Signs of Dysregulation
Mind (Thoughts)	• Can consider more than one perspective/point of view • Can hear words and make sense of them • Has positive, hopeful growth mindset • Thoughts reflect confidence and competence (self-efficacy) • Can consider options and choices • Can analyze costs and benefits of behaviors • Has resilient thoughts (bounce back) • Focused on task • Mind is alert and flexible; can go with the flow • Mindful of feelings, behaviors, surroundings, and senses • Self-aware of stress or early signs of dysregulation • Is actively regulating thoughts (e.g., "It will be OK, I can handle this") • Can plan, prioritize, and organize	• Fixated, stuck on a thought, dwelling, perseveration • Inflexible; unable to consider behavioral options • Unaware of surroundings; unaware of what you are experiencing (senses) • Can hear words but unable to make sense of them (not processing language or social cues) • Wandering thoughts • Mind clutter; too many thoughts, too much on my mind • Negative self-talk: negative thoughts about self or others • Thoughts of incompetence ("I can't do it") • Thoughts of quitting, giving up • Hopeless thoughts ("Nothing ever works out, I'll never be successful") • Blaming thoughts • Angry or frustrated thoughts • Hyper alertness to emotional landmines

(continues)

TABLE 2.1 (*continued*)

	Signs of Regulation	Signs of Dysregulation
Mood (Feelings)	• Feels in control • Feels safe, secure, and settled • Has comfortable feelings (e.g., happy, calm, patient, confident) • Feels motivated ("I can") rather than overwhelmed ("I can't")	• Unsafe • Alone; no one understands • Bummed out, unmotivated • Sad, depressed • Over-excited, impatient, over-whelmed, unsettled • Angry, furious, enraged • Nervous, tense, worried, anxious, scared • Ashamed or embarrassed • Shut down; like I can't communicate what I want or need
Body (Behaviors)	• Body is in control • Just right energy • Body is relaxed but not tired • Smiles • Full on your seat • Eyes track the speaker • Ears listen to the speaker • Can make sense of the speaker's words • Voice is relaxed; tone is friendly • Connected and engaged • Body is socially respectful; provides space and is safe, gentle • Humor is appropriate to the context (not disparaging, denigrating or cutting)	• Sick, unwell • Tired, low energy, moving slowly • Awkward in seat (on edge of seat, slumping, head on desk or in hands) • Over-energized; body is jumpy, fidgety, wiggly, shaky • Can't control verbalizations, blurting, impulsive verbals • Body out of control; impulsive movements and actions • Aggressive voice, loud and angry tone • Unexpected language • Biting sarcasm • Body is unsafe: not providing space, physically aggressive or threatening • Body showing disengagement from academics, social situation

Note. © 2020 by Eric Mann. Adapted with permission.

the will—to put words to how they are feeling. This basic understanding of how a young person's brain functions is critical because it helps us adjust our expectations and accept that kids are doing the best they can with the brains they have.

> Kids are doing the best they can with the brains they have.

5. LSCI is an approach that helps adults calm a young person's overactive emotional brain (through Stage 1 of the LSCI process, known as *Drain Off*) and

bring language to emotion (through Stage 2 of the LSCI process, known as *Timeline*) so that kids are better able to access their neocortex and utilize the problem-solving part of their brain (through Stages 4 to 6 of the LSCI process).

6. With LSCI, our goal is always to drain off the intense emotions triggered in the limbic brain, then assist kids in moving their perceptions, thoughts, and feelings from the part of the brain that doesn't have language to the part of the brain that does. In doing so, we help kids gain insight into the destructive nature of their behaviors and learn skills to better manage problem situations. More details on the six-stage process of LSCI is provided in Chapter 7.

In the next chapter, we look at another essential element of the healing process validated by neuroscience, trauma-informed practice, and LSCI's usage over the decades: the power of positive relationships.

"I don't care
what you know
until I know
that you care."

3 THE PRIMARY IMPORTANCE OF POSITIVE RELATIONSHIPS

Relationship is *connection*. According to the Canadian Mental Health Association (2019), social connections are known to boost both mental and physical health, including lowering anxiety and depression, helping us regulate emotions, increasing self-esteem, building empathy, and actually improving our immune systems. Adults and young people "connect" for many reasons, each having to do with their own unique needs. Adults are motivated to guide and teach young people, seeing themselves as helpers and advocates or as nurturers and care providers. Children and adolescents connect for safety, protection, learning, and nurturance. They respond to the experience, power, wisdom, knowledge, compassion, and skills of adults. Kids model the behaviors and attitudes of adults they admire and are more willing to listen to adults with whom they feel a connection. In *Help for Billy: A Beyond Consequences Approach to Helping Challenging Children in the Classroom*, Heather Forbes (2012) explains:

> Teachers are humans. Students are human. Merge these two vital forces and what comes to fruition is a powerful teacher-student relationship. This relationship far outweighs any other technique created by educators to further a student's academic achievement. Humans as a species are designed to be in relationship and to be in community. Relationship is what defines humanity. When relationships are neglected or placed secondary to other goals, such as academics, both students and teachers suffer. Integrating this relational concept back into the classroom is the solution."

Indeed, an adult's effectiveness with young people is often directly proportional to the quality of their connection with them. LSCI is built on relationship.

Relationship is also *regulation*. For our purposes, we define regulation as a calm brain state and say that a well-regulated person is one who can effectively access the higher-level functions of their thinking brain in order to select helpful responses to stressful experiences. Neuroscience shows us definitively that a well-regulated adult who is connected to a young person through a trusting relationship has the capacity to help calm the brain of a young person in distress. This phenomenon, called *co-regulation*, is a truly amazing function of our brains and a testament to the power of connection between human beings. LSCI works because emotions are contagious (Desautels, 2016) and *regulated* adults can use their *connection* with a young person to create calm.

The interpersonal abilities to *connect* with others and to *regulate* emotions come quite naturally to many educators, psychologists, counselors, social workers, youth care workers, and others who choose to work in a professional capacity with challenging children and adolescents. And yet, there are circumstances, interpersonal dynamics, systemic pressures, and personality mismatches that sometimes thwart even the most relationship-oriented persons. Before we move on with our study of the foundational skills of LSCI, it is critical to acknowledge—and to overcome—common challenges to forming the positive relationships that are at the heart of the LSCI process.

What Gets in the Way of Forming Positive Relationships With Young People?

We begin with an urban legend that, although debunked by the US Navy, provides a great representation of power struggles between adults and youth:

> This is the transcript of a radio conversation of a US naval ship with Canadian authorities off the coast of Newfoundland in October 1995. Radio conversation released by the Chief of Naval Operations 10-10-95.

> *Americans: Please divert your course 15 degrees to the north to avoid a collision.*
> *Canadians: Recommend you divert YOUR course 15 degrees to the south to avoid a collision.*
> *Americans: This is the captain of a US Navy ship. I say again, divert YOUR course.*
> *Canadians: No. I say again, you divert YOUR course.*

> *Americans: This is the aircraft carrier USS Lincoln, the second largest ship in the United States' Atlantic fleet. We are accompanied by three destroyers, three cruisers, and numerous support vessels. I demand that YOU change your course 15 degrees north, that's one-five degrees north, or countermeasures will be undertaken to ensure the safety of this ship.*
>
> *Canadians: This is a lighthouse. Your call.*

Like the captain, many of us have learned the hard way that kids know how to short-circuit authoritarian attempts at control. Also like the captain, we can find ourselves feeling powerless because we don't know alternatives to traditional discipline strategies, which are ineffective with many young people and can cause damage to our relationships with them. LSCI teaches practical strategies that take professionals past rigid discipline and toward a more effective way to connect with challenging children in order to create genuine, lasting changes in their behavior. As Forbes (2012) reminds us, "True 'power' and 'control' do not come through authority, but through relational influence."

Unfortunately, most professionals, including the captain, do not have explicit training in how to effectively respond to kids' problem behaviors and use relationship to bring about lasting change. Rather, in our haste to take care of problems quickly and efficiently, we can be quick to speak and slow to listen. Despite our good intentions to care for kids, we can fail to recognize that *the problems kids cause are not the causes of their problems*. As a result, we address kids' surface behaviors (e.g., disrespect, yelling, cursing, rule-breaking, aggression) but fail to find out what is causing those behaviors. Instead of making things better, we sometimes make matters worse. LSCI, with its focus on the importance of forming positive relationships between adults and kids, offers a process that can turn that around.

> The problems kids cause are not the causes of their problems.

Three Outcomes of a Conflict

There are three possible outcomes when an adult-child conflict emerges.

Outcome 1: Adult-Child Relationship Unchanged

In many schools and treatment settings for children and youth, the staff reaction to a crisis or conflict is punishment. Many settings have an established list of "consequences" for specific infractions. There is little or no consideration of the circumstances surrounding the situation or the young person's perception of the event. For many challenging youth, these rote punishments have little effect on changing behavior because they address only the symptoms and not the perceptions, thoughts, and feelings that underlie the behavior. The young person does not feel that the adult is genuinely concerned about them, and so an opportunity to build a more positive relationship is missed. In this type of situation, nothing changes except that the likelihood of future problems increases.

Consider the following example:

> Jon is a 16-year-old student who attends a large suburban high school. Every day, he meets his girlfriend as they pass in the hall during the third period class change. He walks her to her class then races down the hall only to be late for his English class at least three times per week. Mr. Gore, the teacher, usually makes a sarcastic comment such as, "Well, if it isn't the late Jon Smith!" as he hands him a detention slip. Jon has not changed his behavior and is now beginning to cut detention, which could lead to suspension.

Outcome 2: Adult-Child Relationship Damaged

Unfortunately, there are times when the pressure of professional expectations or the tension of a tiring day can get the best of an otherwise caring adult. Just like young people, adults can become emotionally overloaded and find their behaviors driven by their limbic brain rather than their neocortex. In these moments, adults may humiliate, degrade, or belittle a young person. They say things they would not normally say and behave in ways that are uncharacteristic. Even though these behaviors might be unusual, when they happen and are not quickly repaired, hurtful interactions with an unregulated adult can severely damage the adult-child relationship. In some cases, the damage extends to the young person's entire school or treatment experience.

> What if Mr. Gore was frustrated on a Monday morning after a stressful weekend at home and replaced his usual sarcastic comments with cruel, berating ones in front of all of Jon's classmates? What if Mr. Gore threatened to do something humiliating like meeting Jon at the end of his second period class and personally escorting him to third period? What if Mr. Gore decided to teach Jon a lesson by lowering his class grade, thereby affecting his overall GPA? For too many students, these "what ifs" are a daily relationship-damaging reality.

Outcome 3: Adult-Child Relationship Improved

The skills of LSCI help professionals move away from a relationship-damaging focus on behaviors and consequences to a relationship-building emphasis on regulation and connection. Throughout this book, we will show you how interventions framed in the spirit of relationship bring about long-term changes in a child's beliefs, thoughts, feelings, and behaviors and how this simple shift from "behavioral" strategies to "relational" ones can make all of the difference in the life of a child.

> LSCI training gives the adults in a child's *life space* the knowledge, skills, and ability to genuinely connect with kids, ask questions about problem situations, listen well to the answers, decode deeper meaning, and respond in ways that are at once calming and dignifying. An LSCI-trained teacher would understand the importance of connecting with Jon on a personal level early in the school year so that should trouble ever arise, he could use the foundation of their positive relationship to encourage adherence to class rules. An LSCI-trained teacher would maintain enough self-awareness to realize that their frustrated, sarcastic reactions to a student only escalate problem situations and would use specific skills to manage and reduce their own counter-aggressive, conflict-fueling behaviors. Schools and organizations that have LSCI infused into their culture are ones in which young people seek out adults as helpers rather than regarding them as adversaries. LSCI offers adults and kids alike both the mindset and the skillset to turn problem situations into long-term learning opportunities.

Research from Harvard University's Center on the Developing Child (2020) highlights the value and impact caring adults can have on a child's life:

> The single most common factor for children who develop resilience is at least one stable and committed relationship with a supportive parent, caregiver, or other adult. These relationships provide the personalized responsiveness, scaffolding, and protection that buffer children from developmental disruption. They also build key capacities—such as the ability to plan, monitor, and regulate behavior—that enable children to respond adaptively to adversity and thrive.

The importance of positive relationships in a young person's life can never be overstated.

The Neuroscience of Positive and Negative Adult-Child Relationships

Why Kids Dwell on the Negative

Neuropsychologist Rick Hanson suggests that our brains are like Velcro for negative experiences and Teflon to positive ones (2020). From an evolutionary perspective, humankind's instinct to dwell on perceived dangers and threats makes perfect sense; to live to see another day, cave people always needed to keep the threat of dangerous encounters with saber-toothed tigers in mind. The trouble is, our twenty-first-century limbic brains do not distinguish between a tiger's roar and a teacher's raised voice; both are perceived as threatening and both activate the body's fight, flight, or freeze response. The good news is our brains remain wired to protect us. The bad news is our brain's wiring can be over-protective at times.

As a result of the human brain's negativity bias, negative interactions with adults produce more activity in a young person's brain than do positive ones. What's more, negative experiences are more rapidly transferred to the brain's long-term memory than positive experiences. This explains why an otherwise good day can so quickly be remembered as the "worst day ever" by a child.

For young people who have experienced trauma (see Chapter 2), the impact of the brain's tendency to hold on to negative interactions is even greater. Harsh words, raised voices, attempts at behavioral coercion, and punitive warnings from adults all set off alarm bells in the child's hypersensitive limbic brain. The adult-child connection is especially fragile and particularly susceptible to relational damage.

Children who lack a close relationship to an important adult, who lack an awareness of being loved and protected (or who perceive themselves as unloved or unworthy) suffer intense emotional pain. The resulting anxiety can be debilitating. It compounds other problems of general development. Without alleviation, this pain can persist into adolescence and adult life, permeating self-esteem, heightening sensitivity to stress, and compounding the problems of forming and maintaining satisfying relationships with others.

How Relationships Can Be Used to Create Something Positive

It's not all bad news when it comes to negative experiences and the brain, however! As noted earlier in the chapter, helping adults have the ability to create calm in dysregulated kids, through co-regulation and the influence of mirror neurons. Mirror neurons are neurons that respond to actions that we observe in others (Acharya & Shukla, 2012). What is especially interesting is that mirror neurons fire in the same way when we actually recreate that action ourselves. This means that when an adult chooses to communicate positive regard and to model a calm response to a stressful situation, the mirror neurons in a young person's brain can pick up on and directly mimic that goodwill and calm. At all times, an adult has a choice to make: do we want to escalate a problem situation by role modeling an angry, aggressive, or hostile response? Are these the emotions and behaviors we want a child to

> Helping adults have the ability to create calm in dysregulated kids, through co-regulation and the influence of mirror neurons.

mirror? Or so we want to turn down the heat on a conflict by responding with calm, logic, and a problem-solving mindset? The choice is ours. (We will discuss this concept in further detail in Chapter 6: *The Adult's Role in Breaking the Conflict Cycle.*) For now, it is helpful to keep in mind that connection and self-regulation allow adults to model positive responses that young people can pick up on and mirror during stressful situations. Mutual goodwill is the foundation of emotional regulation, problem-solving, and long-term behavioral change.

> Connection and self-regulation allow adults to model positive responses that young people can pick up on and mirror during stressful situations.

What Comes First: Changing the Child's Behavior or Changing the Adult's?

While most youth-oriented intervention programs focus squarely on strategies for changing the challenging behaviors of kids, LSCI is unique in its core belief that behavioral change begins with the adults. We believe that change starts with adults modeling the behavior they want to see from young people. LSCI challenges practitioners to:

- Acknowledge their role in escalating or de-escalating a conflict
- Choose neocortex-based *responses* over amygdala-driven *reactions*
- Use their inherent authority to create connection and calm rather than conflict and chaos

When adults shift their focus from changing others to changing the way they respond to others, that's where their real power lies and that's where their greatest effectiveness begins.

> When adults shift their focus from changing others to changing the way they respond to others, that's where their real power lies and that's where their greatest effectiveness begins.

Attributes of Adults Who Conduct Successful LSCIs

Adults who do successful LSCIs seem to hold and convey some fundamental beliefs about a young person's needs for protection, gratification, and responsibility—basic immunizations against excessive stress and anxiety.

Protection by adults provides emotional support while enhancing a youth's capacity to face stress constructively. Protection gives young people confidence that they will not be exposed to embarrassment, ridicule, or failure. Protection gives assurance that adults will not violate a student's privacy—that family issues and personal information will not be publicly exposed. Protection also assures that adults will maintain an environment where young people will not be hurt by others. Protection is a fundamental premise in every LSCI.

Gratification is a necessity of life. Somehow, every young person must have hope that things will get better and that experiences will bring joy. Without hope and joy, life loses meaning and there is little, if any, energy available for learning or for social-emotional growth. A young person's storehouse of memories must contain, on balance, a greater number of positive than negative emotional memories. Effective LSCI expands this memory bank and uses a youth's need for gratification as a motivation for change. LSCI holds out the promise of better things to come—through change!

Responsibility is the basis for solving problems and coping successfully with stress. Responsibility requires value-directed behavior, in which a young person recognizes the need to self-regulate. A youth's capacity for responsibility evolves through the development of a coherent sequence of thoughts and feelings about obligations to themselves and others. Whatever the extent of a young person's sense of responsibility, it is a necessary theme to be introduced in some form into every LSCI. When adults keep in mind that ultimately a young person must assume responsibility, the natural impulse to take over and tell the youth how to handle a problem or solve a crisis is restrained.

These three basic psychological concepts are conveyed by adults who use LSCI successfully. These messages contribute to a climate that counters the negative impact of stress, adverse experiences, frustrations, and disappointments experienced daily by young people. These concepts are the antidotes to a child's feelings of unworthiness and helplessness in controlling what happens to them. Throughout the book you will see these concepts applied.

How Do You Want to Be Remembered by the Young People in Your Life?

Using the brief exercise that follows, we challenge you to think about how, 20 years from now, you'd like to be remembered by the young people with whom you work. Consider the questions below and record your thoughts in the space provided:

1. Identify an adult from your childhood who made a positive difference in your life. Record the person's name and briefly explain what they said or did to make you feel valued and worthy.

_____

_____

_____

2. Now, identify an adult from your childhood who made a painful or negative impression on your life. In the space below, briefly explain what they said or did to cause you pain and/or a loss of trust.

_____

_____

_____

3. The things said and done by adults have a lifelong impact on kids—and on the future generations that they, in turn, encounter. We must be ever mindful of the words we speak and the actions we take with the kids in our care. *How do you want to be remembered by a child?*

_____

_____

_____

"You think you know
what I said.
But what you don't
know is,
what I said is not
what I meant."

4

THE PSYCHOLOGICAL WORLDS OF YOUNG PEOPLE IN STRESSFUL SITUATIONS

The LSCI Conflict Cycle™ (see Figure 4.1) explains the circular and escalating dynamics of conflict between adults and children. It breaks down specific antecedents of problem situations to shine a light on areas for crisis prevention and offers critical insights about the adult's role in either fueling problem situations or ending them before they spiral out of control. In this chapter, we analyze six key concepts related to the psychological world of a young person during a stressful situation. These concepts are foundational to understanding adult-child Conflict Cycles. In Chapter 5, we analyze the final element of the LSCI Conflict Cycle (the only element that adults have control over) and then put all of the concepts together to show you how crisis dynamics play out in real life.

Key Concept 1: The Impact of Stress

Stress is a normal part of life. At times, it serves a useful purpose. Stress can motivate adults to meet important deadlines at work and can prompt kids to study hard for a test. While not all types of stress are bad, when young people become overwhelmed by the stressors in their lives, crises become more likely. In this section, we distinguish between *universal stressors* (developmental stress, physical stress, and reality stress) embedded in the process of growing up and *traumatic stressors* (see Chapter 2) created by adverse childhood experiences. Both types of stress profoundly affect a child's burgeoning self-concept and beliefs about the world.

> While not all types of stress are bad, when young people become overwhelmed by the stressors in their lives, crises become more likely.

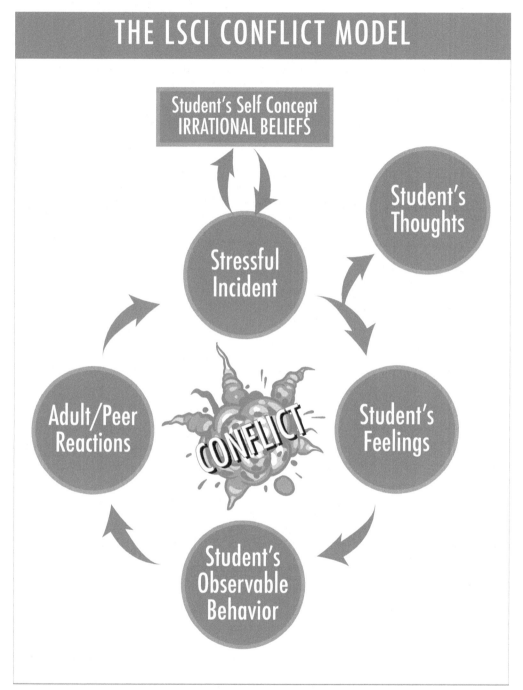

Figure 4.1. The conflict cycle.

Developmental Stress

Developmental stress refers to the normal age-related changes human beings go through over the course of a lifetime. In Chapter 9, we closely examine five types of developmental stressors that occur in a predictable sequence in all children and youth: abandonment, inadequacy, guilt, independence–dependence conflict, and identity. Every stage of development imposes its own characteristic demands on a developing child or youth.

For some kids, developmental stressors are handled in stride on their pathway to becoming independent adults. For others, "developmental arrest" occurs when adverse experiences prohibit a child from mastering the psychological challenge of a stage. Having an awareness of how developmental stress and developmental arrest impact a young person's inner world is essential in understanding their outward behavior.

Physical Stress

Physical stressors are felt by millions of young people every day. Common stressors in this category include:

- Threats to safety
- Lack of adequate shelter
- Lack of sleep
- Hunger
- Poor diet and nutrition
- Poor hygiene
- Illness or disability

Young people living in communities where they feel safe and have their basic physical needs consistently met have the luxury of going to school ready to learn. Kids who live in persistent states of deprivation, on the other hand, can have a harder time complying with rules to sit quietly, focus on instruction, and attend to challenging material when their brains and bodies are preoccupied by basic physical needs. Attentiveness to this disconnect between adult-child goals is critical to avoiding relationship-damaging power struggles and conflict.

Reality Stress

Reality stressors are frustrating unplanned events. They happen spontaneously and not from any organized attempt to upset a young person. Common examples of reality stress in a kid's life may include spilling something on clothing, an embarrassing moment with peers, not being able to open a locker, a forgotten homework assignment, getting a bad grade, arriving late to a class, or misplacing a smartphone. For many kids, reality stress often comes from multiple sources at once.

Universal Stressors vs. Traumatic Stressors

When adults' reactions are supportive and oriented toward helping young people manage universal sources of stress, kids develop resilience and crises may be averted.

When adults are unsupportive, however, and a youth's emotional resources are overwhelmed, developmental, physical, and reality stressors can be experienced as trauma. As you learned in Chapter 2, the memories of unmitigated stressors are stored in the brain's limbic system and can resurface in the form of challenging behaviors. Unmitigated stressors are antecedents for crisis.

> Unmitigated stressors are antecedents for crisis.

Can the Impact of Stress on Young People Be Mitigated?

It is critical to note that the impact of traumatic stress on a child can, in fact, be mitigated. We know from Chapter 3 that positive relationships provide the "personalized responsiveness, scaffolding, and protection that buffer children from developmental disruption . . . and enable children to respond adaptively to adversity and thrive." What's more, Perry and Szalavitz (2017) remind us that "the more healthy relationships a child has, the more likely he will be to recover from trauma and thrive."

Key Concept 2: Self-Concept and Irrational Beliefs

What kids believe about themselves is more important in determining their behavior than any facts about them. A young person's self-concept and personal belief systems are rooted in the experiences of their earliest years of life and continue to develop as they age. When a young person experiences chronic stress, when adults have been unsupportive,

> What kids believe about themselves is more important in determining their behavior than any facts about them.

neglectful, or abusive, and when the child has felt powerless to improve conditions, the impact on their psychological world is profound and enduring.

Consider This (Dawson & McBride, 2014)

Think of a young person you know who has been exposed to traumatic stress during childhood. Consider the impact of this experience(s) on the child's developing beliefs about self (self-concept), beliefs about others, and beliefs about the world. Record your thoughts from the perspective of the young person you are holding in your mind.

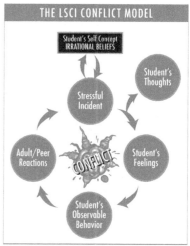

Figure 4.2. Self-concept and irrational beliefs.

I am . . . (*What have they been told about themselves, again and again?*)

_____

_____

_____

_____

All adults are . . . (*What has their experience been with caregivers?*)

_____

_____

_____

Life is . . . (*What has life or the world taught them?*)

_____

_____

_____

We share this powerful exercise during LSCI trainings. Below are two examples completed by participant groups from the perspective of a young person in their care:

Example 1:
Subject: An elementary school-aged student, diagnosed with ADHD, whose parents were both incarcerated due to opioid abuse. The child's living situation was inconsistent, as he moved between the homes of relatives every few weeks.
I am . . . *annoying, wild, stupid, a pain, going to end up in jail someday*
All adults are . . . *unreliable, mean, unfair, impatient*
Life is . . . *hard, impossible, pointless, unpredictable, out of my control*

Example 2:
Subject: A high school student who is a survivor of sexual abuse.

I am . . . *dirty, unloved, to blame, disgusting, damaged, not safe*
All adults are . . . *scary, dirty, not trustworthy, manipulative*
Life is . . . *not worth living, scary, tough, difficult, unstable*

To bring logic, order, and some sense to their stressful worlds, young people make generalized interpretations about why bad things happen.

- They hear the words adults use about them (e.g., "a pain in the ass," "disgusting") and internalize these descriptions as part of their own self-concept.
- They develop one "schema" for adults—they are all untrustworthy and mean.
- Their developing beliefs, based on their actual experiences, lead them to conclude that life is hard, the world is scary, and they are powerless to control the bad things that happen to them.

While it is apparent to us that the bad things that happen during childhood won't inevitably last forever or be repeated by other adults, kids don't have this benefit of broad life experience that tells them that "things can be different." Rather, kids are more likely to overgeneralize. *Overgeneralization* is the process of taking single events and broadly applying them to all circumstances.

There are benefits to this kind of "pathological" thinking. For kids who feel that they have no control over their world, overgeneralization makes their world more predictable—and therefore seem more manageable. Have you ever wondered why kids continue to act out even when they know they are going to get in trouble? Consider the following example:

Jonathan grows up in a family where both parents are alcoholic. He is constantly yelled at when his parents are intoxicated. He goes to school and meets his teacher, Mr. Fisher, who is firm, fair, friendly, and does not raise his voice at students. What is Jonathan going to try to get Mr. Fisher to do? *Yell at him!* Why is this so important to Jonathan?

- Eliciting a familiar response from Mr. Fisher gives Jonathan's life a sense of being predictable and manageable rather than overwhelming because at least he knows what to expect.
- Kids like Jonathan don't have to risk getting hurt by beginning to trust Mr. Fisher or believing he could be different from the other adults in Jonathan's life.
- When Jonathan elicits a predictable response from Mr. Fisher, it makes him feel like he has a sense of control. In his subconscious calculation,

it's better to *cause* the adult's reaction than to find yourself a surprised, powerless victim of it.

- Jonathan doesn't have to take responsibility for his behavior because the fault lies elsewhere (with the unfair, scary adult).

It is critical for adults who work with kids that exhibit challenging behaviors to understand why kids behave the way they do—to realize that kids are instinctively driven to imitate, replicate, and duplicate their histories with adults again and again. If we allow ourselves to take their behavior personally (more on how to avoid this in Chapter 6) and if we engage in conflict with the young person, we accidentally acknowledge that their conclusions about adults are valid. Our goal is to help young people *change* their poor self-concept and negative beliefs. When we do this, we can help young people change their lives!

Now that we understand how some young people develop their beliefs about themselves and their world, it's time to look at how beliefs impact the ways kids perceive their world—especially stressful situations.

Key Concept 3: Perceptions

As we age, we tend to learn there are many ways to perceive things. For example, if we were to all witness a car accident, we could be certain that we would have multiple and varying accounts of it among us. We also know that sometimes our perceptions can be inaccurate. We know that stress, exhaustion, and other factors can color our perceptions. As a result, we are usually able to listen to an alternative viewpoint and reconsider our own.

A young person, on the other hand, may have a much more difficult time accepting varied points of view. Because trauma results in a fundamental reorganization of the way the brain manages perceptions (van der Kolk, 2014), kids in stress can be especially concrete and rigid in their perceptions. In those moments, attempts by an adult to offer a contrary point of view may be considered suspicious or confusing.

Adults can make the mistake of believing that kids are simply being stubborn when they insist that their perception of an event is the only correct one. The idea that the child *"knows the truth about what happened but won't admit it"* can trigger a hostile reaction from adults.

Consider This

Look at the image in Figure 4.3. What is the first thing that you see?

Can you see an alternate image?

Figure 4.3. My Wife and My Mother-in-Law.

This image, known as "My Wife and My Mother-in-Law," is drawn so that a viewer may either observe a young woman with her head turned to the right or an old woman with a large nose and protruding chin. *The image you see depends on your perception.*

As an optical illusion, this image is fun to view. It can be entertaining to try to see both images. Now, compare how you feel when you look at this image to how you feel during a conversation with a young person whose way of "seeing" a problem situation is different than yours. These conversations are rarely as fun and light-hearted. That's because adults, like children, can become rigid in their perceptions during times of stress and conflicting viewpoints. At times, we all dig our heels in and insist that our way is the right way.

In professional interactions, adults are expected to be able to show flexibility and to broaden their personal view of a situation by considering a young person's point of view. This can be hard to do, especially when pride is involved, others are watching, and/or we feel the need to assert our authority and "be right."

It's important to acknowledge that young people, driven by their self-concepts, beliefs, and histories of feeling powerless relative to adults, experience this same intense need to be right.

Feeling heard and understood—having your perception acknowledged and validated—is a universal need. An adult's willingness to un-dig their heels from an "absolute" way of seeing things and to be open to listening to an opposing point of view is a gift that we give to young people, especially those who are accustomed to having their viewpoint dismissed. Our flexibility signals to the child that we are different from their pre-conceived notion of "*all adults are . . .* and that, in time, we might actually be worthy of their trust.

> An adult's willingness to listen to an opposing point of view is a gift that we give to young people, especially those who are accustomed to having their viewpoint dismissed.

Returning to the discussion of "My Wife and My Mother-in-Law," imagine for a moment that you and a young person with whom you work are looking at the image together. You can only perceive the image of the wife and the youth can only perceive the image of the mother-in-law. Suppose as you talk to the child about your differing views of the image, you tell them that there will be consequences if they don't "admit" that the image depicts a young woman with her head turned to the right. What would go through the young person's mind if you punished them for their sincerely held perception that the image features an old woman with a large nose and protruding chin? Would the punishment change the way the child perceived the image? Or would it simply change (or affirm!) the way they perceived you? And adults like you?

The "My Wife and My Mother-in-Law" image lends us four critical insights to working with young people:

1. We all have unique ways of perceiving our world. Knowing how a child perceives a situation is always the starting point for teaching an alternate perception. The LSCI Timeline (see Chapter 7) equips adults with skills to uncover a child's unique perceptions.
2. A child's ability to consider other points of view has to do with the availability and approachability of an adult who will listen and dialogue with the child. LSCI provides a framework for communication that makes young people feel heard and understood and thus more willing to hear and understand alternate ways of perceiving a situation.
3. Punishment does not change perceptions. Two people can look at the same image, see it completely differently, and both be 100% correct in their perception of it. Is there an old woman in the image? *Yes.* Is there a young woman? *Yes.* Likewise, an adult and a child can perceive the same situation differently and both be "right." Trying to prove a personal point of view is a no-win, conflict-fueling situation.
4. When adults are willing to dialogue with a young person about the ways they perceive a stressful event, they open the door for a range of benefits, including better communication, mutual understanding, increased trust, and the opportunity to teach kids more flexible ways of viewing the world.

Key Concept 4: Thoughts and Thought Errors

As adults, our thinking is usually driven by our neocortex: logical and orderly. We establish predictable environments, make schedules, and

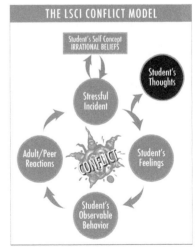

Figure 4.4. Thoughts and thought errors.

have plans to follow each day. When something interrupts the flow of the day, we seek to bring things under control quickly. Young people, in contrast, are more likely to respond emotionally when things go wrong and to have less of an ability to think rationally.

During stressful situations with young people, how many times have we found ourselves lecturing kids (a neocortex-driven response) while the kid is crying or yelling (a limbic brain reaction)? While it is a mark of professionalism and skill for us to remain in our logical brains during a conflict, it is a mistake when we fail to realize that a child is in a state of emotional turmoil and therefore unavailable to reason for the time being.

The neurobiological explanation for this is clear (see Chapter 2 for full detail). When a child is in a stressful situation:

- Their brain directs them to fight the perceived danger, flee the situation, or freeze up. Listening quietly, following directions, and thinking rationally are *not* a part of the fight, flight, or freeze reaction. The resulting behavior of young people is instinctual, rather than willful or intentionally defiant.
- Trauma changes not only how kids think and what they think about but also their very capacity to access the thinking part of their brain at all.
- Because kids in stressful situations cannot effectively access the language centers of their brain, demanding that they "use their words" at that point in time is futile.
- The only worthwhile goals in the moment are to keep the child physically safe and help drain off the intensity of their emotional reaction.

Cognitive Traps

We can identify five rigid patterns of thinking known as Cognitive Traps. Each of these thinking errors flows from a young person's self-concept and beliefs and can serve to distance the youth from taking any responsibility to change behaviors.

1. **Mental filter:** The young person selects a single negative detail and inflates its value. For example, a teacher says, "This paper is very well written. Your logic is easy to follow. Your sources are well-documented, and your research is comprehensive. Perhaps a summary paragraph at the conclusion would help tie it all together." The young person concludes:

   - "I knew I screwed this up. The teacher is just trying to let me down easy."

Occasionally, we see this thinking in young persons who announce at the start of the day that they are going to have a perfect day. At the moment of their first problem, they believe their goal is shattered and they feel all is lost. They can't recover from the single negative event.

2. **Discounting the positive:** The young person discounts his achievements. Positive experiences don't count.

   - "So I got an 'A' on my project—big deal. Everyone is going to get an 'A.'"

3. **All-or-nothing thinking:** The young person processes information in extremes. They tend to use words like "always" and "never" and struggle to recognize the "in between" areas of their world. The cognitive trap of thinking in negative extremes is sometimes referred to as *catastrophizing*.

   - "My teacher is never going to forgive me. She will always hate me."

4. **Jumping to conclusions:** The young person interprets situations negatively with no supporting data.

   - "No, I didn't tell the teacher about it when Jack stole my hat. Why should I, he wouldn't have done anything anyway."
   - (Teacher) "Dane, you'll have to stay here until you finish this worksheet." (Dane) "You knew I couldn't do all of this work before Gym. You just wanted me to miss it."

5. **Magnification and minimization:** The young perfect inflates or diminishes the importance of a behavior, in order to justify their reactions.

   - *Magnification:* It takes her, like, an hour to respond to any of my texts, so I took her phone. Clearly she's not using it anyway, so now I'm using it!
   - *Minimization:* It was just a joke. I don't know why she has to be so sensitive about everything. She totally took it the wrong way!

6. **Emotional reasoning:** The young person feels bad, so believes he is bad.

   - "I forgot to turn in my permission slip for the field trip and now I won't be able to go. I'm such a loser."

7. **"Should" statements:** The young person takes a narrow perspective on issues. "Should" statements often serve to reduce or remove responsibility for behavior and therefore limit opportunities for change.

- "Miss Foster should accept my paper even if it is incomplete and not very organized. At least I turned something in!"

Embedded in the LSCI process is ample time for kids to share their thoughts with adults. When attuned to common cognitive traps, adults can help kids understand—and ultimately change—distorted thought patterns that lead to painful feelings and often result in destructive, disruptive behavior.

> When attuned to common cognitive traps, adults can help kids understand—and ultimately change—distorted thought patterns that lead to painful feelings and often result in destructive, disruptive behavior.

Key Concept 5: Feelings and Defense Mechanisms

During LSCI trainings, we talk about the three choices we all have for expressing feelings.

1. **Accept and Own Personal Feelings**
   Ideally, our goal for young persons is to help them accept and own their feelings. We do this by helping them de-escalate intense feelings and put language to emotion once they are calm. Being able to accept and own feelings requires self-regulation skills, self-awareness, and an engaged neocortex. *As adults, we want to help kids develop the skills they need to accept and own their feelings.*

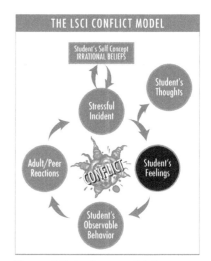

Figure 4.5. Feelings and defense mechanisms.

2. **Act Them Out**
   Some young people become quickly flooded by their feelings; they experience a feeling and they spontaneously act it out through behavior. Their motto seems to be *act first, think later.* In neuroscience terms, their behavior is amygdala-driven. We say that these young people don't just have feelings; they are "had" by their feelings. *As adults, our goal is to help prevent kids from becoming overwhelmed emotionally and lashing out.*

3. **Deny and Defend**
   Some youth experience feelings such as anger, sadness, or guilt as intolerable and try to deny their true feelings by employing *defense mechanisms.* Defense

mechanisms operate at an unconscious level and serve to guard against psychological pain. We all use defense mechanisms from time to time. Defenses can be very useful when we are under stress and can't face something at the moment. When defense mechanisms are used as a person's primary way of coping with uncomfortable feelings, however, they become problematic. *As adults, our goal is to replace defensive behaviors over time with skills for coping with intolerable feelings.*

The Use of Defense Mechanisms

Because unresolved uncomfortable feelings are so closely linked with problems behaviors, an essential skill of LSCI is being able to recognize the characteristic defense mechanisms employed by young people. A working knowledge of common defense mechanisms helps the LSCI practitioner:

- Decode a child's behavior on a deeper level (see Chapter 6)
- Accurately diagnose the Central Issue of a young person's crisis (see Chapter 7)
- Respond more effectively

Below we identify seven defense mechanisms adults need to keep in mind when working with young people:

1. **Denial:** Disowning feelings associated with painful events.
   - **Sample denial statement from a young person:** "I don't even care that I haven't seen my mom in two months. I can take care of myself!"
   - **Sample helpful response from an adult who can see beyond the defensive words and recognize the underlying uncomfortable feelings:** "I'm wondering if it's easier for you to say that you don't care about seeing your mom than it is to talk about how much you miss her."

2. **Rationalization:** A conscious effort to defend an action which has produced a feeling of underlying guilt.
   - **Youth:** "If that kid really cared about his bicycle, he would have locked it up instead of just leaving it in his front yard. He was practically asking for me to take it."
   - **Helpful adult response:** "Is it possible that when you tell yourself that the kid didn't care about his bike, it makes it easier for you to justify stealing it from his yard?"

3. **Projection**: Attributing undesirable feelings onto someone else rather than dealing with those feelings. Projection frequently sounds like blame or a false accusation.

- **Youth**: "I forgot to bring my math book. I'm going to be in so much trouble because all of the teachers in this school hate me."
- **Helpful adult response**: "It's really painful to believe teachers dislike you. I know that sometimes when we are feeling badly about ourselves, it's easier for us to deal with those feelings by blaming others for having them. Saying a teacher hates you might be easier than admitting that you're really upset at yourself right now. Is that possible?"

4. **Displacement**: Transferring an emotional reaction to a substitute when it cannot be directed at the one who causes it.

- **Example**: A young person who had an argument with a parent before leaving for school acts out his feelings by arguing with the bus aide.
- **Helpful adult response**: "You seem really angry this morning that I said hello to you. Did something happen earlier to make you feel so upset?"

5. **Sublimation**: Changing negative feelings and impulses into positive, socially acceptable behavior. *This mature defense mechanism lays behind many success stories.*

- **Example**: An angry adolescent who wants to hurt someone takes his energy out on the football field and has an especially good practice.
- **Helpful adult response**: "I noticed how you channeled your angry feelings in a really positive way today."

6. **Conversion**: Transferring distress to a physical symptom such as illness or pain.

- **Example**: A young person lacks the physical coordination to do well in PE and is made fun of by his peers. Over the first three months of school, he develops severe headaches just before PE class.
- **Helpful adult response**: A helping adult could recognize the pattern of headaches prior to PE and advocate for the student by (1) having the PE teacher establish firm rules and expectations for sportsmanship in class to reduce teasing behaviors, (2) role-playing effective ways to cope with teasing from peers, (3) if a physical disability is involved, helping determine accommodations so that the child can find more success in PE class.

7. **Regression**: Temporarily returning to self-soothing behaviors of an earlier stage of development rather than handling uncomfortable feelings in an age-appropriate way.

- **Example:** A middle school student has recently been separated from his mother due to her incarceration. He begins to suck his thumb and his grandmother reports that he has started wetting the bed.
- **Helpful adult response:** A helping adult would recognize that there has been a change in the youth's behaviors and seek to understand if there are any stressful events causing the change. The adult can offer the student a safe place to talk about their feelings and offer strategies to cope in an age-appropriate way.

Our goal in using LSCI is to help kids *accept and own* the full range of their feelings, rather than *acting them out* or *defending against them* in self-defeating ways. The skills of LSCI help us to recognize and respond effectively to common defense mechanisms so that we can get to the real root of what's driving a child's problematic behavior.

> The skills of LSCI help us to recognize and respond effectively to common defense mechanisms so that we can get to the real root of what's driving a child's problematic behavior.

Key Concept 6: Behavior

We have spent a great deal of time so far in this chapter studying a young person's psychological world. There can be no doubt that the life experiences and stressors endured by a child in their earliest years have a significant impact on the development of the child's self-concept and beliefs about the world. Likewise, it's clear that a young person's self-concept and beliefs influence their perceptions of events, which in short order initiates a series of thoughts and feelings about the events.

When we analyze these things *on paper*, it is easy to acknowledge the complexity of a young person's inner world. An iceberg (see Figure 4.7) provides a perfect metaphor to help adults realize that there is far more to a

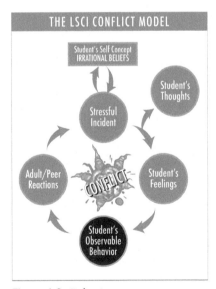

Figure 4.6. Behavior.

young person's behavior than meets the eye. And yet, a young person's behavior—just the very tip of the iceberg—is generally what demands our immediate and total

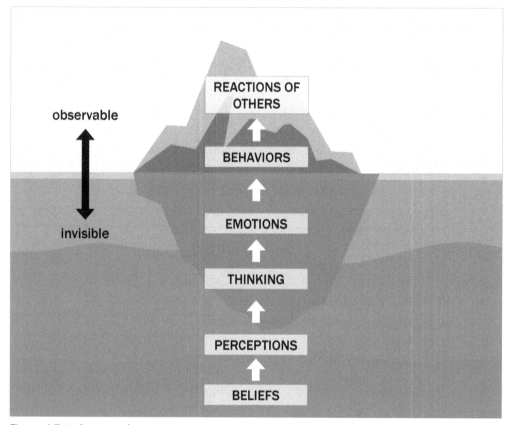

Figure 4.7. Behavior iceberg.

attention. In real life, as opposed to on paper or in hindsight, there are no flashing lights to warn adults about an underlying set of rigid perceptions triggered by a stressful event or an amygdala-activating cluster of faulty thoughts and intolerable feelings. Rather, it is usually only the disruptive behavior(s) itself that makes us aware of a problem.

A foundational skill of LSCI is to *look beyond behavior*. It is essential that adults recognize that behavior is a symptom of a problem, not just a problem in and of itself. Behavior is an outward reflection of a child's inner psychological world, driven by all of the unique beliefs, perceptions, thoughts, and feelings they have. *If adults are not thoughtful and aware, we will react to the behavior as if it is occurring in isolation—forgetting that there are a whole set of conditions driving it.* When we do this, we risk defaulting to rote punishment or amygdala-driven, relationship-damaging reactions.

It is essential that adults recognize that behavior is a symptom of a problem, not just a problem in and of itself.

LSCI challenges traditional thinking about why kids act out. We often hear that kids act out because they want power, control, or attention. It's true that we *all* want a sense of power and control over our environment. We *all* want some attention and interaction with other people. These are good things. If kids didn't want them, we'd really be worried about them. As paradoxical as it might seem, the problems that kids create are often an attempt to gain feelings of power and control or to feel seen and heard.

It is also important to note that acting up and acting out are not just random. Rather, they are often predictable. If you think of a young person whose behavior challenges you the most, you can probably predict with a good deal of accuracy what kind of problem he's going to get into next. Nawrocki (2018) writes, "With most kids, a crisis is a predictable and repetitive part of a cycle of ineffective behavior. For young people to be able to change a pattern of behavior into something more effective and socially acceptable, they must see that pattern. The best way to show them that pattern is for a caring adult to [enter] into the middle of a crisis with them."

LSCI offers a set of skills and a consistent verbal framework that allows adults to enter the life space of a child in crisis and to help them understand—and change—their self-defeating pattern of behavior.

Consider This

Before concluding this chapter, we invite you to spend a few minutes thinking about the predictable and repetitive patterns of behavior exhibited by your most challenging children and then to consider the possible underlying causes or meaning of the behavior. For example:

Student's Behavior:
Anna is a first grade student who persistently tries to run out of her classroom. The classroom teacher and Anna's aide have become extremely frustrated by her behavior because of the disruption it causes to the learning environment and because Anna laughs as she runs out of the room. She often tries to find an enclosed space in which to hide. The adults believe that Anna tries to run out of the room because she thinks hide-and-go-seek is a fun game. On her report card, they label her behavior as "attention-seeking."

Possible Cause or Meaning of Student's Behavior:
Anna is diagnosed with autism. She often becomes anxious in school during transitions or when new experiences are presented.

- Running out of the classroom could be a sign of Anna's survival-based instinct to flee from the perceived threat of a transition or unfamiliar task.
- When Anna seeks out an enclosed hiding space, it is possible that she is looking for a space that she perceives as safe.

- Rather than thinking of Anna's behavior as "attention-seeking" and choosing to ignore it, it might make more sense to think of it as "safety-seeking" and aim to teach Anna strategies for coping with feelings of anxiety at school.

If a student refuses to go to class, what might be an underlying reason for the behavior? (Think beyond defiance.)

_____

_____

_____

If a young person fails to complete any schoolwork at home, what might be an underlying reason for the behavior? (Think beyond laziness.)

_____

_____

_____

If a child lashes out suddenly at a group of kids, what might be an underlying reason for the behavior? (Think beyond bullying.)

_____

_____

_____

Use the space below to think about other predictable or repetitive problem behaviors of young people and possible underlying causes:

_____

_____

_____

Although a person's outward behavior is the primary thing that draws adult attention and concern during problem situations, this chapter underscores how superficial behavior really is in comparison to the events, beliefs, perceptions, thoughts, and feelings that drive it. To effectively reach and teach young people, adults must understand the importance of looking beyond pain-based behaviors and tuning in to a child's private psychological world. The LSCI process provides helping professionals with a consistent verbal framework to do just that. It is only when adults gain insight into the underlying dynamics of conflict that they can begin to change problematic surface behaviors. As you will see in the next two chapters of this book, change begins with the behaviors of the adult.

> To effectively reach and teach young people, adults must understand the importance of looking beyond pain-based behaviors and tuning in to a child's private psychological world.

Stress establishes beliefs.

Beliefs generate perceptions.

Perceptions produce thoughts.

Thoughts trigger feelings.

Feelings drive behavior.

Behavior incites others.

Others increase stress!

5

THE LSCI CONFLICT CYCLE

The LSCI Conflict Cycle™ is a way of looking at crisis by analyzing the interactions among a young person's stressors, perceptions, thoughts, feelings, behavior, and the reactions of others in the environment. This circular concept, developed by Dr. Nicholas Long in 1965, represents the idea of conflict between two opposing forces: needs within the young person clashing against the expectations of others. Healthy adjustment results when the conflict between these two opposing forces is minimized or resolved; maladjustment results when these two opposing forces continue to conflict. Conflict Cycles that are not broken will inevitably explode into crisis.

In Chapter 4, we took a detailed look at the first six elements of the Conflict Cycle—the experiences, beliefs, perceptions, thoughts, feelings, and behaviors that make up a young person's private psychological world. In the next section, we look at the remaining element of the Conflict Cycle: the adult's behavior in a conflict situation. When you are faced with a stressful situation with a young person, do you resort to amygdala-driven, possibly relationship-damaging emotional reactions? Or are your responses thoughtful, measured, and driven by your neocortex? In this chapter, we put all the pieces of the Conflict Cycle together and look at an example of how these dynamics play out in real-life interactions with young people.

The Remaining Piece of the Conflict Cycle: The Reactions of Adults and Peers

Here, we examine the only element of the Conflict Cycle that adults have any control over—their reactions to a young person's behavior. To begin this section, we pose a very basic, and critically important, question: *During a crisis, will the adult make the problem situation better or worse?*

An amazing aspect of the Conflict Cycle is how young people under stress can transmit their feelings of anger, frustration, and helplessness to adults, to the point that adults may behave in counter-aggressive, impulsive, or rejecting ways. Counter-aggressive *adult reactions, in turn, create new stress for the youth.* The young person now must deal with the adult's rejection or anger in addition to the original stress.

For an adult to respond with any counter-aggressive behavior is self-defeating. If you act out the feelings you have and "do what comes naturally," your behavior will perpetuate the cycle of conflict by mirroring the young person's aggression or inability to control behavior. *As a result, the youth becomes the one determining the adult behavior.* The more involved you become in struggling with a young person, the more likely it is that you will be the one who ends up in crisis. Even if the child loses the battle, by getting you to express open dislike, hostility, or rejection, he wins the emotional war by demonstrating that adults are hostile and cannot be trusted.

What must adults do to stop this destructive cycle? They must understand the dynamics of conflict as represented in the Conflict Cycle. *They must be aware of the existence of their own negative thoughts and feelings and make a conscious, professional choice not to act on them!* Awareness and self-control are required to manage counter-aggressive reactions to a young person's behavior and to intentionally disengage from cycles of conflict. Effective adults reject the instinct to win out over a young person; it is not necessary.

> Effective adults reject the instinct to win out over a young person; it is not necessary.

In Chapter 6, we will further explore the pivotal role that adults play in breaking a Conflict Cycle. We'll explain the skills adults need to control their responses to young people and to prevent themselves from being drawn into relationship-damaging, unprofessional cycles of conflict. Fortunately, the structured and goal-oriented nature of the LSCI process helps adults stay focused on underlying causes of behavior, rather than on surface behavior itself. When adults look beyond behavior—*when they become curious instead of furious*—they are better equipped to engage the skills of helping. This is the goal of LSCI.

The Sequence of the LSCI Conflict Cycle

A Conflict Cycle follows this basic sequence:

1. A *STRESSFUL EVENT* occurs which activates a young person's irrational beliefs.
2. BELIEFS generate a youth's way of perceiving the world.

3. PERCEPTIONS may lead directly to feelings or may first produce negative thoughts

4. These *NEGATIVE THOUGHTS* trigger intolerable feelings.

5. *FEELINGS*, not rational forces, drive inappropriate behaviors.

6. Inappropriate *BEHAVIORS* incite adults.

7. Adults take on the young person's feelings and may *MIRROR* his behaviors.

8. This negative adult *REACTION* increases the young person's stress, often becoming the next *STRESSFUL EVENT*, and a second cycle of conflict ensues, escalating the incident into a self-defeating power struggle.

9. The young person's *SELF-FULFILLING PROPHECY* (irrational beliefs) is *REINFORCED*; the youth is not motivated to change thinking or behavior.

> The Conflict Cycle provides a paradigm for understanding how a youth in stress creates feelings comparable to their own in adults, and if the adult is not trained, how the adult may mirror the young person's behavior.

Unless the first cycle is interrupted by a constructive, calming adult response in Step 7, the Conflict Cycle spirals into a crisis. Figure 5.2 illustrates the spiraling phenomenon. The Conflict Cycle provides a paradigm for understanding how a youth in stress creates feelings comparable to their own in adults, and if the adult is not trained, how the adult may mirror the young person's behavior.

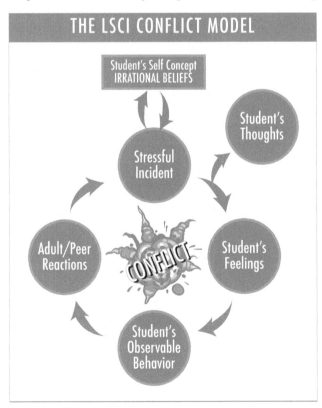

Figure 5.1. The conflict cycle.

Example of a Conflict Cycle

It is useful to develop the habit of analyzing each component of the Conflict Cycle: stress, beliefs, perceptions, thoughts, feelings, behavior, and the reactions of others. Doing this as you work through the initial

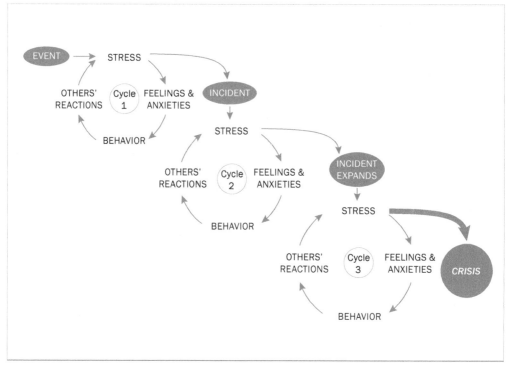

Figure 5.2. Unbroken, the conflict cycle spirals into crisis.

stages of LSCI with a young person helps keep the central points clear. From time to time you may find yourself digressing from the real issue, or a young person may unload a lot of feelings or thoughts that cloud the issue. This should not be a problem if you have the components clearly sorted out in your own mind.

To illustrate how to use the Conflict Cycle to analyze an incident, we return to "The Math Problem Crisis" detailed in Chapter 1. You may recall that the teacher, Ms. Westerman, is using LSCI with Dane, a student who has tested limits by taking advantage of a miscommunication between Ms. Westerman and the classroom assistant. The original stress spirals into three Conflict Cycles before the cycles are broken by Ms. Westerman through her use of LSCI. By stripping away all but the essential information about the events that led to the LSCI intervention, an analysis can reveal major differences between adults and young people in their perceptions, thoughts, and feelings about stressful events.

1st Cycle of Conflict

The original stress that started Cycle 1 was Dane's frustration with a math worksheet. His past failures with math had established a mindset: *"I hate math; I'm a failure."* This mindset triggered feelings of impatience, frustration, and anger which were expressed in his behavior: Dane didn't try to arrive at the correct answers but turned in his paper anyway. Ms. Westerman responded to this action by requiring Dane to correct the paper before going to his extra gym class.

2nd Cycle of Conflict

Cycle 2 began when the classroom assistant, unaware that Dane had been given special directions by Ms. Westerman, announced that everyone should turn in papers and go to gym. Dane immediately recognized this as an opportunity to default on his understanding with Ms. Westerman. He felt a sense of relief at this serendipitous opportunity. He went to gym knowing he was violating a trust but hoping it would go unnoticed.

3rd Cycle of Conflict

Cycle 3 began when Ms. Westerman discovered the situation and called Dane from the gym. Dane was now on the spot and filled with "righteous indignation" that he should be held accountable for a communication error between the staff. He expressed his angry feelings to Ms. Westerman verbally, but her response was disarming.

Breaking the Conflict Cycle

Ms. Westerman broke the Conflict Cycle by recognizing and acknowledging Dane's stress. She reviewed the sequence of events with him and demonstrated understanding about why he chose his course of action to relieve his extreme stress. Then, she took him to the next step of insight. She led Dane to see that, even though accepting responsibility is difficult, the rewards for doing so are great. Throughout the interview Ms. Westerman acknowledged Dane's fledgling attempts to *accept and own* his role in the problem.

As Ms. Westerman went through this intervention, she touched on the themes of LSCI in every stage. Sometimes she addressed the themes by reflecting on what she saw in Dane's responses or body language. Other times, she defused the intensity by countering it with affirmations and praise of Dane's maturity and the personal responsibility he showed in handling the crisis. At no time was there a sense that Ms. Westerman blamed Dane for having a problem. What is important is that the adult saw the crisis as a sequence of stress, perceptions, thoughts, feelings, behavior, and reactions of others within the context of Dane's personal history and that she used it as an opportunity for growth rather than as an occasion for conflict and punishment.

What Makes Some Young People Prone to Engaging Adults in Conflict Cycles?

In Chapter 4, we explored the predictable yet problematic patterns of behavior repeated by some young people. In this final section of Chapter 5, we take a closer look at the question of "What makes some young people prone to engaging adults in Conflict Cycles?" We propose that self-defeating patterns of behavior begin with the sources of stress in a child's life that, in turn, shape a young person's developing self-concept and beliefs.

Early in life, infants gain a sense of security when their environments are safe and predictable. As children grow older, they learn that they have some control over their environment and can predict and understand certain cause–effect relationships. But what if things are not stable at home? What if other responsibilities leave parents little time to teach these lessons to children, or what if children experience abandonment, neglect, or abuse? Among the ill-effects of adverse childhood experiences is the inner sense of unrest for the child, the sense of being unable to understand or to control events in their life. There is a need to allay this anxiety and human beings will go to great lengths to do so.

Children need to understand why bad things happen and to have some sense of control over their lives. Understanding comes in the form of an emerging self-concept and set of beliefs about the world. Below, we define this in terms of two types of self-concept prominent in young people who exhibit challenging behaviors.

Self-Concept of a "Bad" Kid

Some children growing up under adverse conditions may form the belief that they were abused, neglected, or abandoned because they are, by nature, "bad." Otherwise, why would adults hurt them? Their experience with adults may have taught them that adults are not to be trusted, that they enjoy bringing pain and suffering to children, and that unless the child fights them, they will hurt the child. In the experience of these students, these beliefs are founded in reality.

Self-Concept of a "Weak" Kid

Other children who have grown up feeling victimized and fearful may conclude that they are "weak and worthless." They may believe that adults are fearsome and powerful. Since they depend on adults for survival, they have learned that the best way to deal with adults is to be quiet and withdrawn. Students will create data to support their beliefs through *self-fulfilling prophecies*. In school, these children may be the quiet students who sit at the back of the room and fade away. When a teacher tries to help them, these children are silent and withdrawn. These students can frustrate adults because nothing seems to reach them. Adults may take the student's silence and withdrawal at face value, labeling them as "unmotivated" or "lazy." When this emotional disconnection takes root, the teacher may begin to withdraw from the "failing" student and turn their attention to more "rewarding" students. Masterfully, these trauma-impacted students manipulate teachers into providing data to reinforce their belief that they are weak and worthless young people.

Why Self-Fulfilling Prophecies Are Problematic

The beliefs become problematic, however, when young people overgeneralize and apply them to all adults. Some kids are unable to distinguish between the small number of adults in the world who will harm them and the vast majority of professionals who truly want to help them. Young people who have endured trauma tend to treat all adults as if they were in the first category. They successfully reinforce their self-fulfilling prophecy by engaging authority figures in Conflict Cycles. They unconsciously, and self-destructively, find ways to anger adults through disruption, defiance, disrespect, silence, or withdrawal. In response, some adults will end up saying something hurtful or apply rote punishments that fail to change behavior. This is, at some level, reassuring to these young people. The adult has reinforced the young person's self-concept as a bad kid and has followed through with something painful, just as the youth had predicted. The ability to predict and control life events is comforting because it overrides the dreaded feeling of helplessness.

> The ability to predict and control life events is comforting because it overrides the dreaded feeling of helplessness.

Summary of the Conflict Cycle

LSCI sees crisis as the product of a young person's stress, kept alive by the reactions of others. Conflict Cycles occur when a *stressful event* activates a young person's self-concept and personal beliefs, which have been formed over the years by the child's experiences and interactions. Beliefs, in turn, generate the youth's characteristic pattern of perceiving, thinking, and feeling. When *negative thoughts* trigger uncomfortable feelings, the young person may act out. Inappropriate *behaviors* incite adults and if untrained, the adults will *mirror* the young person's behaviors. When this happens, the adult's negative *reaction* becomes the next *stressful event* for the child, igniting a second cycle of conflict. This is the circular and repeating nature of the Conflict Cycle.

Conflict can become contagious to groups of young people. In schools, learning can be brought to a standstill by a single, spiraling conflict between a teacher and student. Yet, a problem situation also represents a potential turning point and opportunity for new learning. A conflict can be one of the best times to teach young people how to handle stress constructively. LSCI provides the framework for doing this.

> A conflict can be one of the best times to teach young people how to handle stress constructively.

In Chapter 6, you will learn how to break the Conflict Cycle, based on your knowledge of its component parts. When cycles of conflict are prevented or interrupted before they spiral out of control, adult-child relationships can be strengthened, new problem-solving skills can be learned, and problem situations can be turned into valuable learning opportunities.

Crisis reveals

character . . .

ours!

6

THE ADULT'S ROLE IN BREAKING THE CONFLICT CYCLE

n a crisis, young people are seldom aware of connections between stressful events and what they think, what they feel, how they behave, and how others respond. Instead, their responses to stress tend to be challenging behaviors that perpetuate conflict and crisis. Not only are most young people unable to recognize feelings, they are also incapable of talking about them in the heat of the moment. But unless a young person becomes able to do these two things, it is difficult—if not impossible—for them to make a lasting change from behavior driven by feelings to behavior regulated by rational processes.

The reality is that some adults are equally inept at this process. An adult can be of little help to a student until they (1) regulate their own emotional reactions to a young person's unwanted behavior, (2) recognize that the young person's behavior is an expression of their underlying feelings, and (3) know how to convey this insight to the youth. An adult cannot teach something that they don't themselves understand. Learning to regulate their own feelings and behavioral responses is a major part of learning to use LSCI effectively.

In this chapter, we focus on the specific skills adults need to manage their personal feelings and behaviors so that they are emotionally available to teach young people how to do the same. When youth recognize feelings and connect them to their own behavior and the reactions of others, the Conflict Cycle can be broken. This is the goal of Chapter 6.

This chapter is divided into two strategic areas for breaking cycles of conflict:

1. **The adult's role in conflict:** We identify skills adults can use to manage their role in typical Conflict Cycles. The goal of all adults should be to reduce

the volatility of a problem situation by thoughtfully employing conflict de-escalating responses.

2. **The art of listening:** We identify five critical skills of listening that allow young people to feel heard and understood. We look especially deeply at the skill of Decoding, the listening skill that helps adults respond to youth in ways that build bridges between their private psychological world and their public behavior.

The Adult's Role in Conflict

In Chapter 4, we examined the essential elements of the LSCI Conflict Cycle, including understanding a child's beliefs, perceptions, thoughts, feelings, and behaviors. Remember that as a helping adult, have very little—*if any*—control over these elements. As much as we would love to, we cannot change or rewrite a young person's history of adverse experiences. We can't instantly alter their self-concept and beliefs (although we can have a positive impact on these things over the course of time). Likewise, in the heat of a stressful situation, a youth's instinctive, amygdala-driven feelings and behaviors are beyond adult control.

> The only thing that an adult has control over during a crisis with a young person is their own response.

And so truly, the only thing that an adult has control over during a crisis with a young person is their own response. We have a distinct choice: will we make the problem situation better, or will we make it worse?

Here in Chapter 6, we focus on the only part of the Conflict Cycle that is under our complete and sole control. *What sets LSCI apart from all other cognitive-behavioral models and crisis intervention programs is its focus on the adult's response during a child's Conflict Cycle and the practical skills we offer to turn a crisis into a learning opportunity.* As Haim Ginnot wrote:

> "I have come to the frightening conclusion that I am the decisive element. It is my personal approach that creates the climate. It is my daily mood that makes the weather. I possess tremendous power to make life miserable or joyous. I can be a tool of torture or an instrument of inspiration, I can humiliate or humor, hurt or heal. In all situations, it is my response that decides whether a crisis is escalated or de-escalated, and a person is humanized or de-humanized. If we treat people as they are, we make them worse. If we treat people as they ought to be, we help them become what they are capable of becoming."

—Haim G. Ginott, *Teacher and Child: A Book for Parents and Teachers*

Skill 1: Q-Tip

Young people bring their personal histories and beliefs about adults into each interaction they have. To bring order and predictability to their world, kids attempt to imitate, replicate, and duplicate what they have experienced in the past in their present interactions. (See Chapter 4 for further explanation.) In a very real sense, you represent all adults and authority figures a young person has known. In many cases, this is not a favorable archetype.

> A young person's behaviors are not directed at us on a personal level, but rather reflect past experiences that they are playing out with us.

It's important for helping adults to maintain awareness that a young person's behaviors are not directed at us on a personal level, but rather reflect past experiences that they are playing out with us. When we understand the powerful influence of a child's psychological world, we can make the conscious decision to *Quit Taking It Personally* (Q-Tip) when a child behaves in certain ways.

Personal Plan for Button Pushing

Some young people seem to have an uncanny ability to figure out an adult's vulnerabilities. They go "fly fishing" for signs of distress in us until they hit the mark perfectly. Whether we have strong feelings around family, race, religion, gender identity, sexual identity, physical appearance, personal values, being liked, etc., kids are often able to pick up on our personal issues and "press our buttons" to get us to lash out—just as they expect us to do.

Before moving on with the text, consider your responses to the questions presented on the following page. Use this enhanced level of self-awareness to make the decision to *Q-Tip* when it comes to reacting to challenging behaviors of children.

When we *quit taking it personally,* we are much better able to resist a young person's instinctual drive to engage us into a patterned cycle of conflict. Keep in mind: *your ability to stay grounded in your neocortex and consistently choose rational, conflict de-escalating responses is the only part of the Conflict Cycle you have control over.* In LSCI, self-awareness is a tool, a skill, and the key to responding effectively.

Skill 2: Respond Like a Thermostat

If our ultimate goal is to teach young people that they have choices when it comes to their behavior (rather than being haplessly controlled by their emotions) we must begin by role modeling positive choices of our own, particularly in terms of how we respond to our kids' behaviors.

> Skilled adults interrupt destructive Conflict Cycles with young people when we manage the temperature of a stressful situation—like a thermostat—rather than simply mirroring it—like a thermometer.

What am I sensitive about?	What do I think and feel when a young person tries to push my buttons?	What is my typical response?	How can I change my typical responses?

Figure 6.1. Personal plan for button pushing. © 2014 by C. Dawson & A. McBride. Reprinted with permission.

When we practice self-awareness and when we understand how a child's inner psychological world fuels outward behaviors, we can respond like a thermostat, rather than like a thermometer, during a stressful situation. To be clearer with our analogy, consider the following:

- A thermostat controls the temperature of a room. It is used with purpose to turn the heat either up or down, depending on need.
- A thermometer, on the other hand, simply reflects the temperature that already exists. If a child is hot, the thermometer reflects his heat. If a child's temperature continues to rise during a conflict, so does the thermometer's reading.
- Skilled adults interrupt destructive Conflict Cycles with young people when we manage the temperature of a stressful situation—like a thermostat—rather than simply mirroring it—like a thermometer.

Skill 3: Use Personal Calming Strategies

It goes without saying that our students do not always behave in ways that endear them to us. As the responsible adults, however, our response to the young person's behavior is the critical factor. We will either reinforce the student's self-fulfilling prophecy, or we will present him with an alternative example. A critical skill of helping adults is to develop and employ a reservoir of personal calming strategies that enable us to regulate our own emotions. Only a calm brain can calm another brain.

Only a calm brain can calm another brain.

Personal calming strategies are unique to each individual. What soothes one person might aggravate another—and vice versa. Adults working with challenging children should make a Personal Calming Plan that specifies the self-soothing strategies that work for them and that they will employ in order to regulate their emotional responses. Common activities that can trigger the brain's relaxation response include:

- Slow, deep breathing
- Brief grounding and mindfulness exercises
- Counting backward from 20
- Movement and physical exercise
- Acknowledging conflict-fueling feelings as they develop ("I am getting frustrated; I am becoming angry")
- Using positive self-talk ("I can handle this")
- Taking a brief break from a heated situation
- Getting a drink of cold water
- Taking a step back to give personal space to yourself and to the child
- Visualizing a calming image
- Lowering the lights, lowering voices, lowering the temperature
- Ask a well-regulated colleague to help. This is not a sign of weakness but rather an indication of wisdom that only a calm brain can calm another brain. We all need each other at times!

The more adults practice personal calming strategies, such as breathing, mindfulness and exercise, the more readily their brains can return to a relaxed state during a stressful situation. Make your calming responses more automatic by rehearsing them regularly, including during the times when you are already regulated.

Skill 4: Choose Teaching

When a young child is learning to tie her shoes and she does it incorrectly, we teach her the skills she needs.

When a student is learning how to multiply fractions and he makes a mistake, we teach him the proper way to solve the problem.

> **What if we applied a teaching model to emotional skills, like we do to practical and academic ones?**

When a teenager is learning to drive and brakes too abruptly, we teach her to apply the brake pedal more smoothly.

But when a young person is managing a frustrating situation and lashes out verbally, we tend to punish him straightaway.

What if we applied a teaching model to emotional skills, like we do to practical and academic ones? What if instead of resorting to rote punishment when kids melt down, we took time to learn about the problem and then taught kids the skills they need to manage it? *LSCI believes that adults are more effective when they teach young people the skills they need to solve a problem than when they punish them for having a problem in the first place.*

> **When a young person exhibits unwanted behaviors as the result of a dysregulated limbic brain, responding with threats and punishment only worsens the problem.**

Consider the differences between traditional punishment models vs. an LSCI-inspired model of discipline in Figure 6.2.

Traditional Punishment	LSCI-Inspired Discipline
Based on a system of punishment and reward	Based on teaching and helping kids solve a problem
Governs all situations and is applied rigidly	Applies to all situations because of its flexibility in taking situational factors into account
Relies on a rote behavior = consequence (b=c) formula	Gives misbehavior a context; youth see how their actions impact others
Based on treating all young people equally	Based on treating all young people fairly
Fuels an adversarial adult-child relationship	Cultivates a trusting adult-child relationship based on mutual respect and concern
The adult is powerful; the child is relatively powerless	The adult is powerful in his ability to guide the child toward better outcomes; the child has the power to choose his behaviors
Supports the labeling of children into "good" and "bad"	Focus is on the behavior as a "bad choice," not on the student as a "bad kid"
Bandage approach: no emphasis on skill-development; kids learn little	Long-term approach in which children develop new skills that can be applied to future situations; kids learn and grow
Puts children down	*Builds children up*

Figure 6.2. Traditional discipline vs. LSCI-inspired discipline.

Why Punishment Doesn't Make Good Neurobiological Sense

When a young person exhibits unwanted behaviors as the result of a dysregulated limbic brain, responding with threats and punishment only worsens the problem. The only solution that makes good neurobiological sense lies in calming the brain in order to move back to a state of calm and safety at the body level (Forbes, 2012). In fact, when a frustrated adult uses amygdala-driven strategies to change a young person's behavior, their actions are—by definition—irrational. Further, this fear-based strategy will ensure that a cycle of non-thinking, reactive behavior is perpetuated between the youth and the adult.

Punishing children is quite different from disciplining them. Discipline uses positive ways of guiding children to develop self-regulation skills and confidence. Positive discipline relies on the adult engaging the problem-solving part of his brain and making decisions based on helping young people understand their feelings and manage their behavior. Effective discipline has everything to do with the adult controlling his counter-aggressive feelings in the moment and making decisions that help a child in the long term.

The Art of Listening

The art of listening is the path to self-regulation for challenging children and youth. We know that our emotional responses are directed by our limbic brain and they're done so non-verbally and subconsciously. We know that language and logical responses to emotions are directed by the neocortex. The process of using LSCI with young people helps them learn to bring language to emotion. When kids learn how to communicate positively about their emotional experiences, they become more able to regulate their behavior.

> The art of listening is the path to self-regulation for challenging children and youth.

How we listen to kids is critical. When we're listening, we're always trying to link emotions and language and get them to work together. Mann and Muscott (2014) propose five core skills for effective listening to kids:

1. **Attending Skills**

   Attending skills communicate that the adult is there to listen, is attentive to the young person's needs, and wants to hear what the youth has to say. Attending skills are demonstrated non-verbally through positive facial expressions, body language, and posture. There are also verbal components to effective attending behavior, including using a relaxed, non-threatening tone of voice and simple phrases of acknowledgement. See Figure 6.3 for examples.

Non-Verbal Attending Skills	Verbal Attending Phrases
• Head nods	• *"I see."*
• Smiles	• *"You seem to be starting to relax a little— that's great."*
• Expression of genuine curiosity about the young person's point of view	• *"I want to hear what you have to say."*
• Relaxed but frequent eye contact	• *"Can I get you some water?"*
• Engaged posture	• *"Are you ready to walk through what happened so I can really understand your point of view?"*

Figure 6.3. Attending skills and phrases.

2. Reassuring Skills

Reassuring statements communicate that you care about the young person and care about the issues that are important to them. Effective reassurance communicates that you want to help solve the problem together, along with an optimism that you and the youth can figure out what to do.

Sample reassuring statements:

- "I am here to help."
- "I want to understand exactly what happened."
- "I want to understand things from your point of view."
- "I'm sure we can figure this out together."
- "We're going to work this out."
- "It takes real courage to talk about what you are thinking and feeling."
- "The more I hear things from your point of view, the better I'll be able to help."

3. Affirming Skills

Affirming statements communicate a positive view of the young person by recognizing positive qualities they possess or desirable behaviors they exhibit. They can defuse defensiveness, emotional flooding, and resistance. Affirmations offer support for young people, communicating understanding of what they feel without demeaning or disapproving. Perhaps the most important results from abundant use of affirmations are changes in a young person's attitude toward the adult who affirms them. Affirmations communicate that the adult likes the young person, believes that there is a better side of the young person, and is an ally for bringing out better qualities. Almost all young people are hungry for this mirror of a positive image. It is their only hope to be better than they have been before!

Sample reassuring statements:

- "I like the way you're using words."
- "You're doing a great job settling down and getting ready to talk about this."
- "Thank you for telling me that."
- "Thank you for being patient."
- "You are handling a difficult situation really well."
- "I can see that was hard for you to say."
- "You are really trying to get yourself together."

As you can see, affirming phrases can be easily adapted to the age of the young person with whom you are speaking. One of the most valuable parts of LSCI is the flexibility it affords adults to adapt wording, pacing, and level of insight to the developmental needs of each young person. (We devote Chapter 20 to demonstrating how the LSCI framework can be adjusted to meet the needs of very young or developmentally delayed students.)

4. **Validating Skills**

Validating statements effectively convey to a young person that you non-judgmentally accept their thoughts, feelings, and behaviors as important and real to them. Validation begins with putting language to a child's emotion. In accurately identifying the emotion that underlies a child's statement or other outward behavior, the adult helps the child feel heard and understood. In turn, a validated child is more willing to continue expressing their thoughts and feelings through words. An unvalidated child, on the other hand, is likely to shut down, become defensive, or act out further. Consider the examples in Figure 6.4.

Validation is a powerful skill that lets kids know that an adult is genuinely attuned to them and can hear beyond their angry, defensive words.

Youth's Statement	Instinctive but Invalidating Adult Response	Thoughtful, Validating Adult Response
I can't do anything right.	That's not true! You do lots of things right.	*You're feeling frustrated* that things didn't turn out the way you expected.
Everybody here hates me.	That's ridiculous. Why would I spend all this extra time with you if I hated you?	*You felt embarrassed* when the kids were laughing. You thought they were laughing at you.

Figure 6.4. Invalidating vs. validating responses. © 2007 by J. Whitcomb. Reprinted with permission.

Helping name an emotion for a child is a brain-based strategy for connecting the limbic, feeling brain with the language centers of the neocortex.

5. Decoding Skills

Decoding means connecting what young people are doing and saying to what they are feeling. Decoding has three purposes: (a) to teach young people to recognize specific feelings that drive their inappropriate behaviors, (b) to build a youth's confidence that they do not have to be victims of their own bad feelings because there are alternative behaviors they can choose, and (c) to convey that talking about feelings may not be as awful as anticipated. Unless decoding is done, feelings continue to fester, finding outlets in all sorts of unacceptable behaviors.

Decoding begins with objective observation of young people's behavior and careful listening to what they say. Accurate decoding also requires sensitivity to body language and to what is implied and left unsaid. From this information, the adult makes connections for the young person between their outward behaviors and inner feelings. To fail to decode is to ignore the most potent force driving the behavior of the young people with whom you work.

The accuracy of your decoding will be evident in the young person's responses. Typically, a youth will react when you decode accurately. The reaction may be vigorous denial or passive quietness. In either case, the decoded message has touched the child's concerns. When decoding misses its mark, young people generally do not change their level of affect. They may continue the same behavior, appear to be genuinely disinterested, or simply go on to another subject without an emotional change.

As young people learn that talking about feelings and connecting them to behavior is not invasive, they gradually start to do this themselves. They begin to decode for you, explaining what they did and the feelings that were part of their behavior. It is essential to keep in mind that when you decode, or when young people learn to decode their own behavior and that of others, it is not the end of the LSCI. Young people must also learn to change their behavior in ways that bring about better feelings and more satisfying results. For this reason, we use different types of decoding during the first three stages of LSCI (detailed in Chapter 8), while exploring the problem, the issues, and the feelings involved. Then, as we work with young people to plan and implement solutions during the last three LSCI stages, we prefer to use less decoding and to focus instead on new, more appropriate behaviors and the more pleasant results (better feelings) a child can expect from a change.

The First Level of Decoding: Acknowledging

We begin decoding by simply acknowledging that feelings are embedded in a young person's words and behavior. This basic level of decoding does not attempt to interpret complex responses or characterize feelings in any particular way. It requires no understanding about the child's psychological world or situational

Feelings are embedded in a young person's words and behavior.

factors. It is particularly useful when you haven't used LSCI with the young person before, know very little about the child or an incident, or when you need to convey acceptance and support while disapproving of behavior.

The intent in acknowledging feelings is to communicate your awareness that a young person is feeling unhappy (awful, miserable, terrible, angry, sad, etc.). When acknowledging feelings, you are not asking the young person to describe feelings or motivations. Neither are you condoning the inappropriate behavior they used to express their feelings. You are not making interpretations about why or how. You are not even asking the person to talk about the feelings yet. By simply acknowledging the presence of feelings, you are not intruding too rapidly into a young person's private psychological world. This respect for a youth's feelings can help establish your credibility and lead to trust. It is essential to acknowledge feelings during LSCI, especially during Stage 1 of LSCI.

The following are examples of how we use this type of decoding to acknowledge feelings in ways that need no response on the young person's part:

Mikayla
When asked to put away her iPad, Mikayla blurts out, "Go away!"
Adult decodes: "It's frustrating for you to stop a good game before it's finished. You can come back to it at the next break."

Calvin
Calvin goes to his desk and buries his face in his arms after backing down from a challenge to fight on the playground.
Teacher decodes: "Being challenged to a fight can make anybody feel scared and confused."

Decoding behavior by simply acknowledging feelings can enable you to defuse the intensity of a child's feelings and even prevent a crisis from occurring. The following were observations made by two teachers that illustrate the potential for crisis:

"He came to school today with a chip on his shoulder." [Student is angry about something and will use any opportunity to unload the anger.]

"She's an emotional basket case." [Student is so emotionally overloaded that feelings spill over into anything she does.]

Unless there is some intervention, the teachers can predict that the underlying emotion will continue to grow and a crisis will occur in the near future. Acknowledging the child's feelings helps the young person feel understood and therefore connected to the decoding adult. These relationship factors are powerful in diminishing the intensity of the feelings and undoing need to act out in order to feel heard.

The Second Level of Decoding: Surface Interpretation

Connecting freely expressed, undisguised feelings to specific behavior is the next level of complexity in decoding. This strategy, called surface interpretation, is explaining the emotional meaning expressed in the behavior. For this type of decoding, the behavior is so obviously related to feelings that decoding can be done in a straightforward way. It is easy to recognize the expressed feelings and respond to them. For example, there is a direct connection between the action of a young person throwing a book across the room and associated feelings. To accurately decode that behavior for the youth, you need to have information about the sequence of antecedent events and know enough about the child's history, self-concept, and psychological world to understand how the event could be stressful. Depending on such information, the adult might decode the book-throwing behavior in one of several ways:

> Surface interpretation is explaining the emotional meaning expressed in the behavior.

- "You thought the work was too difficult, but throwing the book won't make the problem go away."
- "It made you angry when they didn't wait for you to finish, and the book was handy."
- "Throwing the book told me that you were frustrated with the assignment, and that's really important information for me. It's OK just to tell me next time."

The following are several other examples of decoding that carry clearly conveyed messages explaining feelings communicated by young people' behavior:

Carter
Carter is not chosen to play on his friends' team, so he walks off the playground without saying anything to anyone.

Teacher decodes: *"It made you sad when no one picked you to play during recess and cursing at me was a way to show me that something was bothering you."*

Mia

Mia loses control and flips over an art table because her friend will not share paints. Adult decodes: *"You do things for friends and then when they don't do things for you, you feel betrayed. It makes you lash out."*

Sometimes adults are afraid to make such statements because they fear that young people will interpret the decoded message as tacit approval of inappropriate behavior. This may be true, unless the adult continues to emphasize how feelings cause behavior that results in reactions from others that are not always in the student's best interest. During the first three stages of LSCI, decoding with such follow-up discussions occurs frequently. The adult guides (and sometimes leads) a young person from acknowledgment of feelings, through interpretation of surface feelings associated with the behavior, to the unpleasant reactions of others. Such discussions are essential before you and a youth converge on a solution during the last three stages of the LSCI to break the Conflict Cycle.

The Third Level of Decoding: Secondary Interpretation

Vigorous denial by a young person in reaction to decoding usually requires a third, more difficult type of decoding we call *secondary interpretation*. Secondary interpretation requires shifting focus from the young person's original behavior to the young person's denial. It also requires decoding a second time, connecting feelings to the denial. Secondary interpretation of denials are reformulations of the original decoding, put in ways that are more palatable and supportive but just as accurate.

When young people are first exposed to decoding, it is not unusual for them to react with strong denial of what you say. It often is uncomfortable and hard for them to believe that you can understand and talk about the feelings behind their behavior. In these situations, secondary decoding reiterates the original message in a less threatening and more supportive way. Here are examples of decoding with a second interpretation that focuses on the denial:

> Secondary decoding reiterates the original message in a less threatening and more supportive way.

Charlotte

Charlotte stalks suddenly into the room: "I'm not doin' shit today."
Teacher decodes: "You've got other things on your mind today?"

Charlotte: "Like you even care?"

Teacher decodes: "When you're under a lot of pressure, it's hard to think about schoolwork."

Elijah

Elijah throws his pencil on the floor: "This freakin' work is bullshit!"

Teacher decodes: "This is a tough assignment; would you like some help?"

Elijah: "I don't need help and I don't care!"

Teacher decodes: "This work is so hard it seems like you'll never get through it. That can frustrate anybody."

Lucas

After a fight in the bathroom, Lucas shouts at the staff, "You're picking on the wrong person!"

Staff decodes: "It's hard to face up to a problem when you have hurt someone."

Lucas: "No! You've got it all wrong! That's not what happened. I was just standing there."

Staff decodes again: "I'm interested in hearing how you explain it."

You have probably noticed that this type of decoding requires no specific answer from the student. The intent is to get the message out in the open, to be built upon as the young person can tolerate the insights. When a youth responds to this secondary interpretation with less emotion, less denial, no further response, or changes the subject, you know that the message has connected.

Summary of Decoding

Used extensively during the first three stages of LSCI, decoding is the means of making connections for the young person between outward behavior and underlying feelings. Depending upon the student's behavior, there are three types of decoding. The least complicated form of decoding requires only acknowledgment that feelings are present. More complicated forms of decoding involve interpretation of surface feelings conveyed through behavior and secondary interpretation when a young person denies the first decoding.

Through decoding, an adult conveys support and understanding of what a young person is feeling during crisis. Decoding that is accurate and supportive enhances the trust between the adult and child. The young person sees the adult as understanding and as a reliable source of support in a difficult time. The young person also begins to learn about the connections between their behavior and the reactions they get from others. By changing behavior, the young person sees that outcomes can be changed for the better.

Summary of Breaking the Conflict Cycle

While most youth-oriented programs focus squarely on changing the problematic and patterned behavior of young people, LSCI is unique in recognizing that effective change begins with adults. This represents a new vision for helping young people; instead of relying on kids to change what they do in order for things to get better, LSCI doubles down on adults, knowing that when they commit to breaking the Conflict Cycle, they engage the most potent tool of change available: the power of a positive relationship. By choosing logical, language-based responses during crises and using the art of listening skills to regulate young people's emotions, LSCI-trained adults bring about lasting, positive changes in young people.

> LSCI is unique in recognizing that effective change begins with adults.

"The problems I cause
are not the causes
of my problems."

THE STRUCTURE OF LSCI

SCI is a six-stage verbal strategy for providing active intervention in young people's lives during times of stress and crisis. Oftentimes during a conflict, a young person will say or do something that takes us by surprise. We may feel intense anger, want to storm out of the room, or freeze up. In the heat of the moment, we can become unsure of what to do. That's why LSCI is both so practical and so powerful; it gives us a cognitive roadmap for how to respond effec-

> LSCI is a consistent, six-stage verbal framework that enables adults to be at their best, even when a young person is at their worst.

tively during a stressful situation. We always know where we are in the LSCI process and where to go next. In this chapter, we share the consistent, six-stage verbal framework that enables adults to be at their best, even when a young person is at their worst.

The time shortly after crisis is a productive time for youth to learn new social skills and gain new insights into their patterns of reacting to stressful situations. Because current behaviors have failed them and emotional distress is intensified, young people are more receptive to change immediately following a crisis than at any other time. By using LSCI, the adult conveys to a young person that (a) problems can be solved, (b) the young person has an advocate in the adult, (c) the adult sees the good qualities in the young person, (d) the young person has the skills to solve the crisis, and (e) even though the young person must change certain behaviors, he or she is still a valued individual.

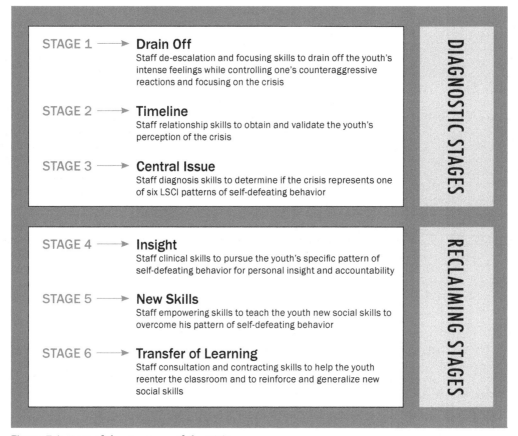

Figure 7.1. Map of the six stages of the LSCI process.

The Six Stages Of LSCI

The six stages of LSCI can be divided into "three and three": the first three stages focus on the skills to diagnose the type of crisis and the central issue, while the last three stages address the outcome goals. See Figure 7.1 for a map of the six stages of LSCI.

Stage 1: Drain Off (De-Escalate the Stressful Situation)

SYNOPSIS OF STAGE 1

Since emotions often run high in the immediate aftermath of a crisis, the first stage in LSCI is used to convey soothing support through the five core listening skills (Chapter 6). Using effective listening, adults drain off the intensity of a young person's emotions to the point where the youth can engage the higher functions of their brain (the neocortex) and begin to talk about the incident in a rational way.

Intensely angry feelings, "shock" words, and inappropriate behaviors are almost always present as you intervene in crisis and begin LSCI. This is the point at which well-meaning but inexperienced staff get hooked into the Conflict Cycle with young people. Rather than acting as a thermostat to regulate the child's emotional intensity, the adult unwittingly acts as a thermometer, mirroring the young person's intensity. Through the LSCI stages, it is critical for adults to remember to act on what is best for the young person instead of acting on their own feelings and counter-aggressive impulses.

Sometimes, the Drain Off stage is brief and only takes a sentence or two. With other LSCIs, it may take as much as half an hour to diminish emotional flooding so that a young person can begin to talk. If emotional intensity does not diminish to a point where the young person can use words, do not go further into LSCI. Instead, try Surface Management skills, which we describe in Chapter 9 as part of the helping process.

Table 7.1 illustrates the dynamics, goals, and skills of the Drain Off stage. A young person is ready for the next stage when they (1) believe that an adult is genuinely interested in helping them and (2) begin to use words instead of being dominated by emotions.

TABLE 7.1		
STAGE 1: DRAIN OFF		
Youth	Adult Goals	Adult Skills
Drain Off	De-escalation	Drain Off and Emotional Regulation
I'm upset and out of control!	Drain off the youth's intense feelings and de-escalate inappropriate behaviors	Understand the dynamics of the Conflict Cycle and the adult's role in conflict
		Provide verbal and non-verbal support
		Co-regulate to lend calm to a youth's dysregulated state
		Use active listening skills to support the youth and begin a dialogue

During and Immediately After a Crisis

During stressful situations, the limbic brain becomes hyper-aroused and the young person's body is mobilized for the fight, flight, or freeze response (see Chapter 2 for further detail). Cortisol and adrenaline flood the youth's body. Access to the language centers of the brain are greatly diminished. A young person may be so overwhelmed by emotional flooding that dialogue is not yet possible. If you find this is the case, pause before concluding that the young person is beyond help or that a verbal intervention won't work. Use the skills described below to help the child *become* ready to dialogue. Nothing is gained by diving into the later stages of LSCI prematurely.

1. **Support the Young Person**

    While waiting for the young person to have greater access to the language centers of their brain, the adult can use attending, reassuring, and affirming statements to convey support. Calmly communicate that you hear and see that the young person is upset but that the situation is not beyond solution. Sometimes these messages can be communicated non-verbally through your body language and facial expressions and sometimes by a few simple words, sounds, or statements, such as the following:

    - *I am here to help.*
    - *Would you like a cup of water?*
    - *We're going to work this out.*
    - *Should we take a quiet walk before we talk?*
    - *It takes strength to talk about what you are feeling.*
    - *I can tell you're almost ready to talk. You're breathing deeply and you've stopped yelling.*
    - *In a few minutes we're going to figure out why you're so mad today.*
    - *When you are upset it is difficult to remember what happened, but let's give it a try.*

2. **Co-Regulate**

    If a young person does not make eye contact or respond to these types of verbal prompts right away, don't rush to the conclusion that he is being defiant, uncooperative, or willful. Rather, consider that the child is not yet neurologically ready to engage; he likely remains dysregulated. As noted in Chapter 6, adults can use co-regulation to calm the brain of a child. Co-regulation typically involves using a warmth, soothing tone of voice, verbal acknowledgement of the young person's distress, and words of encouragement. Sometimes the best model of co-regulation is simply being with a young person in quiet stillness until they are ready to engage with you, rather than insisting that they process events on a school schedule or someone else's timeline. Remember: *crises do not happen by appointment.* The skills of LSCI enable us to drain off the intense emotions of a young person whenever the situation calls for it, rather than when it is convenient.

When the young person begins to give more eye contact or verbal responses, it usually means that a shift is taking place from an emotional mode to a rational mode for dealing with the problem. Now you have a way to begin the Drain Off stage. By converting difficult feelings and destructive behaviors into words, you and the young person have the tools for problem-solving.

3. **Begin a Dialogue Using the Three-Part Message**
When a young person starts to talk about the incident, you probably will not know exactly what happened prior to the conflict, what type of LSCI will be needed, or what the outcome goal will be. The Three-Part Message (Freado, 2014) is a simple, natural, and effective framework to initiate productive dialogue in any LSCI. It consists of these elements:

Part 1: Recognize and acknowledge the young person's emotional state
Part 2: Express a need to know more
Part 3: Commit to try to understand

In practice, the three-part message might sound like:

- I can see that you are very upset right now. Something very important must be going on.
- I understand that you're very angry, but I don't know what you're so angry about. I'd really like to hear what happened from your point of view.
- It seems like you are having a really hard time right now. Let's see if we can make sense of what happened to you.

When a young person begins to talk, you have moved automatically into the next LSCI stage. But if words are slow in coming, it may require further effort on your part (see below for *Your Role in Stage 1*). The important point is to *begin a dialogue about the incident. It is not important to confront lies or straighten out distortions in perceptions during this first stage, nor is it necessary for you to get your own position on the matter out in the open.* In fact, doing so this early in the LSCI process often reactivates the young person's stress response and shuts down any progress that had been made.

If a young person continues to be dominated by emotions or has not begun to focus on the incident, don't go further into the LSCI. Continue to focus on the incident, on your ability to help, and on the young person's potential to talk about it. (Chapter 9 contains a discussion about emotional flooding and how to respond to young people who will not talk.)

Your Role in Stage 1

Begin Stage 1 by being a representative of fairness for all: an accepting, impartial adult who shows concern for the young person's situation (the crisis, feelings, or conflict). You are setting the tone for the relationship that will follow throughout the six LSCI stages. Questions and statements such as the following help to convey the idea that adults can listen, understand, and be objective and fair:

- "This is a difficult situation, but we can work on it together."
- "Sometimes things seem terrible, but there are always different ways of looking at them."
- "I want to understand exactly what happened."
- "Every problem has a solution. We'll figure this out together."
- "I can tell this is a serious situation to you. It calls for some serious thinking about what will be helpful to you."

The young person must have confidence and trust in you. Provide support and a sense of optimism that the problem can be handled. Convey your belief in the importance of being fair. Communicate your confidence in the young person. Let the young person know that you understand and respect the young person's feelings even though you cannot accept the behavior. Focus on the young person's positive attributes that can be used in solving the crisis. With practice, you will develop increasing verbal skills for even the most difficult problem. In time you will find few, if any, young people failing to respond to your strategies for getting the LSCI rolling in Stage 1.

As You Transition to Stage 2

You are ready to phase into Stage 2 when the young person responds to you with words (or in some instances eye contact or a nod) that acknowledge a willingness to go along with you on the topic. The following are examples of ways to transition to Stage 2, affirming your confidence in the young person, your support, and your confidence in a good outcome:

- "When you talk about a problem like this, it begins to make sense out of confusion." [affirmation of the young person's ability]
- "This is a difficult situation, but we're not going to give up until we better understand . . . [affirmation of your support for the young person]
- "Even the worst problem can be understood." [affirmation of hope]

- "I can see this is hard for you to talk about, but you're managing to work through it." [affirmation of the young person's self-control]

Stage 2: Timeline (Bring Language to Emotion)

SYNOPSIS OF STAGE 2

This is an intensely interactive stage: The young person talks and the adult listens, asks questions, clarifies, and decodes. The exchange between adult and young person during this stage has two objectives:

1. *For the young person*, there must be a decrease in emotion and an increase in rational words and ideas, organized around the sequence of events—a Timeline. If these do not occur, the young person cannot benefit from the problem-solving phases later in the LSCI.

2. *For the adult*, the goals are to increase understanding and clarify details about the young person's perceptions, thoughts, and feelings about the incident, to begin to decode behavior, and to construct an answer to the question, "Is the incident the issue, or is some underlying concern the real issue?" The answer will shape the rest of the LSCI.

As Table 7.2 shows, our goal is to encourage the young person to tell a personal story and to feel understood. The decoding process is used along with questions to clarify the young person's perceptions about the "when," "where," and "who" of the incident, and the events leading up to it.

Stage 2 phases into Stage 3 when the talk has produced a review of the time, place, and people involved in the incident, along with the youth's perceptions, thoughts, and feelings. The adult then has a sufficient understanding of the young person's reactions and point of view to begin to focus the following stage on the Central Issue.

What Happens in Stage 2?

Stage 2 is a young person's chance to "tell it like they see it." Stage 2 is a skill-building exercise in using rational words to process a problem. This is not easy for young people whose typical reactions to an incident are anger, denial, evasion, distortion, confusion, guilt, shame, or verbal counterattack.

For the adult, Stage 2 is a skill-building exercise in attempting to view the situation from the young person's unique perspective. We want the youth to replay for us a mental recording of the incident. This can be more challenging than it might

Youth	Adult Goals	Adult Skills
TABLE 7.2		
STAGE 2: TIMELINE		
Timeline	**Bring Language to Emotion and Build Relationship**	Interviewing
This is what happened to me as I remember it!	Encourage the youth to tell their story and to feel understood	Empathy skills
		Attending skills
		Reassuring skills
		Affirming skills
		Validating skills
		Decoding skills
		Non-verbal observing skills

seem, as the young person's perceptions may be distorted by personal history, cognitive traps, defenses, and the intensity of the moment. The adult will have to help the young person organize the sequence of events and put it into proper relationship with surrounding circumstances. Because an incident triggers a young person's private psychological storehouse, it has infringed on personal space. Talking about the incident should provide an opportunity to bring out deeper or different issues and concerns that may be preoccupying a young person's thoughts and energy.

Young Person Talks About the Incident

When the incident is first identified during Stage 1, a young person's reaction usually is loaded with defensiveness and intense denial of concern or responsibility. An emotional intensity exists that obscures objectivity. The young person tries to justify what has happened by blaming you or others, insisting that the incident occurred in a specific way, or initiating talk that is off the topic.

As the young person begins to focus on the incident in Stage 2, you will notice a change in the tone of the dialogue from a predominance of emotion to an increasingly rational tone. When this happens, don't be misled into thinking that LSCI is nearing an end because the young person is using rational behavior. Cooling down and talking rationally are *not* the only objectives in this stage. Until you make a preliminary choice about whether the incident is really the Central Issue, the LSCI should not move to the next stage.

Listen for Signal Flares

As young people become more comfortable with you and more spontaneous in their talk, they occasionally drop small comments or make side remarks that seem to have little bearing on the incident or the discussion. We call these "signal flares." Unless you are actively listening and looking for them, you may let them pass as unrelated comments or as attempts by the young person to get off the subject. It can be difficult to discern a youth's intent when the discussion wanders from the subject. Signal flares often represent the first attempt by a young person to let you know that there is another, central issue that goes beyond the incident.

A signal flare is a representation of the private psychological world we examined in Chapter 4. When you spot a signal flare, it may or may not be the right time to respond to it. If you choose to respond, a simple verbal reflection of the young person's words is usually enough to highlight the fact that you hear it and recognize it as important. This response usually is enough to get the topic under way. If the young person does not respond verbally but body language says there is an interest in further talk about the topic, try a follow-up question. If young people are not ready to talk about a private issue, they usually initiate a shift in the conversation or show such agitation that it is apparent the topic is too uncomfortable to pursue for the moment. In this case, let it go but remember it for later use.

Adult Asks Questions to Increase Understanding and Clarify the Incident

For the adult, Stage 2 is used to increase the young person's awareness of the complexities of the incident. This is the stage for teaching the young person to look at the incident as a sequence in time. Since LSCI usually takes place because of a situation that the young person could not handle, the first focus is on the "here and now." We are not asking why a problem occurred, but rather where, when, who, and what regarding the problem. The following are some examples of questions to ask about the problem:

- "When did this happen?"
- "What happened before that?"
- "What happened next?"
- "Did this happen before or after you got up to get your supplies?"

After confirming the Timeline, explore the setting through questions such as the following:

- "Where did this happen?"
- "Where were you when he said that to you?"
- "Did this happen at the . . . ?"
- "Has this happened at that same place before?"
- "What was going on?"

These types of questions easily flow into questions about the people involved and who said what to whom and when, such as the following:

- "Who made the first move?"
- "Who was there?"
- "Who else was there?"
- "What did they say (do)?"
- "Then what did you say?"
- "What did they do after you said that?"
- "Could you repeat what you just said?"
- "I'm not sure I understand. Please say that again."
- "Let me summarize what I heard, and you correct anything I didn't get right."

It sometimes helps to use words that evoke specific visual images about the incident. Such graphic imagery aids many young people in making the shift from raw emotion to using words in thinking and talking about the incident. The following are some examples of ways to enhance your questions with imagery:

- "Was he wearing a red shirt?"
- "Was he that great big guy that looks like a wrestler?"
- "Did she scream at you?"
- "Where did they run after that?"
- "Were you sitting in the front of the bus?"
- "Can you hear that noise when it's dark?"

Bearing in mind that stressful situations create physiological responses (Porges, 2015); make it a habit to tune in to the sensations a young person feels in their body during and after a problem incident by asking questions such as:

- What do you notice in your body?
- Can you feel your heart beating faster?
- I notice that your fists are balled up and your body is tense.

As Stage 2 gets under way, use the discussion to separate the various issues embedded in the incident. From each remark the young person makes and each accompanying behavior, you must choose whether to respond. Respond to those remarks that seem to hold promise for greater understanding and insight. Also respond to remarks that seem to hold significance for the young person, even if they do not for you. Through this selective process, you increase understanding and clarify the incident. You also increase the young person's investment in the process. It is a balancing act that requires considerable mental agility.

Your Role in Stage 2

Your role during Stage 2 is to convey a sincere interest in hearing the young person's perceptions about what happened and obtaining more facts about the incident. The more information you have from the young person, the more opportunities you have for understanding and clarifying. To do this we find these five strategies useful: questioning, listening, observing, reflecting, and interpreting (decoding).

1. Questioning

   Questions are the most direct way to expand the information you have about the incident and the extent to which the young person has invested emotionally in it. (How much of the child's private psychological world is embedded in the incident?)

   Generally, the first questions ask for facts about the incident and explore the sequence of events—the Timeline. Examples of these basic questions appear in the previous section. Use more complex questions as you begin to explore the extent to which the young person can view the incident from the perspectives of others. You want to know if the young person can associate personal behavior with resulting reactions from others. Questions also can reveal the extent to which a young person is relying on adults to provide external control, and what kinds of issues the young person sees as important in the incident. The following are examples of questions that expand the information base:

   - "How would he describe what just happened?" [perspective of others]
   - "Could there have been something that set him off?" [cause and effect]
   - "Is this a problem for kids to handle by themselves?" [source of authority]
   - "Is fairness (kindness, leadership, friendship) an issue here?" [values]

2. Active Listening and Active Remembering

   Listen carefully to what a young person says. Key words and ideas are the cues you use to form your own responses. The young person's view is the starting point, giving you a base from which to structure the remaining LSCI stages. It also is important to remember what the young person says. In later phases of an interview, or in subsequent interviews, you should be able to recall and reuse important or vivid points made by the young person during these earlier stages. When young people act out and trigger counter-aggressive impulses in adults, we tend to be quick to speak and slow to listen. In LSCI, we must reverse that and learn to be quick to listen and slow to speak.

3. **Observing**

Observing is an important part of active listening. The body language a young person uses to accompany a statement often tells more than words. A young person's behavior also reveals a lot about the impact you are making.

You can be confident that the talk has validity if a young person participates, responds with intense emotion, or shows a pronounced increase in body movement. Occasionally, a young person will be very still, making no remarks and showing no behavioral response. This reaction almost always indicates interest in hearing an elaboration of the idea you just brought up.

If the talk is not on track, a young person will show boredom or disinterest and may bring up another topic. This strategy also may be used by some young people when content is too close to private reality. You can usually tell the difference by the amount of agitation or emotion accompanying the response.

4. **Reflecting**

Reflections are words that mirror an idea or an observed behavior back to a young person. They are used to convey that the young person's idea or behavior is worthy of note (or in the case of a negative point, that it has not escaped your notice). Reflections require no responses from young people because they are statements of fact. A reflection does not intrude into a young person's space and is not judgmental. It is among the best strategies for minimizing defensiveness and keeping a sensitive topic going. It also is useful with young people who have problems with authority because it does not require a defensive response. Typically, a young person will respond to a reflection by elaborating on the details and expanding the content spontaneously; if not, go back to questions again—more facts and observation are needed.

If you have not used reflections before, you may feel a bit awkward simply turning an observation or a remark back to a young person without adding your own ideas. The following are examples of simple reflections, where the young person has made the first statement and the teacher has simply rephrased it:

- "It didn't sound fair to you."
- "You were sitting there minding your own business."
- "You didn't mean to make her mad."
- "You think he is the one I should talk with."
- "You were feeling good about what you had done until he made that remark."

Did you notice that these examples are not stated as questions, although they could be? Reflecting involves no questions, so responses are not necessary. These examples do not reflect negative feelings or negative behavior. Also, they are non-judgmental, without innuendo that the young person somehow really might need to reconsider. This technique is very effective during the first stages of LSCI when you want to encourage young people to freely express their views and feelings about the incident.

5. **Decoding**

When you make a statement that connects meaning or feeling to a young person's surface behavior or words, you are interpreting, which is a form of decoding (see Chapter 6). Interpretation expands a young person's awareness of connections between behavior and private beliefs, perceptions, thoughts, and feelings. Construct your first interpretations from reflections about the young person's behavior and words. Reflections provide credibility to the interpretation because they give observed evidence. This is a neutral way to link what is publicly observed to what may be private for the child. The following are examples of the way reflections and interpretations are used together in decoding behavior:

- "When a young person puts his hands over his ears [reflection of behavior], he is telling me that this topic is uncomfortable for him to hear [interpretation of feeling]."
- "I've noticed that each time you get around him, you end up in trouble [reflection]. Maybe he enjoys seeing you out of control [interpretation]."

In the first example, the third person pronoun is used to provide psychological space for the young person. Because the interpretation does not directly address the young person, there is enough distance for the young person to hear the message without having to be defensive. The young person is not forced into a position of having to respond. The reflection and interpretation are simply matter of fact.

When a young person's response suggests that decoding has been accepted, follow it with a question. This helps the young person begin to deal with the new material. Usually a yes or no question is the easiest to answer, particularly if the interpretation is heavily laden with private concerns.

With sophisticated young people and those who have had previous LSCIs, you can begin to shift responsibility for decoding and making interpretations to the young person, using statements and questions like the following:

- "That comment must have hurt your feelings."
- "What went through your mind when she said that?"
- "What is your idea about why that remark set her off?"

- "Do you think your comment had anything to do with the way you were treated by them last week?"
- "Some people really know how to make other people feel bad."

While you or a young person are decoding, you are seeking answers to the question, "What is the real issue here?" Decoding is the simultaneous mental process used to translate interpretations of behavior into broader networks of meaning, connecting the obvious to the not-so-obvious. Decoding should shape the direction of your LSCI, moving it toward a focus on the surface incident or toward a more private, underlying issue. (If you are still hesitant about decoding, review Chapter 6. Decoding is a skill that must be used for effective LSCI.)

As You Transition to Stage 3

Stage 2 begins to merge into the next stage when the young person has reviewed the incident and you have used interpretations, decoding, and affirmations of the young person to forge links of confidence, mutual trust, and personal connection. Inaccurate interpretations, failure to decode, or a shortage of strong affirmations will dilute the confidence the young person may have in you: "This adult is like all the others and doesn't really understand (or care)!" Through accurate interpretations and sensitivity to the young person's psychological world, however, the young person begins to believe, "This adult really does understand!" When this happens, the young person will be ready to go with you into the next LSCI stage.

The following are examples of ways to bridge into Stage 3:
- "This is what I hear you saying . . ."
- "You've described the situation clearly. Let's review what you have said."
- "It's interesting how something that you intended to be nice backfired and led to all this trouble."
- "It seems like the problem that got you in here to talk isn't the real problem after all."

Stage 3: Central Issue (Select a Goal)

SYNOPSIS OF STAGE 3

Stage 3 builds a conceptual structure about what is significant in the incident. At the moment of the incident, the young person's life space includes both public and private realities. It is the adult's job in Stage 3 to sort it all out and make decisions about which reality predominates and what is needed. Stage 3 is the decision-making point for selecting a therapeutic goal.

The key processes in Stage 3 are to explore the young person's view of the incident and underlying concerns until you have sufficient understanding to (a) concisely state the central issue, (b) assess the young person's perceptions, thoughts, feelings, and motivation to change behavior, and (c) decide what the goal should be for this particular intervention.

Table 7.3 illustrates the dynamics of Stage 3. In this stage a logical outcome will begin to take shape and the information is used to structure the remainder of the LSCI. In Stage 3 you are preparing the young person to consider another perspective of the situation, one that requires the young person to accept some responsibility for a part in creating the crisis. What is difficult at this point is that we have the insight; we know the young person's patterns of perceiving, thinking, feeling, and behaving and how they most likely contributed to the crisis. We need to fight our impulse to bring this insight into the bright light of day. The goal of the LSCI is to plant a seed of insight which we hope will take root over time and eventually grow into a new realization of repetitive patterns of self-defeating behavior. The art of Stage 3 is "preparing the soil" to accept the seed of insight which we hope to plant in Stage 4. Stage 3 gives way to Stage 4 when the issue has been stated concisely by the adult or young person and the adult has chosen an Intervention. (The chapters in Part 2 provide in-depth discussions of how to conduct each Intervention.)

What Happens in Stage 3?

Preliminary information needed to identify the central issue is obtained in Stages 1 and 2. As Stage 3 begins, you have an initial idea about whether the incident itself, or an underlying concern, is the central issue. During Stage 3, this idea is tested and expanded by obtaining information in greater depth, looping back for more verbal exchanges, and performing more decoding. At Stage 3, we are assessing the situation for potential insight gain. Will the young person benefit from short-term intervention to quickly return to the ongoing program, or is this event so characteristic of the young person's repetitive patterns of perceiving, thinking, feeling, and behaving that we will use the LSCI to maximize the insight potential?

> Will the young person benefit from short-term intervention to quickly return to the ongoing program, or is this event so characteristic of the young person's repetitive patterns of perceiving, thinking, feeling, and behaving that we will use the LSCI to maximize the insight potential?

Youth	Adult Goals	Adult Skills
TABLE 7.3 **STAGE 3: CENTRAL ISSUE**		
Central Issue	Select a Goal	Differential Diagnosis
So this is the central focus of my problem!	What I need to do to determine: [A] If this problem is characteristic of how this youth perceives, thinks, feels, and behaves when under stress [B] If this problem is best managed by short-term intervention in order to get the youth back into the classroom or program [C] If this problem is best managed by using one of the LSCI interventions	Understand the youth's history and current life stressors Understand the six LSCI interventions and be able to select the most appropriate one for the problem situation State the central issue behaviorally with age-appropriate language

Find the Central Issue and Form a Concise Statement

The first decision in Stage 3 is whether to focus on the incident or to put your effort into unfolding some of the underlying anxieties associated with the incident. To focus on underlying concerns is difficult and complicated. Yet unless this is done, a young person's private reality remains untouched and unresolved. Emotional volatility builds up as a young person attempts to function while avoiding a private burden. Through LSCI, underlying concerns can be better understood and dealt with in a satisfactory way. When emotional tension is reduced, rational problem-solving becomes possible.

With increasing information comes greater clarity about the incident and underlying concerns. This information must be distilled into a single statement that represents the central issue. The central issue should be clearly stated in one or two simple sentences before continuing further into the solution stages.

In some interviews the adult summarizes the central issue; in others the young person will be able to blurt out some version of the central issue. The following are examples of statements about central issues. These examples state the incident as the central issue:

- "It seems that joking around with others leads to problems."
- "The way you see it, you are the one who is always picked on."
- "You tried to follow the rules, but it's really hard to do right when everyone else is breaking the rules."

- "You think he deserves trolling because he trolled you."
- "She thinks she knows everything and that annoys you."
- "You really didn't mean to hurt him. It's hard to stop yourself."

Assess the Young Person's Perception, Insight, and Motivation to Change

Following a concise statement of the central issue, think through the preceding dialogue to summarize, in your mind, how the young person views the incident and the extent of the young person's sense of responsibility. From the previous stages, you should be able to see the events as the young person has seen and felt them. Some young people have extremely restricted perceptions, but others are clearly able to view an incident from another's point of view. It is essential to understand how your particular young person views the event. You also should have an idea about the young person's view of adult authority and who should solve the problem, the young person or the adult.

This information will help you evaluate the young person's motivation to change and assume responsibility for the crisis. It also will give you an indication of the young person's readiness to give up old defenses and rationalizations for new or different behavior in the future. With this information, you and the young person are ready to move on to selecting an intervention based on the young person's current perceptions, thoughts, and feelings.

Select the Appropriate Intervention

Once the issue has been clearly stated, and you have assessed the young person's psychological world and motivation to change, the question becomes, "What do I want to happen, now that the young person may be open to change?"

Almost every central issue can be managed within one of LSCI's six interventions. The original names given by Redl (1959) are in parentheses, with the exception of the Red Flag intervention. The Red Flag intervention was developed by Dr. Nicholas Long through his work with students in the New York City public schools, District 75. The following is a summary of each of the six Interventions.

The Red Flag Intervention
Goal: Identify the Source of the Stress

Young Person's Perception:	"Everybody is against me! No one understands what's going on with me and no one cares!"
Uses:	With young people who overreact to normal rules and procedures with emotional outbursts and who attempt to create a no-win situation by engaging adults in a

power struggle that ultimately results in more rejection and feelings of alienation.

Goal: To identify the source of the problem: is it a *Carry In* problem from another setting, a *Carry Over* problem from another situation within the setting, or did an event in the current setting *Tap In* to emotional unfinished business?

Focus: Helps young people recognize that they are *displacing* their feelings on others and alienating the sources of support they need to handle their stress.

Young Person's New Insight: "Someone does understand my real problems and can read beyond my behavior. I need to talk to adults about my real problems and not create new ones here."

The Reality Check Intervention (Reality Rub Reclaiming Intervention)
Goal: Organize Perceptions of Reality

Young Person's Perception: "I am being treated unfairly!"

Uses: With young people who demonstrate any of the following:
(1) Misperceptions of reality due to triggering of personal sensitivities
(2) Blocked perceptions of reality due to intense feelings
(3) Restricted perceptions of reality due to perseveration on a single event
(4) Private reconstruction of reality
(5) Manipulation of reality to test limits

Goals: • To help the young person organize thinking so that a more accurate perception of reality emerges
• To bring the young person to the realization that there is "more than meets the eye"
• To help the young person begin to understand his or her contribution to the problem

Focus: Organizes the young people's perceptions and the sequence of time and events

Young Person's New Insight: "Maybe there is another way to look at this situation. I can see how I might have contributed to making it worse, and what I need to do about it."

The New Tools Intervention
Goal: Build Social-Emotional Skills

Young Person's Perception: "I want to do the right thing, but it always comes out wrong."

Uses: With young people seeking approval of adults or peers but lacking appropriate social behaviors to accomplish this

Goal: To teach new social behaviors that the young person can use for immediate positive gain

Focus: Instructs in specific social behaviors that will have immediate payback in desired responses from others; developmentally, reflects emerging independence and responsibility

Young Person's New Insight: "I have the right intention, but I need help to learn the skills that will help me make friends, achieve, and get along with adults."

The Benign Confrontation Intervention (Symptom Estrangement Intervention)
Goal: Challenge Unacceptable Behaviors

Young Person's Perception: "I do what I have to do even if it hurts others." "I have to take care of 'Number One.'" "I have a reputation to maintain. I have no need to change."

Uses: With young people who are comfortable with their asocial behavior through receiving too much gratification; those who practice aggression, passive aggression, manipulation, or exploitation of others.

Goal: To make a behavior uncomfortable by confronting the rationalizations and decoding the self-serving narcissism and distorted pleasure the young person receives from the unacceptable behavior.

Focus:	Helps young people realize that they are paying a high price for justifying the exploitation of others; they are tricking themselves into believing their cause is just.
Young Person's New Insight:	"Maybe I've been cruel. Maybe I've been tricking myself into believing this behavior is justified."

The Regulate and Restore Intervention
(Massaging Numb Values Intervention)
Goal: Strengthen Self-Control

Young Person's Perception:	"Even when I'm upset, a part of me is saying, 'Control! Stop yourself,' but I don't." "I'm worthless. I hate myself."
Uses:	With young people who, after acting out, are burdened by remorse, shame, inadequacy, or guilt about their own failures or unworthiness; those with a destructive self-concept; and those who have a negative social role.
Goal:	To relieve some of the burden by emphasizing a young person's positive qualities; to strengthen self-control (Regulate) and build the young person's confidence that they are a valued person with qualities like fairness, kindness, friendship, or leadership potential (Repair).
Focus:	Expands young person's self-control and confidence through abundant affirmations and reflections about existing socially desirable attributes and areas where the child exhibited self-control. Developmentally, this goal requires a shift in source of responsibility from adult to young person.
Young Person's New Insight:	"Even under tempting situations or group pressure, I have the capacity to control myself."

The Peer Manipulation Intervention
(Manipulation of Body Boundaries Intervention)
Goal: Expose Peer Exploitation

Young Person's Perception:	"It's important to have a friend even if the friend gets me into trouble." "I'm going to teach him a lesson!"

Uses:	With young people who are neglected, abused, scapegoated, isolated, or who seek out destructive friendships by acting out for others; with young people who are unwittingly set up by passive-aggressive peers to act out.
Goal:	To help a young person see that another young person (or adult) is manipulating events in a way that is working against the young person's best interests.
Focus:	Provides insight into reasons for the behavior of others; views social interactions from the perspective of motivations and behaviors of others; developmentally, this goal requires considerable maturity on the young person's part as the young person learns to understand how others think, feel, and behave.
Young Person's New Insight:	"A friend is someone who helps you solve problems and feel good rather than someone who gets you into trouble." "I can make my own decisions; I don't need to 'take the bait' when someone is trying to get me in trouble."

Examples of LSCIs using each of these Interventions can be found in Chapters 10 through 15. These chapters illustrate how each of the Interventions uniquely shapes the strategies and content of the remaining stages in every LSCI.

You may be asking, "Why put off selecting an outcome goal until Stage 3?" Sometimes, with young people we know well, we have an idea from the very beginning about what the young person's characteristic perception is, what the central issue will be, and what Intervention is needed. Even so, it is necessary to establish the facts and observations about the crisis and obtain the young person's current perception. Without establishing these, the young person will not become sufficiently involved to own a solution as it is developed.

Your Role in Stage 3

Stage 3 requires a lot of decoding, thoughtful observing and listening, and good verbal skills for questioning and interpreting behavior. We have described these processes in the previous stages, but it is necessary to return again and again to Stage 2 as you form a statement of the central issue in Stage 3. You will find yourself in an information loop—questioning, interpreting, decoding, and hypothesis building. While sifting through the maze of responses you hear and observe, you also must form your own questions and responses in ways that begin to shape the direction of the LSCI. Your task is to decide upon a particular outcome goal.

As You End Stage 3

Stage 3 transitions when a statement has been made about the central issue and you have chosen one of the six Interventions. With the end of Stage 3, the problem phase ends, and the solution stages begin. The following are examples of ways to end this stage and bridge into Stage 4:

- "This situation is beginning to make sense. When a person understands a problem, it can be solved."
- "This has not been a good day for you, but we know what's wrong now, so we can do something about it."
- "Now that we know what the problem is, you (we) can make a plan for what to do about it. We've made so much progress already!"

Stage 4: Insight (Highlight a Pattern of Behavior)

SYNOPSIS OF STAGE 4

In Stage 3, we made a decision based on what we learned from the young person in Stage 2. We determined either (a) the crisis was best managed by a short-term milieu intervention, or (b) the incident offered enough material characteristic of the young person's pattern of self-defeating behavior that we would attempt to help him gain insight into the pattern. If we have decided to go forward with a full LSCI, we have selected one of the six outcome goals. In Stage 4 our task is to bring the young person to insight; that is, to help them begin to recognize the rigid patterns of perceiving, thinking, feeling, and behaving that have been driving their inappropriate behavior. This is neither an easy task or a "quick-fix" for a young person. Human beings tend to resist change. We tend toward familiar patterns and resist abandoning old ways—even if a part of us knows that those old ways were self-defeating. It is somewhat like the person clinging to a life preserver in the ocean, who is afraid to give it up to climb into a rowboat. In this stage, we ask the young person to trust us to help find *new and better solutions* to old problems. In a single LSCI intervention, a young person can be said to "gain" insight rather than to "master" it completely. True insight comes gradually, over time, and through repeated LSCI conversations. Table 7.4 illustrates the dynamics of Stage 4.

	TABLE 7.4	
	STAGE 4: INSIGHT	
Youth	Adult Goals	Adult Skills
Insight	Highlight Pattern of Behavior	Intervention Skills
Now I understand how I contribute to my problems and how I make them worse!	Facilitate the youth's insight into the pattern of self-defeating behaviors; implement the selected LSCI	Carry out the selected LSCI successfully

This stage begins the "problem-solving" or "long-term insight development" part of LSCI. The following three questions are to be answered during this stage:

- If a young person's crisis is an opportunity to learn new insights into patterns of self-defeating behavior, what would be the message of these insights?
- How are these insights translated into a plan to change a young person's behavior?
- What will the young person see as a satisfactory solution that can be "owned?"

Often, there are two solutions to be dealt with: one is the reality issue surrounding the incident; the other is an underlying issue that may have become evident during the previous stages. When possible, the young person should come up with alternative solutions and then select the course of action that seems best. If the young person is not able to do this, the adult helps the young person by providing guidelines, values, or rules. For young people to have genuine ownership of solutions, the choices should be ones that they value as beneficial. Stage 4 bridges to Stage 5 when a solution is chosen, and the young person puts the solution into words.

What Happens in Stage 4?

In the Insight stage, we use the information that we collected in the Timeline to reframe the student's perception, thoughts, and feelings about the issue. This can be explained with an analogy of a camera and a cameraman; as the youth is telling his story in the Timeline, he is showing us his video of how he saw the situation. The adult's task during the Timeline is to listen carefully and "see" the video from the young person's point of view. As the video runs, we may pick up on problems with the camerawork, such as times when either the camera was focused too narrowly on just one small aspect of the event or times when the view was so wide, it missed an important detail.

In Stage 4, as the young person shares his "video," we provide structure to the conversation by asking purposeful, focused questions that relate to the central issue identified in Stage 3. Likewise, the questions we ask help the young person focus on the missing pieces of the video, such as when the camera was taking a myopic, telescopic, or even blurry view. Our overall goal is to help the student edit the videotape of the event. Through the Stage 4 process, the young person begins to see the event from a new perspective. When that happens, that's a glimmer of Insight. Several things can happen at that point.

One thing that happens frequently is back-peddling. As the young person begins to recognize that the adult is onto something, you may see her go back and try to cover her tracks a little bit so that they're not so easy to follow. But the adult continues to ask questions, listen, and clarify:

- Oh, there's one more thing that I have to ask you about . . .
- There's one more thing I don't understand . . .
- Do I remember this correctly? Help me through this again.
- Wait a minute. Fifteen minutes ago, didn't you just say the opposite?

Through questions and clarifications, we help the child end up with a more accurate video that sheds a new light on the sequence of perceptions, thoughts, feelings, behaviors, and reactions that contributed to the problem. Young people slowly gain new insights into their role in the problem and are then better equipped to consider (in Stage 5) what new skills they need to prevent this problem from recurring.

During this stage, the nature of LSCI changes distinctly. The tone is upbeat; the focus is on personal insights and new solutions which make things better. Before this point, LSCI has been diverging, exploring, and expanding for a full understanding of the incident and the central issue behind it. Now, with the central issue identified, new solutions become the focus.

If a young person's crisis were an opportunity to learn a new insight into patterns of self-defeating behavior, what would be the message of this insight?

Each of the six interventions has a specific insight message that the young person hopefully will discover as they identify, examine, and review their pattern of dysfunctional behavior. The interviewer's task is to encourage the young person to see this crisis not as an isolated, one-time happening, but as a chronic pattern of dysfunction that the young person turns to when they become frustrated, angry, and overwhelmed. How an interviewer accomplishes this task is both an art and a skill. However, a young person will learn the following from a successful LSCI Intervention:

1. **The Red Flag Intervention**
   "When life gets stressful and I get mistreated, I believe everyone is against me. I'm so upset that when I come to school, I overreact to the smallest frustration and blow up. I take out my anger at a teacher or a classmate and blame them for my anger and sadness, not even realizing that I'm taking my feelings out on the wrong person. Instead of reaching out to those adults who can help me, I alienate them. I need to change the pattern of behaviors and ask for help instead of creating a new problem at school."

2. **The Reality Check Intervention**
   "Maybe when I get upset, I distort what happened, what I saw, what I remembered, and what I heard. Sometimes I come to the wrong conclusions before checking out the facts. When I do this, I make the situation worse. I need to stop this pattern of behavior."

3. **The New Tools Intervention**
   "I want to have friends and learn, but somehow things go wrong, and I'm rejected and feel embarrassed. I have learned I have the right intentions but the wrong behaviors to achieve what I want. Adults recognize my good intentions, and I am motivated to learn new social skills that will improve my relationships in school."

4. **The Benign Confrontation Intervention**
   "Sometimes I find clever ways to justify my aggressive behavior toward others. I feel powerful knowing that others fear me, but lately I am on the hot seat and adults are coming down on me, so I've been paying a high price for my behavior. Maybe it's not worth it. Maybe I'm fooling myself into believing I have a right to do what I want, when I want. Maybe a part of me enjoys the pleasure of threatening and hurting others. Maybe this is not the way to live. I don't want to be cruel—just cool. Perhaps I need to change some of my behavior."

5. **The Regulate and Restore Intervention**
   "When I get upset, I find ways of beating myself up both physically and psychologically. Nobody else needs to mistreat me: I have a successful way of doing that all by myself. When I feel bad, I try to get others to punish me because I think I deserve mistreatment. But I am learning that I'm not a terrible person. I do have some self-control skills, and others believe in me—they believe that I can change and feel better about myself."

6. The Peer Manipulation Intervention

"I want to have friends but sometimes I pick the wrong ones and I end up in trouble. A friend should be someone who helps me and not someone who gets me into trouble. I'm not going to let my friends control what I do anymore! Adults have helped me recognize my pattern of destructive peer relationships and with their help I would like to find new and more positive friends. In my case, I have not been aware of how [name of other young person] successfully manipulates me to respond to his teasing behavior until I blow up and end up in trouble. I do not want him to control me in the future, and I need to develop a plan to achieve this goal."

How are these insights translated into a personal plan for improving the young person's behavior?

This is the critical step in the LSCI process. If the young person's insight into their repetitive pattern of self-defeating behavior doesn't lead to a personal plan to change and improve this behavior, the process becomes a hollow intellectual experience. An LSCI Intervention mobilizes a young person to translate new insights into a plan to develop new skills in order to improve self-concept and interpersonal relationships. During this guided process, the young person is encouraged to consider as many alternative plans as possible. Some will be unrealistic and inappropriate; but by discussing the pros and cons of each plan, the young person will take responsibility for personal change as they practice a problem-solving approach.

> An LSCI Intervention mobilizes a young person to translate new insights into a plan to develop new skills in order to improve self-concept and interpersonal relationships.

The adult can assist in this important process by raising the following questions about the young person's plan:

- What do you hope to accomplish by using this plan?
- How many new skills do you think you need to learn?
- Are some of these skills more important than others?
- How long do you think you will have to show these new behaviors before others recognize the change?

The young person's plan should be realistic and attainable and implemented in degrees, not in expediential leaps.

What is a satisfactory solution?

Satisfactory solutions are those that young people believe will work to their benefit. The most acceptable solution from an adult viewpoint may not be seen as satisfactory by a young person. If a young person does not really buy into a solution, the time has been wasted.

Your Role in Stage 4

The adult's responsibility during Stage 4 is to guide. How much guidance you provide should be adjusted to the young person's view of adults and who has responsibility for solving problems. Your influence can widen a young person's consideration of alternative ways to solve a problem. The following are some examples of ways to encourage a discussion of alternatives:

- "There are lots of ways to go about solving this problem."
- "That's a solution that might work. Can you think of another way?"
- "Let's count how many different ways you can think of to handle this situation."

An important part of being an effective guide in this stage is to see that the young person describes as many alternative solutions as possible. The benefits and problems associated with each alternative should be considered. To do this you will need to ask questions and reflect on real consequences. The best help you can provide during this stage is to suggest guidelines, rules, and values that are relevant to the incident and alternatives the young person is struggling with. Through your responses, you can influence the young person to carefully consider solutions that the young person might not otherwise consider.

Exercise caution so that you do not jump in too soon and influence the young person toward a solution. If you provide the solution, or the young person sees you as having already made up your mind, the chosen solution will be owned by you and *not* by the young person.

As You Transition to Stage 5

This is the point in LSCI when the adult and young person begin to merge in agreement about a solution. Among the alternative solutions discussed, one will begin to take shape as being more satisfactory than others. The process is a series of trade-offs. The young person is seeking relief from the stress of the incident. You are seeking the most constructive solution for the young person's psychological world, outward behaviors, and the outcome goal that you selected in Stage 3. Keep in mind the desired change in the young person's level of insight that each different intervention cultivates. Gains in insight are an essential part of a satisfactory solution. The solution also should provide for enhancement of the young person's self-concept and confidence to face the people who were involved in the stressful incident. The solution also must be realistic and achievable. It must fit into the real situation the young person faces and be within his capacity to use successfully. The young person must feel ownership of the solution. Stage 4 draws to a close as the young person puts the chosen solution into words. Sometimes you may have to summarize it first and then ask the young person to tell it to you again. With other young people, you can end the stage with requests such as the following:

- "We've talked about a lot of ways to handle this. Which seems the best to you?"
- "It seems pretty clear that you've considered all the choices. Which will work best for you?"
- "You have thought this through carefully. Let's review the choices."

Stage 5: New Skills (Teach and Empower)

SYNOPSIS OF STAGE 5

This is the stage for realistic teaching and rehearsal of new skills that can be used in future problem situations. The focus is on specific behaviors—*what to do* and *when*. Both negative and positive aspects are anticipated, and a working Plan for Success is formed for putting the solution into action. Table 7.5 illustrates the dynamics of Stage 5.

TABLE 7.5 STAGE 5: NEW SKILLS		
Youth	Adult Goals	Adult Skills
		Teaching New Ways to Perceive, Think, Feel, and Behave
New Skills	**Teach and Empower**	
These are the social-emotional skills I need to make positive choices and improve my interpersonal relationships!	Teach social-emotional skills that will improve the youth's self-concept, interpersonal skills, and behaviors.	Social-emotional skills Self-control skills Self-regulation skills Role-playing skills

What Happens in Stage 5?

Stage 5 is used to teach, practice, and plan for applying the new skills that the chosen solution will require. The question is, "Will this solution work for the young person?" Behind this simple question is the major concern of intervention programs—will there be a carryover effect? Stage 5 is the place to teach the new social-emotional skills that help turn the gains of the previous stages into lasting positive outcomes. Because it tends to be difficult for people (of all ages) to replace old behaviors with new ones, Stage 5 requires that adults help kids carefully plan for success and abundantly affirm the young person's ability to approach problems in new ways.

The Adult's Role in Stage 5

In Stage 5, adults help young people expand their social-emotional skills, rehearse new behaviors, accept consequences, anticipate challenges, and affirm benefits of behavioral change.

1. **Develop a Plan for Success**
   The first task of this stage is to help the young person plan for how they will make use of their new insight (however nascent). While plans can be discussed verbally, they become more impactful and enduring when they are written down. The simple act of putting plans on paper can serve as a deepening of a commitment to goals. A Plan for Success should include answers to the following questions:

   1. What happened?
   2. What did I learn from the situation?
   3. What solutions were agreed upon?
   4. What are the benefits of this solution for me?
   5. What new skills have I practiced?
   6. Who or what was hurt?
   7. What do I need to do to make things right?
   8. Do I need to apologize to anyone? If so, to who and why?
   9. Are there any consequences as a result of what happened? How will I show responsibility?
   10. What will I do when something like this happens again in the future?
   11. Who are two people I can go to for help when I feel upset or triggered?
   12. What are three strategies I can use to calm myself down when I begin to feel upset?
   13. What are some likely things that may happen when I return? How can I respond in an effective way?

Do not be intimidated by the number of questions listed above. Not every young person will need to answer every question during every LSCI. On the other hand, encouraging kids to reflect on the incident and create a written plan for the future is one of the best ways to transform the short-term benefit of the LSCI conversation into long-term changes in perceptions, thoughts, feelings, and behaviors. A template for a Plan for Success is provided in Appendix B of this book. The plan can be customized for different ages, stages, and settings.

2. **Teach and Rehearse New Skills**

   Identifying and practicing new social-emotional skills is the "main event" of Stage 5. Sample statements to begin the conversation include:

   - "You have come up with some good ideas here. What will you say to him when we leave here?"
   - "This is a really good plan. Let's pretend I am that person; what will you say to me?"
   - "It's not always easy to do what we've been talking about. Let's figure out how to put this plan into action."
   - "This is going to take a lot of courage on your part. How will you begin?"

3. **Help the Youth Accept Consequences**

   While young people will often ask questions about consequences at the beginning of an LSCI, Stage 5 is the most appropriate time to explore the issue. If kids seem preoccupied with consequences during the Drain Off and Timeline stages, acknowledge their concern, affirm their feelings, and reassure them that as soon as you understand more about what happened from their point of view, you'll be able to have a more informed conversation about any consequences. While the most important outcomes of LSCI are improved adult-child relationships, new insights, improved social-emotional skills, and plans for better behaviors, preparing young people to accept consequences with responsibility is an essential outcome of Stage 5.

   The following are examples of statements that help a young person prepare for the consequences resulting from an incident:

   - "It's clear you have a good plan. When we go back into the room, he will be expecting you to apologize. What will you say?"
   - "This talk shows your best qualities. You're going to be able to (repair the damage, handle the suspension, explain it to your parent, face the judge, talk with the principal, apologize)."

- "I'm sorry you have to (face the consequences), but once it's over, I know you're going to handle something like this in a better way next time it happens."

Such statements affirm your belief in the young person's capacity to accept the consequences in a responsible way. They also provide support for the most unpleasant part of an incident: enduring the consequences.

4. **Help the Youth Anticipate Challenges**
Young people often fail to anticipate that events won't always unfold the way they expect. When the unexpected occurs, this is a stressor. If unprepared to handle it, this stressful event can be the start of a whole new cycle of conflict! To help young people anticipate challenges to their Plan for Success—and avoid resorting to old, reactive coping strategies—use statements such as the following:

- "What will you do if . . . "
- "What if he doesn't listen?"
- "What if she tells you it doesn't matter that you had a reason for breaking the rule?"
- "Do you think they'll believe you next time?"
- "It will be hard to say no to your friends when they try that again. What will you do?"
- "The next time they tell you to do that, you are going to feel just as angry. What will happen?"
- "They may ignore you. What then?"

This effort should provide expanded insight into social exchanges, both positive and negative.

- Begin with a future scenario that repeats the present incident
- Lead the young person through a replay while the young person describes the new behaviors to be used
- Help the young person imagine how others will respond

The difficult part is to balance the amount of reality you expose the young person to with their capacity to anticipate future stress. If a young person is just beginning to try new behaviors, it may not be the time to expand the horizon to foresee all possible problems. On the other hand, if a young person has already participated in a series of LSCIs with you and there does not seem to be carryover into real-life situations, you may need to spend more time on rehearsal.

5. **Express Confidence in the Youth**

The importance of expressing confidence in a young person's ability to carry out a plan for success during this stage cannot be overemphasized. Your confidence is the fuel for their change. Your support for the youth is the mirror in which they see a changed self. Your expressed belief in their ability to use new behaviors gives them the confidence to follow through. Many young people are engulfed by self-doubt, but a trusted adult's affirmations can make real change possible. Without such a change in a young person's private psychological world, there will be no real, lasting benefit from LSCI.

6. **Point Out Potential Benefits**

Benefits are not easily anticipated by most troubled young people. They seem to live with a sense of immediacy that precludes planning. They also seem to operate under a cloud of pessimism, always ready to see the worst possible side of every person and event. To a large extent, experience has been the teacher, and their experiences have been downers. Teaching young people to look at the future with optimism requires optimism and enthusiasm on the part of the adult. The following are examples of statements that convey future benefits:

- "If you can do this, people will give you a break. They'll treat you with (respect, fairness, love, kindness, understanding)."
- "When you start making these changes, people are going to start saying, 'Wow, I want to be around her.'"
- "When you handle things this way, people will say you are a person they can count on."
- "Your friends are going to look up to you."
- "People will see you as (a leader, a really nice person, a friend, someone they enjoy being with)."
- "This will give you the chance to show the really nice things about yourself."

As You Transition to Stage 6

When a young person tells how the current issue will be handled and responds constructively to the idea that the issue will likely come up again in the future, they are ready for Stage 6. You know that LSCI has been successful when the young person provides constructive and realistic responses to the present situation and future incidents. You will have a sense that the young person is realistic about the current consequences and ready to try a new solution, recognizing that it will not be easy to implement but will be worth the effort in future benefits. The following are examples of ways to end Stage 5:

- "This has been tough talk, but it's going to pay off for you!"
- "You have a view about this that will really work for you."
- "Things will be better when you handle it this way."
- "It won't be easy, but I believe you can do it!"
- "You can do this, even if it's hard to do."

Stage 6: Transfer of Learning (Get Ready to Resume the Activity)

SYNOPSIS OF STAGE 6

The last stage in LSCI is the plan for the young person's transition back into the group. This stage helps the young person prepare for reentering and participating in an ongoing activity. It also is important to use this stage to close down private topics or feelings brought out during LSCI. Table 7.6 illustrates the dynamics of Stage 6.

The topic shifts in this last stage. The incident and the central issue have been put to rest, at least temporarily. A solution has been worked out. The critical task of Stage 6 is to help the young person transition successfully back to the group and apply their Plan for Success. The discussion centers on:

1. What has happened while the young person has been away (from the class, from the group, from an activity, etc.)
2. What the young person will do to restore relationships upon return
3. How others will react as he rejoins the group

TABLE 7.6		
STAGE 6: TRANSFER OF LEARNING		
Youth	Adult Goals	Adult Skills
Transfer of Learning	Ready the Youth to Resume the Activity	Planning and Follow-Up Skills
This is how I need to behave to get more of my needs met when I return to my class or group!	Prepare the youth to return to the classroom and follow up with the adults involved in ensuring the youth's successful transition	Understand group dynamics in the classroom or program Collaborate with significant adults to ensure youth's successful transition Work with youth to establish a Plan for Success

Affirmations of the young person's new insights and competence for carrying out the Plan for Success are essential for lasting positive outcomes.

Stage 6 ends when the young person is under rational control, has described the behaviors needed for successful reentry, and conveys a responsible attitude.

What Happens in Stage 6?

Stage 6 generally begins with questions such as the following:

- "What is your group (class, friend, etc.) doing now?"
- Who do you need to talk to to resolve the conflict that occurred?
- "When you left the group, they were working on their independent projects. Do you think they are still at it?"
- "We've been in here for quite a while. Is there work you will need to get done?
- Is there anything else to take care of before returning?

Such questions shift the focus from the young person to another place and other people. The questions are designed to help a young person begin to think about the peer group, the activity that has gone on while the young person has been away, and the expectations for participation and appropriate behavior. In Appendix B of this manual, you will find an LSCI Reentry Checklist, a tool that helps adults attend to the most important tasks of reentering the group after an LSCI.

Like the first LSCI stage, the last stage often is brief because the young person usually is eager to put the problem aside and get back to the group. This response is typical of young people who believe that there has been a satisfactory solution. These young people also have developed some additional confidence in themselves during the LSCI.

The moment of reentry into a group is a powerful one. A young person has usually left the group because of crisis and conflict. Reentry poses its own set of stressors, challenges, and opportunities.

The Expectation to Participate

In this stage, the adult's role is to help a young person understand and accept responsibilities for appropriate participation in anticipated activities. We have seen young people make substantial progress in highly successful LSCIs, and then lose it all because they had not been sufficiently prepared for the demands made on them when they reentered their group. The fewer surprises the better. The following are examples of ways a young person can be prepared for the expectation to participate:

- "They are keeping your work for you. You will have time to finish it before lunch."
- "The project will be over by now, and they will be working on something new. The teacher will tell you how to do it."
- "I know you are sorry to have missed the field trip because of our talk, but we have done something important in here today. They'll want to tell you about the trip when they get back. That will give you the chance to use what we have been practicing in here."

By reviewing the behavior needed for successful reentry and participation before a young person returns to the group, the young person has increased assurance that the reentry can be handled smoothly and without further embarrassment. When you include affirmations of the young person, you increase self-confidence. Without feelings of confidence, young people seldom make it back to the door before anxiety floods and the young person is out of control again.

Regression and Resistance

Occasionally, you may have a young person who participates in LSCI with cooperation and collaboration until the talk turns to returning to the group. If a young person loses control, appears to suddenly reject everything that has gone on previously, seems reluctant to return to the group, or tries to control the reentry process, something is producing anxiety about the reentry. The young person may have one of the following problems:

1. The young person may have more to say than has come out in the LSCI
2. The young person may lack the confidence to make the shift back to being a participating group member
3. The young person may have difficulty separating from the interviewer

Consider each possibility. You may find that you need to go back to an earlier stage to bring out something that has been overlooked. Or you may have to review again the plan you and the young person rehearsed in Stage 5, perhaps modifying it to be more realistic about what the young person can do successfully. Or you may have to examine the quality of the relationship that has developed between you and the young person. The young person may be feeling the anxiety that comes with separation from you. Your role in that relationship may be the significant force, fueling resistance to reentry or spiraling negative behavior. We discuss ways to handle this in the following chapter on the helping process and potential pitfalls.

Reactions of the Peer Group

The success of a young person's reentry is directly related to how effectively someone deals with the peer group while the young person is away. It requires close teamwork to reconnect the young person and peers. Too much emphasis on the young person's problem in front of peers tends to highlight the deviance, while ignoring the disruption to the group or the discomfort of group members communicates either the adult's desire to ignore it or inability to handle it.

In the complex dynamics of a peer group, the reentry of a member who has been away will almost always cause disturbance in other members of the group. This reaction is intensified dramatically when the absent member left the group under less-than-pleasant circumstances and may have transgressed against members of the group. Even if not directly involved, members watch a crisis with fascination, closely identifying with trouble and vicariously projecting themselves into the situation.

When the young person reenters, it often excites the group again, and these reactions need to be anticipated. Sometimes the reactions will be directed against the reentering young person, sometimes against the adult, and often against each other. Anticipating these reactions often heads off trouble.

The adult who remains with the group must deal with the reactions of group members during the time the young person is away. Spiraling anxiety can be diluted or avoided by sensitive observation and redirection of each member to something personally successful. During this time group members want to be reassured that they are "safe," the adult in charge is looking after their needs, and the absent young person is being treated fairly. The following are examples of statements made by adults to reassure the peer group:

- "You're doing so well with this project that you should be able to show him the finished product by the time he gets back." [The message: everything is under control, and the young person will return to participate.]
- "When we see a friend having to leave the room, we wonder what is happening to her. She is okay, and when she works out the problem with the teacher, she will be back." [The message: the young person is not being hurt; she is problem solving.]
- "When a problem gets out of hand, it is a good thing to go out with an adult to talk." [The message: a talk with an adult is the way to solve a problem.]

Your Role in Stage 6

The relationship between adult and young person is significant in every stage of LSCI. However, this final stage validates the relationship developed in the preceding stages. If you have not been on target, the young person will present some of the problems we have described in the section on regression and resistance. If you have been accurate in identifying and conveying the type of adult role the young person needs, using the type of strategies that influence the young person, the young person will respond constructively to this last stage. The relationship you have established through your adult role should provide the young person with confidence that reentry is something that can be handled in a satisfactory way.

The view a young person holds about adults changes as a result of increasing emotional maturity. The following are illustrations of how these changing roles are conveyed by adults during Stage 6:

- "If this trouble starts again when you go back, remember that you decided to tell the teacher before you get in trouble." [Adults provide protection, power, and approval.]
- "I've noticed how you can control yourself even when others are losing it. When you go back, keep your attention on the assignment and you will be the winner!" [Adults' attitudes and views are best, and so they should be imitated and internalized.]
- "This is your chance to show the other kids who you are. When you go back in there cool and calm, they'll know you have the situation under control." [Adult mirrors the young person's best self, one who can be independently responsible.]

By the time you have reached Stage 6, you have established a level of trust with the young person. He has decided to share with you some of his psychological world, trusting that you can help relieve stress and make things a little better. She has developed a plan, and you have an investment in her success. Committing oneself to a goal, especially when it relates to a change in habitual behavior, is no small task. Consider what adults do when they set and commit to a goal; for example, the goal of losing 20 pounds. They surround themselves with "reminders" of the goal, such as a calorie intake record, a chart by the bathroom scale, a lunch with measured portions. They also engage in positive self-talk ("nothing tastes as good as slim feels") and reward themselves for incremental weight loss achievements (that new pair of jeans they've been wanting at 10 pounds, a new wardrobe at 20 pounds). If adults construct such behavioral and cognitive strategies to achieve their goals, it is expected that children and youth will also need support as they attempt to reach their goals.

The interviewer should be sure to collaborate with other important adults to establish conditions under which the young person can practice new skills and enjoy a measure of success as he approximates these goals. A wide variety of behavioral and cognitive strategies are available to help the young person, including behavior check-ins and contracts with various adults in the setting, environmental prompts such as posters and signs, and charts showing the young person's progress toward the goal. If the young person is to be successful in changing a repetitive pattern of behaving, our support is essential.

As You End Stage 6

The end of Stage 6 usually signals the end of the LSCI. The young person understands that the next stage is to rejoin the group and participate in a responsible way. If LSCI has been effective, emotional intensity has been reduced, events make more sense, the young person's insight has changed, a plan for success has been established, the adult-child relationship was improved, and the child's self-concept has been enhanced. The LSCI outcome goal has been accomplished, and the young person is left with changes in emotional memories—a modified psychological world now including a set of positive experiences coping with conflict. These are the ingredients of confidence. They carry over as the young person leaves the privacy of the LSCI setting and begins to put these changes into action.

The following are statements that end the LSCI, conveying confidence that the young person can carry out the Plan for Success. We put them in a sequence of young people's increasing emotional maturity.

- "The next time he starts that stuff, what are you going to do so you won't be in trouble?"
- "You've made a lot of progress today. When you go back to the group now, keep thinking about our plan and you will have a good day!"
- "You know what to expect from the others when you go back to class. It's going to be tough, but I have confidence that you can handle it now without getting into trouble again. If you spot trouble beginning, let's come out here and talk again before it happens."

LSCI is a realistic, practical, brain-based, field-tested way to interact with young people that builds positive relationships, enhances trust, and brings about genuine and lasting changes in a youth's characteristic way of perceiving, thinking, feeling, and behaving.

Is one successful LSCI enough to see significant behavioral improvements?

LSCI is not a once-and-done process. Rarely, if ever, does a young person fully grasp a new insight or permanently adopt a new set of behaviors after just one helpful interaction with an adult. Indeed, there exists no magic wand intervention that instantly reverses challenging patterns of behavior—for adults or kids! *If someone tries to tell you that their program or model or plan will change challenging children overnight, they either don't understand the psychological worlds of young people or they are knowingly deceiving you.*

LSCI is the opposite of a miracle cure; it is a realistic, practical, brain-based, field-tested way to interact with young people that builds positive relationships, enhances trust, and over time brings about genuine and lasting changes in a youth's characteristic way of perceiving, thinking, feeling, and behaving. View each LSCI as one step forward on a walk we take with a young person. Each intervention expands a young person's self-confidence, emotional regulation, impulse control, insight, and ability to change behavior; every LSCI is a step toward eventual independent problem-solving and emotional maturity.

USING LSCI WITH A GROUP

The focus of this chapter is the basic LSCI stages used with an individual young person, but the application for use with a small group of young people is similar. We use this LSCI process frequently with two young people, or a group, when they have been party to the problem situation. A group LSCI sometimes follows an individual LSCI when one young person has played a central role in a problem incident but the group has been involved. Bringing the issue back to the group emphasizes group responsibility and individual responsibility to maintain a satisfactory group. Sometimes we begin with a group LSCI when a problem situation is clouded by the involvement of everyone. As we go through the LSCI stages with the group, several central issues begin to emerge. Usually, this is followed by one or more individual LSCIs, as particular perpetrators, instigators, and victims are identified.

When using LSCI with a group, the adult must take the central role and maintain control. Relationships in a group are usually tentative and volatile and can be destructive to individuals if care is not exercised to provide psychological protection for everyone participating. Face-saving and posturing for peers are major elements that you will find in most group LSCI interventions. Individuals under stress must be supported when emotionally charged discussions begin. Individual group members also must learn how to participate in group discussions constructively and be respectful of each other's space. Just as individual young people must learn how to discuss feelings and actions, young people in groups must learn group communication and social skills if they are to deal with problem situations more successfully in the future.

The Do's and Don'ts of Implementing LSCI

To be successful in using LSCI with young people, be sure that you:

The Do's:

- **Do** maintain a mindset that crisis is a time for teaching and learning, not judging and punishing.
- **Do** avoid getting pulled into a Conflict Cycle. Manage your own emotional responses consistently through every LSCI.
- **Do** control the pacing of the intervention, spending as much time as is needed with each stage. Thoroughness in the early stages sets the stage for success in the later stages.
- **Do** remember that LSCI does not always occur in stages that are as neat and linear as outlined in this book chapter. In real life, you will likely find yourself cycling back through Stages 2 and 3 several times to clarify, decode, or expand an issue. You might even need to return to Stage 1 briefly if you touch upon an emotional issue with a young person and they become emotionally flooded. This is an expected part of the process.
- **Do** use listening skills and thoughtful questions to point the young person in the direction of important insights.
- **Do** support the youth in arriving at the insight on his own to maximize his feelings of ownership and his commitment to making behavioral changes.
- **Do** take time to rehearse new skills. It has taken the child a lifetime to develop their self-defeating patterns of behavior; they will need time to unlearn old ways and to become comfortable with new ones.
- **Do** be mindful of what the young person needs in order to transition back to a class or group successfully. Nothing undoes the success of an LSCI more quickly than for a young person's plan for success to be met by residual anger, hostility, or rejection from adults and peers.
- **Do** keep in mind that a child's psychological world cannot be changed by a single LSCI; it is through repeated use that lasting changes in beliefs, perceptions, thoughts, feelings, and behaviors result.
- **Do** remember the details of completed LSCIs, so that you can build continuity into the next one with the same young person.
- **Do** select conditions under which an LSCI can be conducted such that privacy and freedom to talk are provided.

The Don'ts:

- **Don't** rush through Stage 1 to try to get to the Timeline stage if the young person is still out of control or emotionally flooded. Take your time to help the young person become better regulated.
- **Don't** begin LSCI if *you* are overwhelmed by the crisis; wait until your own reactions are rational, objective, and completely under control.
- **Don't** rush the LSCI process. Helping young people feel heard and understood—and cultivating genuine, lasting changes in behavior—takes time! While time is hard to come by for adults who are managing groups of kids, it is also true that a challenging child will get our time one way or another. The question is how do we prefer to spend this time?

  - Do we want to spend the time managing the aftermath of aggressive outbursts and emotional flooding that result from a child feeling misunderstood or disconnected? (Think paperwork, phone calls, conferences, meetings, restrictions, behavior plans, etc.)
  - Would we rather invest time in a relationship-building, perspective-changing conversation with a child? The choice is ours.
  - A thorough LSCI takes time—as do all efforts to build relationships in any context. Consider the time it takes to use LSCI with a child as an investment. The time you put into building the relationship, making the child feel heard and understood, helping the child develop new insights, and teaching new skills pays long-term dividends. Ultimately, the child will likely require less and less of your time because of the front-end investment you've put in by using LSCI.

- **Don't** feel that you must complete all six stages each time you begin LSCI.

  - If time is an issue, go directly from Stage 3 to Stage 6, and close the LSCI with the message that you and the young person will talk again.
  - The use of Drain Off skills can help calm a child in the moment until a better time is available to complete the process.
  - The Timeline stage can go a long way in helping the child develop more organized thoughts about the events leading up to the crisis.
  - Take advantage of colleagues who are also trained in LSCI. If you are unable to conduct a thorough LSCI with a child in the moment due to the constraints of your setting, perhaps another trained professional can step in.

"Who's in charge here?"
"Who's going to handle this problem?"
"How do I know it's going to be all right for me?"

UNIVERSAL CONCERNS OF YOUTH UNDER STRESS

Questions to Consider Before Beginning LSCI

Young people bring their life experiences and developmental anxieties into every classroom, group, and stressful situation. To them, you represent all authority figures. No matter how positive, professional, or caring you are, there is no avoiding the fact that a youth's past interactions with other adults will have an impact on their current encounters with you. In many cases, you will be the unwitting recipient of their negative beliefs, feelings, and attitudes toward other adults.

Three questions from a youth's history with adults arise repeatedly during LSCI:

1. *Who's in charge here?*
2. *Who's going to handle this problem?*
3. *How do I know it's going to be all right for me?*

These universal concerns are pervasive and ever-present. When unresolved, they preoccupy a young person and influence the LSCI. To use LSCI successfully, an adult must recognize the specific form these concerns are taking and deal with them proactively. It is essential to recognize that a young person's behavior is likely not directed against you as an individual but against you as a representative adult. Knowing this can diminish the counter-aggressive feelings you may experience and help you disengage from the conflicts that often arise when behaviors are taken personally.

> It is essential to recognize that a young person's behavior is likely not directed against you as an individual but against you as a representative adult.

Learning to recognize developmental anxieties and universal concerns about emotional security is a major part of learning to use LSCI effectively. This chapter provides those insights. First, we outline a framework for identifying the developmental anxieties that are a natural part of personality development for all children and youth. Then, we describe how adult roles and strategies are matched to each child's developmental view of authority, motivation, and values. When adults can recognize the underlying developmental anxieties and concerns of young people, and connect them to behavior, the Conflict Cycle can be broken and an LSCI can be successful.

Developmental Anxieties

Anxiety is a private, chronic reaction to unmet emotional needs and stress. For some young people, early life experiences produce debilitating developmental anxieties. These are the young people we call "at risk." They live with traumatic events, insecurity, unpredictability, alienation, helplessness, and/or failure. The developmental stressors these young people experience may be similar to those of other young people of the same approximate age, but there is a difference: young people who are traumatized by adverse childhood experiences are seldom able to successfully navigate the normal crisis of each developmental stage.

There are five general types of developmental anxieties, encompassing complex interpersonal and intrapersonal processes from birth through adolescence: abandonment, inadequacy, guilt, conflict, and identity (Wood, Quirk, & Swindle, 2007). By identifying the developmental anxieties in the young people with whom you work, you will have a framework for decoding their behavioral responses to stress. This information also will give you direction for selecting specific intervention strategies. We summarize the salient points of each developmental anxiety below.

> By identifying the developmental anxieties in the young people with whom you work, you will have a framework for decoding their behavioral responses to stress.

Abandonment (Approximately Birth to Age Two)

"No one cares!"

Abandonment is the fundamental anxiety arising from fears of physical or psychological deprivation, abuse, or abandonment. It occurs as a normal developmental crisis in infants and children under age two. The need for basic nurturing predominates behavior. If unresolved, anxiety about abandonment permeates personality development and all subsequent relationships. In older children, adolescents, and adults, this anxiety is expressed in attempts to satisfy primitive needs at any cost: by eating, hoarding, stealing, and pursuing both sexual gratification and superficial emotional attachments. To resolve developmental anxiety about abandonment, a young person needs:

1. Consistent care from a primary caregiver
2. Expressed, unconditional affection
3. An environment that provides consistency, pleasure, comfort, care, and security

Inadequacy (Preschool Years)

"I can't do anything right."
 "You won't like it."

In normal development, the anxiety of *inadequacy* typically becomes the emotional crisis of preschool-aged children as they become increasingly aware of the expectations of the important people around them. The dynamics of this anxiety include self-doubt and fear of the unknown, the need to avoid failure by denying association, and the avoidance of experiences with uncertain outcomes. Imagination runs rampant, and young people see most events as clashes between right and wrong, good and bad. Punishment often seems imminent from powerful adults and other external sources (magical forces, nature, rules, authority). Kids typically experience a sense of lack of control. When anxiety about inadequacy continues in school-aged young people, they seek to avoid blame, criticism, punishment, and failure at any cost. The driving motivation is to cover up mistakes (by blaming others, denying responsibility, lying, or by avoiding failure or being put in a position of looking "bad"). Anxiety about inadequacy can be overcome as young people:

1. Learn skills to become successful
2. Build self-confidence
3. Receive adult approval as individuals who can accomplish things
4. Learn that problems have solutions (not just punishments)
5. Begin to see themselves as having some power to control events around them

Guilt (Early Elementary)

"I'm no good. I'm a loser."

Guilt is a more complex form of inadequacy, in which the source of judgment about a young person's unworthiness changes from others to self. Typically, this is a normal developmental crisis for young people during their first three years in school (about six to nine years old). Guilt signals the presence of a basic value system. The expectations and rules of others are accepted as one's own. The young person then serves as judge and jury to the self, determining that personal inadequacy (failure) deserves punishment.

If it is unresolved, guilt arrests a young person at a developmental level where self-denigration predominates. Failure to meet the standards of others is absorbed as excruciating evidence of unworthiness. Older young people with this anxiety often allow themselves to become scapegoats, exploited by adults and bullied by peers. Their behavior may be outrageous. They perform unacceptable acts to prove their unworthiness and to be punished as atonement. Or they may violate rules so clumsily that it is evident that they want to be caught.

Another defensive strategy seen in young people with guilt is passive-aggressive behavior (see Chapter 18). These young people are so aware of expected standards of behavior and so in need of approval from others that they believe they cannot afford to put themselves in the position of being rejected. Yet, they are so troubled by their personal failings and so angry at others for their miserable situation that they express their anger in deliberate but hidden ways.

Developmental guilt normally resolves as:

1. The young person emotionally expands through successful experiences with friends and adults. Adult sanction of this new independence is essential.
2. Young people begin to see that there is more than one point of view and that there are other ways to judge a person's worth. This insight frees young people to explore alternative ways to achieve recognition, relieving their sense of guilt.

The Independence–Dependence Conflict (Upper Elementary)

"I want to, but they won't let me."
  "Try and make me!"

This developmental anxiety first emerges as an *independence–dependence* tension between a young person's need for independence and a continuing need for adult approval (dependence) during the upper elementary school years (about nine to twelve years old). In some young people it may be evident even earlier. It is usually triggered when a young person begins to identify and conform to new peer group values. As a strong, independent sense of self expands with social experiences and increasing self-confidence, anxiety takes the forms of willfulness, aggression, defiance, independence, and resistance to authority.

Typically, the developmentally based anxiety over this conflict is resolved when:

1. The young person has learned that conformity brings its own rewards and can be traded off for new personal freedoms and recognition
2. The old saying, "With freedom comes responsibility," is the understanding that resolves this developmental anxiety and fortifies the young person for approaching adolescence

In contrast, if this clash between the need to be an independent person and the requirement to submit to authority (in order to be affirmed by adults) is unresolved, a young person is ill-equipped to take on the next developmental stresses in adolescence. Such young people continue to resist authority and fight the system. They manipulate, act out, aggress, and transgress, continually seeking to meet their intense dual needs to control and to receive affirmation and admiration. These young people are inevitably caught in Conflict Cycles because their behaviors inevitably evoke negative reactions from others. Instead of obtaining the recognition they crave, they often find themselves with reputations as "bad kids."

Identity (Adolescence)

"Who am I?"

  "Am I a person who can handle this?"

The question of psychological *identity* is the classic anxiety of the adolescent years. It takes form as young people begin to experiment with new self-images as distinctly individual persons. Young people are acutely aware of new psychological and physical freedoms which simultaneously bring demands to be responsible and successful. The dynamics of this developmental anxiety are an extension of the previous one—the clash between a need for independence and lingering dependency needs. The pervasive concern in adolescence is about how teens appear to others in relation to how they appear to themselves. Self-doubt and self-confidence interplay as young people alternately believe, and then doubt, their ability to handle challenges.

If it is unresolved, developmental anxiety about self-worth and self-identity dominates attitudes, values, and behavior. Adolescents who are not able to resolve anxiety about self-worth and their place in society express their vacillations with all of the defensive behaviors described in the previous section. They try every means they can to obtain gratification, assuage their feelings of uselessness, and express their anger at being in such a state. For them, getting caught in Conflict Cycles may become a way of life.

Resolution of this identity crisis normally takes a number of years for most adolescents. It is such a major part of personality formation that it often continues into adult life as careers and interpersonal relationships are forged. This developmental anxiety is resolved as young people receive clear evidence of their success in new situations in which they can use new skills, try out new attitudes and values, and begin to see themselves recognized by others as independently successful.

Summary of Developmental Anxieties

Every stage of development has its own characteristic stresses and anxieties making demands on a developing child or youth. As each developmental anxiety is successfully resolved, a young person acquires increasingly mature, age-appropriate behaviors and insights. Equipped with these new behaviors, a young person is prepared to face the new stresses produced during the next stage of development. If unresolved, however, a developmental anxiety at one stage contributes to the stresses of the next stage of development, compounding the young person's problems and having a negative impact on the young person's capacity to develop further. Central to every LSCI is the need to recognize developmental stressors in a young person's life and to identify the developmental anxiety that predominates.

> As each developmental anxiety is successfully resolved, a young person acquires increasingly mature, age-appropriate behaviors and insights.

Before You Begin an LSCI

We suggest that before beginning any LSCI, you seek to answer the three questions (featured at the beginning of this chapter and again below) that pertain to a youth's history with adults, while simultaneously keeping in mind the context of the young person's stage of development and developmental anxieties. Because the meanings and feelings behind these questions are complex, we use the rest of this chapter to study the questions one by one.

Question 1: "Who's in Charge Here?" (Authority, Adult Roles, and Influence)

Authority is a term with many meanings, referring variously to those in command, the source of support for a statement, the defense of an action, the power to influence thought or behavior, a person's expertise, or the granting of independence or freedom. We use the term here to include all of these meanings because the adult using LSCI effectively must be able to convey all these forms of authority, as needed. What we *do not* mean in using the term is blind obedience, which defines a different approach—an authoritarian one.

Adult authority stands as one of the most dynamic forces in the lives of all young people. Whether they accept adults or reject them, young people generally acknowledge the authority and power of adults. They also have strong social and emotional needs for adults, even if they reject them. Young people recognize that adults possess special knowledge and skills and have power to make rules, decide what is right and wrong, judge, reward, and punish. Adults also solve problems, dispense care, and affirm young people. Adults are an important source of approval and disapproval. Young people tend to see themselves in the mirror of the views adults hold about them.

At every age, young people are influenced by their needs from significant adults. The way adults have responded to those needs in the past shapes the behavior young people use with adults in the present. Young people's histories are a series of fulfilled and unfulfilled expectations. When their expectations about adults have been met, they are left with feelings of well-being and they trust that adults can be counted on to handle problems, encourage, praise, provide, and do what is needed. Unmet expectations, on the other hand, leave youth with a range of unsettled feelings, confusion, and mistrust in adults.

Changing Roles of Adults

Different behaviors from adults convey different types of authority. In the normal process of growing up, the type of adult authority needed by kids changes as they mature. The evolving roles of adults in the child developmental process are well known. When used purposefully with young people at particular stages of development, specific adult roles can promote healthy social and emotional development. Figure 8.1 contains a synopsis, highlighting typical adult roles based on normal social and emotional development of young people in various age groups. By determining where a young person is in this developmental progression, you can select the general type of adult authority and role needed to facilitate a young person's particular stage of development.

> By determining where a young person is in this developmental progression, you can select the general type of adult authority and role needed to facilitate a young person's particular stage of development.

It is helpful to keep a particular role in mind as you begin LSCI with a young person. When you do this, you will find the gap narrowing between your expectations and the young person's needs. This lowers stress and reduces the tendency for a young person to displace anger onto you as a stand-in for other adults who have failed to fulfill their expectations in the past.

Adult Strategies That Influence a Young Person's Behavior

Once you have determined the type of adult authority and role you should convey in a particular LSCI, you have a range of intervention strategies you can choose from

What's Important to a Child		The Adult's Changing Role
"My needs"	"I am what I am given." (Infants and Toddlers)	Satisfier of needs
"Please adults"	"I can do, so I am what I will ... with your help." (Preschool Children)	Teacher of standards Provider of approval
"Be fair"	"I am what I can imagine I will be." (School-Age Children)	Upholder of authority Director of behavior
"Fit in ... and be responsible"	"I am what I can learn from others." (Middle School Children)	Social role model Group facilitator
"Do what's right and care for others"	"This, I believe ... so I can stand tall." (Teens)	Counselor Advocate Confidant

Figure 8.1. A child's expanding spirit. *Note.* From "Vibes, Values, and Virtues," by M. M. Wood, 1996, *Reclaiming Children and Youth, 5*(3), p. 17. Copyright 1996 by M. M. Wood. Reprinted with permission.

to convey the role effectively. Because there are so many strategies to choose from, we find it helpful to group them according to *style of influence* and fit them to an individual young person's view of adults. Adult styles of influence, when used selectively, can cause young people to do spontaneously what they might not ordinarily do on their own. When an adult is able to assist young people in changing behavior, a major gain has been made toward independent regulation of behavior.

The most frequently used styles of adult influence can be grouped into four general forms: motivation, relationship, shared skills, and consequences. The following is a brief summary of each of these styles.

Motivation

Motivation is the preferred form of influence, in which the adult is able to affect a young person's behavior while not directly controlling it. The emphasis is on using indirect, motivating strategies that enable young people to act spontaneously and to self-direct in acceptable ways. Within this style, youth experience intrinsic positive feedback, leading them to successful outcomes without the appearance of undo adult influence. Peer pressure, mobilized by an adult, is an example of influence through motivation.

Strategies that influence through motivation are highly effective with young people who are struggling between the need to be independent and the need to be cared for by adults. Those who think they need to be independent of adult control often relax their defenses when they begin to experience success on their own and then receive recognition from others for their accomplishments. Strategies that motivate are especially effective with young people who distrust adults and who have developed passive-aggressive strategies. Similarly, young people who are driven by unresolved developmental anxieties of abandonment or inadequacy can be supported by adults who motivate them to respond to an event in a way that brings them satisfaction.

Relationship

Relationship is a style of influence that relies on the adult's connection with the young person. Young people tend to respond well to adults who have characteristics that they admire and like, such as warmth, humor, enthusiasm, friendliness, fairness, helpfulness, and approval. Youth are also influenced by the mannerisms of admired adults. Because young people imitate appealing adult characteristics, it is essential that adults provide positive models of behavior to influence young people in helpful ways.

Adults are using relationship as a way of influencing young people when they say:

- "Please do this for me."
- "I really like it when you do that."
- "That is really good work!"
- "I think that's the best you've ever done."
- "I'm proud of you."

The effectiveness of this style of influence is evident when you hear young people say:

- "Miss Barkley, how do you like this?"
- "I knew you wouldn't like what they did."

- "I made this for you."
- "I did what you wanted me to do."

You also can see the results when you observe young people:

- Looking toward adults at a time when others are misbehaving
- Listening quietly and intently to what an adult is saying
- Directing the bulk of their social communication toward adults
- Spontaneously recalling what an adult has said to them on previous occasions
- Volunteering bits and pieces of their most private thoughts and feelings

Relationship strategies are most effective when they are used in combination with other forms of influence. When they are used as the primary style influence, adults risk fostering dependency and restricting a young person's development toward independence. Also, adult-child relationships run the risk of turning into person-to-person bonding when the adult does not exercise necessary authority or the young person fails to assume independent responsibility. Appropriate boundaries are important in any adult-child relationship.

Shared Skills

Shared skills is a style of influence that conveys an adult's ability to help a young person solve a problem. The goal is to teach new social-emotional skills. Young people develop trust in adults who can manage a problem successfully and calmly. Likewise, they respond to the expertise of adults who accurately decode behavior. An adult is using this style of influence when they make statements like the following:

- "You don't need to worry; staff can help you with this kind of thing."
- "I've had other young people with this problem, and this is how we handled it."
- "I've been watching how you were doing in that difficult situation; you figured it out correctly."
- "Your behavior tells me that something else is really bothering you."

When adults are effective in helping young people solve problems, the result is trust, admiration, and a positive relationship with the adult. An adult who shares skills with a young person creates a climate of security which, in turn, gives the young person a new freedom to learn because their energy is no longer misdirected into defensive behaviors.

Consequences

To be effective, consequences should be seen as direct, natural results of a behavior. Unfortunately, young people who have a history of adverse experiences with adults often misperceive consequences as being the result of the adult's cruelty, bias, or unfairness. Examples of adult strategies that influence through behavioral consequences include:

- Time-out
- Denial of privileges
- Physical proximity (standing over a young person)
- Office referrals
- Parent conferences
- Suspension
- Expulsion

When adults continually use strategies that are punitive and threatening, young people feel powerless. Powerless youth either give up (which arrests development) or begin to acquire negative feelings and defensive, oppositional behaviors toward adults. With a few exceptions, strategies focused on consequences seldom contribute to creating positive relationships or an environment conducive to LSCI. When you find it necessary to use consequences to influence a young person's behavior, keep the encounter short and look for ways to change to strategies based on other forms of influence.

Summary of Question 1: *Who's in Charge Here?*

The answer to the first question raised in this chapter, "Who's in charge here?" is simple: *it must be the adult!* But this answer does not imply authoritarian control. Rather, it requires an adult to convey the type of role that will produce the greatest possible social and emotional development for the young person.

Study the strategies you typically use to influence young people. If you find that you are relying on only one adult role and using only one style to influence young people, resolve to broaden your repertoire. To be effective in LSCI, you should be able to use strategies from all four types of influences to convey the adult role needed by each individual young person.

Question 2: "Who's Going to Handle This Problem?" (The Existential Crisis)

The previous discussion focused on adult authority and the need for adults to influence the psychological and interpersonal climate in positive ways. While an adult must always have control of the environment, this does not imply that they are responsible for the solution to every problem. In this section, we consider the second major question raised in this chapter: *Who resolves the problem situation? Is it the adult's or the young person's responsibility?*

Few young people are capable of managing stressful situations independently when LSCI is needed. Yet, in LSCI, young people must begin to learn to assume responsibility for their behavior and its consequences. The long-term goal of LSCI is to teach young people to regulate their own behavior and to meet their own emotional needs in appropriate ways without dependence on adults. We view this gradual transfer of authority and responsibility for problem-solving from adult to child as occurring in three phases centering around a major developmental event in the lives of all children and youth. We call this developmental event the *Existential Crisis.*

The Existential Crisis is a phase in social-emotional development when a young person's belief in the absolute, omnipotent authority of adults begins to falter (Wood, Quirk, & Swindle, 2007). It is called existential because it deals with new awareness about the limitations of adults for taking care of life events in satisfactory ways. This uncertainty about adults leads a young person to question authority and to look for other sources of security. It is called a "crisis" because it raises concerns about alternatives to adults taking care of problems, with the possibility that the young person must be responsible. Most young people doubt their own ability. Yet they must change, learn new behaviors, and take on new consequences. The challenge is nearly overwhelming to some young people.

As we begin each LSCI, we have found it helpful to determine which phase the young person is in:

- If the young person is in the pre-existential phase, the LSCI will need to be directed and controlled by the adult.
- If the young person is going through the Existential Crisis, the LSCI must provide abundant adult support and direction but also must begin to shift responsibility for problem resolution to the youth.
- If the young person is in the post-existential phase, the LSCI focus should be on assisting them to handle the problem situation with independence and a focus on personal responsibility.

To help you recognize which of these general phases your young person is in, the text below reviews the dynamics involved and the management strategies that are appropriate for each phase.

The Pre-Existential Phase

In the pre-existential phase, a young person's emotional need is for an expert adult who directs behavior, makes rules, handles problems, provides protection, and arranges for satisfaction of needs. To pre-existential young people, adult authority is all-powerful. Every first-grade teacher knows about pre-existential young people:

- "Teacher! Teacher! . . .
- "He's not playing by the rules."
- "Make her give it to me."
- "He's bothering me."
- "I'm going to tell my mother."

Notice how each remark is directed to the adult, even though the issue involves peers. Such responses are normal for young people under age nine. In the view of a typically developing pre-existential young person, adults are responsible for solving the problem. These young people look to them for protection, problem-solving, and maintenance of law and order.

Adults use many behavior management strategies for young people in the midst of this pre-existential phase that are also useful during the problem-solving stages of LSCI. The following are several examples:

- Rules and procedures
- *First-then* statements (*First,* you put the books away; *then,* we will play outside)
- Affirmations (smiling faces, grades, privileges, selection by teacher as "leader," checks)
- Prescribed consequences
- Token systems
- Adults as behavioral role models

At some point you will have to take these young people through the Existential Crisis and into the post-existential period. The management issue here is one of gradually shifting the source of authority and responsibility from external controls to controls from within. It will not happen if you continue to maintain external control at all times; young people will simply continue to rely on you to set standards and then will test and defy you as they experiment with independence.

During LSCI, there are many opportunities for strengthening internal control and self-regulation, as kids have the chance to explore alternatives and make choices. LSCI offers opportunities for individual input, exploration of "what happens when . . . " alternative rules to live by, and more effective behaviors. Every successful choice moves responsible, independent development one step closer to self-governance and responsibility.

The Existential Crisis

Typically, this period starts at about the time children begin school and continues for several years until the young person has completed the shift from relying on adults as the sole source of authority and behavior control (pre-existential) to a view of authority as coming from more than one source. When the Existential Crisis is resolved, young people are able to consistently assume responsibility for control of their own behavior.

During the Existential Crisis, young people have doubts and uncertainty about adults. This leads to testing adult authority and credibility, defying directions, ignoring rules, denying responsibility, and shifting blame to others. During this phase, young people vacillate unpredictably—one minute they conform to adult expectations and the next they defy these same standards. Examples of strategies that are useful during LSCI with young people who are in the Existential Crisis phase include the following:

- Providing positive feedback and praise
- Offering verbal reflection of words, actions, and feelings
- Decoding meanings behind behavior
- Assuming responsibility for rule maintenance and consequences

The volatility and lack of stability in adult-child relationships make this period particularly difficult for many adults. It requires us to use pre-existential strategies (adult authority and control) at one time and then switch to post-existential strategies (adult guidance but not control) when a young person begins to show control and responsibility for self-regulation. By recognizing and understanding the dynamics of the Existential Crisis, you can prepare to provide changes in your own strategies, loosening and tightening control as needed.

Should we be concerned about younger young people who go through the Existential Crisis too early because of trauma and adverse life experiences? What about older young people who have failed to resolve the Existential Crisis satisfactorily; will such deviations in the normal sequence of development affect their behavior and the way their behavior is managed by others? The answer is clearly "Yes!" These will be young people who have difficulty trusting adults and therefore resist taking adult direction. They will seek reassurance and recognition while still lashing out at the adults from whom they seek approval and support. These youth have a strong drive to assert themselves while at the same time feel compelled to test the limits of adult control and authority. They often avoid taking responsibility for their own behavior and tend to blame others, as admitting failure can be overwhelmingly painful.

The Post-Existential Phase

As young people turn increasingly to peers for behavioral models and affirmations of themselves, there is gradual detachment from psychological dependency on adults. Adults now become mirrors for young people to see themselves as others see them. Their evolving role is to encourage young people toward independent, self-regulated behavior. As this course to independence is charted, adults are needed as backstops when challenges become overwhelming and behavioral skills are insufficient for successful navigation through stressful situations.

Effective teachers in middle and high school know about post-existential young people and develop teaching styles that allow independence while providing sufficient direction for young people to achieve success. These adults serve as role models for effective interpersonal relationships and independent problem-solving. Post-existential young people know they have responsibility for self-regulation and generally exercise some degree of responsibility for problem-solving. In LSCI with kids in the post-existential phase, you will see the youth making an effort to resolve conflict and make suggestions that show a sense of responsibility for the problem and its resolution.

Summary of Question 2: *Who's Going to Handle This Problem?*

In summary, the answer to the second question in this chapter, "*Who's going to handle this problem?*" is that it must be the young person, with adult support to the extent that the young person needs an adult in order to have a satisfactory resolution. To determine this need, we use the Existential Crisis as the reference point, using the three-phase guide summarized in this section.

Begin every LSCI with a quick review of how your young person views adults:

- Some young people will have the pre-existential view that adults must solve problems and are responsible for crisis resolution.
- Other young people will be experiencing the Existential Crisis, in which they will swing between attempts to solve a crisis on their own and retreating to a pre-existential position, deferring to adult authority and denying responsibility.
- Post-existential young people will make attempts to resolve a crisis, even if their skills and judgment are seriously lacking.

From this information, you will be able to balance the extent to which you assist and direct a young person during each LSCI or choose to leave the selection of a solution and implementation plan to the young person.

Question 3: "How Do I Know It's Going to Be All Right for Me?" (Motivation to Be Responsible)

The question we raise in this section considers a young person's motivation to be responsible for personal behavior and problem resolution. While we are concerned with making the transfer from adult authority to youth responsibility, the young person is concerned that their personal needs will not be met. Young people behave in ways that they think will produce results they value. Likewise, they try to avoid causing results they do not value. Values are the internal rules young people (and adults) live by. They are the fixed points of reference for daily behavior—the glue that holds together the structure we know as personality and character. What young people care about is what they value. Their values shape their choice of activities, influence their reactions to stress, and regulate their behavior.

What the young person cares about the most during a crisis situation is avoiding the unpleasant feelings of stress. This is their fundamental value. The Conflict Cycle presented in Chapter 5 is fueled by this motivation for self-protection. Any attempt to break the cycle (see Chapter 6) must guarantee that emotional stress will cease. Satisfactory resolution of crisis must be constructed from this fundamental value. Unless emotional protection is provided, young people will not be able to change established patterns of defensive and unacceptable behavior. Young people must believe that, in the end, they will be alright. When they believe this, they will participate in problem-solving. If they doubt that their interests are being considered, they will raise their defenses.

> Young people must believe that, in the end, they will be alright. When they believe this, they will participate in problem-solving.

Assurance of emotional protection is only the first element in successful crisis resolution. Central to every goal in LSCI is the idea of learning independent responsibility for behavior. This gradual transition from guaranteed protection to independent, self-regulated behavior is not an easy task. To exchange dependence on others for independent responsibility requires a powerful motivation.

How do we provide this motivation for behavior change? Think of providing motivation as building solutions to a stressful situation based on (a) a gradual change in a young person's values, and (b) a gradual shift away from emotional dependency on adults toward emotional independence. The following is a review of these ideas in a framework that is helpful in identifying a young person's values and levels of emotional dependency. From such information, you will be able to build motivations during LSCI for youth to change their behavior.

Identifying a Young Person's Values

Young people's values develop in a natural sequence that can be summarized in five general stages: personal needs, adult approval, fairness, responsibility for self, and responsibility for others (Wood, Quirk, & Swindle, 2007). The basic value begins with the premise that one's own needs are paramount. Any behavior that meets personal needs is satisfactory. Gradually, young people move from that orientation to a belief that adults' standards are the ones that bring personal benefits. Therefore, their behavior should conform to please adults and avoid punishment. As young people develop further, their views broaden to include justice and fairness as guidelines for regulating their own behavior. When fairness first emerges as a value for regulating behavior, young people are concerned that they receive fair treatment from others. Gradually, their view of fairness expands to include fairness for others. Finally, young people embrace society's values of responsibility for self-regulation, justice, and care of others. Empathy and altruism also are added as values that regulate behavior.

Figure 8.2 summarizes this sequence of values and provides examples of solutions to problems that would be considered satisfactory to young people holding these particular values. (We refer to this sequence again in Stage 4 of LSCI.) In this illustration, the band of dotted lines indicates the approximate place in the developmental sequence when the Existential Crisis occurs. The two concepts tie together a young person's changing values and evolving views of authority. Concern about personal needs begins to blend into the notion that satisfactory interactions with others bring satisfactory results for oneself. With this development, a young person's sense of responsibility begins to broaden to include the possibility of giving up something in order to get something in return.

The arrows in Figure 8.2 indicate ways to challenge young people to consider solutions at the next stage in the sequence of values. As you bring LSCI to the solution stages, you have two basic choices: (a) encourage young people to choose solutions at their present stage of values, or (b) challenge young people to consider solutions at a higher stage. Sometimes it is necessary to guide young people to choose solutions that are a part of their current value system. These solutions may bring specific benefits, better feelings, concrete incentives, or adult affirmation and approval. These are pre-existential solutions, necessary because the young person may have tenuous confidence in making choices or doubts about your reliability as an adult authority. Such young people will resist making choices, leaving it up to adults instead. However, if you continue to fill the adult-as-authority role too long, you may restrict the young person's development, and responsible independence will not develop. When you notice themes of fairness in a young person's remarks, you can be confident that they are moving beyond the Existential Crisis and may be ready for more personal

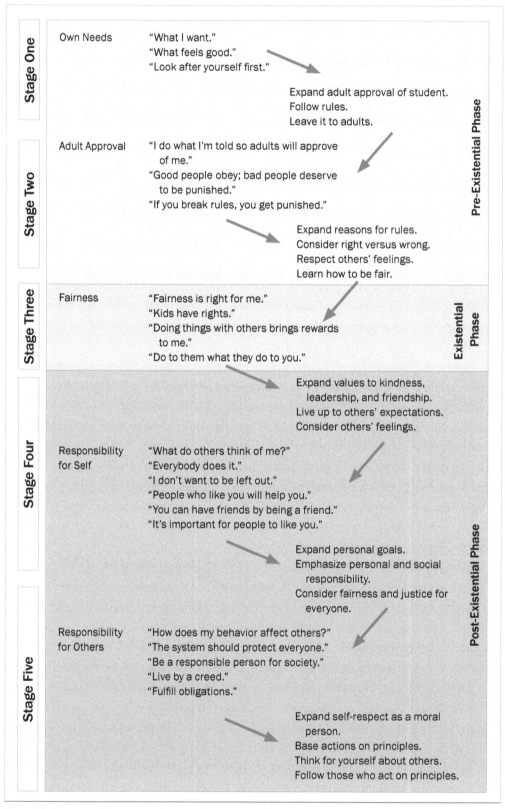

Figure 8.2. How values are used in Developmental Therapy–Developmental Teaching to enhance and expand a child's maturity. *Note.* From *Teaching Responsible Behavior: Developmental Therapy–Developmental Teaching for Troubled Children and Adolescents* (4th ed.), by M. M. Wood, C. A. Quirk, and F. L. Swindle, 2007, pp. 58 and 97, PRO-ED. Copyright 2007 by PRO-ED. Reprinted with permission.

responsibility. You'll know that it is time to challenge the young person to consider solutions at the next stage. You probably will find the young person receptive to new ideas for solutions with themes of friendship, leadership, consideration, responsibility, and kindness.

One caution about challenges: sometimes adults tend to foster solutions that are beyond a young person's current ability to handle successfully. If a planned solution has no value to the young person or the expectation requires too great a leap forward for the young person to accomplish, the desired behavior will not be forthcoming, and the plan will fail.

Identifying a Young Person's Emotional Dependence

A goal of most intervention programs, like the goal for LSCI, is learning independent control of behavior. When a young person exits a program, the expectation is that the learning will generalize (independently) into other settings. It is enormously frustrating to most adults when young people fail to achieve this goal. This failure may indicate chronic emotional dependence. Emotional dependence sustains the pre-existential values held by some young people about adults. Young people who are emotionally dependent still fear that their own needs may not be met by significant adults. As long as a young person clings to this view, the young person will not be able to assume independent regulation of personal behavior. The young person will be preoccupied with meeting emotional needs and protecting feelings.

Another form of emotional dependency results when a young person has been deprived of emotional care and support or has failed to form primary attachments to an adult. The fundamental need for emotional attachment can supersede all other motivators. Secure attachment provides children and youth with confidence that they are valued by others. Normally, an infant's primary caregiver is the first source of emotional significance. When a child's need for emotional attachment has been satisfied, they do not have to struggle to attain it. They use it as a base of confidence to venture beyond the attachment to pursue new relationships and independence.

On the other hand, if attachments fail or never develop, emotional dependence results. A young person has to put major effort into seeking and holding on to substitutes. Failed attachment is a major part of the first developmental anxiety, abandonment. If this anxiety is left unresolved, the young person may seek substitute forms of gratification (e.g., work, hoarding, overeating, addiction) that erode interpersonal relationships and can severely modify the course of an individual's personality development. Such young people often lack empathy and sensitivity to the feelings of others. They bend rules to gratify their own needs, operating from a "look out for number one" basis. As you proceed to Part 2 of this book, you will see this most prominently in the Benign Confrontation pattern (Chapter 13).

The developmental counterforce to attachment is separation, a drive for independence. Young people show a willingness to forgo primary attachments as they mature, seeking independence. The success of the separation process depends on the previous success during the attachment phase of emotional development. Successful separation centers around the balance adults achieve between providing security and comfort (dependency needs) and simultaneously allowing freedom (independence needs). This is the daily challenge for children, youth, and adults.

If the separation process is experienced without success, psychological independence may not be achieved. Fear of failure, fear of inadequacy, and fear of not measuring up to the expectations of others can spiral into a restricted personality. Such young people fail to take initiative, resist change, pander to others, and follow those who will control and direct them (inadequacy, a developmental anxiety). These young people also may be selected as scapegoats or isolated by their peers.

Whenever the attachment process or the separation process fails, anger is a major by-product. A young person feels anger toward family members who have failed to nurture and protect them and anger at those who have ridiculed or criticized the young person's attempts at independence. These failed relationships from home and community permeate the young person's view of adults at school and in the community. They bring this emotional baggage with them. Teachers, counselors, and other authority figures become the recipients of the anger these young people hold toward adults outside of school.

In contrast, resolution of the conflict between attachment and separation produces emotional independence. It is clearly observable in most young people by upper elementary school. These young people believe that adults really care about them and will provide emotional protection, while at the same time permitting young people the freedom needed to be independent. Such young people have no need to be preoccupied with protecting themselves emotionally. Keep in mind, however, that all young people continue to experience stress, and they never will be totally independent of their need for emotional support and relationships with adults they admire. Emotional independence increases in direct correspondence to the extent to which dependency needs (attachment) are met and independent experiences are successful.

Summary of Question 3:
How Do I Know It's Going to Be All Right for Me?

In summary, the answer to the third question in this chapter, "How do I know it's going to be all right for me?" is that young people must believe that their emotional needs will be met. Until they are secure in this belief, they will not move toward appropriate, independently regulated behavior. When a young person believes that a solution is possible and desirable, they will take ownership of it. To produce lasting change from LSCI, solutions must be owned by the young person, not the adult.

Values are the internal regulators of young people's behaviors. To have an effective outcome of LSCI, resolutions must be framed within the context of current values held by the young person. The belief that something beneficial will occur in exchange for using a new behavior is a fundamental motivation for change.

The gradual transfer of responsibility from external control to appropriate, independent, self-regulated behavior also depends upon successful transition through the Existential Crisis, from emotional dependence to emotional independence. Emotional dependency is a major roadblock toward independent responsibility. When you use LSCI, awareness of a young person's level of emotional dependency is essential. It is a major force in the eventual progress made toward accomplishing LSCI goals.

Note that age does not necessarily determine views about authority or the values held by young people. We see many adolescents who respond to stressful situations with simple, self-protective values and also encounter young children who attempt to use more complex values. When they are not successful in their independent attempts to solve a crisis with these values, youth tend to slip back to more primitive values.

Examples of Authority, Responsibility, and Motivation

The topics covered in this chapter are sometimes difficult to apply at first reading. It may be helpful to integrate the information by considering the following example of Henry.

Henry

A fight breaks out on the middle school bus. Henry is a known instigator and has a history of aggressive behaviors and suspensions. His view is that he is being picked on by the others and is simply defending himself. The angry bus driver reports Henry to the assistant principal. Henry cools his heels in the outer office for an hour or so until the assistant principal returns for a talk. The result is a call to Henry's mother and another suspension. Henry (H) explains all of this to the coach (C) as he prepares to leave school.

> H: I got busted again.
>
> C: The bus?
>
> H: It wasn't my fault! Leon had some bleach in a spray bottle, and he threatened to spray me with it.

VALUE: Modeling adult standards of right versus wrong.
EXISTENTIAL PHASE: Post-existential. Young person tries to handle the problem
    independently.

C: What did you do?

H: (*defensively*) I told him to put it away or I'd kick his ass! It's my right to protect myself!

VALUE: Rights for self.
EXISTENTIAL PHASE: Post-existential.

C: You thought Leon might really be serious?

H: You can't ever tell about Leon!

C: So, what happened next?

H: He didn't put it away, so I told the driver that Leon had some bleach.

VALUE: Adults are powerful and should protect young people.
EXISTENTIAL PHASE: Crisis. Independence was not working, so adult authority was needed.

C: What did she do?

H: She told us to get off the bus or settle down. Then she turned us both in.

C: Now you're suspended! What will happen when you get home?

H: I guess my mother will get mad about them throwing me out of school when it wasn't my fault. So, she'll come down here and straighten out that principal. She won't let them pick on me!

VALUE: Adults are powerful.
EXISTENTIAL PHASE: Pre-existential.

C: Will she punish you?

H: Nah, she'll wait for my dad.

C: What will he do?

H: He's always telling me to stick up for myself. He says there's only one way to settle some scores. He'll tell me, "Next time, Henry, just beat the shit out of Leon, so he'll know not to pick on you again!"

VALUE: Adult authorizes punishment for bad kids.
EXISTENTIAL PHASE: Pre-existential.

Henry tries to solve this problem on his own, at a fairly advanced value level. Without success from his first attempts to handle the problem himself (post-existential), Henry gradually regresses to a pre-existential attitude that it is someone else's problem (his mother's) and he will follow the authority of the powerful adult in his life (his dad).

Track back through this scenario again to identify the vacillations in the adult roles and types of influence conveyed to Henry:

Bus driver	[sent Henry to office for punishment] *Role:* Upholder of law and order *Influence:* Fear of consequences
Assistant principal	[sent Henry home for punishment] *Role:* Upholder of law and order *Influence:* Fear of consequences
Coach	[no shared skills; perhaps friendship?] *Role:* Counselor, friend *Influence:* Not clear
Mother	[wait for father] *Role:* Advocate *Influence:* Shared skills [taking care of basic need for protection] and fear of consequences
Father	*Role:* Teacher of behavior *Influence:* Fear of consequences

Henry's attempts at emotional and behavioral independence crumble under pressure. We can be fairly confident that Henry is still emotionally dependent on the approval, power, and authority of adults.

It is clear that each adult is responding to Henry from a personal "style," with no thought of Henry's potential for social-emotional problem-solving and what he needs in order to learn to regulate his own behavior and resolve the crisis independently. The coach was a key. He could have used this crisis to reinforce Henry's emerging attempts to solve problems in appropriate ways. It was a time for LSCI!

If you had been the coach and carried the LSCI forward:

- What role would you have taken?
- What type of strategies would have been helpful in influencing Henry to change his behavior?
- What existential phase should you emphasize?
- What value level should be used as you and Henry approach the resolution phase of LSCI?

These are the same questions to be answered as you begin every LSCI.

"There is nothing so small that it can't be blown out of proportion."

9 THE HELPING PROCESS AND POTENTIAL PITFALLS

n Part 1 of this book, you have learned the foundational concepts and skills needed to carry out successful LSCI interventions. We started with a basic understanding of how a young person's brain responds to stress and trauma and showed you how LSCI prioritizes establishing positive connections with kids as the basis of its trauma-informed approach. Then, we took a thorough look at the psychological worlds of kids, examining the development of their self-concept, beliefs, perceptions, thoughts, and feelings. We put these foundational elements together to bring you the LSCI Conflict Cycle, our major paradigm for explaining the circular and escalating dynamics of conflict between adults and children. In Chapter 6, you learned the key role that adults play in breaking the Conflict Cycle, including studying five listening skills that are essential ingredients in every successful LSCI. Then in Chapter 7, you learned the six stages of the LSCI process, our consistent verbal framework for (1) de-escalating crises, (2) helping a child put language to emotion, (3) identifying a self-defeating pattern of behavior, (4) guiding a child toward insight into their problematic pattern, (5) practicing new skills to replace older, problem behaviors, and then ultimately (6) successfully reentering their class, milieu, or group. Finally, in Chapter 8, you learned how to recognize developmental anxieties and universal concerns about emotional security held by young people.

In Part 2 of this book, you will put all of this knowledge together as you learn to carry out each of the six LSCI interventions. Before we turn to Part 2, however, we conclude this part of the book with a look at three remaining elements of the helping process. First, we'll review Surface Management, strategies adults can use to try to prevent minor conflicts from blowing up into major crises. Then, we'll look at potential pitfalls and ways that effective LSCIs can get derailed. Lastly, we'll talk about the differences between short- and long-term LSCI interventions and how to take every opportunity to bring insight and lasting behavioral change to young people.

Surface Management Strategies

Ruckert's Law states that *"there is nothing so small that it can't be blown out of proportion."* Indeed, for young people (and not-so-young-people!) during stressful situations, the most minor irritation can sometimes become a major issue that incites overwhelming emotions and disrupts an entire day. Whenever an adult can prevent a conflict from becoming a crisis, they should try to do so! The more experience young people have managing emotions in calm ways, the better for their development of self-regulation and problem-solving skills (not to mention the more peaceful for all those in the vicinity). LSCI offers a continuum of classroom and behavior management strategies.

> The more experience young people have managing emotions in calm ways, the better for their development of self-regulation and problem-solving skills

Fritz Redl (1966) first described ways to provide Surface Management—situational strategies that assist a young person in keeping emotions and behavior under rational, neocortex-based management. The following section summarizes 15 Surface Management strategies:

1. **Support From Routines**

   In some groups, problems arise because young people do not know what is expected of them. The establishment of clear rules and routines meets this need. Consistent daily management and gentle reminders are the best tools to support positive behavior. The following are several examples:

   Group Norms:

   - "Smartphones must be in your locker or in your backpack."
   - "Before we eat, we always wash our hands."
   - "Hats and hoods come off whenever we are inside the building."
   - "When we walk in a line, we keep our hands at our sides."

   Individual Expectations:

   - "Each day I quietly remind Jared before class that he must finish his assignment before he can read."
   - "When Kayla starts complaining in a loud voice that someone is bothering her, I tell her to use a calm voice and politely let the person know that it bothers her."

- "Noah likes to make sarcastic remarks to get attention. I remind him that one of our rules is to remain quiet so that others can get their work done. This seems to be enough to drain away his interest in getting someone else upset."

2. **Apply Accommodations Through an ACEs Lens**

   Many students with histories of trauma arrive at school in a survival brain state (see Chapter 2). They are emotionally dysregulated and physically unable to meet the demands of a classroom environment. By this point in your reading, it should be clear that no amount of traditional limit setting, redirection, or consequences (no matter how kindly they are given) will succeed in making a child's brain more regulated or their body better able to remain still in a seat. What we can do, however, is apply accommodations through an ACEs lens, thus creating the conditions in classrooms and schools in which kids feel safe and secure, know that there are trusted adults with whom they can speak, and have access to quiet spaces with sensory tools they can use to become more regulated. When trauma-informed accommodations occur naturally through daily procedures, routines, transitions, and meetings, we meet a child's emotional needs and prevent the types of disruption, defiance, and shut-down that show up otherwise (Desautels, 2019). In Appendix A of this book, we provide Desautel's comparison of traditional school-based accommodations vs. accommodations that use an ACEs lens for your own use and adoption.

   > We can apply accommodations through an ACEs lens, thus creating the conditions in which kids feel safe and secure, know that there are trusted adults with whom they can speak, and have access to quiet spaces with sensory tools they can use to become more regulated.

3. **Planned Ignoring/Positive Attention**

   Many young people engage in negative behavior to receive attention from adults or peers. For these youth, negative attention is better than no attention. Effective adults should make it their practice to ignore inappropriate attention-getting misbehavior whenever possible and give descriptive praise to those who are acting appropriately.

   - "I notice that many of you are sitting quietly and raising your hands before you speak."

   When a child stops making noise and raises his hand before calling out, the appropriate behavior should immediately be acknowledged and affirmed:

   - "Thank you for sitting quietly."
   - "Thank you for remembering to raise your hand."

Be aware that older students may prefer praise to be private rather than public.

4. **Signal Interference**

There are several non-verbal signals that an adult may use to prompt kids to discontinue unwanted behavior. These strategies include eye contact, hand gestures, snapping fingers, clearing throat, facial signals, and body postures. These non-verbal techniques are most effective at the beginning stages of misbehavior, especially when there is a positive relationship with the young person.

5. **Proximity Control**

Adults need to be highly aware of the early stages of misbehavior by constantly scanning the room and looking and listening for any signs of unrest. At the first signs of a young person having a problem, it can be helpful to move closer to him. The physical proximity of the adult is often enough to reduce unacceptable behavior.

6. **Interest Boosting**

Sometimes the purpose of an activity or content of a lesson appears meaningless to the lives of a young person. This can be alleviated by getting to know the youth and what is important to them. Incorporating their interests into lessons can improve motivation.

7. **Humor**

Laughter triggers the release of the neurotransmitter dopamine, which creates a sense of euphoria in the brain. Laughter also releases endorphins, brain chemicals that are known to trigger positive feelings in the body. By handling an incident with humor, the adult can reduce the overall tensions of a situation and boost the young person's mood, all while retaining respectable leadership of the group. Please note: humor should always be genial and kind. There is no place for sarcasm or ridicule.

8. **Hurdle Help**

Some students misbehave in school when they do not understand some aspect of the work. If this occurs, help the student overcome the hurdle. The overall strategy is to help the child with the task at hand in order to prevent misconduct.

9. **Diversion and Redirection**

Sometimes a growing restlessness becomes evident with a young person, group, or class. Rather than concentrate on the over-excitement, it may be wise to change the nature of the activity or redirect kids to a new focus of interest/activity.

10. Antiseptic Bouncing

Antiseptic bouncing is a strategy that can be used when a young person first begins showing signs of emotional dysregulation, such as talking to himself, fidgeting, or clenching fists. It involves giving the young person a task to do outside of the classroom or group space (hence, the "bounce"), such as bringing a note to the office or returning a book to the library. The experience of physical movement and the brief change of scenery can trigger a very effective emotional reset, allowing the youth to calm down and avoid potential problems.

> The experience of physical movement and the brief change of scenery can trigger a very effective emotional reset, allowing the youth to calm down and avoid potential problems.

11. Encouragement Rather Than Criticism

"Catching the child doing something good" is a more effective way to shape behavior than criticizing misbehavior. Praise students by giving specific, descriptive examples of their academics and behavior that highlight positive gains. Young people are better able to "own" concrete examples of their accomplishments than generic praise.

12. Prompting/Anticipation Planning

Transitions and new situations can be hard for some children to manage. Often a brief description of what the situation may be like or what limitations may be anticipated will enable a young person and/or group to feel more relaxed in the face of a challenging event.

13. Maintain Communication When Relationships Are Breaking Down

In an intense crisis, some young people withdraw and become uncommunicative or go into a prolonged anger, sulking and refusing to talk. Unless this defense is penetrated, the world of hostile fantasy can be more destructive to them than the world of reality. The purpose of this Surface Management strategy is to redirect young people away from emotional withdrawal by engaging them in any kind of conversation until they feel more comfortable with their thoughts and feelings. Occasionally fidgets, food, or humor are effective ways of thawing a young person from a frozen sulk. The following are descriptions of how two teachers used this type of Surface Management to stay in touch with young people until they could be reached for an LSCI:

Liam's Teacher:

Liam had to use his study hall to complete his math assignment. He sat at his desk, folded his arms, looked at me with blazing eyes, and said, "I'm not doing anything or saying anything, so leave me alone!" When I tried to talk to him, he covered his ears with his hands. I sat down at the table near him with the materials I was using to make a board game for reading. The pieces were race cars. Although I was silent, I made certain Liam saw them. It wasn't long before he asked, "What's that for?" Now we were in a communication mode and ready to begin LSCI.

Mason's Teacher:

Mason kept staring out the window the whole time I was talking to him. After many futile attempts to get a response from him, I asked Mason to draw a finger picture on the windowpane and I would try to guess what it was. Halfheartedly he drew a circle that I said was a purple elephant taking a bath in a white Volkswagen. With great effort Mason tried to hide his smile. Then I said, "I'll do one now, for you to guess." Mason nodded that he was interested and guessed my quick design to be an engine falling off a pickup truck and smashing into pieces on an interstate. That imagery made our entry into the first stage of LSCI.

14. Rewards/Reinforcement

Receiving a reward or reinforcement is one way to acknowledge and promote behavior that is appropriate. Reinforcement should always be paired with verbal praise so that the young person understands the direct connection between behavior and the reward. Initially, the youth may need instant gratification to encourage personal growth. Start where the young person is developmentally and gradually delay the reinforcement or increase expectations so that the child can progress. Success breeds success.

15. Consequences vs. Threats

Young people have choices when it comes to their own behavior. This is a fundamental concept of LSCI that we should always articulate to kids, as awareness of choice and personal control cultivates neocortex-driven responses. It is often helpful to clearly state the consequences of the choices that young people may make. Encourage them to choose wisely. Threats undermine relationships, put the locus of control on the adult, and create anxiety. Consequences encourage responsible decision-making.

Threats undermine relationships, put the locus of control on the adult, and create anxiety. Consequences encourage responsible decision-making.

After Surface Management Strategies Are Used

If Surface Management strategies have been successful, young people feel supported, adult authority is established, emotions are regulated, and rational words are used as the primary way to communicate. In many cases, Surface Management can preempt the need for LSCI.

In many cases, Surface Management can preempt the need for LSCI.

Potential Pitfalls in Using LSCI

Although we ordinarily prefer to use a positive focus when preparing adults to use LSCI, it can be helpful to show how problems arise and provide specific suggestions for how to rectify them. We have identified 12 responses adults use that can create unnecessary problems. Everyone makes these mistakes at one time or another when using LSCI. The important lesson to be learned is the value of self-monitoring so that you recognize why a particular LSCI goes astray and what you can do to improve it next time.

1. **Beginning LSCI When a Young Person Is Not Ready**
   Never go beyond Stage 1 until the young person has given you some verbal response. Don't even think of it! Silence can be a powerful device for de-escalating a young person and mobilizing them toward verbal interaction. There are several ways to use silence effectively as you wait.

   Silence can be a powerful device for de-escalating a young person and mobilizing them toward verbal interaction.

   - *Thinking Silence:* Some young people need time to get themselves under control, to consider how to express themselves, or to think through the feelings and facts surrounding an event. The body language they use is generally not emotional. When you suspect this is going on inside a young person's head, respect the silence and sanction it with a statement such as, *"It's helpful to think about what happened before we talk."*
   - *Silence as Confusion:* If the young person's behavior suggests anxiety or confusion, it is possible that the young person lacks a grasp of what happened or has insufficient verbal ability to get talk started. Sometimes young people will pick or twist their fingers, squirm, or kick their feet to convey their confusion or inability to respond. If you suspect this, try tapping into some concrete, key recollection with a statement or question such as the following: *"Tell me what you heard"* or

"What was the very first thing that happened?" Such openings from you may help the young person connect to a timeline or remember a vivid aspect of the incident that can begin LSCI.

- *Silence as Uncertainty of Trust:* Often, young people are uncertain as to whether they can trust an adult with their thoughts and feelings. Their silence is the result of their indecision about opening up. Adults can communicate their genuine interest in the young person's well-being, along with their sincere desire to understand more about what's happening, using this three-part message (see Chapter 7):

  - *"I can see you're really upset right now."*
  - *"Something is going on that's really important for you."*
  - *"I'd really like to understand."*

- *Silence as Resistance:* Sometimes silence is used by young people to test their independence or resist adult authority. If there is no response, go back and try decoding with greater depth using statements such as the following:

  - "Some young people don't talk because they don't trust adults to understand and help."
  - "I have the feeling this discussion is upsetting you. It's okay to tell me that you don't want to talk."
  - "I see it's difficult to continue. I wonder if your silence is connected to something I said."

In the rare instance when these last statements do not produce some verbal response, the young person may be (a) developmentally below the level of comprehending your words or (b) testing you to the limit.

Every adult who works with challenging young people has encountered the youngster who "digs in" and refuses to engage in a dialogue or bring a matter to closure. We have two strategies to suggest. Rather than engage in a power struggle, point out that you recognize this issue is difficult for the young person to discuss:

- "It is so hard for you to talk about this that you would rather be silent. Perhaps the issue goes deeper than you are ready to share."

A second strategy is to note the resistance and divert the discussion to relationships that may be at the center of the resistance:

- "Let's set this aside for now and talk about how you are feeling about me (your teacher, friends, etc.)."

The young person's refusal to talk may have more to do with a relationship than with feelings about the event being discussed. Ultimately, we have to bring the dialogue to closure, but we want to avoid developing a stalemate.

2. **Allowing an Adversarial Climate to Develop**
Nothing sabotages LSCI more quickly than when an adult allows themselves to be cast into the role of the young person's adversary. Often this tone creeps into an exchange without the adult being aware of it. Sarcasm, exasperation, impatience, disbelief, and cynicism may also convey adversarial attitudes. During Stages 2 and 3, the potential is there to set up a win-lose dynamic. The young person is determined to win and so is the adult. Guard against this; it has no place in the helping process!

> Nothing sabotages LSCI more quickly than when an adult allows themselves to be cast into the role of the young person's adversary.

When you sense an adversarial tone creeping into your LSCI, aim to change it as swiftly as possible. Interject an affirmation of some valuable attribute in the young person. Align yourself with the young person and express conviction that you believe in their ability to deal with the crisis. If the young person observes you conferencing with another adult prior to your conversation, don't allow him to jump to the conclusion that you are "on the adult's side." Rather, acknowledge the conversation openly by saying something like, "As you know, Mr. Reed shared with me his thoughts on what happened. I'd really like to understand your point of view, however. Let's begin there." Remember that what we want is a collaborative, win-win dynamic.

3. **Reflecting Negatives**
As feelings come out during LSCI, it is often the adult who initiates the topic by decoding what a young person is feeling. Guard against reflecting negatives, such as "that was terrible" or "that was an abusive experience." These statements only reinforce the young person's belief that they are worthless or that the situation is hopeless. Instead, try "I'm impressed by how calm you are staying in this kind of situation."

4. **Becoming Counter-Aggressive**
In Chapter 6, we looked extensively at the adult's role in a Conflict Cycle and shared our belief that an adult has the power to make a situation better or worse, depending on their response to a young person's behavior. Although we know that some young people have a way of engaging adults in Conflict Cycles,

we also know that counter-aggressive behavior is self-defeating. To disengage from power struggles and stop counter-aggressive behaviors, adults must:

- Recognize that the dynamics of the Conflict Cycle are in play
- Q-Tip: Quit taking it personally
- Respond like a thermostat
- Use personal calming strategies
- Choose teaching over punishment
- Apply the art of listening

All of these skills are described in detail in Chapter 6.

5. Treating Complex Feelings in Trivial Ways

A common adult mistake is to ask a young person, *"How does that make you feel?"* before the young person can tell their complete story. Many of the young people with whom we work would fumble around unsuccessfully if asked such a question. If a young person tries to answer this question at all, the typical answer is *"I don't know."*

Equally unproductive is an adult's response to a young person's answer about feelings that treats the information casually, with marginal compassion, or by trying to minimize the young person's feelings. For example, a young person may say, *"It makes me feel terrible,"* in answer to a question about feelings. If the adult responds, *"It's not all that bad,"* or, *"Come on now, it's not worth feeling that bad,"* the young person's feelings have been invalidated. They have little motivation to continue talking to the adult. In Chapter 6, we explain five listening skills that help adults acknowledge kids' feelings effectively rather than dismissing them inadvertently.

> Adults whose primary concern is their own performance in managing a crisis sometimes listen only to their own voices and their own agendas, and they seldom hear the messages in the young person's words and actions.

6. Failing to Build LSCI Dialogue From a Young Person's Responses

One of the most heard complaints from adults beginning to use LSCI is "I don't know what to say!" Adults whose primary concern is their own performance in managing a crisis sometimes listen only to their own voices and their own agendas, and they seldom hear the messages in the young person's words and actions.

The easiest way to overcome this problem is to actively listen to what a young person is telling you and to respond directly to their statements, rather than speaking from your own point of view or opinions. Paraphrase the young person's statements so that they know you are genuinely listening to what they have to say. Ask follow-up questions using some of the young person's *exact* words or ideas. Begin a statement with the words used by the young person and then tack on your own new ideas or questions at the end. Such bridging between you and the young person conveys that you are listening and hearing.

7. **Invading a Young Person's Psychological Space**

Probably the most serious mistake made by adults in LSCI is intruding into a young person's private psychological space before a young person is ready to share it. Unwelcome intrusion usually happens as an adult begins to make interpretations, decoding the young person's words and actions prematurely. If the interpretation is too private, too bold, or touches a topic too sensitive, a young person will shut down. Such interpretations often leave a young person feeling vulnerable, exposed, and without psychological protection. The child's defensive instinct is to protect themselves from painful feelings. It will be hard to go further in the conversation.

The best way to prevent the activation of a young person's defenses during LSCI is to use *probes*, followed by a neutral statement about the topic. A probe is a follow-up question or statement about a topic not touched upon before. Something in a young person's words or actions might suggest a probe (although we are seldom certain about its accuracy until we try it). A young person's reaction to a probe gives adults the information they need about its accuracy and their willingness to have that topic included in the LSCI.

Fly-fishing makes a nice metaphor to explain probes. In fly-fishing, the lure is lightly cast onto the surface of the stream. The fisherman casts with some knowledge that this is a likely spot to find a fish. However, there is no guarantee that the fly has landed in the right spot. So, the fisherman moves up and down the area, casting again and again, until the connection is made. Probes are used in the same way. An interpretation is "cast" in the general direction you believe may be significant. When you get a "strike," you will know it from the young person's response (or notable lack of response). In short, you have interpreted accurately, and the new bit of information goes into your decoding network. As the dialogue with a young person continues, your probes take on greater accuracy and you will find yourself decoding increasingly more relevant interpretations about increasingly more sensitive and significant subjects. The young person is letting you into their private psychological space.

Carefully gauge a young person's willingness to let you into their psychological world. If you sense resistance, or there is an increase of emotional intensity, it may be a sign that the young person is not comfortable revealing more at this time. Respect the young person's privacy and return to discussing the events of the incident.

8. **Injecting Personal Comments About Yourself**
   As the personal, psychological world of a young person unfolds, a caring adult often becomes caught up in compassion for the emotional suffering of the young person. When this happens, it is natural for adults to want to let young people know that they share similar experiences and feelings. This is a well-meaning attempt to support a young person, but it is seldom interpreted that way by young people. When an adult brings personal experience into a discussion, young people often see the adult as more centered on themselves than on the young person ("All she wants to do is talk about herself"). This problem occurs more frequently than imagined, and it is usually not recognized or is vigorously denied by the adult. The following are some statements made by adults projecting their own personal experience unnecessarily into LSCI:

   - "I have felt that way myself."
   - "When I was your age that happened to me."
   - "My best friend did the same thing to me."
   - "People like that make me angry, too."

Instead of taking over the conversation by talking about your personal experiences, substitute expressions of empathy and compassion:

   - Acknowledge specific strengths of the young person, to express your confidence in their ability to resolve the crisis: "You're the oldest of five kids, so you have lots of experience taking care of others. Now you have a chance to take care of yourself by turning this situation around."
   - Validate the feelings of the young person to help them feel understood and supported: "You feel betrayed by your best friend. This is a painful time for you but also a turning point where you have the opportunity to change the friendship for the better."

9. **Allowing Young People to Reverse Roles With You**
   Young people with strong control needs sometimes use the first three stages of LSCI to test their ability to influence adults. Such young people are usually very verbal and experienced at getting their needs met. In fact, we have seen young people who take charge of their LSCI, controlling the questions, the answers, the movement through the stages, and even the stopping point of the intervention. This can happen to anyone, but don't let it happen to you.

The strategy most frequently used by such young people is to ask the adult pleasant personal questions or to make observations about the adult's personal characteristics. The following are some typical statements and questions used by young people to reverse roles (the young person becomes the interviewer):

- "Are you married?"
- "Do you have kids?"
- "Are you a real teacher?"
- "Your hair (belt, dress, shirt, etc.) is beautiful."
- "You are really strong."

If an adult responds with detail to these harmless questions, the young person may begin to form the impression that topics for LSCI can be controlled by the young person, and that an adult who can be controlled is a less reliable adult. More blatant testing of adult authority invariably follows:

- "Why do I have to be here?"
- "Why didn't you take Emma out of class too?"
- "How long do we have to stay in here?"
- "You don't understand the situation!"
- "This isn't your business; it's between him and me."
- "You don't want to be fair; you only want to get me in trouble!"

If you let yourself react emotionally to such statements, the young person has found a way to control you and take charge of the LSCI. Equally damaging is ignoring a young person's attempts to control, thereby creating the impression that things get by you or that you do not know how to respond. Paradoxically, showing yourself to be inept or vulnerable to manipulation by a young person is frightening to the young person. The unspoken message is that the adult cannot control the situation. Young people must believe that the adult can handle the crisis competently and not abdicate authority.

If an adult fails to communicate competence in handling the minor attempts of young people to reverse roles, the youth will almost always continue to pursue the adult, testing for vulnerability. Typically, the role reversals become more overtly confrontational and personal as these young people try to exert power over an adult that they perceive to be vulnerable to manipulation. The following are some typical examples of young people attempting to control adults with personal attacks (notice the implied attempts to elicit counter-aggression):

- "Your breath stinks!"
- "You don't even know what's going on."
- "I'm going to get my dad to come down here and get you fired!"
- "I can kick your ass whenever I want to."
- "You're too fat to help anyone."
- "I'm leaving and you can't stop me!"

By now, your decoding skills should be working, and you should recognize that these are desperate remarks based on concern, anger, or fear. There are several ways to respond to young people who try role reversal. The following are possible responses to first attempts, when a young person uses innocuous questions or statements to see the extent of your vulnerability:

- Turn the question back to the young person, rephrasing it to ask a personal question of the young person.
- Use an affirmation to commend the young person's interest in others.
- Make a statement such as, "*What's important in this conversation is you (or what happened)*." Then continue the talk about the incident.

If a young person continues personal verbal attacks, decoding is essential. The young person must know that you understand the feelings behind the attack and that there is another way to help the young person out of the desperate situation. The following are several examples of effective statements adults have made in response to the previous examples:

- "When we're talking about things that are uncomfortable, it doesn't help to try to change the subject."
- "I can see how upset you are, but there are ways we can solve this problem."
- "It seems to me that you made a choice, and now you regret it."

10. Failing to State the Central Issue Simply and Concisely

As you and a young person go through the first three stages in LSCI, it is easy to get bogged down in details, specifics, and information overload. It requires mental organization to analyze a large amount of complex and often disparate information. You may not know exactly what it all means, what is important, and what is simply off the track. Yet it is essential to make a concise and clear statement about the central issue before you leave Stage 3.

We find that the best help in this situation is observing the young person. Their behavior usually provides an indication of what is truly significant. Test your observations by decoding. The young person's response will give you an indication of your proximity to the central issue. Sometimes young people protest loudly but then show by body language that they are waiting for your next statement. At other times they will be unusually silent, waiting for you to follow up on the idea. When you sense that you are on the right track, ask the young person to put the central issue into words with statements such as the following:

- "What is really important in all of this?"
- "We've talked a lot. Some of this is really important if things are going to get better for you. Let's list the important points."
- "I think what we are talking about gets right to the heart of the problem. Do you agree?"

If the young person is not able or willing to respond, try to extract the essential focus from the young person's viewpoint with lead-ins such as the following:

- "It seems like what we have been talking about really is . . ."
- "What I hear in all of this is . . ."
- "It is really hard for kids to have to face . . ."

Once you or the young person have made a simple summary of the issue, you are ready to move the LSCI into the problem-solving stages. *Do not go forward until that concise statement has been made.* If you do, you will have no basis for choosing a therapeutic goal and nothing to which you can attach a crisis resolution plan.

11. Jumping to Solutions Prematurely

Once an issue is out in the open, adults tend to leap to the finish to "fix it." This same type of reaction also slips into the adult's response when a young person describes the incident and the adult says, "Didn't you know that would happen?" Without waiting, the adult often goes ahead and tells the young person a better way to handle the incident, or the adult reminds the young person of the rules that should have been used to govern the behavior. In either case, the adult is providing the solution prematurely. *Neither of these responses is appropriate during LSCI Stage 4, when what is needed is to encourage the young person to consider all possible solutions and to select the best one(s).* Hold off on expressing your opinion about the best solution, for two vital reasons:

1. First, you do not want to preempt the young person's process of thinking through the choices. To do so would close off the opportunity to consider the results and consequences of each alternative. This is an essential part of accomplishing the LSCI goal.

2. Second, if you provide the solution (rule, guideline), it is yours, not the young person's. *You will own it, but the young person will not!* Remember that the preferred result for LSCI Stage 4 is a young person-selected solution. Also remember that you should not leave Stage 4 until the young person states (or restates) the solution that has been chosen.

12. **Failing to Consider Negative Solutions and Consequences**

It is common to find adults attempting to lead young people away from mentioning inappropriate or negative solutions during LSCI Stage 5. This desire to skirt any thought of inappropriate behavior is understandable, but not useful. By sanctioning a review of the inappropriate solutions, an adult helps a young person rationally anticipate and weigh the consequences. We have found it helpful with some young people to role-play the various choices and vicariously play out the negative consequences.

> By sanctioning a review of the inappropriate solutions, an adult helps a young person rationally anticipate and weigh the consequences.

Consider the reality of implementing a resolution to a crisis that involves new behavior. It is likely that the young person will try out the new solution with the best of intentions. But the ineptness of the young person in carrying out a new skill or a negative response from someone may produce a feeling of failure. To reduce this likelihood, it is helpful to always rehearse the new behavior with the young person during Stage 5. Take the role of the potential adversary. When the young person tries the new behavior, respond negatively to the young person. If the young person is overwhelmed, confused, or reacts in anger to your role play, the new alternative has not been sufficiently practiced. You have not prepared the young person well enough, or the chosen solution is beyond the young person's ability to accomplish successfully. You may have to go back to Stage 4 and reconsider solutions with the young person.

If the young person handles the practice role play, in which you respond negatively to the new behavior, you have increased the odds that the young person can react to the next real incident with the new behavior. The LSCI has been a success.

Summary: Quick Tips to Avoid LSCI Pitfalls

1. Respect silence; understand its functions. Use it wisely.
2. Think of LSCI as two-way communication between allies. Set up win-win situations. Monitor your choice of words and tone of voice to convey respect and support.

3. Reflect positives. Credit a young person's good intentions and provide genuine affirmations whenever possible.

4. Use calming strategies. Disengage from power struggles.

5. Validate the young person's perceptions and feelings.

6. Listen actively. Respond directly to kids' statements. Paraphrase and ask follow-up questions.

7. Use probes to gain information and increase understanding without raising a child's defenses.

8. Show empathy. Aim to understand the psychological world of the young person.

9. Portray competence, leadership, and a solutions focus. Young people feel safe when trustworthy adults guide the LSCI process.

10. Always have the young person make a concise and clear statement about the central issue before you leave Stage 3.

11. Give ample time to problem-solving and solutions. Encourage the young person to consider all possible solutions and to select the best one(s). Resist the temptation to express your opinion about the best solution.

12. Communicate optimism: reassure the child that positive change will produce satisfying results. Use role play and rehearsal to help kids anticipate and overcome challenges to desired outcomes.

Outcomes of Effective LSCIs

In the final section of this chapter, we explore both short and long-term outcomes of LSCI and look at what it really means to carry out an effective LSCI intervention.

Diagnostic vs. Reclaiming Interventions

In Chapter 7, we explained the structure of LSCI, detailing the tasks and objectives of all six stages of the process. At first glance, one might think that a "successful" LSCI Intervention is one in which all six stages are completed. Does this mean that an adult who was interrupted after carrying out a helpful Drain Off and Timeline but before she could clearly state the Central Issue was *unsuccessful* in implementing LSCI? No. Does this mean that her time, energy, and connection with the young person were wasted? No again. Does this mean that an adult who left the LSCI process incomplete should feel inadequate? Of course not.

Before moving on to learn the six interventions in Part 2, it's important to establish a meaning for the phrase "successful LSCI Intervention." The way to do this is to define a successful LSCI as a short-term or a long-term intervention with different outcome goals and benefits. Ideally, every LSCI-trained adult would have the time and resources to carry out a full intervention. Without a doubt, we always want to help kids achieve insight, new skills, and lasting behavioral changes. When conditions are not ideal, however, an abbreviated LSCI still has powerful potential.

Why Some LSCIs May Be Cut Short

Let's look first at typical reasons why an adult may not always be able to carry out the full six stages of the LSCI process with a young person:

- Time constraints (e.g., end of the class period, end of the day)
- Conflicting schedules (child or adult is scheduled for another activity/class/appointment)
- Too many concurrent crises (sometimes everything goes wrong at once)
- The crisis was complicated, involved several young people, and/or was not observed by any adults
- The crisis was the child's first experience with the LSCI process; engaging all the way through to a resolution was beyond the young person's capacity
- Staff mood and energy (the self-aware adult understands and acknowledges when they are not in the right psychological space to carry out the LSCI process)

Diagnostic Interventions

If any (or all) of these variables unexpectedly prevent you from being able to carry out all six stages of the LSCI process, it's important to know that important short-term outcomes can still be achieved through the diagnostic stages of LSCI, including:

- The young person will experience a de-escalation of emotions in connection with a trustworthy adult
- The young person will have the opportunity to put language to emotions and feel heard as they tell their story
- The young person will understand the sequence of his crisis and begin to connect actions with reactions
- The young person will have a brief cognitive understanding of why this crisis happened

Core Benefits of the Diagnostic Stages of LSCI

- The youth's relationship with a helping adult is enhanced
- The young person learns that a personal crisis does not have to lead to punishment, alienation, and rejection

- The young person experiences that she can be accepted at her worst and still be treated with respect
- The experience provides building blocks that lead to future self-awareness and behavioral changes
- The young person is more motivated to return to his previous setting and will do what is necessary to be accepted (apologize, accept consequences, etc.)

Although a short-term intervention is incomplete, there is no doubt that it can be defined as a meaningful and successful experience for a young person.

The Critical Need for Reclaiming Interventions

At this point, you may be wondering, *if there are so many benefits to a diagnostic intervention, why take the time to do a full LSCI?* For all the genuine and worthwhile benefits of carrying out just the first three stages of LSCI, the fundamental objectives *missed* by ending the process prematurely are:

1. To increase the young person's self-awareness and insight into their self-defeating pattern of behavior. (To be unaware of a pattern is to be destined to repeat it.)
2. To consider, discuss and practice new skills to replace older, problematic behaviors. (To be unaware of appropriate, pro-social skills leaves the young person incapable of making needed changes.)
3. To have the experience of successfully reentering a situation and repairing damaged relationships. (To reenter a class the scene of a problem incident without a plan for success can prove to be a recipe for failure for the young person.)

The reclaiming stages of LSCI hold the essential elements that enable a young person to achieve long-term learning and make lasting behavioral changes. Whenever—and however—possible efforts should be made by professionals to carry out all six stages of the LSCI process with young people.

> The reclaiming stages of LSCI hold the essential elements that enable a young person to achieve long-term learning and make lasting behavioral changes.

Tall order? Maybe. We know that LSCI is a complex process that can be lengthy at times. Worth it? Absolutely. The long-term benefits and lasting changes cultivated through the six-stage LSCI process are worth every second of time we spend making young people feel heard, valued, understood, and respected. Remember: kids are going to get our time one way or the other. Do we want to spend that time dealing with disruptions, overcoming hostilities, reacting to resentments, anticipating aggression, managing the fallout created with other students, conferencing with staff and parents, and then doing it all over again the next day? Or do we want to spend that time connecting with a vulnerable young person, de-escalating their emotions, clarifying their perceptions, processing their thoughts, and teaching more desirable behaviors? As adults, the choice is ours to make almost every single time.

PART 2

In Part 2 of this book, we take you beyond the foundations of LSCI to illustrate how the full verbal framework is used to address six distinct patterns of self-defeating behaviors.

During the first three LSCI stages, your task is to formulate the Central Issue that will become the focus of the LSCI Intervention. In shorthand terms, the self-defeating pattern and corresponding outcome goals we explore in Part 2 are:

- Chapter 10: Red Flag Intervention—Identify the real source of the stress
- Chapter 11: Reality Check Intervention—Organize perceptions of reality
- Chapter 12: New Tools Intervention—Build social-emotional skills
- Chapter 13: Benign Confrontation Intervention—Challenge unacceptable behavior
- Chapter 14: Regulate and Restore Intervention—Strengthen self-control
- Chapter 15: Peer Manipulation Intervention—Expose peer exploitation

The outcome goals are presented in the form of action statements to highlight the adult's role in shaping the therapeutic focus. The goal you select will shape Stages 4 to 6 of the LSCI. It will guide what you do and say and will structure the way the crisis is resolved. If effective, the LSCI process cultivates new insight and understanding of the stressful incident along with the perceptions, thoughts, feelings, behaviors, and reactions that escalated the conflict.

Chapters 10 to 15 detail the LSCI Interventions used to accomplish these therapeutic goals. You will see that the basic stage-by-stage process is consistent, no matter which outcome goal is selected. This is the beauty of the LSCI framework; it gives adults a cognitive roadmap to where they are in a conflict situation and where to go next to lead young people to desired outcomes. What changes from intervention to intervention is the direction of the solution, the amount of your guidance and directness needed, and the outcome for the young person.

Nothing comes from nothing.

THE RED FLAG INTERVENTION
Identifying the Source of the Stress

Young Person's Perception:

"Everybody is against me! No one understands what's going on with me and no one cares! I can't take it anymore!"

Uses:

With young people who overreact to normal rules and routines with emotional outbursts and who attempt to create no-win situations by engaging adults in power struggles which ultimately result in further rejection and feelings of alienation.

Goal:

To identify the source of the problem; is it a *Carry In* problem from another setting, a *Carry Over* problem from another place within the current setting, or a *Tap In* to a personal, unresolved trauma?

Focus:

Helps young people recognize that they are displacing their feelings onto others and alienating the sources of support they need to help handle stress.

Young Person's New Insight:

"Someone does understand my real problems and can read beyond my behavior. I need to talk to adults about my real problems instead of creating new ones."

Brandon

Brandon is a 13-year-old boy living in a group home that provides residential services for at-risk adolescents. Early in the school day, Brandon became extremely angry, tearing up his papers and yelling at his teacher. Other school staff became aware that a problem was unfolding when they heard furniture banging and Brandon walked out of his classroom, growling and threatening to harm anyone who came near him. He paced around a small area of the hall, mumbling that someone was going to "get f---d up."

Keep this image of Brandon in mind as you read about the Red Flag intervention. We will return to Brandon's story at the end of the chapter to show you how LSCI was used to transform the situation.

While working with students in the 1980s in New York City schools, Dr. Nicholas Long picked up on a pattern in which young people like Brandon ignited explosive conflicts early in the day or early in the start of a new class period. The conflicts were especially puzzling to observers because they seemed to come out of nowhere. With the wisdom that "nothing comes from nothing," Dr. Long examined the pattern of problems and discovered that they were often a result of some sort of unfinished business that a young person was carrying in, carrying over, or tapping into during an otherwise benign situation. The unresolved stressors would trigger an intense, unexpected emotional reaction in the child and often create massive counter-aggressive feelings in those on the receiving end of their wrath since the behavior appeared so unfounded. Red Flag crises have been described as "an open invitation to a power struggle" because a young person seems determined to fight with whatever adult they can catch in their Conflict Cycle.

As Dr. Long studied this dynamic further, he realized that many young people hold their emotions inside temporarily, believing they can't deal with the problem openly or honestly in the moment. They wait until they're in a safe, predictable place, and then let all of their anguish and stress go. These youth displace their anger onto an unsuspecting, undeserving teacher, counselor, classmate, or friend in this "safer" setting. The problem with this emotion management strategy is twofold:

1. The young person sparks an explosive crisis that creates new problems, in addition to the original one(s).
2. Through unexpected and conflict-fueling behaviors, the youth tends to push away the very people in his life that he needs to help and support him.

The LSCI Red Flag Intervention helps young people learn new skills to regulate intense emotions triggered in their limbic brain and use neocortex-guided strategies to manage stressors in a more productive way. Our outcome goal with the Red Flag is to help young people recognize their tendency to displace anger and to gain insight that their pattern of alienating friends and supports is self-defeating.

Our outcome goal with the Red Flag is to help young people recognize their tendency to displace anger and to gain insight that their pattern of alienating friends and supports is self-defeating.

Use the Red Flag Intervention With Young People Who . . .

1. **Overreact to Minor Requests or Incidents With a Massive and Uncharacteristic Emotional Outburst**
   A key diagnostic characteristic of the Drain Off stage in this intervention is the explosive emotional reaction of the young person. A Red Flag crisis can be difficult to manage because the young person is actively resistant to help. Over the years, we have found that the Red Flag is among the most frequently used of LSCI's interventions, especially in school settings where adults may be unaware of stressors that students are carrying in to school from elsewhere.

2. **Attempt to Engage Adults in a No-Win Power Struggle**
   No matter how accommodating and patient the adult is, the young person seems determined to escalate a minor situation into a no-win power struggle. The youth often creates massive counter-aggressive feelings in adults. The adult tendency is to threaten or resort to rote punishment because the young person makes us feel helpless and angry.

3. **Displace Their Anger Onto an Unsuspecting Person**
   A central theme of Red Flag situations has to do with the dynamic of displacement, one of the defense mechanisms identified in Chapter 4. During the Timeline stage, the adult often discovers that the source of the stress that the young person was feeling at the moment was not grounded in the immediate setting or the immediate events, but rather in some past experience that had left residual unfinished business. The young person had an emotional "sore spot," and when an otherwise innocent comment or occurrence bumped up against that sore spot, it set off an onslaught of impassioned dumping. The unfortunate victim who happened to be available became, in the young person's eyes, the source of the stress and received the full wrath.

4. **Inadvertently Alienate the People They Trust the Most**
   One of the most self-defeating aspects of Red Flag situations is that young people push away the people they trust the most. Because select adults or

peers have been kind and patient with them in the past, kids perceive them as a "safe" place to express their inner feelings. Yet because their feelings are so intense and had been so well-hidden, the unsuspecting, undeserving recipients become defensive, angry, and alienated rather than drawn to help and support the child.

Three Types of Red Flag Problems

We recognize three types of Red Flag conditions: the *Carry In,* the *Carry Over,* and the *Tap In.*

1. **Carry In Situations**

   The *Carry In* situation occurs when a young person has had a recent negative encounter or experience that occurred *before entering* the setting in which the crisis develops. There has been an argument or incident at home, in the community, or on the bus which the young person was unable to resolve satisfactorily. Often, the young person is in a position in which real feelings cannot be expressed to the offending party for fear of retaliation or punishment. Rather than telling a step-parent that he is angry at being accused of stealing or telling the bully on the bus he can no longer tolerate his abuse, the young person comes into the classroom loaded with feelings and explodes at the slightest reasonable request.

2. **Carry Over Situations**

   The second type of Red Flag, the *Carry Over,* is very similar to the *Carry In* except that the offending event has occurred within the same setting as the following expression of emotion. For example, instead of telling Mr. Bruno, the no-nonsense physical education instructor, that derogatory remarks about lack of coordination are not appreciated, the middle school student bottles up his feelings and takes them out an hour later on his art teacher, a trusted adult whom he perceives as "safe."

3. **Tap In Situations**

   The third type of Red Flag, the *Tap In,* is somewhat more complex, as the issue for the young person is much deeper. In this situation, an old wound exists as a result of abuse, abandonment, neglect, or other trauma. As we know from Part 1 of this book, many challenging children have endured traumatic stressors that keep their limbic brain functioning in a state of hypervigilance and hypersensitivity. When something taps in to a memory of past trauma, van der Kolk (2014) explains that the youth's brain reacts as if the event were happening in the moment. The child can experience feelings of fury, terror, rage, or shame, as if they were reexperiencing the event rather than simply remembering it. When old pain is triggered, young people react with an intensity that is incomprehensible to the uninformed observer—especially those who are completely unaware that a triggering event even occurred.

Examples of Young People Who Can Benefit From a Red Flag Intervention

Raya

Raya is a nine-year-old girl who is small for her age and fears older, larger kids. This morning on the bus ride to school, a middle schooler named Chris grabbed Raya's lunch box, took what he wanted, crushed the remainder, and threw it at Raya. Raya arrived at school feeling weak, miserable, abused, ashamed, and angry. In the safe environment of the classroom, she exploded at her teacher, refusing to do any work and saying the teacher was unfair for calling on another student before calling on her. (Carry In)

Malik

Malik is 16 years old and has been attending an alternative high school for about six months. Usually he enters the building, greeting the staff and removing his baseball cap according to the school rules. On this morning, however, he does not greet the staff and refuses to remove his cap. When he is told to report to the office, he swears at the staff and continues to walk down the hallway toward his classroom. When a teacher signals to Malik to turn around, Malik becomes aggressive, attempting to push past the teacher. He screams and swears. When Malik has finally been restored to calm and the teacher begins a Timeline, Malik reveals that his stepfather and mother got into a terrible argument the previous evening, and when Malik stepped in to protect his mother, his stepfather pushed him into the wall. His mother left the house with Malik and his younger sister. They spent the night at a neighbor's house, and when Malik left for school this morning, his mother told him not to go home at the end of the day. She would call to tell him where they would spend that night. (Carry In)

Jamal

Jamal, a 15-year-old young person with a learning disability and oppositional defiant disorder, takes American history with a teacher who is sensitive to his difficulties and supportive of his efforts. On this day, however, his teacher is out sick. A substitute teacher is in charge. The substitute teacher decides that students will read aloud from the textbook, not realizing that Jamal has great difficulty reading. When it is Jamal's turn to read, he is torn between following directions or choosing a diversion that will relieve him of the stressful task. He decides to say "Pass" when he is called upon to read. The substitute writes a note for the regular teacher, calling Jamal's behavior defiant. Jamal is furious but says nothing in class. The next period, he enters his English classroom. When his teacher tells him to work on his journal, he explodes in an angry torrent of curses and accusations. (Carry Over)

Sylke

Sylke is 14 years old and has been struggling with dyslexia all of her life. Her parents, who immigrated from Eastern Europe, cannot understand why Sylke reads at a third-grade level. Despite explanations from the school psychologist, they still believe she is just not trying. Her parents criticize her for poor grades and allow her brother to refer to her as "stupid." They tell her that if she doesn't like to be called stupid, she should work harder in school. Although Sylke does poorly with academics, she is athletic and excels in sports. During gym class, the group is playing volleyball and it is Sylke's turn to serve. She uncharacteristically botches the serve, placing the ball right in the middle of the opposing team's court. It is set up for a slam and the other team scores. A competitive boy on Sylke's team turns to her and says loudly, "You stupid idiot, why did you do that?" Sylke goes after him, knocking him to the floor and punching him in the face. (Tap In)

How Trauma and Adverse Childhood Experiences Shape the Red Flag Pattern

Young people who experience an upsetting event and are able to withhold their emotional expression until they reach a safe setting demonstrate a degree of emotional control not available to all traumatized children. Their fight, flight, or freeze reaction is under some level of regulation. These youth have enough structure in their lives to know that "safe spaces" and "less-safe spaces" exist, and they possess enough self-control to wait until they are in a safe space to "let it out." This is a hopeful indicator when it comes to our ability to teach young people new social-emotional skills for regulating behaviors.

It is also true, however, that young people who wait to express their anger, resentment, or fear until they are in a safe space have a paradoxical problem; the real-life struggles that are the source of their stress require support systems, but their unleashing of abusive or violent behavior upon "safe" individuals tends to alienate would-be supporters. In that way, the child's underlying belief that he is unworthy of support is validated.

The LSCI process gives us a framework to look beyond behavior—to recognize unexpected and explosive behaviors as indicators, or "red flags," that something else is driving the behavior. After Draining Off intense emotions, we use the Timeline to figure out what that hidden something actually is. By identifying the Central Issue, we help the young person gain Insight into their pattern of displacing anger and alienating sources of support. In teaching New Skills for coping with intense emotions, we empower the young person to connect with helpers rather than engaging them in destructive self-fulfilling prophecies.

> The LSCI process gives us a framework to look beyond behavior—to recognize unexpected and explosive behaviors as indicators, or "red flags," that something else is driving the behavior.

The Adult's Tasks in a Red Flag Intervention

The Red Flag intervention requires a good deal of skill on the part of the interviewer, as most young people are not inclined to approach an adult and announce calmly that something is bothering them. In fact, there are those who know only one way to engage adults—by making them angry. The irony is that most young people really do want to tell their story to an adult who can help, or at least understand. Yet, these helping adults are the very ones the young person drives away with disrespectful or even abusive comments and behaviors. To be successful, the adult must avoid being drawn into conflicts that elicit counter-aggressive feelings. The adult's task is to discover the true source of the stress and help the young person understand the damaging effects of their pattern of displacement.

> The adult's task is to discover the true source of the stress and help the young person understand the damaging effects of their pattern of displacement.

Sequence of a Red Flag Intervention

Stage 1: Drain Off

The Drain Off stage in the Red Flag intervention is often intense and sometimes extensive. Young people have been holding in painful feelings and the impact of releasing them takes a toll on their brain and bodies, in terms of heart rate, blood pressure, and stress hormones that all need to return to normal levels before the logical brain can be accessed.

The first task the adult faces in confronting a Red Flag situation is to stay calm and avoid becoming counter-aggressive. This is not easy, as frequently the crisis will occur early in the day, or early in the class period, and there are few if any observable antecedent events that might explain a behavioral response of such great magnitude.

The most innocent comment or request, such as, "Please open your math book," might ignite an explosion from a young person. For the adult, it doesn't add up. Furthermore, our good relationship with the young person, which helps so often in dispersing tension in other situations, seems to have evaporated. The young person rages against every effort of the adult to help and to understand, and even the most patient adult begins to feel anger creeping into non-verbal messages.

The adult's tasks in this first stage are to:

- Realize that the young person's behavior was an uncharacteristic over-reaction to a minor request or incident. Recognize that the youth is *too* angry, sad, fearful, or frustrated for the situation. Remind yourself that *nothing comes from nothing.*
- Manage your own reactions. Tell yourself to be a thermostat, not a thermometer.
- Be aware that at this stage, the young person may still want to keep the conflict going. Resist all invitations to a power struggle.
- Use listening skills to break the Conflict Cycle (see Chapter 6). Maintain reassuring communication, validate feelings, and use plenty of affirmation.
- Use the three-part message (see Chapter 7), including de-escalating phrases such as:
  - I see how stirred up you are. I don't know what happened in the classroom, but I really want to hear about it from your point of view. Let's take a walk and breathe for a few minutes before we try to figure this out.
  - I can see you're very angry, but I don't know what you're so angry about. I'd really like to understand what is happening.

Stage 2: Timeline

The intensity of the emotion and the seeming overreaction detected in the Drain Off stage should prompt you to remember that *nothing comes from nothing.* Adults should calmly and systematically use the Timeline to look beyond behavior, seeking to identify the source of the problem. You are trying to establish the most recent point of relative calm and trace events forward until you find the first moment of distress. This process is a delicate one, as young people usually will not come right out with the problem. They will, instead, drop hints or clues and wait for you to decode them. A skilled interviewer will recognize these as "offers" to the adult to ask the kinds of questions that will enable the young person to ease into the sensitive topic. With support, the young person will reveal the true source of the stress.

The adult's tasks in the Timeline stage are to:

- Discover the "video" of the event as it exists in the young person's mind. Use questions to work backward in time to a point before the triggering event occurred. Ask questions such as:
  - How was the first part of your day? What kind of mood were you in when you came to school?
  - Were you upset about something before Mr. Matthews asked you to turn in your homework?
  - Did something happen earlier in the morning that made you angry even before you got on the bus?
  - It looked like you were really agitated when you walked in the room. Did anything unusual happen last night?

- Then, move forward to discover how the youth perceived, felt, thought, acted, and reacted to others. Guide them to talk about their feelings, moving the issue from the part of their brain that does not have access to language to the part of the brain that does. Summarize the order of events frequently to help organize them for the young person.
- Use a diagram of the Conflict Cycle to help kids make important connections between previous events and current triggering events, perceptions, thoughts, feelings, behaviors, and reactions from others. The Conflict Cycle paradigm is a very useful guide to help young people connect to the original source of their stress.
- Continue to stay attuned to the young person, validating his feelings and decoding his behaviors. Guard against remnants of the young person trying to cast you in an adversarial role. Reassure him that you are allies working together on the same problem.
- Provide abundant affirmation. This serves at least two purposes: (1) it brings a sense of relief that someone else understands the real problem and is supportive, and (2) it encourages the continuation of the interview.

Stage 3: Central Issue

The Central Issue in a Red Flag crisis is that the young person has displaced their anger. *Carry In* and *Carry Over* issues can range from mild to quite serious situations. They can be as irritating as a teacher giving a detention to a young person who doesn't feel it is deserved, or as disturbing as witnessing a physical

> The Central Issue in a Red Flag crisis is that the young person has displaced their anger.

confrontation between parents. *Tap In* issues are usually more intense as the young person reveals past traumatic events and seeks to be supported in personal pain, grief, or fear.

The adult's tasks in the Central Issue stage are to:

- Summarize the Timeline using the Conflict Cycle paradigm to shed light on the original source of the stress (Carry In, Carry Over, Tap In) that has emerged through the conversation.
- Concisely state the central issue of displacement.
- Assess the youth's perceptions, thoughts, feelings, and motivations to change.
- Determine that the Red Flag intervention is the most suited to the desired outcome and resolution of the crisis.
- Prepare the young person to consider that they displaced their feelings onto an undeserving and unsuspecting source.

Stage 4: Insight

In sharing about an underlying source of stress, the young person has taken a risk. The adult now has a responsibility to support the young person. Support comes in many forms—acting as a confidante, seeking help from other professionals, or in cases where abuse is suspected, notifying Child Protective Services. Adults should assure young people that they do not have to handle the problem alone. It is very important to note, however, that solving the complex underlying problem is *not* a goal of this intervention. There are times when the life issues a child reveals are so serious that an adult may disregard the goal of the LSCI and begin immediately to assemble a team to address the underlying problem. We recommend guarding against this. *Both* the underlying problem *and* the child's self-defeating way of handling it are important to the child's long-term success. *Both* need to be addressed.

Even in the context of new awareness of an underlying issue, the *here and now* part of the Red Flag intervention remains very important. For both their long- and their short-term well-being, we need to help the young person become aware of the damage caused to good relationships when feelings are displaced onto friends and supporters. It benefits the young person to understand that the very people who can be counted on for relief from the real problem are the ones that their behavior is driving away. This goal is on a par with the goal of addressing the under-

> It benefits the young person to understand that the very people who can be counted on for relief from the real problem are the ones that their behavior is driving away.

lying problem. What plan can work if the young person unwittingly continues to "bite the hand that feeds"?

In Stage 4, our goal is to help the young person develop the insight that *"I need to talk to adults about my real problems and not create new ones. Adults can understand my personal pain and look beyond my behavior. I need to stop this self-defeating pattern of behavior that alienates the people I need the most."*

The adult's tasks in the Insight stage are to:

- Help young people recognize the original source of the problem. Acknowledge their initial attempts to manage the problem on their own and affirm their ability to proceed with their day, given the nature of the original problem.
- After the youth feels supported, ask:

  - Who were you really mad at?
  - Who received your anger?
  - Is this a pattern? Has something like this happened to you before?

- Teach the dynamics of displacement.
- Help the young person see that by lashing out at helping adults and friends, he is weakening his support system to deal with the real problem.
- If the young person acknowledges that this is a pattern, reassure him that together you've learned something very important. Assure the youth that you will help and support him in changing this pattern.

Stage 5: New Skills

The purpose of Stage 5 is to help the young person consider and practice the social-emotional skills needed to be successful should a similar problem occur again. The focus should be on replacing old behaviors with new, more effective ones. It is essential to convey hope and affirm the young person's ability to carry out a plan for success.

> It is essential to convey hope and affirm the young person's ability to carry out a plan for success.

The adult's tasks in the New Skills stage are to:

- Acknowledge that real problems come with intense emotions.
- Help the young person anticipate and plan for future situations that will trigger strong feelings. Discuss ways to recognize and check rising feelings.
- Establish a "check-in" procedure with an adult the youth trusts.

- Rehearse new emotion management skills through role play and discussion.
- Affirm the benefits of the young person making changes in behavior.
- Provide a window of realism while conveying confidence in the young person's ability to employ the plan for success.

Stage 6: Transfer of Learning

The last stage of LSCI prepares the young person for a transition back into the classroom, group, or interpersonal situation. Because the conditions under which the young person left may have been quite intense or disruptive, it is critical to help the youth plan for how to successfully cope with other people's reactions, lingering feelings, and any programmatic consequences. It is also important to use this stage to resolve or follow up on any significant sources of stress that may have been identified.

The adult's tasks in the Transfer of Learning stage are to:

- Empower the young person to be successful by summarizing their new insights and affirming their competence for carrying out the plan for success.
- Discuss what has happened while the young person has been away from the group and engaged in LSCI; plan for what the young person will do when they return, and how others may react as they rejoin the group.
- Collaborate with other important adults to establish conditions under which the young person can practice new skills and enjoy a measure of success as they approximate their goals.
- Encourage restorative practices to resolve issues involving adults and peers.

Now that you have a thorough and comprehensive understanding of the adult's stage-by-stage tasks in a Red Flag intervention, we return to Brandon, the teenage student we met at the beginning of the chapter. We give you the opportunity to "listen in" on the way a helping adult used Drain Off skills to de-escalate Brandon's intense emotions and then helped the teen recognize the original source of stress by constructing a Timeline. By identifying the dynamic of displacement and helping Brandon consider better ways of managing emotions in the future, the adult gave Brandon a powerful experience of feeling understood, seeing adults as sources of support, and understanding ways to engage supports rather than create new problems.

Example of LSCI Used to Identify the Source of Stress: A Red Flag Intervention

"I can't hold it in forever, you know!"

Background Information

Brandon is 13 years old, tall, overweight, and of mixed racial background. He has no direct knowledge of his father and, until placement in a group home, lived with his mother and younger sister. He is considerably larger than the other young men in his group, giving him a menacing appearance when he is angry. He has been aggressive with peers and adults prior to and during the earlier parts of his placement in this program. In recent months, however, he has been working with the program, gaining new trust, taking on more responsibility, and earning additional privileges. His nature seemed to be much gentler than his reputation would have one believe. Brandon acknowledges that he gets really mad sometimes and uses his size and strength to intimidate.

The adult who conducts the LSCI Red Flag intervention with Brandon is not someone that Brandon knows well. Rather, he is a consultant (C) to the residential program in which Brandon (B) resides. Despite their lack of a previous relationship, note how the consultant uses the early stages of the LSCI process to establish a positive rapport and create the conditions necessary to help Brandon feel heard and understood.

The Incident

It was obvious from a glance into the room that Brandon was very upset about something. A few minutes later the commotion in the classroom spilled out to the hall. There was his loud voice, part growling, part yelling. Then there was the sound of furniture banging. Brandon came out of the classroom with a very aggressive posture. Soon several staff members formed a semicircle around Brandon, who was threatening harm to anyone who came near him. From some distance away, I asked his teacher, Miss Nancy, if it would be all right if I tried to talk with Brandon. She readily agreed and there was no objection from the others.

Stage 1: Drain Off

> C: *I waited a few minutes and let the other adults in the area recede before I approached and asked Brandon if there was anything I could do to*

help him relax. He quietly but firmly suggested that I could leave him alone. I told him I would stand back and check back with him shortly. He was not quite ready as he paced around in a small area of the hall talking, mostly to himself, about how someone was going to "get f---d up." Stage 1, the de-escalation phase, had begun.

C: I can see you're very angry, but I have no idea what you're so angry about. I'd really like to understand what is going on with you.

After making these statements, the interviewer purposefully let silence happen so that Brandon could consider his choices. Letting silence happen is an important skill that many adults find difficult to embrace without training and support.

By this point, all the other students had now settled in their classrooms and the adults had gone back to their primary tasks. Two of them stayed within range but out of sight of Brandon in case things escalated again. After approximately 3 to 5 minutes (those intervals always seem longer than they are), I approached Brandon again:

C: I appreciate you taking some quiet time. I hope it helps you feel settled enough to talk with me.

Brandon did not say anything, which I interpreted as evidence he was more settled.

C: *(Walking slowly to the doorway of a room adjacent to the classroom)* Brandon, when you are ready, please come in and sit down with me.

B: *(Silently walks to the adjacent room and sits across from the Interviewer at a small table)*

C: Thank you for trusting me to talk with you about this problem. Would it be all right if Heather and Ron *(two program staff members)* stay in the room while we talk? The way I'm going to talk with you is what I'm teaching staff to do. If you are okay with letting them sit in and listen, you would be giving them a great learning opportunity. Together, we can help staff get better at what they do.

B: It's all right with me as long as it's only you and me that talk.

We all agreed and were able to proceed.

Stage 2: The Timeline

C: Brandon, things were really tense as soon as you came to school. Did something happen earlier this morning that caused you to be so upset?

B: I don't want people on my back all the time. People just need to leave me alone.

C: Someone was bothering you this morning?

B: Miss Heather came in to get us up like every morning and kept yelling at me to get up so I could get breakfast and get to school on time.

C: She yelled at you like that in a loud and angry sounding voice?

B: No, but she kept saying "get up, Brandon, get up, Brandon." (*Said with a sneering voice*)

C: Brandon, I have to ask, did she say it like that with that tone?

Brandon just smiled slightly and looked at Miss Heather, who was in the room with us.

C: So she said it in her normal voice but she said it a few times?

Brandon nodded affirmatively.

C: Do you think she really just wanted you to get up on time for breakfast and school or do you think she was trying to get you angry?

B: She was just being nice but I didn't want to get up, so I yelled at her and said some really bad things.

C: What did Miss Heather do then?

B: She just said I should make a good choice and she would be in the kitchen waiting for me.

C: So she gave you some space. Did you get up then?

B: Yeah, but all I got for breakfast was an apple and some toast to eat in the van.

C: So you were late, but she made sure you had something to eat anyway?

Brandon nodded affirmatively and looked sideways in Miss Heather's direction.

C: Were you upset about something before Miss Heather came in to wake you?

B: I was mad the whole weekend.

C: The whole weekend? Was there something going on in the house that you were having a hard time with?

Brandon put his head down. I could see tears dripping from his eyes.

C: Brandon, it looks like something happened that really has you upset. It could be lots of things, maybe with the other boys or the staff. Whatever it is really seems like it's important to you. Please give me some idea about what happened if you are okay talking about it with me.

Brandon continued to sit in silence with his head down.

C: We don't have to talk about it if you don't want to. I can see it is something important to you.

B: It's my mother again.

C: Again? I don't know what you mean when you say that.

B: She was supposed to bring my sister and come to visit me on Friday, but she didn't come.

C: Your mother and your sister were supposed to visit on Friday, but they didn't come. I'm really sorry to hear that, Brandon. I can see that really was upsetting to you. Anyone would probably be upset in a situation like that. What happened that they didn't come to visit?

B: I don't know.

C: You don't know? You weren't able to talk with her?

B: No, she didn't call and she doesn't have a phone.

C: You still don't know what happened, through the whole weekend?

B: *(Shakes his head no.)*

c: No wonder you're upset. You said *again*. This has happened before?

b: She hasn't come for visits before, but she called. This time she didn't call so I'm mad but I'm also scared something happened.

c: If she doesn't have a phone, how do you usually talk with her?

b: My aunt lives down the street and she has a phone.

c: Did you call your aunt's house?

b: Yeah, but nobody answered the phone.

c: Did the staff working this weekend try to help you find out what happened?

b: They let me keep calling and they let me call my therapist and she said she will try to find out, too, but she never told me anything. I told her she better find out something or she'll be sorry.

c: Three days must seem like a really long time when things like this happen.

b: It's really long. It was her birthday. I got dressed up and had a present for her. I made a cross from wood and painted it for her.

c: Oh, Brandon. No wonder you're so upset. Did you have problems with other people over the weekend?

b: I didn't really do anything. I yelled at the other guys and the staff, but it was no big deal.

c: You held all those upset feelings in pretty much all weekend but this morning they just came flying out. What happened this morning that made it harder to control?

b: I can't hold it in forever, you know! First Miss Heather was on my back in the house, then Miss Nancy started on me as soon as I came in to school. My mother didn't come to visit me and these women are on my back.

c: If I understand this right, you weren't very pleasant with anyone since this happened Friday but you were a little harder on the women you talked with than the other guys or male staff. Is that right?

b: (*Nods*)

c: This kind of thing gets in your way a lot, doesn't it?

b: (*Nods again*)

Stage 3: The Central Issue

In Stage Three of LSCI, the Central Issue stage, we decide what kind of intervention to use, based on what is the most important issue for the young person and the pattern of self-defeating behavior we discern from listening to their story. In this case, we used a Red Flag Tap-In Reclaiming intervention. When his mother didn't show up for this visit, Brandon's long-held painful feelings about his family were stirred up again. He took out his anger in increasing doses with the people in the house, his therapist, Miss Heather, and then Miss Nancy.

C: Brandon, this kind of waiting and wondering and worrying that you are going through is so hard. When something like this happens, it helps to talk through it. Otherwise, you just keep turning it over in your mind and it's like one of those wheels in a hamster cage. Lots of spinning, but the hamster never gets anywhere. Who do you think would be a good person to talk to about this?

B: Probably my therapist.

C: Would it be OK with you if I called her and told her about our conversation? I know that when she learns this has been bothering you, she will want to talk with you about it. What do you think?

B: Yeah, I guess.

C: OK, I'll give her a call. Maybe you could benefit from a good talk with her. I really admire how you were able to tell me about how you felt and she would appreciate knowing it too.

B: OK.

C: OK. There's just one more thing—can I try to summarize? You've had a lot on your mind this weekend. It was your mother's birthday and you put a lot of care and effort into making a gift for her. You were really looking forward to a visit from her and your sister on Friday, but they did not show up. That has happened before, but those times, you've been able to get in touch with her to know what happened. This time, you haven't been able to reach her. That has created a lot of intense feelings for you that you've been trying to keep to yourself.

B: (*Nods.*) I haven't been able to stop thinking about what might have happened. I'm really mad and really scared at the same time. It's crazy.

C: That makes perfect sense that you feel that way. Ever since Friday, all of your feelings about missed visits in the past and worry about what's happening now have been stirred up. I'm wondering if you've been taking those feelings out on the people in the house, your therapist, Miss Heather, and then Miss Nancy.

B: Yeah—I guess. I just couldn't keep it all inside!

C: That's a very mature insight, Brandon.

Stage 4: Insight

Situational insight is one way we teach self-control using LSCI. We try to help the young person recognize that in many of these crisis situations, they have some responsibility for how things turn out. But it is also important that we help them realize they also have some control and power to make things turn out differently. Many adults talk with young people in trouble about being responsible. Helping them understand that they can also have control about choices and behaviors and power to change outcomes can be a powerful experience. It is most useful if we lead the young person to insight rather than giving it to them, as is typical for helping adults who might say, "All you have to do is . . ." Leading them to insight works through effective questioning.

C: Now that you are thinking more about how your feelings from the weekend impacted your actions at school today, would you change anything if you could do any of this over again?

B: If I could change things, do you think I would be here?

C: I understand that you'd like things to be different with your family, that it is a really big thing in your life. That may be something that's too big for you to change and I know that could be really frustrating. Is there anything else that happened in this that you could make be different?

B: I tore up papers in the classroom, do you mean that?

C: That's something you might have some control over, do you think? What could you have done differently?

B: I could have just told Miss Nancy to give me some space because I was upset about my mom.

C: That's a good example. Anything else?

B: I said some really bad things to Miss Heather this morning.

C: That's another good example. What could you have done differently about that?

B: I could have just gotten up. *(Looking at Miss Heather.)* Miss Heather, I'm really sorry I said those things to you. You were just trying to help me, but I was so mad about what happened with my mom, I just didn't care about anything.

HEATHER: Thank you for apologizing, Brandon. I think I understand how badly you felt about what happened with your mom and now I know you're still worried. Maybe I can help find out if she's all right and what happened.

B: OK.

C: Do you have any ideas how we can help you so things don't get worse for you when you get so angry about things?

Stage 5: New Skills

Stage Five of the LSCI process, the New Skills stage, is another opportunity for us to teach practical skills or support skills the young person already has. In this case, I was assessing Brandon's ability to see alternative behavior choices. If he has ideas that will be positive alternatives, we can help him through practice and ongoing support with reminders of his plan to keep events from getting out of control. If the idea of what to do comes from the young person and if he has some of the skills already, there is a much greater likelihood that we will be successful in helping him because he is personally invested in the solution.

B: I could let people know when I'm mad, but they probably already know that. Staff can remind me that I don't want to make things worse. But when I'm like that, I just don't care.

C: Not long after things like this happen, though, you do care, Brandon. Now you're able to see how some of your choices made a situation that was already really hard for you even worse. Can we say or do something that will help you remember that you will care again soon?

B: Maybe they can just say that and then give me some space.

C: Let's make that our plan then. We'll ask the staff to remind you to think ahead about how you'll feel if you handle things better rather than just act on the bad feelings. Then they can give you some space. Then maybe you can talk things out. Are there people here you can talk with like you just did with me?

B: I would if they listened like you did!

C: That's what we're working on, Brandon, and you just became the best teacher for Heather and Ron since you let them sit here with us. Good work!

B: *(Smiles broadly.)*

C: What needs to happen now so we can move on, besides finding out about your mom?

B: I need to apologize to Miss Nancy and my group and fix the things I messed up. I'll probably lose privileges or something.

C: I think starting with apologies is a great idea. How do you think the apology you gave to Miss Heather worked out?

B: *(Looks at Miss Heather. She smiles at him.)* She was nice. She accepted my apology and said she'd try to help me.

C: Do you remember what you said that made the apology so effective?

B: I said I was really sorry for what I said and that I was really just mad about my mom.

C: What do you think you could say to Miss Nancy?

B: I'll say the same things—I'm sorry about all the yelling and banging things around in class. I shouldn't have taken my anger out on her and the class. I should clean up the mess I made too. When it's just me and Miss Nancy without the other kids around, I'll ask her if she can help me remember to think ahead of time about what I'm going to say and to give me extra space if I look upset.

C: I think that's a great apology and a smart plan.

Stage 6: Transfer of Learning

C: Let's get back with Miss Nancy and check in with the group to see where we go from here.

B: OK.

C: We'll let you know what's going on about finding your mom, so you don't worry that anyone forgot that important thing.

B: Thank you.

C: It's possible that it might take a few hours to get in touch with her or with your aunt. What are you going to do if you feel yourself getting angry or start thinking maybe we forgot?

B: I'll make sure I talk to my therapist and let her know I might need to talk to her again later if I'm getting upset.

C: I think that's a solid plan. Brandon, I have to say that I'm really impressed with how you've handled yourself in this conversation. You started off so angry but you really took control of yourself. I think you learned something about yourself today, which is not always easy to do. We will help you and support you through this process of finding out what happened with your family and helping you manage whatever feelings come next.

B: Thanks.

After the LSCI

Brandon's mother is developmentally disabled and diabetic. We found out that she experienced some medical problems that required a brief hospitalization on Friday. The aunt who usually provided the communication link between Brandon and his mother was out of town. His sister stayed with a neighbor for the weekend. Brandon was able to talk with his mother later that day to know she was all right and wish her a happy birthday. A visit was set up for the following weekend.

Intervention Summary

What we learn from incidents that happen with young people like Brandon is that superficial behavioral approaches to dealing with problems are not enough and they may even make things worse. Brandon did make poor choices and acted in disrespectful and irresponsible ways that did need to be addressed. Programs that react to such behavior with rote punishment, however, fail to address the painful beliefs, perceptions, thoughts, and feelings that so many challenging young people carry around with them.

> Programs that react to behavior with rote punishment fail to address the painful beliefs, perceptions, thoughts, and feelings that so many challenging young people carry around with them.

It is perfectly reasonable that people should be held accountable for their actions. When that accountability includes trusting relationships with significant adults, as well as understanding and restorative responses, more learning will occur, resulting in more meaningful and lasting growth and change.

To the corkscrew,
the knife
looks crooked.

11

THE REALITY CHECK INTERVENTION
Organizing Perceptions of Reality

Young Person's Perception:

"I see things, hear things, feel things, and remember things in my life not as they are, but as I believe them to be."

Uses:

With young people who misperceive reality due to triggering of personal sensitivities, who have blocked perceptions of reality due to intense feelings, who have a restricted perception of reality due to perseveration on a single event, who privately reconstruct their own reality, and who manipulate reality to test limits.

Goal:

To help young people organize their thinking so that a more accurate perception of reality emerges, to bring them to the realization that there is "more than meets the eye," and to help them begin to understand their contributions to the problem.

Focus:

Organizes the young person's perceptions and sequence of time, events, cause, and effect.

Young Person's New Insight:

"Maybe there is another way to look at this situation. I can see how I might have made it worse and what I need to do about it."

Isabella

Isabella is a 16-year-old high school student who tends to be impulsive and say whatever is on her mind. In class, students are assigned to complete a 10-question worksheet. Isabella takes her time on the first five questions, looking up the answers in her history textbook and responding correctly. After 15 minutes, however, she loses interest in the task. She guesses at the last five questions, recording responses without doing any research. When the teacher finds Isabella reading a magazine at her desk and realizes that only 50% of her responses are correct, she asks Isabella to put the magazine away and look up the correct answers before leaving class for the day. Isabella lashes out at her teacher, insisting that she did the work and that teachers are just out to hassle kids. Isabella then storms out of the room. When her teacher follows her, Isabella tells her teacher, "Leave me the f--- alone" and blames the teacher for causing the problem.

Have you ever been in a situation with a young person in which your perception of events was so different from theirs that you felt like you were talking about two totally different incidents? Have you been convinced that the student must be delusional because there was no way that they could believe their own version of events? Have you ever questioned your own sanity, wondering if you remembered events incorrectly since the student seemed so sure that she was right? If any of these experiences or emotional reactions ring true, chances are good you have interacted with a young person who could benefit from a Reality Check intervention.

The LSCI Reality Check intervention helps young people reorganize and clarify reality by discussing their perceptions of a problem incident and, with the adult's assistance, identifying what is real versus what is perceived or believed. For kids caught in this self-defeating pattern, the stress of a situation triggers the limbic brain and disconnects the youth from their ability to accurately recall sequences of events, connect cause and effect, and separate feelings from behavior. These young persons have been described as having "social blindness" or "tunnel vision" because they often intensely focus on an unwanted action by someone else (e.g., a remark, a laugh, an act of aggression) without considering their own behaviors. The common characteristic among young persons for whom this type of LSCI is appropriate is the inability to connect cause and effect in a series of interpersonal exchanges culminating in a problem incident.

> The common characteristic among young persons for whom this type of LSCI is appropriate is the inability to connect cause and effect in a series of interpersonal exchanges culminating in a problem incident.

Originally called a "Reality Rub-In" (Redl, 1966), this type of LSCI has its foundation in the characteristic way a young person perceives, thinks, feels, and reacts to an incident. Redl describes the rationale for this therapeutic goal:

The trouble with some of our youngsters, among other things, is that they are socially nearsighted. They can't read the meaning of an event in which they get involved unless we use huge script for them and underline it all in glaring colors besides. Others are caught in such a well-woven system of near delusional misinterpretation of life that even glaring contradictions in actual fact are glided over by their eyes unless their view is arrested and focused on them from time to time. More fascinating even are the youngsters whose preconscious perception of the full reality is all right but who have such well-oiled ego skills in alibiing to their own consciences that the picture of a situation that can be discussed with them is already hopelessly repainted by the time we get there. It is perhaps not necessary to add how important it is, strategically speaking, that such children have some of this "reality rub-in" interviewing done right then and there, preferably by persons who themselves were on the scene or at least known to be thoroughly familiar with it. (p. 44)

Use the Reality Check Intervention With Young People Who . . .

1. **Misperceive Reality Due to Triggering of Personal Sensitivities**
   This is the most common form of a Reality Check crisis. Young people come to us with a history (that we are not aware of until we take the time to listen to their story and enter their psychological world). Their history influences the way they perceive, think, and feel about life's events. During stressful situations when the limbic brain is activated, kids' perceptions become more rigid and their feelings become more intense. They are convinced that what they saw, heard, and remembered is *exactly* what actually happened during the crisis. In the heat of the moment, these young persons cannot be talked out of their convictions and are more likely to believe their own account of a crisis than any objective evidence.

> During stressful situations when the limbic brain is activated, kids' perceptions become more rigid and their feelings become more intense.

Liam

Liam is a ten-year-old student who is in the office due to acting out in class. It is his second time this week being removed from the classroom and he is worried about being suspended. His father is a strict disciplinarian and does not hesitate to spank Liam. As the crisis interventionist entered the office, he looked at Liam and began taking off his jacket, as it was warm in the room. Liam dove under the table shaking with fear. In his world, when a man takes off his jacket, it means he is going to hit you.

2. Have Blocked Perceptions of Reality Due to Intense Feelings

Sometimes, feelings such as anger, fear, and sadness become so intensely activating to the limbic brain that young people become temporarily unable to access the language centers of their brain or to effectively process sensory messages (see Chapter 2 for a full explanation). The stressed young person literally does not accurately see, hear, or remember what is happening around them. They are so angry they "see red." They are so frightened they are "scared out of their minds." They are so sad they cannot think and so anxious they cannot remember what they hear. Until the intensity of their feelings is drained off, they will continue to behave in irrational and suppressed ways.

Miguel

Miguel is a 16-year-old resident of a group home. One day at school, he is very agitated and cannot settle down. He leaves his area, wanders from the classroom, and becomes irritated and oppositional when given a direction. The assistant principal begins walking with Miguel and convinces him to sit down. Almost immediately, Miguel says, "I have to go to court and I didn't even do anything wrong! Why do I have to go to D.H.?"

By doing a careful Timeline, the assistant principal discovers that Miguel's social worker visited him earlier in the day. Miguel "remembers" that his social worker told him that he was going to court and afterward, would either live with his father or go to "D.H." (D.H. is the common reference for the detention home where juvenile offenders are held.) The assistant principal asked Miguel if there was anything else the social worker said. Miguel replied, "I don't know, something about 'S.'" Now the assistant principal has an insight. The social worker told Miguel that his custody would either revert to his father, in which case he would return home, or that his custody would remain with D.H.S., the Department of Human Services, in which case Miguel would stay at the group home.

The actual placement is not an issue for Miguel because he is comfortable living with his father or at the group home, which is just a few miles away. Miguel was fearful of having to go to the detention home; this was the source of his stress. Because of anxiety, Miguel's perception of the reality of what his social worker said was skewed.

The assistant principal was able to use the six-stage LSCI framework to guide Miguel in understanding how the intensity of his anxiety blocked his ability to realistically perceive the situation and how, in turn, the error in perception fueled problematic behaviors such as leaving the classroom.

3. Have a Restricted Perception of Reality Due to Perseveration on a Single Event

This pattern occurs when a young person responds to a crisis by focusing their awareness only on one part of the sequence of the crisis. These young people perseverate on a particular act, as if it exists without context and represents the entire crisis. In this type of Reality Check intervention, the adult's job is to help broaden the young person's awareness and see the "big picture" of events rather than continuing their tunnel vision on a singular detail.

The adult's job is to help broaden the young person's awareness and see the "big picture" of events rather than continuing their tunnel vision on a singular detail.

Samara

Samara is a high school sophomore. She takes 15-year-old Jaxon's phone and taunts him that she is going to send embarrassing texts to a girl Jaxon likes. This continues for several minutes until Jaxon becomes very upset, grabs Samara's arm, wrenches it backward, and grabs his phone back. Samara starts yelling and insisting, "Jaxon put his hands on me! He should be suspended!" Samara feels that the staff are being unfair when they do not automatically punish Jaxon. For the rest of the day, Samara insists, "It's not fair! Jaxon should be in trouble. I didn't do anything to deserve that!" Samara only focuses on Jaxon's actions without seeming to understand her role in the conflict. She doesn't recognize her behaviors that led up to the problem, only the last moments when she felt she was wronged.

4. **Privately Reconstruct Their Own Reality (Accurate Perception of Reality, Faulty Conclusion)**

   The three previously described types of distortions of reality all involve intense feelings that alter the young person's perceptions. In this fourth type of Reality Check situation, however, a young person does not deny, misperceive, or restrict sensory experiences. Rather, they are able to describe the events with accuracy but still come to the wrong conclusions. The adult's role is to help the youth consider alternate interpretations of reality and reach a more accurate conclusion.

Kaitlyn

Thirteen-year-old Kaitlyn is often absent from school, doesn't turn in homework, and rarely completes classwork. She receives an "F" on her report card. She accurately perceives the grade and knows that she is failing but concludes, "The teacher doesn't like me, that's why I'm failing." She has an accurate perception but comes to the wrong conclusion.

5. **Manipulate Reality to Test Limits**

   Young people engaging in this pattern purposefully test the limits of the adults and the setting. They look for loopholes in policies and procedures and use them to justify their behavior. The clever young person shapes reality to fit their own needs. The adult's role in this type of Reality Check intervention is to help the young

The adult's role in this type of Reality Check intervention is to help the young person understand the "spirit of the law" and move beyond their self-defeating insistence on the "letter of the law."

person understand the "spirit of the law" and move beyond their self-defeating insistence on the "letter of the law."

Shawn

Miss Foster tells her fourth grade class to walk quietly in line to the gym. Nine-year-old Shawn, who is first in line, walks but sets a pace so fast that the others cannot keep up with him. When Miss Foster removes him as line leader, Shawn becomes angry and non-compliant because he insists that he wasn't doing anything wrong. Shawn knew what Miss Foster expected of a line leader and was testing the limits.

The vignettes shared above illustrate some of the problems that are suited to the Reality Check intervention, the goal of which is to organize reality to broaden a young person's perceptions and insights. We suspect that you have found similarities with some of your own students among these descriptions.

How Trauma and Adverse Childhood Experiences Shape the Reality Check Pattern

In Chapter 2, we learned that young people with high ACEs scores and/or those who have experienced trauma may experience chronic hyper-arousal of their limbic system. When the amygdala is perpetually on alert for signs of danger, it is prone to misperceive the behavior of others. Young people who see the world through a lens of potential threats are great candidates for the reorganization of perceptions and clarification of cause and effect that happen through the Reality Check intervention.

It is helpful to remember that the brain instinctively searches for memory evidence that supports existing beliefs and perceptions. If a young person believes that others are cruel or unfair, then their brain sticks like Velcro to instances where this belief is reinforced and separates like Teflon from evidence that counters this deeply held belief. For example:

On Thursday morning, high school freshmen Diego and Miles agree to play basketball after school. During last period, however, Miles texts Diego that he can't play because he remembered that he has to take his brother to an appointment. Diego becomes furious and texts back, "YOU LIED TO ME!" He slams his phone down on his desk and yells out that he will never trust Miles again. Miles texts Diego back with an apology for having forgotten about the appointment and asks if Diego can play over the weekend, but Diego is unmoved. He continues to yell and curse that Miles is a liar who cannot be trusted, ever.

To process the situation, Diego could benefit from a Reality Check intervention that helped him gain insight into how quickly his brain attached to a negative belief, concluding that Miles was an untrustworthy liar, rather than a forgetful friend who tried to apologize and make amends for his mistake.

An additional trauma-related behavior of young people who exhibit the Reality Check pattern is that their history of feeling powerless relative to adults drives an intense need to be right in stressful situations. Feeling "right" makes them feel strong. Admitting that they are wrong would cause them to feel to feel weak and vulnerable—conditions that their limbic brain drives them to avoid. While fixed beliefs can offer a measure of comfort at times, flexibility is a social skill that enables people to adapt to new situations and adjust to changing circumstances. The Reality Check intervention is effective because it helps kids *consider* new ways of perceiving and thinking without setting up rigid right-wrong, win-lose, powerful-powerless dynamics.

> The Reality Check intervention is effective because it helps kids *consider* new ways of perceiving and thinking without setting up rigid right-wrong, win-lose, powerful-powerless dynamics.

Recall the "My Wife and My Mother-in-Law" image from Chapter 4. In viewing this image, we suggested that a child's ability to consider multiple points of view has to do with the availability and approachability of an adult who will listen and dialogue with the child. The Reality Check intervention provides a trauma-informed framework that helps young people feel heard, understood, and thus less threatened by the prospect of considering alternate points of view.

The Adult's Tasks in a Reality Check Intervention

With the Reality Check intervention, the adult's goal is to correct the young person's distorted perceptions about a problem incident. To accomplish this outcome, the adult helps the youth reduce the emotional intensity of their reaction to the crisis, carefully reconstruct the details of the incident, consider causes and effects, gain insight into the self-defeating nature of the behavior, and organize new insight into a plan for improved behavioral responses.

Sequence of a Reality Check Intervention

Stage 1: Drain Off

The Drain Off stage in the Reality Check intervention can be demanding. Young people may be experiencing a mixture of outrage, anger, defensiveness, and self-righteousness over their perception that they are right, that someone else has wronged them, and that they did what they had to do to protect themselves.

The adult's tasks in this first stage are to:

- Recognize that young people in stress have rigid ways of perceiving the world and may only be able to see from their point of view at first. They are not "just being stubborn," but rather, their perception is a belief statement.
- Manage their own emotions and guard against taking a child's pain-based behaviors personally.
- Use plenty of affirmations such as *"I can see that was hard for you to say"* and *"You are really trying to get yourself together"* to encourage further dialogue.
- Attend to the young person through calming non-verbal behaviors, re-assure them that you will help them solve the problem, validate their feelings, and begin to decode the underlying meaning of their troubling behavior.

Stage 2: Timeline

The Timeline stage in a Reality Check intervention is likely to be complicated and difficult to understand. Adults must patiently and persistently use this stage to help the young person organize perceptions into an accurate, logical sequence of events and to broaden their perspective about what may have happened. A thorough Timeline is the key to a successful Reality Check intervention.

A thorough Timeline is the key to a successful Reality Check intervention

The adult's tasks in the Timeline stage are to:

- Help the young person trace through the sequence of events, identifying who, where, when, and what happened. Identify cause and effect relationships.
- Discover the "video" of the event as it exists in the young person's mind. Use questions to work backward in time to a point before the stressful event occurred. Then, move forward to discover how the youth perceived, felt, thought, acted, and reacted to others. Summarize the order of events frequently to help organize them for the young person as you begin to shed light on a new reality.
- Use a diagram of the Conflict Cycle to help kids make important connections between events, perceptions, thoughts, feelings, behaviors, and the reactions of others. The Conflict Cycle paradigm can bring order to the young person's chaotic recollection of the incident.
- Continue to frequently validate, reassure, and affirm feelings and behaviors that were natural under the circumstances. It is essential to com-

municate to the youth during the Timeline that you are allies working together on the same problem.

- Request clarification of "questionable" points. *"What you are saying is very important and I want to be sure I have it right."*
- Watch for *signal flares*, the seemingly insignificant comments or asides that may signal an important issue. If one appears, try repeating the key word or phrase or use a follow-up question. Don't push it if the youth doesn't want to continue, but remember the comment and return to it at another time.
- Observe the youth's body language very carefully. Denial, agitation, interest, changes in body language, or silence can be indicative that you are on a meaningful track.
- Decode the youth's comments. Help the youth to connect underlying perceptions, thoughts, and feelings with surface behavior. Attempt to zero in on the answer to the question, *"What's the real issue here?"*

Stage 3: Central Issue

The Central Issue in a Reality Check crisis is that the young person has a distorted perception of the conflict due to personal sensitivities, intense emotions, tunnel vision, faulty conclusions, or testing limits.

The adult's tasks in the Central Issue stage are to:

- Review the Timeline using the Conflict Cycle paradigm to shed light on the changing "video" of the event that has begun to emerge through the conversation.
- Concisely state the central issue.
- Assess the youth's perceptions, thoughts, feelings, and motivations to change.
- Determine that the Reality Check intervention is the most suited to the desired outcome and resolution of the crisis.
- Prepare the young person to consider another perspective of the situation.

Stage 4: Insight

In this stage, our goal is to help the young person develop the insight that *"Maybe there is another way to look at this situation. I can see how I might have contributed to making it worse and what I need to do about it."*

The adult's tasks in the Insight stage are to:

- Help the young person begin to recognize the rigid patterns of perceiving, thinking, feeling, and behaving that have been driving their behavior.
- Continue using the information gathered through the Timeline to articulate a new "video" of the event in which the young person can perceive

the event from an alternate point of view and recognize their own role in the problem situation.

- If the young person accepts their role in the problem, ask if anything like this has happened before and explore the possibility of a pattern of behavior; if you know the youth, you can remind them of past experiences that fit the pattern.
- The Insight goals of the Reality Check are to help the young person:

  - Organize thinking so that a more accurate perception of reality emerges.
  - Realize that there is "more than meets the eye."
  - Understand their contribution to the problem.

- Avoid "giving" the young person the Insight, as this diminishes their sense of ownership of the new way of thinking. Rather, use questions to explore possibilities, shed light on patterns, and lead the youth to consider new ways of organizing reality.
- Acknowledge and affirm that the young person has learned something valuable and important for their life through engaging in the conversation.

Stage 5: New Skills

The purpose of Stage 5 is to help the young person consider and practice the social skills needed to be successful when they encounter a similar situation in the future. The focus should be on specific behaviors—what to do and when. Affirming a young person's ability to carry out the plan is essential for success at this stage. It is almost always difficult for young people to use new behaviors and new approaches to a problem. Without practice and abundant encouragement, they tend to fall back on old ways of behaving.

The adult's tasks in the New Skills stage are to:

- Develop a plan for success that includes both current and future situations.
- Rehearse new skills through role play and discussion.
- Anticipate challenges and consequences.
- Affirm the benefits of the young person making changes in behavior.
- Provide a window of realism while conveying confidence in the young person's ability to employ the plan for success.

Stage 6: Transfer of Learning

The last stage of LSCI prepares the young person for a transition back into the classroom, group, or interpersonal situation. It is important to use this stage to close down private topics or feelings brought out during LSCI.

The adult's tasks in the Transfer of Learning stage are to:

- Discuss what has happened while the young person has been away from the group and engaged in LSCI; plan for what the young person will do when they return and how others may react as they rejoin the group.
- Empower the young person to be successful by affirming their new insights and competence for carrying out the plan for success.
- Collaborate with other important adults to establish conditions under which the young person can practice new skills and enjoy a measure of success as they approximate their goals.

Now that you have a thorough and comprehensive understanding of the goals of the Reality Check intervention and the adult's stage-by-stage tasks, we return to Isabella, the young girl we met at the beginning of the chapter. In the pages that follow, you will get a bird's eye view of how her teacher, Ms. Foster, managed Isabella's intense emotions, facilitated the construction of a Timeline, identified the central issue of the conflict, and carried out the Reality Check process through completion.

Example of LSCI Used to Organize Perceptions of Reality: A Reality Check Intervention

"It's Friday, and I want out of here!"

Background Information

Isabella is a 16-year-old student attending an alternative school in a large urban area. Since her parents divorced three years ago, Isabella lives with her mother, who has a hard time managing Isabella's demanding behavior. Because Isabella can be so oppositional, her mother seems always to be directing and correcting her—pleasant conversation has all but ceased to exist. Isabella has poor impulse control, saying whatever comes to mind without filtering her thoughts for the effects her words may have on others. As a result, she can infuriate adults and peers and engage them easily in Conflict Cycles. Isabella is clever and a source of great amusement to her peers. At school, she often finds herself in trouble for "mouthing off." When confronted, Isabella can become verbally abusive and sometimes leaves the classroom or the building without permission.

The Incident

It is Friday afternoon, 30 minutes before school is dismissed. Isabella has had a trying day, finding it difficult to follow directions and complete her work. Yet, she has managed to stay just short of receiving disciplinary action. As the group completes a history assignment, Ms. Foster goes from desk to desk, checking each young person's work. When she reaches Isabella, she finds her reading a magazine, her completed worksheet sitting on her desk. Ms. Foster checks the answers and finds that the first five are correct, but the second five questions are not. The following dialogue takes place between the teacher (T) and Isabella (I).

T: You did these pretty quickly, Isabella. It looks like the first five are correct, but did you look up the answers for the other five?

I: (*Without looking up from her magazine*) I didn't have to look them up—I knew the answers.

T: Please put away the magazine and get out your history book. I would like you to look up the correct answers and finish the assignment before you leave.

I: (*Angrily*) I told you I don't have to look them up—are you deaf or something?

T: Isabella, the last five are wrong and you need to correct them.

I: That's bull! Those answers are good enough and you know it. I did the work so just get away from me. (*With increasing intensity*) You people around here are pathetic! All you want to do is hassle us. Then you think you can tell us we got problems! (*Stands up and begins to pace*) I've got a problem all right—putting up with your BS! Every day it's the same damn garbage! (*Shouting*) I'm not taking it anymore! (*She walks out of the room into the hallway as Ms. Foster follows, asking the classroom aide to take over monitoring the group; Isabella is leaning against the wall*)

T: Take it easy, Isabella. I don't think there needs to be an argument here.

I: Can't you understand f---ing English? I said leave me the f--- alone!

Stage 1: Drain Off

T: Isabella, it's Friday afternoon and it's been a long day for you. I can see you're very upset right now—let's try to work something out. You don't need to take it beyond this level.

I: Yeah, like you don't want me in as much trouble as you can get me in.

T: You think I want you in trouble.

I: Don't give me that innocent act. You know exactly what's going on.

T: Something is going on that's really important for you. I'd really like to understand what happened because, although it's been a long, rough day, you've been staying out of trouble. You don't want to have trouble now, so let's take a minute and work through this.

I: Fine.

T: Great, thank you for being willing to talk about this. Let's start with how you were doing when we started history?

I: When history started, I was thinking that I had less than an hour before I could get away from you.

The teacher feels her anger rising. She makes a conscious decision to ignore Isabella's personal comment instead of reacting to it verbally. She also takes a brief pause to regulate her emotions before responding Isabella. Although she does not explain her actions verbally, she is aware that young people are always watching—and often learning— from how the adults in their lives manage intense emotions. Role modeling calming skills can be a powerful part of the LSCI process.

T: So you were looking forward to finishing the day and starting your weekend.

Stage 2: Timeline

I: Yeah.

T: You weren't angry or upset then, just wanting to finish up the day.

I: Right.

T: Then I handed out the assignment sheet and said that it was due at the end of the period. How were you feeling then?

I: I started it, didn't I?

T: Yes, you did—I noticed that you got to work on it right away. That was great! Was the work difficult?

I: That's baby stuff and it's boring as hell!

T: So, you were having some thoughts about the assignment. You were thinking that it was busy work and you were feeling bored.

I: Who cares about state history anyway?

T: I can understand how you might not find it the most interesting thing to read. So, you got bored after looking up the answers to the first five questions?

I: Hell yes! What do you think?

T: Do you remember anything about how you were feeling physically when all of this was going on?

I: What do you mean?

T: Like, do you remember feeling like your heart was racing or maybe your face was feeling really hot?

I: None of that but I know I had a really tight feeling in my chest. I still kind of have it now, but it's not as bad.

T: Did it feel like it was hard to breathe?

I: No, more like I just needed to scream or hit something—you know, to release the pressure!

T: What did you do when you felt that way?

I: I knew I'd get in more trouble if I made any noise, so I took a few deep breaths and told myself over and over to settle. Then, I just got back to work and answered the other questions from what I remembered from class.

T: Wow! I'm impressed! You were aware of the uncomfortable feelings welling up in your body and you made a conscious decision to calm yourself down with some deep breaths? That's terrific. A few months ago, you wouldn't have been able to show that self-control, would you? You would have screamed or lashed out right away. That's is amazing progress and I am really proud that you thought to calm yourself down.

I: (Nods slightly)

T: So, you took some deep breaths until you felt more grounded, but you were still bored with looking up the answers so you decided to give the last five your best shot from memory. Then, I came to your desk and saw that your paper was finished and you were reading a magazine. Is that right?

I: Yeah, I was done. You always say, "Don't bother anybody when you finish your assignment," so I wasn't.

It may be tempting for many adults to take Isabella's bait at this point and quibble with the self-serving way in which she has interpreted the *teacher's rule to remain quiet after completing work. By controlling her reaction and using affirming statements (see below) rather than defensive, conflict-fueling ones, this interviewer skillfully avoids Isabella's efforts to entangle her in the Conflict Cycle.*

T: That's true, you were keeping to yourself and not bothering anyone. I noticed and I appreciate that. So, then I looked at your work and told you the last five were wrong and I wanted you to correct them. Is that right?

I: Oh, you're conveniently leaving out the part where you threatened me. Of course, you don't remember that, do you?

T: You heard me threaten you?

Stage 3: Central Issue

I: You said you were going to keep me after—and it's Friday!

T: So that explains it! Isabella, let's think through this together. What I said was that I wanted you to finish the assignment before you left. You had plenty of time to do it, and you know how you are with homework—you don't do it on weekends. So, I was just trying to get you to finish it up in class. That's all. I had no intention of keeping you after school today.

I: Yeah, right.

T: Have I ever kept you after school because your work was not done correctly?

I: You've made me miss breaks and be late to lunch to correct work.

T: True, but have I ever caused you to miss the bus because of it?

I: No, I guess not, but who's to say you weren't going to do that today?

T: You were thinking I was going to do something different today than I've done in the past and that worried you. I understand that. Tell me, where's the evidence that I was going keep you after today?

I: Well, it sure seemed like that's what you meant.

T: You know, in a way, I'm kind of glad this happened.

I: What do you mean?

T: Because it's a great opportunity to learn something. Do you see how you jumped to a conclusion before you had evidence that your conclusion was right?

I: Maybe.

T: Think back, what was going through your mind when I told you to finish the assignment correctly before you left?

I: You don't want to know.

T: Give me a clue—with respect, please.

I: I was thinking how f---ed up it was of you to keep me after on Friday just because of five questions.

T: And how were you feeling when that went through your mind?

I: I was mad as hell!

T: And how did you show me you were "mad as hell"?

I: Well I didn't throw anything or leave the building, did I?

T: That's true, you showed some control for someone that angry. Do you remember what you said?

I: I said something about all you teachers are sick.

Stage 4: Insight

T: That's right, and you left the room without permission. And all of this because of what you "assumed" I was saying. Is it possible that you let your emotions get the better of you? Instead of staying calm, thinking it through, and asking me if you would have to stay after, you let your feelings take over.

I: (Silence)

T: Has anything like this ever happened before?

I: (Slight smile) Once or twice.

T: That smile tells me you know this is a problem—jumping to conclusions, getting angry, and lashing out?

I: Yeah, well, I have a hot temper.

T: You do have a hot temper at times—and just knowing that about yourself is a giant step toward being able to change it, so I'm proud of you for that. A hot temper has to be controlled by a cool head or it gets you into a lot of trouble.

I: Tell me about it.

T: Do you see how you tend to make your problems bigger? Do you see that today you almost created a problem that could have gotten you suspended?

I: Yeah, I guess.

T: Isabella, if you could solve this problem—avoid jumping to conclusions and acting on your emotions—life would be so much easier for you. Think of how smoothly your afternoon would have gone if you had not jumped to conclusions. What can you do to work on this?

I: I don't know because when I'm doing it, I don't know that I'm jumping to conclusions. I just feel myself getting mad.

Stage 5: New Skills

T: That's an observation we can work with—the fact that you feel yourself getting mad. And when you get mad, what happens?

I: I just get mad.

T: What do you do when you get mad?

I: Whatever—I'm like on autopilot.

T: So, when you feel yourself getting mad, it's kind of like a warning?

I: I guess.

T: What does that warning feel like?

I: Everything rushes to my head and I just want to get away.

T: So, your body gives you a signal that you're about to lose it— everything rushes to your head. It's great that you recognize the signal, because you can use it like a traffic light to stop before things get out of hand.

I: Yeah, sometimes I do.

T: So, you have already practiced this, and how have you done?

I: Depends; not that great, really.

T: What can you do, then, when you feel that warning signal about anger coming on?

I: I could tell myself to chill, or something. I could tell myself to stop, so it won't get any worse.

T: Sounds like a pretty good strategy. When you feel yourself getting angry, what will you say to yourself?

I: I don't know, something like, "Chill—don't talk." Something like that.

T: Do you think it would help to silently count to ten before saying anything?

I: I don't know—maybe.

T: And when you have your emotions under control, might it be helpful to check on the reality of your conclusions—maybe ask the person what they meant? That way, you will know for sure what the person intended instead of just assuming you know what they meant.

I: What do you mean?

T: I mean, check the facts. For example, today when I told you to finish the work before you leave, you might have asked, "Do I have to stay after if I don't finish it?" Then you would have known that you wouldn't have to stay. If you had known that, would your reaction have been different?

I: I guess I wouldn't have been so mad.

T: Exactly. So, what you're saying is that in some situations you can actually feel yourself getting angry. When that happens, you will . . .

I: Tell myself to relax and be cool.

T: Then when you have your emotions under control, you will ask the person . . .

I: I'll ask the person, "What do you mean?"

T: Yes, you'll get more information. You'll check out your assumptions. Can you do it?

I: I'm going to try.

Stage 6: Transfer of Learning

T: OK, you've got a plan and you can try it out right now. When we go back to the room everyone will be finished with their work, but I'm going to give it to you as homework. Can you handle it?

I: Yeah.

T: What are you going to do if you feel yourself getting angry?

I: I'll just chill and count to ten and not say anything, then I'll make sure I know what's going on.

T: OK—let's see how you do. You know, I have to say that I'm impressed with the way you were able to handle this talk. You really want to do well, and you want to manage things for yourself. That's half the battle.

I: Thanks, Ms. Foster.

Intervention Summary

Using the verbal framework of the Reality Check LSCI intervention, Ms. Foster transformed a potential crisis into a learning opportunity for Isabella. The helping adult recognized the situation as another example of Isabella's tendency to misperceive reality due to stress or anxiety. In using the Timeline stage effectively, Ms. Foster was able to recognize that Isabella's vital interest was being able to leave on time. One can see how quickly Isabella's perception of the situation, and subsequently her feelings and attitude, changed when that threat to her freedom was nullified. Ms. Foster understood the hostility she received from Isabella was associated with the problems she is experiencing in her relationship with her mother. Ms. Foster decided that she would not decode this openly for Isabella, as displacement was not the central issue. Yet she acted on this awareness by consciously avoiding Isabella's attempts to draw her into a power struggle through sarcastic comments and swearing. Additionally, in her role as mediator, Ms. Foster considered Isabella's motivation and readiness to contribute to the plan to change her behavior. She guided the planning in Stage 5 but invited Isabella's suggestions and incorporated them into the plan. As Isabella is consistently supported in acting on the plan for success and helped to recognize when she is not using the plan, her ability to "think twice" will improve. As it does, conflicts with adults will decrease in frequency and, ultimately, her perception of herself as a competent young adult will be strengthened. This is the goal of the Reality Check intervention.

"I try to do
the right thing
but it always comes out
wrong."

THE NEW TOOLS INTERVENTION

Building Social-Emotional Learning

Young Person's Perception:

"I want to do the right thing, but it always comes out wrong."

Uses:

With young people seeking approval of adults or peers but lacking appropriate social behaviors to accomplish this.

Goal:

To teach new social-emotional skills that the young person can use for immediate positive gain.

Focus:

Help the young person realize he or she has the right attitude and intentions, but the wrong behavior. Since behavior is easier to change than attitude, the young person can successfully learn new social-emotional skills.

Young Person's New Insight:

"I have the right intention, but I need help to learn the skills that will help me make friends, achieve, and get along with adults."

Sophia

Twelve-year-old Sophia is in tears. She fell down in front of a group of her peers, who laughed at her instead of helping her get up. Sophia hit one of the girls who was laughing. A staff member told Sophia she would have to go meet with her social worker. She was angry and indignant; why should she be the one in trouble when the other kids were laughing at her?

Do you work with young people who try to do the right thing, but it always seems to turn out wrong? Young people whose social-emotional development lags behind that of their peers often find themselves in frustrating, confounding interpersonal situations. In relation to same-age peers, they tend to experience difficulty making and keeping friends, recognizing social cues, understanding sarcasm or other intended humor, managing emotions, and intuiting social norms. Teaching social-emotional skills to young people is a major way that adults can help them succeed.

> Teaching social-emotional skills to young people is a major way that adults can help them succeed.

Many young people use inappropriate or self-defeating patterns of social behavior. We identify three major explanations for this:

1. **Developmental Reasons**
   Developmentally, it is not unusual for early school-aged children to lack mastery of specific social behaviors such as starting conversations, joining play, and disagreeing without arguing.

2. **Neurodevelopmental Reasons**
   Diagnostically, deficits in social interaction are a defining feature of autism spectrum disorders (ASD) (Frye, 2018). In addition, the social maturity of children with attention deficit disorder (ADD/ADHD) can be up to three years behind that of their peers. Kids with both ASD and ADHD may have difficulty reading verbal and physical social cues, misinterpreting remarks, and/or understanding jokes. Because their responses and reactions to others are often inappropriate, it can be difficult for these kids to make friends.

3. **Trauma and Adverse Childhood Experiences**
   For young people who have experienced trauma, deficits in social-emotional skills often have to do with deprivation in terms of the role modeling of skills and the interpersonal attentiveness required for these skills to fully bloom. We will discuss this in greater depth later in this chapter.

Whether it be age, social inexperience, trauma, or a neurodevelopmental condition that underlies the lag in social-emotional skills, many of these kids have positive intentions behind their inappropriate behaviors and possess the desire to succeed. We have found over the decades that the New Tools intervention is particularly effective and well-suited to helping these young people.

> Using the New Tools intervention, an adult sees beyond inappropriate surface behavior, recognizes the (neuro)developmental need, and helps young people build the social-emotional skills they need to succeed.

Using the New Tools intervention, an adult sees beyond inappropriate surface behavior, recognizes the (neuro)developmental need, and helps young people build the social-emotional skills they need to succeed. The outcome goal of New Tools is to bring about change in a young person's ineffective interpersonal behaviors by teaching new, more adept social behaviors that bring about desired reactions from others. To accomplish this goal, the adult helps the young person realize that their current ways of expressing intentions do not bring the results they hope for. The adult uses the framework of LSCI to help the youth understand the connection between their positive intentions and the new behaviors needed to bring about these desired results.

Fritz Redl (1966) described this form of LSCI as widening a young person's "adaptational skills." In crisis and under stress, kids' defensive behaviors often break down or change form. Redl sees this as a significant time to make therapeutic gains:

> Use many of their life experiences to help them draw visions of much wider ranges of potential reactions to the same messes. . . . Even the seemingly simple recognition that seeking out an adult to talk it over with is so much more reasonable than lashing out at nothing in wild fury may need to be worked at hard for a long stretch of time with some of the children I have in mind. (p. 46)

Use the New Tools Intervention With Young People Who . . .

1. **Have the Correct Attitude and Intentions but Lack the Appropriate Social-Emotional Skills to Be Successful**
   Young people for whom the New Tools intervention is most effective are those who want to belong to a peer group, have friends, be admired by others, and have a close relationship with someone. They aspire to do well academically and to achieve in athletics, arts, technology, and

   > They have the motivation to do well but their social-emotional deficits often get in the way of desired outcomes.

other endeavors. They have the motivation to do well but their social-emotional deficits often get in the way of desired outcomes. Indeed, their behaviors often produce quite the opposite reactions in others from the ones they anticipated. The New Tools intervention is well-suited for youth who want to have friends but who communicate this by shoving, hitting, bragging, touching, or making offensive remarks about others. Likewise, the intervention works well for kids who want adult approval but who try to achieve this by contradicting, boasting, disavowing interest, posturing as know-it-alls, cheating, or clowning. When, as adolescents, these kids may take on negative, alienated postures as defensive covers for their interpersonal deficits and history of social failures, it helps to have an LSCI-trained adult who can see the New Tools pattern that underlies the sullen behavior.

2. **Experience Confusion, Frustration, or Shame by the Failures They Experience**
A key diagnostic characteristic of the Drain Off stage in this intervention is that while the young person may seem extremely angry, indignant, or tearful at first, with reassurance, validation, and decoding, these feelings often morph into confusion, frustration, sadness, and/or shame. The young person does not actively resist the adult's help as they might during the first stage of other LSCI interventions; rather, kids who exhibit the New Tools pattern typically want adults to help them understand where things went so wrong. They are baffled by the unexpected turn of events and need an adult ally to help them gain social insights and understanding.

> Kids who exhibit the New Tools pattern typically want adults to help them understand where things went so wrong.

Examples of Young People Who Can Benefit from a New Tools Intervention

Alex

Whenever eight-year-old Alex wants help with his math assignment, he taps his pencil on his desk. If the teacher ignores him, he calls out disruptively, "Come over here! I said, 'Get over here!'" Versions of Alex's disruptive and disrespectful behavior toward the teacher are fairly commonplace whenever adults make assignments for Alex to do work independently. What is Alex's intention? His intention is to accomplish the task successfully, but it is obscured in his defensive attempts to capture the teacher's attention and reassurance without appearing to need help. New Tools conversations that recognize Alex's intention to succeed academically and help him develop the interpersonal skills he needs to appro-

priately enlist aid from a teacher can bring about significant long-term gains for Alex in a school setting.

Logan

Logan is a 16-year-old young man who, due to developmental delays, frequently has difficulties interacting with others. He often uses phrases from TV shows or songs to communicate. He wants to have friends and wants to be liked but is often made fun of and excluded by his peers. A group of youth are playing Monopoly in the living space of their group home. Logan starts playing music for everyone to hear. He then gets up and starts to rap incredibly inappropriate and sexual song lyrics to his peers. The kids get angry and tell him to shut up and leave them alone. Logan gets upset and walks away to his room, where he punches holes in the wall. When processing the incident with an adult later that afternoon, Logan indicates that he wanted to be "one of the guys" and that he knows to be "one of the guys" you have to "do things like sex and stuff." He said he thought that if he sang vulgar sexual lyrics, then his peers would think that he was sexually experienced and therefore "cool" enough to be included in their group of friends. Logan had the right intention of wanting to make friends and be involved, but he went about it the wrong way.

How Trauma and Adverse Childhood Experiences Shape the New Tools Pattern

Before moving on to study the impact of trauma and adverse childhood experiences on young people, it may be helpful to further define social-emotional learning and the important role that social skills play in a young person's life. Social-emotional skills have dozens of functions, including enabling kids to:

- Manage emotions
- Connect with others
- Make and maintain healthy relationships
- Experience empathy and compassion
- Gain awareness of thoughts and feelings
- Express themselves appropriately
- Solve problems and resolve conflicts
- Manage stress
- Make appropriate decisions

Young people start learning social-emotional skills from the day they are born. Babies develop early social-emotional skills through caregivers who consistently meet their needs, provide safety, and model emotions through face-to-face interactions. From toddlerhood through adolescence, social-emotional skills are continuously cultivated by kids' caregivers through everyday modeling, responsiveness, encouragement, co-regulation, and specific instruction (e.g., "This is how to ask a friend to play," "This is how to say I am sorry").

As noted earlier in the chapter, deficits and lapses in social-emotional skills can be directly connected with a young person's stage of development or a neurodevelopmental challenge such as ASD or ADHD. In other cases, however, a child's inappropriate interpersonal behavior can be seen as evidence of deprivation and trauma. According to the CDC (2020), adverse childhood experiences such as neglect, abandonment, and inconsistent caregiving can impair a person's ability to form connections with others, regulate emotions, and form healthy, stable relationships. When primary caregivers are absent, abusive, neglectful, or inconsistent, young people grow up without fundamental role models for how to interact in socially acceptable ways. Since relationships are the agents of change (Perry, 2017), a young person with under-developed interpersonal skills is hampered by two problems: (1) the lack of social-emotional skills and (2) the inability to connect with an adult who can teach them the social-emotional skills they need to be successful. LSCI is a process that can reverse both problems, successfully connecting young people with helping adults and then, through the positive relationship, building the social-emotional skills kids need to go on to build additional supportive connections with others.

An especially challenging part of the New Tools pattern is that young people often unwittingly create exactly the social situations they fear and hope to avoid. For example:

Oliver is a high school freshman with a history of alienation from teachers and peers in middle school. When his family moves to a new state, he is excited about the opportunity to make a fresh start in a new school. Oliver is nervous about the change, however; he desperately wants to feel liked and accepted in his new school but carries the belief that he is unlikable and incapable of having positive relationships. On the first day of school, Oliver keeps his earbuds in all day and refuses to speak to any of his teachers or classmates. On his walk to seventh period, he pulls his sweatshirt hoodie over his head and makes finger guns at kids walking by him in the hall. When asked to speak with the school counselor, Oliver expresses outrage: "I knew this place would suck just like my old school! You people are all the same—just trying to make problems for kids and assuming we're all going to shoot up the school or something!"

His behavior, driven by his self-concept and beliefs about others, led him to behave in ways that brought about the exact outcome he hoped to avoid. *This is the essence of self-defeating behavior.*

Keep in mind that Oliver truly wanted a fresh start and to be liked in his new school! Yet his behavior, driven by his self-concept and beliefs about others, led him to behave in ways that brought about the exact outcome he hoped to avoid. *This is the essence of self-defeating behavior.* To get the fresh start he craves, Oliver needs an adult who is trained to look beyond his threatening surface behavior and uncover the anxiety that is driving it. Oliver needs help understanding the cause-and-effect patterns of his school experiences and to learn new social-emotional skills that can help him elicit the type of friendly responses that he craves from teachers and peers, rather than the repetitive reactions of fear, alienation, and punishment.

Internalizing vs. Externalizing the Impact of Traumatic Stress

Before leaving this topic, an interesting distinction when talking about the impact of trauma and adverse childhood experiences is the one made between "externalizers" and "internalizers." Externalizers are those who tend to outwardly express emotional pain, lashing out verbally and physically toward others. Kids who engage in Red Flag and Reality Check patterns of behavior (as well as the Benign Confrontation and Set Up patterns covered in upcoming chapters) tend to externalize their feelings. Internalizers, on the other hand, tend to turn their pain inward, experiencing embarrassment, personal shame, and guilt along with feelings of worthlessness and powerlessness. Young people who benefit from the New Tools intervention tend to internalize problem incidents, seeing themselves as deserving of the rejection and punishment that their inappropriate social behavior sometimes elicits.

> Young people who benefit from the New Tools intervention tend to internalize problem incidents, seeing themselves as deserving of the rejection and punishment that their inappropriate social behavior sometimes elicits.

The Adult's Tasks in a New Tools Intervention

A trusting relationship with the helping adult is essential to the effectiveness of the New Tools intervention. For this reason, it is less often used during the initial stages of a young person's time with a teacher or in a new program setting, when kids typically spend time defending against adult help and support. Once beginning trust develops and a young person wants to experience interpersonal successes, the adult can serve as a model for the youth and use a range of techniques to build social-emotional learning.

In comparison to the two LSCI interventions we have studied thus far—and to the

> The child is beyond *active resistance,* meaning they want to do the right thing but lack the social-emotional skills to be successful.

three remaining interventions featured in Chapters 13 to 15—many people find the New Tools intervention easier to learn and practice. This is because in a New Tools crisis, a young person has good intentions and genuinely wants help from adults. The child is beyond *active resistance,* meaning they want to do the right thing but lack the social-emotional skills to be successful. There is often a strong sense from early on in a New Tools conversation that the adult and child are on the same side. The adult's task in the New Tools intervention is to help the young person make the connection between the good intention and the wrong behavior and then to teach the child how to apply new social-emotional skills to real life situations to bring about more desired outcomes.

Sequence of a New Tools Intervention

Stage 1: Drain Off

In a New Tools crisis, a young person may present initially with anger or rage. With the use of Drain Off skills, however, these intense emotions typically "soften" into feelings of confusion, frustration, anxiety, shame, or embarrassment. The young person's amygdala has been hijacked by the unexpected reaction they received from others when they were trying to do something positive.

The adult's tasks in this first stage are to:

- Maintain reassuring communication, letting the child know that you are there to help and you want to understand what happened from their point of view.
- Validate the young person's feelings through phrases such as *"You're feeling confused about why things didn't turn out the way you expected."*
- Use plenty of affirmation to acknowledge and encourage the youth's efforts to calm down.
    - *"You're doing a great job settling down and getting ready to talk about this."*
    - *"I can see that was hard for you to say."*
- Manage your own reactions. For some, the New Tools intervention evokes little counter-aggression because the young person is relatively open to help. Yet others report finding it frustrating to work with young people who don't pick up on social cues. In all types of LSCI crises, the adult must regulate their own thoughts, feelings, behaviors, and reactions. Our task is to help, not to express exasperation at who "should have known" that an inappropriate joke would cause an angry reaction.

Stage 2: Timeline

Perhaps the hardest part of the New Tools Intervention is to initially identify a young person's positive intentions and desire for socially rewarding results. This is the task during LSCI Stages 2 and 3. Using decoding skills, the adult should validate these intentions if a young person is not able to convey them directly. Then, it is important to support and affirm the young person by reinforcing that what they want from others is desirable and achievable. Throughout the process, providing empathy, warmth, and real concern for the young person's feelings is essential.

The adult's tasks in the Timeline stage are to:

- Discover the "video" of the event as it exists in the young person's mind.
- Use questions to work backward in time to a point before the stressful event occurred. Ask questions such as:

  - *Why don't you begin by telling me a little bit about how your day started . . .*
  - *Were you upset about something before you were with the kids at recess?*
  - *You said that when you fell down, the kids were laughing. Tell me what caused you to fall . . .*
  - *You told me that you and Lexi have been becoming better friends lately. Did something happen to change that?*

- Then, move forward to discover the sequence of events that seemed to cause the stressful event. Seek to have the youth verbalize how they perceived, felt, thought, acted, and reacted to others. This powerful part of LSCI helps move the stressor from the limbic brain to the neocortex, where access to the brain's language centers can aid in effectively processing the events.
- Make sure to ask questions that enable the young person to articulate their intentions:

  1. *What were you trying to do when you grabbed her shoulder?*
  2. *What did you imagine would happen when you gave Mr. Felker that picture?*
  3. *What were you hoping she would say when you told her who you liked?*
  4. *When you hid her phone, what did you think she would do?*

- Use paraphrasing and restating to highlight the connection between their good intention and the inappropriate behavior.
- Summarize the order of events frequently, using a diagram or sketch of the Conflict Cycle. It is particularly important in a New Tools crisis to be explicit with concrete details that a child can readily grasp.

- Provide abundant affirmation to encourage the young person to keep exploring the conflict and to confirm that you are an ally and a support who shares the child's desire for a positive outcome.

Stage 3: Central Issue

The Central Issue in a New Tools crisis is that the young person has the right intentions and attitude but the wrong behavior.

The adult's tasks in the Central Issue stage are to:

- Summarize the Timeline using the Conflict Cycle paradigm to shed light on the child's positive intention.
- Concisely state the central issue.

> The Central Issue in a New Tools crisis is that the young person has the right intentions and attitude but the wrong behavior.

Stage 4: Insight

In Stage 4, our goal is to help the young person develop the insight that *"I want to do the right thing, but I need help to learn to do some things better. I know if I get help and practice, things will improve. I can learn to choose the right action and be successful in making friends, fitting in, getting along, following rules, getting good grades, and achieving success in the things I try to do."*

The adult's tasks in the Insight stage are to:

- Clearly articulate the Insight for the young person who, more so than others, likely needs you to be very clear about what you now understand:
- *Wait a minute. Hold on. Are you saying:*
  - *You teased _____/you grabbed _____ because you wanted to connect with her, because you were copying how the other kids acted, because you wanted to fit in, etc.?*
  - *You copied _____'s homework because you are really trying to get good grades this term?*
  - *You shouted out in class because you wanted to show the teacher that you had finally figured out the answer that had been stumping you?*
- *You have the right intention/idea/attitude! You were trying to make friends/fit in/do the right thing/get good grades/please the teacher, etc.*
- *We have the same goals for you that you have for yourself.*
- *Having the right intention is the hard part! Remember at the beginning of the year when you didn't care about making friends/following rules/succeeding*

academically? But now you do! What you're telling me is that you were trying to do those things. That's great! That's progress!

- *It's easy to learn the skills you need, now that you have the right idea! Let's figure out a better way to help you go about achieving your goal. I'll help you.*

Stage 5: New Skills

Stage 5 is particularly important to the long-term success of a New Tools intervention, as the young person's primary need is to learn and practice the social-emotional skills that will help them bring about more desirable outcomes. The focus should be on replacing inappropriate behaviors with new, more socially adept ones. As always, it is essential to convey hope and affirm the young person's ability to carry out a plan for success. Rehearsal of new skills is essential in this dynamic!

The adult's tasks in the New Skills stage are to:

- Teach the social-emotional skill(s) the young person needs to bring about desired outcomes and responses from others. In many cases, the adult and child can use the here-and-now situation as a springboard for brainstorming and practicing new skills. There is also an abundance of material available in print and online for teaching social-emotional skills to young people.

  - The Collaborative for Academic, Social, and Emotional Learning (CASEL) sets national standards for SEL policy, practice, and research and is a great place for professionals to begin looking for resources (www.casel.org).
  - Michelle Garcia Winner's Social Thinking™ methodology provides evidence-based strategies to help people ages four through adult improve social competencies (www.socialthinking.com).

- Help the young person anticipate and plan for things that may go wrong as they try out new social-emotional skills. Put Plans B and C in place, just in case.
- Follow up with the young person soon after the New Tools intervention to ask how things went. Affirm all positives, especially their follow-through on the plan! Help the child recalibrate any efforts that did not turn out as planned.
- Establish a regular check-in schedule with the student. Building social-emotional learning is not a once-and-done process but rather one that is best achieved through consistent conversation, calibration, trial, error,

teaching, and re-teaching. When a young person knows they have an adult ally in their social-emotional learning corner, they are more likely to persist through this ongoing learning process.

- Don't be discouraged if change does not occur rapidly. It is difficult to quickly change old coping strategies that typically have developed over several years to protect the young person from feelings of rejection, alienation, or inadequacy.

Stage 6: Transfer of Learning

The last stage of LSCI prepares the young person for a transition back into the group dynamics or interpersonal situation. Because the conditions under which the young person left were likely painful or embarrassing, it is essential for the adult to help the child plan for how they will calmly respond to peers, adults, and any programmatic consequences.

The adult's tasks in the Transfer of Learning stage are to:

- Summarize the connection between the original positive intention and the new skill(s) the child has learned to try to bring about desired outcomes.
- Affirm the young person's competence for carrying out the plan for success.
- Plan for what the young person will do when they return and how others may react as they rejoin the group.
- Inform other staff of the plan. Ask them to support the young person upon their return and to affirm when the new social-emotional skills are used.
- Encourage restorative practices to resolve issues involving adults and peers.

Now that you have a thorough and comprehensive understanding of the adult's stage-by-stage tasks in a New Tools intervention, we return to Sophia, the teenager we met at the beginning of the chapter. In the pages below, we offer you a bird's eye view of the way a helping adult used Drain Off skills to de-escalate Sophia's initial indignation, then helped highlight her positive intention through the Timeline stage. By connecting her right idea to a wrong behavior, the adult helped Sophia gain new insight into previously misunderstood social dynamics. The adult was also effective in communicating that he was on Sophie's side and eager to help her achieve her goals of making and keeping friends. This New Tools intervention helped a once-alienated teen feel understood, supported, and empowered to achieve desired social outcomes.

Example of LSCI Used to Build Social-Emotional Learning: A New Tools Intervention

"It was a friendly punch."

Background Information

Sophia is a 12-year-old girl who has lived in four foster homes. She has a history of witnessing severe domestic violence in her early childhood. At present, she is significantly behind in her progress toward school graduation. Sophia often finds herself in conflicts that result in physical altercations at school and in her neighborhood. These incidents often leave her confused and struggling to connect with others and keep friends. She enjoys her experience in the after-school program she attends and has made positive connections with a couple of the adults running the program.

The Incident

Sophia punches a peer, accusing the girl of laughing at her. When adult staff intervene and separate Sophia from the group of kids, she is indignant! She wants to know why she is the one getting in trouble when the other kids started the whole thing. "They were the ones laughing!" she insists. "Why am I always the one in trouble?" she demands to know. Below, we observe the conversation between Sophia (S) and a caring adult (A) as Sophia recovers from the incident. You'll notice that the Drain Off stage happens more quickly than in previous interventions you have read. This is accounted for by the fact that there is an established trust between Sophia and the adult, so the de-escalation goal is reached relatively quickly.

Stage 1: Drain Off

A: Sophia, what's happening?

S: You don't care and no one else does either!

A: You sound really sad. I hear you saying that you feel nobody is there for you.

S: Well no one ever listens to me!

A: Can I try?

S: You wouldn't understand.

A: I can tell that something is going on that is really important for you. I'd really like to understand.

S: Haley hates me.

A: You think that Haley hates you. That *is* an upsetting thought. Walk with me, Sophia. Let's take a deep breath together and see if we can figure this out.

Stage 2: Timeline

A: Before we start, tell me a little bit about what you notice in your body right now.

S: What do you mean?

A: Well, from your voice and your words, it seems like you are feeling really sad. I am wondering if you can feel those sad feelings in your body too?

S: You mean like how my head is pounding right now?

A: Yeah, like that. Do you know why your head is pounding?

S: I think it's because I was trying so hard not to cry.

A: It's okay to cry if you want to. Crying is a way to let some of your sadness out. It might even make your head feel better.

S: (*Pauses; let's out a long, deep sigh*) No, I'm OK now. It's not pounding as badly.

A: I'm glad. It's hard to think straight when our heads are pounding, isn't it? It helps to just take a pause like you did. So, who's Haley?

S: Haley's my so-called friend. At least I thought she was.

A: Sounds like something happened between you and Haley.

S: Duh. All I did was go up to her and she pushes me away and laughs with her friends. I hate when people laugh at me!

A: Well, I can understand not liking being laughed at. She pushed you?

S: She pushed me, and I tripped right in front of everyone. They all started laughing at me and I felt so stupid. When I hit one of the girls who was laughing, I got pulled out by the staff and now they're going to make me meet with my social worker. Why should I be the one in trouble when the other kids were being mean?

A: It sounds like things got complicated fast. Where did this all take place?

S: In the hallway.

A: OK. What happened right before Haley pushed you?

S: Nothing. All I did was come up behind her in the hall and grab her by the shoulder.

A: Grab her by the shoulder? What do you mean?

The interviewer is using a clarifying question here to make sure that their understanding of Sophia's intention in grabbing Haley's shoulder is aligned with Sophia's understanding. Asking questions to discern the young person's intentions is a critical part of an effective Timeline.

S: You know, grab her. Like, knock into her. Kind of like a friendly punch from behind. I was trying to surprise her.

A: Do you mean surprise like scare or surprise like being friendly?

S: Being friendly. I wanted to tell her about the media project we've been working on in class.

A: Oh, you were trying to be friendly. You wanted to start a conversation with her?

S: Right.

A: That's great, Sophia. I'm glad to hear you are trying to connect with other kids here. Is Haley someone you usually get along with?

SA: Yeah, we've been working on this project for the last few days and I thought she was my friend.

Stage 3: Central Issue

A: You've told me a lot here and really helped me understand the situation so much better. Thank you for trusting me, Sophia.

S: You're welcome.

A: It is OK if I just say it back to you in my own words so that I can be sure I've understood everything you said? You can correct me if I miss anything. Sometimes it helps me to put everything in order.

S: Sure, that's fine with me.

A: Great. So, you were walking in the hall and you saw Haley. You walked up to her from behind and sort of knocked into her—like a "friendly punch" you called it. Is that right so far?

S: Yes.

A: Great. Let me clarify one thing here: since you were coming up to her from behind, did Haley know you were there? Was she expecting the punch?

Having already clarified Sophia's positive intent in grabbing Haley's shoulder, the interviewer now uses clarifying questions to help Sophia understand how her well-intended act could have been misinterpreted by Haley.

S: Well, no, I mean, how could she? She didn't see me before it happened.

A: Ahh, okay. So, she didn't see you or expect the punch. Do you think you took her by surprise?

S: I guess I did.

A: OK, so you were walking in the hall and you surprised Haley by giving her a friendly punch from behind. You said that you wanted to tell her something about the media project you've been working on.

S: Right.

A: Are you saying that when you knocked into Haley, you were trying to get her attention to talk to you? That you were trying to be friendly?

S: Yeah, exactly.

A: Well, Sophia, that's really good to hear! You were trying to be social. You had the right idea—but something went wrong. You expected Haley to turn around and then you would start talking about the media project. But that's not what happened. What did happen?

S: She turned around and just punched me really hard.

Stage 4: Insight

A: Were you surprised by Haley's reaction?

S: I was shocked!

A: You were completely surprised! That was not the reaction you were going for at all, was it? Sophia, tell me again in your own words what you thought was going to happen. When you saw Haley in the hall and decided to punch her shoulder from behind, what did you expect would happen next?

S: I don't know. I guess I thought she'd be glad to see me. That she'd stop talking with everyone else and talk with me.

A: You wanted her to see you and talk with you?

S: Yes.

A: You know, Sophia, I think you've got the right attitude about all this.

S: What are you saying?

A: Well, here you were, trying to connect your friend. That's something that's been difficult in the past and now you're trying. That's a good thing.

S: Sure, a good thing I got in a fight again, right?

A: No, the fight wasn't that helpful, but I'm talking about what you intended—to connect with your friend and have a good time.

S: Well, then why am I in trouble? And why does it make me feel so bad?

A: I guess one reason might be because when you grabbed Haley by the shoulder, to her it felt more like being punched. And then things got worse after that.

S: Yeah, they did.

A: But even though things got a little worse, you and I have learned something really important. You really wanted the right thing out of this—conversation with a new friend. That's the hard part—getting to the point where you are ready and eager to reach out to other kids and form friendships. The trouble is that you went about getting her attention in a way that wasn't so effective. But that's an easy thing to fix. We can work together on better ways to get a friend's attention.

S: If I could do that, a lot of my problems would go away.

Stage 5: New Skills

A: Well, I think you've got the right idea about making friends, now we just have to think about some new, better ways to get Haley's—or anyone's—attention when you want it.

s: What do you mean?

A: You know, thinking up ways that you could get someone's attention that don't involve hitting. Have any ideas?

s: I don't know.

A: Well, if you had to get my attention, and you didn't want to hit me, how would you do it?

s: I would say something. I'd say your name.

A: That's a great idea! You'd call out my name to get my attention. What if I didn't hear you? What could you do then?

s: I could say it again. Or I could say it louder.

A: Those are both great strategies. Now, let me ask you this: would you come up from behind or in front of me?

s: In front, I guess. I wouldn't want to scare you. Maybe that's what happened to Haley.

A: You're on to something, Sophia. I think you are right. So, next time you want to start a conversation with someone, you'll try to get their attention by calling their name and approaching them from the front so that you don't take them by surprise or scare them. Let's do a practice run. I'll pretend I'm Haley and you try to get my attention. (*Stands up, walks to different part of the room*)

s: This is weird.

A: Ha ha, I know. But practicing is the best way to learn how to do something new. Do I make a good Haley?

s: (*Laughs*) Fine. "Hey Haley!"

A: (*Pretends not to hear her*)

s: (*Louder*) Hey Haley, what's up?

A: (*Still does not turn around*)

s: (*Walks around the adult to approach from the front*) Hey, Haley, how's it going?

ADULT-AS-HALEY: Oh, hi, Soph. Good, what's up?

s: Not much, just wanted to tell you what we did in class with the media project today.

ADULT-AS-HALEY: Cool.

A: OK—now, let's say that Haley says "hi," but then she turns back and starts talking to her friends. What would you do then? Let's practice that.

S: I don't know. I might feel embarrassed or like she's dissing me. What should I do?

A: What do you normally do if you see that an adult is talking to another adult?

S: I just stand there quietly and wait until they're done with their conversation.

A: That's a perfect thing to do with a friend too. If they say "hi" but then return to their conversation, you don't need to take it personally or feel bad. You can just hang back a bit and wait until they are done talking.

S: If I'm in a hurry, I can just say "hi" and tell them I'll talk to them later.

A: You are really thinking this through now, Sophia! It sounds to me like you have a plan for how to approach a friend, what to say, how to say it, and what to do if they can't give you their attention right away. Can we be sure to check in again so you can tell me how this plan works with kids over the next few days?

S: Sure.

Stage 6: Transfer of Learning

In the distance the adult sees Sophia's peers gathering to head out on a field trip and uses it as a cue to review and generalize Sophia's learning and finish the conversation.

A: Look, there's the group headed out to the van. If you were going to catch up and join them, how would you do it?

S: I guess I'd run over and say "hey" and ask them where they're going. I'd say I want to go, too.

A: Nice idea! Want to try it?

S: Sure.

A: Can I ask you one more thing? You said something about having to meet with your social worker. Any ideas about what you might tell her you learned from all this?

S: I guess I could tell her I'm trying to make friends and not trying to hurt people.

A: She'd probably like to know that about you.

S: Can I go catch up with the others?

A: Sure. And thanks for talking. Let's talk again when you get back, OK?

S: OK. Thanks for listening. I didn't think you had the time.

A: Sophia, I will always make time when you want to talk.

S: OK. See you later.

Intervention Summary

Notice the ingredients present in the final stage of the conversation. First, there is a focus on how Sophia will reenter the activity. Second, there is a connection made with the outcomes or consequence of the incident (e.g., talking with the social worker) and an attempt to connect her new learning to that coming situation. Finally, there is a future connection indicated through the invitation to talk again later. This is important as it communicates the intent of the adult to follow through and reassures Sophia of the support offered to her.

Social interactions require a variety of complex communication skills from young people. Some of these skills include interpreting social cues, recognizing how behavior is affecting others, and understanding how one is perceived by others (Greene, 2008). When young people struggle with such skills it can lead to frustration, misunderstanding, and even violence perceived by others as intentional harm to others.

In this situation Sophia had the right idea (e.g., connecting with a friend), but lacked the skills (e.g., entering a group, recognizing how she was perceived) to carry it out. She was confused, embarrassed, and shamed by the experience with her peers. Given what we know about her background, it is not a surprise this is a pattern in her daily life. Part of this is the result of the prior relational trauma she has experienced from exposure to domestic violence and multiple placements in foster care. She has learned a lot from the social interactions that have been modeled for her in the past.

An interaction like this "involves thought and planning; it is not as spontaneous as it appears" (Stuart, 2013, p. 297). The adult knew the child and had an awareness of her patterns of behavior. It was part of the larger process of being with her and interpreting her experiences (Freeman & Garfat, 2014). This process and intervention can only be facilitated through "being with and participating with people in the everyday moments of their lives" (Garfat & Fulcher, 2012, p. 15).

> Through this brief and focused conversation, a caring adult entered into Sophia's conflict and supported her in making meaning out of it and using it as an opportunity for learning.

Through this brief and focused conversation, a caring adult entered into Sophia's conflict and supported her in making meaning out of it and using it as an opportunity for learning. The stages of LSCI provided the adult with a framework to guide the conversation. It is a much-needed alternative to what this young person might otherwise receive as punishment, lecturing, or further shame—all of which further distance her from connecting with others in meaningful ways. It is an example of a positive strategy many young people need and one step toward reclaiming her from the experiences she missed in her childhood.

"I do
what I have to do."

13 THE BENIGN CONFRONTATION INTERVENTION
Challenging Unacceptable Behavior

Young Person's Perception:

"I do what I have to do even if it hurts others. I have to take care of 'Number One.' I have a reputation to maintain. I have no need to change."

Uses:

With young people who are too comfortable with their harmful behavior, who receive too much gratification from hurting others, and who justify their antisocial behavior in a guilt-free way.

Goal:

To make a particular behavior uncomfortable by confronting the justifications and decoding the self-serving narcissism and secondary pleasure the young person receives from the unacceptable behavior.

Focus:

Helps young people realize that they are paying a high price for justifying their exploitation of others; they are tricking themselves into believing their causes are just.

Young Person's New Insight:

"Maybe I've been deceiving myself. Maybe I can take care of myself without hurting others. Maybe there are other ways to handle things and still maintain my pride. Maybe I am paying too great of a price for my behavior."

Eric

Eric is a 14-year-old middle school student with a reputation for aggressive behavior. During gym, his team lost their softball game. Eric is furious with Mason, his teammate, for making disparaging comments about him during the class. After gym, Eric hurries to be the first student out of the locker room. He waits for Mason in the hallway. When Mason exits the locker room, Eric jumps him. He knocks Mason to the ground, then continues to kick him until school resource officers approach. When Eric sees the officers, he puts his hands up and says, "He's the one who started it!"

Young people for whom the Benign Confrontation intervention was developed often behave in ways that appall and alienate the people in their lives. They may lie, cheat, steal, and hurt others, all while appearing to take pleasure from the pain they inflict. For many adults, it is easy to label these young people as bullies, juvenile delinquents, or antisocial, and to assume that they cannot be helped. What we know, however, is that the young people who work the hardest at severing ties and alienating others are also the young people who need adult connections most desperately.

> Young people who work the hardest at severing ties and alienating others are also the young people who need adult connections most

Likewise, many observers use the negative phrase "manipulative" to describe these youth. Through the trauma-informed lens of LSCI, however, we see them as survivors of complex trauma who have developed strategies to get their needs met. Because they have become adept at doing so, they have little motivation to change their behaviors. (If you are reading this text in order, you'll recognize that the Benign Confrontation intervention, therefore, offers a starkly different approach from the New Tools pattern described in the previous chapter.) The LSCI process can be highly effective with kids who justify unacceptable behaviors and seem unmotivated to change.

Unlike other types of LSCI, this intervention is used to confront behavior by *increasing* the young person's anxiety about what they are doing and saying. It is important to acknowledge that many people prefer to avoid confrontation. This intervention challenges adults to develop a set of skills often outside of their professional comfort zone, as it relies on the process of *benign confrontation* to stir up some anxiety and guilt in an individual who is too comfortable causing others pain. Later in the chapter, we will thoroughly define and explain the skill of benign confrontation, so that you can add it to your professional skill set.

The Benign Confrontation intervention is used with young people who have developed self-defeating ways of protecting themselves from feelings of guilt by shifting responsibility and fault to others. Fritz Redl originally called this approach the "Symptom Estrangement intervention" and described what is needed by these young people as follows:

> The Benign Confrontation intervention is used with young people who have developed self-defeating ways of protecting themselves from feelings of guilt by shifting responsibility and fault to others.

> Our children's egos have, in part, become subservient to the pathological mechanisms they have developed. They have learned to benefit from their symptoms (behaviors) through secondary gains, and therefore are in no way inclined to accept an [adult's] idea that something is wrong with them, or they need help. . . . We use many of their life situations to try to pile up evidence that their pathology [behavior] really does not pay or that they pay too heavily for what meager secondary gains they draw from it. It is not a simple matter of arguing these children into letting go of their symptoms [behaviors]. We must enlist part of their "insight" into wanting the change. . . . And, our actions [adults' daily behavior and values] have to be well attuned to our words in this interview more than others. (pp. 44–45)

The outcome goal of this LSCI intervention is to challenge unacceptable behavior, increasing young people's anxiety about what they are doing and saying to the point that they have some understanding and motivation to change their self-defeating pattern.

Use the Benign Confrontation Intervention With Young People Who . . .

1. Do Not Seem Motivated to Change

These young people generally receive so much natural reinforcement that they do not believe anything is wrong with the way they behave. Simply put: their behavior is netting them what they want. Therefore, they have little motivation to change or give up their power position in the peer group or with adults they can control.

2. Have Well-Developed Verbal Skills That They Use to Try to Control the Conversation

Young people for whom the Benign Confrontation approach is appropriate often use their well-developed verbal skills to avoid talking about an incident or to shift the focus of the conversation. They try blame, distractors, role reversals, and other ploys to divert the adult from the issue. Often these young people switch from one tactic to another until they are successful in confusing and frustrating the interviewer. A consistent strategy among such young people is their attempt to control adults and to divert the focus of the LSCI through justifications and rationalizations.

> A consistent strategy among such young people is their attempt to control adults and to divert the focus of the LSCI through justifications and rationalizations.

3. **Justify Their Aggressive Behavior**
   In this intervention, we will often refer back to the *cognitive traps* and *defense mechanisms* described in Chapter 4, as these young people rely frequently on both to justify their verbally and physically harmful actions. The youth for whom the Benign Confrontation approach was developed do not readily assume responsibility for their behavior. While they do typically admit that they committed the act in question, they adamantly insist that they are not to blame: either it was the other person's fault, the person had it coming, the adult should have known, or they express some other way to deflect responsibility for their actions. Later in this chapter, we further examine three basic justifications used by young people who are caught in this self-defeating pattern.

4. **Cast Themselves Into the Role of Victim and Respond Aggressively**
   Using a series of justifications and rationalizations, these young people try to convince others that they are the actual victim in the situation and that their aggressive responses were merely defensive. For example, a young person in the Benign Confrontation pattern might say:

   - *"He kept staring at me. He knows I don't like to be stared at. I told him to stop. I even warned him about what I'd do if he looked at me again. When he did, I had no choice but to follow through. Otherwise, the other kids would have thought I was weak. So, yeah, I punched him. I actually went easy on him. He should be grateful."*
   - *"I go to work every day and I work hard. My boss is so stingy, he doesn't pay any of us enough. I only took money from the register once and it was only because my boss took out too much in taxes from my check! It wasn't fair. So, I just took back what he should have paid me in the first place."*

5. **Receive Secondary Pleasure From the Pain They Cause to Others**
   For these young people, there is satisfaction in dominating interactions and controlling others. When they inflict pain, hurt, or loss on others, they gain a

sense of power. This feeling of power can seem almost irresistible to a young person who has experienced powerlessness in other aspects of their life. At the same time, empathy and compassion are under-developed skills for these youth. Part of the LSCI intervention process is touching on these core social-emotional deficits with the goal of reawakening them, over time, through the power of connection with a trustworthy adult.

6. **Appear to Be Very Comfortable in Their Approach**
   Because the behavior of these young people nets them what they want (power, control, possessions, etc.) and because their empathy is often under-developed, these kids tend to appear very comfortable when talking with adults about their behavior. A hallmark of the Drain Off stage in this intervention is that the young person typically appears calm and collected, if still a bit hostile and defensive of his "justified"

   > A hallmark of the Drain Off stage in this intervention is that the young person typically appears calm and collected, if still a bit hostile and defensive of his "justified" behaviors

   behaviors. Likewise, the Timeline stage in a Benign Confrontation intervention is typically less like editing a videotape of tangled emotional events and more like gathering facts as an articulate young person weaves a self-serving version of an incident. The child is not afraid to tell you what they did: *yes, they hit someone, yes, they took the money, yes, they lied*—but they are comfortable with the behavior because they have ready justifications for all of it.

Basic Justifications Used to Control the LSCI Conversation

We have discovered three basic justifications young people use to divert adults from the focus of the intervention:

Basic Justification No. 1: "He Started It"
- *"It would never have happened if he had left me alone."*
- *"He was staring at me."*
- *"He gave me the finger."*
- *"She blocked me online."*
- *"He was laughing at me."*
- *"He took my seat."*
- *"She pushed me first."*
- *"He was looking for trouble and he found it."*

Using "he started it" thinking, young people *magnify* (see Cognitive Traps in Chapter 4) the actions of someone else in order to justify their own revenge. Within this basic justification, a youth might try to convince an intervening adult that punching a classmate is the equivalent, deserved response to the classmate's "egregious" act of sitting in their seat on the bus.

Basic Justification No. 2: "It's No Big Deal"
- *"You're making a big deal out of nothing."*
- *"We were just playing around. We already shook hands and made up."*
- *"I guess she didn't get the joke; I was only kidding. She takes everything so seriously."*
- *"It was an accident."*
- *"What's the big deal? I didn't use the (stolen object)."*

Using "it's no big deal" thinking, young people *minimize* their own self-serving behaviors in order to avoid confronting its cruel or excessive nature. For example, following an incident in which a youth steals a staff member's phone, the youth might use the "it's no big deal" justification during an LSCI conversation by saying something like, *"It was just a prank. I was going to give it right back. How was I supposed to know there would be a family emergency and her husband wouldn't be able to reach her for so long? It's not my fault. He could have just called the school phone if he needed to reach Mrs. Bender."*

Basic Justification No. 3: "No One Would Have Done Anything"
- *"I didn't tell staff about it because I knew they wouldn't do anything."*
- *"I'm not a baby. I don't run and tell the teacher. I handle my own problems."*
- *"I have a right to take care of myself."*
- *"My father said if anyone messes with me, I should punch first and ask questions later."*
- *"Everyone has a right to protect their reputation."*

Using "no one would have done anything" thinking, young people *jump to conclusions* about what an adult would have done and justify the independent actions they took despite the availability of an in-charge adult who could have managed the problem. Under the cover of this basic justification, a youth rationalizes taking the matter into their own hands.

These basic justifications are most often used by the young person during the early stages of LSCI, particularly during Stage 2 as the adult builds a Timeline. It is extremely helpful for the reader to become familiar with the three basic justifications, and the variations on how they are articulated by youth, in order to properly diagnose the Central Issue of the Benign Confrontation pattern: that the young person is tricking themselves into believing that their harmful behavior is justified. Also, by listening for rationalizing words and phrases early in the intervention, the skilled LSCI practitioner can come back to them in Stage 4 to help the young person develop Insight into the pattern of self-deceit that occurs when they insist that their behavior is justified, despite plentiful evidence to the contrary.

Examples of Young People Who Can Benefit from a Benign Confrontation Intervention

The following vignettes illustrate typical problems of young people who can benefit from LSCI that challenges their unacceptable behavior and disallows its continuation:

Alani

A book brought to school by Ava for a fifth-grade group project has disappeared. After discussion with the group and a search of the room, the book still cannot be found. As the students get ready to leave for the day, the teacher notices a sizable lump in Alani's coat that turns out to be the book. As the subsequent LSCI begins, Alani shows no remorse or guilt about taking the book from her friend. She calmly defends herself by saying, "I was planning to return it. It's not a big deal." When the teacher continues to probe for the details in LSCI Stage 2, Alani changes her response to, "Ava shouldn't have brought it to school in the first place. Everything gets ripped off around here." During Stage 3, as the teacher begins decoding Alani's behavior, her responses change again: "Someone stole my book about three weeks ago."

Alani's teacher sees the necessity of benignly confronting Alani's defenses (it's no big deal, it's Ava's fault, and everything gets ripped off at this school) by pointing out that she is deceiving herself if she believes she can take somebody else's possessions and say it is okay.

Will, Cayden, and Rob

In the hall, near the high school boys' restroom, Rob flips Will's pen out of his pocket. Will starts chasing Rob. As they run, Rob bumps into Cayden, who is watching from the sidelines. When this happens, Cayden grabs Rob's hand and twists it until Rob drops to the floor in pain. When Rob is on the floor, Will comes over and kicks him in the head. The teacher hears the commotion and finds Rob rolling on the floor in pain. When asked what happened, Cayden and Will reply that Rob has been teasing them, that Rob started it, and that Rob finally got what was coming to him. They show no concern about their cruel tactics, but actually seem pleased about it.

Their teacher takes Will and Cayden to a conference room for a group LSCI that focuses on the event and their inappropriate behavior. The outcome goal for this LSCI is to confront Will and Cayden's defense that they had the right to hurt Rob. The necessary insight for the boys is that it is not okay to justify such a violent response to their class-mate's non-violent flipping of Will's pen. Though the boys initially persist in rationalizing that Rob started it, the teacher benignly confronts this rationalization and causes them each to experience some anxiety over the pleasure they derived from being cruel to Rob.

Wade

During third-grade social studies, students are working independently on a map project. Wade raises his hand for help. As the teacher starts over to Wade, Anthony says, "Why are you helping that dummy?" Wade jumps up and hits Anthony in the face. The teacher pulls Wade away. He immediately justifies his behavior, saying, "I solved the problem because I knew you wouldn't have done anything about it."

The focus of this LSCI intervention with Wade is to confront his justification that he had the right to hit Anthony. During the Timeline stage, the teacher should ask:

- *Who is the person in this class that's in charge of dealing with students when they call each other names?*
- *How did you know I wouldn't have done anything?*
- *Is it possible that if you had given me a chance to address Anthony's behavior, I would have done so, and then you would not have been able to justify hitting him? I'm wondering if hitting him is what you really wanted to do in the first place.*

The goal is to create some anxiety in Wade by pointing out that he is not a mind-reader and that he didn't know what the teacher would have done had he told her. Instead, he used this justification to sanction his harmful behavior without feeling guilty.

How Trauma and Adverse Childhood Experiences Shape the Benign Confrontation Pattern

A youth who exhibits the Benign Confrontation pattern is externalizing their traumatic stress (see Chapter 12 for further detail on internalizing vs. externalizing patterns). Their inner working model—developed through repeated adverse experiences early in their lives—tells them that to survive, they must prioritize their needs over anyone else's. This "me first" way of thinking often creates strong counter-aggressive reactions in

> Egocentrism coming from trauma is not about a feeling of importance, but rather a sense of irrelevance.

adults who observe the unacceptable surface behaviors. Indeed, if judged only by observable behaviors, these kids do appear to be selfish, self-centered, and devoid of empathy. When we practice looking beyond behavior, however, we understand that egocentrism coming from trauma is not about a feeling of importance, but rather a sense of irrelevance. Young people who have never felt important or worthy of love sometimes take a path in which they ruthlessly watch out for their own needs at the expense of others.

Over and over again, we find that the young people who are caught in the Benign Confrontation pattern have endured significant and lasting trauma early in their lives. When we view their unacceptable behaviors through the lens of surviving complex trauma, we are better prepared to respond as instillers of empathy and compassion, role models of trustworthiness, and teachers of better behavioral responses. As helping adults, we have a tremendous opportunity to change the inner working models of these young people over time. LSCI gives us the framework for how to do it.

Externalizing Behaviors of Youth in This Pattern

To enable caring adults to recognize the impact of trauma and adverse childhood experiences on these youth, we identify five characteristic externalizing behaviors:

1. **Self-Serving Thoughts and Defenses**
   Young people in the Benign Confrontation pattern tend to exhibit faulty ways of thinking and get stuck in cognitive traps, such as *magnification*, *minimization*, and *jumping to conclusions* (described earlier in this chapter, under Basic Justifications). They also commonly employ the defense mechanisms of *projection* and *rationalization* (described in Chapter 4 and below):

   - **Projection:** These youth attribute intolerable feelings to others. When a young person casts themself in the role of the victim, rather than the aggressor, they can justify their behavior and alleviate any guilt, e.g., *"He started it, not me. He created the problem, I just solved it."*
   - **Rationalization:** Their ability to justify their aggression frees them from feeling guilt or remorse over their behavior, e.g., *"I gave him a warning. I even told him twice. If he'd have listened to me, I wouldn't have had to hurt him."*

   > Young people that exhibit the Benign Confrontation pattern tend to be estranged from the core social-emotional skills of empathy and compassion.

2. **Lack of Normal Feelings Toward Others**
   As noted earlier in the chapter, young people that exhibit the Benign Confrontation pattern tend to be estranged from

the core social-emotional skills of empathy and compassion. This can show up in several forms, including:

- **A lack compassion for non-violent crimes**: *"What's the big deal? So, we took a few social security checks from their mailbox. It's not like we robbed them inside of their home or caused any physical pain."*
- **Lack of trust for adults**: *"I didn't ask Mr. Peterson for help because he wouldn't have done anything about it. He never helps kids like me."* Kids who have been abused or treated poorly by adults in their past often overgeneralize their hostility and mistrust to all adults.
- **Lack of boundaries regarding ownership**: *"If people don't lock their car doors, what do they expect to happen to their valuables? People steal from me all the time, so I just steal from them."* In this "me first" pattern, kids show little regard for "ownership" and consider it OK to take something if they want it. In their minds (and based on their experiences), if you're bigger, smarter, faster, or stronger, you are entitled to other people's stuff.

3. **Extreme Narcissism**

   Experts at the Mayo Clinic (2020) describe narcissistic individuals as ones who have an inflated sense of their own importance, a deep need for excessive attention and admiration, a belief that they are deserving of special treatment, and a lack of empathy for others. In the Benign Confrontation pattern of behavior, narcissism tends to be prominently displayed through:

   - **Need for instant gratification**: These youth exhibit the need for instant gratification. If they have an itch, they scratch it. If they have an impulse, they act on it. For these kids, hard work and study take a backseat to shortcuts and immediate fulfillment of desires, e.g., *"Why would I work for minimum wage when I can make $1,000 a day running drugs in my neighborhood?"*
   - **Desire for status and superiority**: These young people expect that others around them will recognize their superiority, even without any achievements to show for it. They exaggerate their intelligence, their athleticism, their popularity, and their talents. They can become preoccupied with fantasies about success and wealth. There is an external desire for status—clothes, possessions, attractive friends, etc.
   - **Self-centered**: These kids rarely think that group rules or limits apply to them. They are not interested in hearing about others' problems or points

of view. They monopolize conversations, expect special favors, and take advantage of others to fulfill their own desires.

- **Massive denial, based on rigid pride**: Even when caught red-handed, these young people often refuse to admit mistakes. A superficial bravado and a reliance on defense mechanisms makes them present themselves as infallible.

4. **Active Impulses**

These youth tend to dominate others, seek sensory input, take risks, and face fears. For example:

- **Anger is power**: Power is the ability to have influence over others. These young people know how to intimidate others without resorting to violence. They dominate peers who tend to give in, give up, be subservient, and enhance the youth's status.
- **Sensation seekers**: van der Kolk (2014) notes that traumatized people often seek adrenaline-creating activity (driving fast, breaking rules, evading authority) and background noise (e.g., often wearing headphones) as a way of combatting vague feelings of emptiness and depersonalization. While fear and rage are not experienced as "comfortable" emotions, it is also true that the absence of feelings of duress can feel uncomfortable to a person accustomed to being flooded with stress hormones. It is important for adults to recognize that when a young person seeks pain or danger, it may be their (self-destructive) efforts to simply feel alive.
- **Fear is weakness**: Fear is the brain's response to threatening situations. It prepares us to act in self-preserving ways. Many young people in this pattern equate fear with weakness, however, and go to extremes of behavior to prove to themselves and others that they are fearless, invincible, and therefore strong. They seek adrenaline-boosting activities that help them feel powerful and strong in the face of danger.

5. **Reject Feedback From Adults**

These youth tend to show hostility or indifference toward adults. They see adults as removed or irrelevant, based on their history of poor connections with adult caregivers. When an adult says, "*This is unacceptable*," a young person in this pattern may say, "*I don't have to listen to you.*" They may think to themselves, "*You've got nothing worthwhile to tell me. You can talk to me all day and it won't make a difference. When you get done, I'll do whatever I want.*"

The Function of Externalizing Behaviors

Many young people with histories of trauma in infancy and childhood develop distorted perceptions of reality, self-serving thoughts patterns, and entrenched defense mechanisms as strategies to survive chronic stressful situations. To the outside world, their lack of empathy, aggression, and manipulation appear deplorable. Yet, just below the surface of these narcissistic behaviors, lies a very fragile self-concept that's vulnerable to the slightest criticism. When their bravado is disturbed or peeled back, caring adults realize that many of these young people:

> Just below the surface of these narcissistic behaviors, lies a very fragile self-concept that's vulnerable to the slightest criticism.

- Harbor deep feelings of insecurity and shame
- Are keenly aware of their vulnerabilities and imperfections
- Experience significant depression
- Have difficulty coping with change
- Have difficulty making and maintaining close interpersonal connections

A goal of LSCI's Benign Confrontation intervention is to awaken a sense of human connection in these youth and to foster the social-emotional skills and interpersonal relationships that have been missing from their lives. Through positive relationships, adults can guide these resourceful kids to get their needs met without violating the rights of others.

The Adult's Tasks in a Benign Confrontation Intervention

With the Benign Confrontation intervention, the adult's goal is to create anxiety about the youth's entrenched, self-serving value system. To accomplish this outcome, the adult uses a non-threatening yet direct approach that appeals to the young person's narcissism, exposes their self-deceptions, and ultimately helps the youth choose non-harmful behaviors to accomplish their goals and meet their needs.

When new insights have been achieved, these young people usually need follow-up LSCIs with a change in therapeutic focus to learn substitute social-emotional skills for achieving what they need from others in more appropriate ways. It is also essential that the environment and the adult's own behavior do not continue to reinforce the young person's unacceptable behavior. It takes many LSCIs to bring about lasting changes in the youth's behavior, but the message will get through!

Sequence of a Benign Confrontation Intervention

Stage 1: Drain Off

The Drain Off stage in a Benign Confrontation is often quite brief. Sometimes, it is barely necessary at all. Unlike the other interventions we have studied this far, in which young people are overwhelmed by anger, indignation, frustration, confusion, or embarrassment, youth in this dynamic tend to be very in control of their feelings. We would describe their demeanor as well-regulated. They have access to the language centers of their brain and are able to clearly tell an interviewer about what happened.

The adult's tasks in the Drain Off stage are to:

- Actively manage any counter-aggressive feelings that surface while observing the youth's apparent comfort with their harmful behavior.
- Call on any positive feelings they have about the youth in order to interact in a non-threatening, non-adversarial manner.
- Affirm the youth's willingness to share their story.

Stage 2: Timeline

In the Timeline stage, the youth typically offers a "just-the-facts" personal account of the situation. For the most part, they are truthful in providing information, though the adult must use skilled listening to discern whole truths from partial ones and use careful questions to reveal convenient omissions from the story. While the Timeline may initially seem easy to construct because of the young person's calm willingness to talk, this stage of the Benign Confrontation requires a high level of skill from an adult and must be conducted with great attention to detail.

The adult's tasks in the Timeline stage are to:

- Maintain focused communication, control personal feelings and reactions, and avoid moralizing all while still clearly conveying disapproval of the behavior.
- Appeal to the young person's narcissism, noting the intelligence, planning, or cleverness that it took to carry out a particular behavior. Note: appealing to the young person's narcissism *does not equate to condoning unacceptable behavior.* Effective examples of this technique in the Timeline might sound like:
  - *"Oh, so you are telling me that you've mastered the art of stealing. You quietly watch people in the halls and figure out their locker combinations instead of having to break them open."*

- *"It sounds like you really understand people. You know what makes them tick. You knew just what to say to get Javier angry enough to punch Connor."*

- Identify the young person's basic justification(s) for the unacceptable behavior, e.g., *"He started it"* or *"Nobody would have done anything about it."*

- Use questions to dig into the "fine print" of the young person's story. Listen for what is *not* being said. If something seems to be missing from the story or if facts don't add up, ask about it. Encourage the youth to provide additional information, context, and detail.

- Decode behavior, revealing feelings young people are protecting or gratifying. To this end, you are exposing young people's defenses to themselves. There is always the risk that they cannot hear it and will close down or defend more vigorously. When this happens, secondary interpretations of the denial are required (see Chapter 6 on levels of decoding). Adults must be quick-thinking and verbally facile.

- Illustrate how these young people pay too heavily for the small gains they get from their behavior. Explain that there are more gratifying ways to obtain what they want and to feel better.

Stage 3: The Central Issue

The Central Issue in a Benign Confrontation crisis is that the young person tricks themselves into believing they are justified in hurting or violating the rights of others.

The adult's tasks in the Central Issue stage are to:

- Summarize the Timeline using the Conflict Cycle paradigm to shed light on the sequence of events that has been revealed through the conversation.

- Concisely state the central issue.

- Restate the basic justification(s) used by the young person.

- Assess the youth's perceptions, thoughts, feelings, and motivations to change.

- Determine that the Benign Confrontation intervention is the most suited to the desired outcome and resolution of the crisis.

- Prepare the young person to consider that it is not okay to trick themselves into believing that their behavior was justifiable and that they are paying a heavy price for their self-deception.

Stage 4: Insight

This intervention is named for the skill that takes place during the Insight stage—that of *benign confrontation*. Benign confrontation is not an in-your-face, anger-escalating, make-the-person-admit-what-they-did kind of authoritarian tactic, but rather a quiet and reflective verbal intervention skill in which the adult gently but openly shares thoughts about a young person's unacceptable behavior (Long, Long, & Whitson, 2016). To be successful in carrying out this intervention, adults must strike a delicate balance between communicating respect for the child and directly confronting their unacceptable behaviors. The key to doing so is returning to the information provided by the young person in the Timeline and Central Issue stages.

> Benign confrontation is a quiet and reflective verbal intervention skill in which the adult gently but openly shares thoughts about a young person's unacceptable behavior.

The adult's tasks in the Insight stage are to:

- Summarize earlier stages of the intervention, zeroing in on details that the youth is trying to avoid in their retelling of the story.
- Identify specific behavioral justifications they used and help the young person begin to recognize their pattern of self-deception. For example:
  - If a youth justifies revenge by magnifying the issue and saying, "*He hit me first. I have a right to defend myself,*" helpful adult responses include:
    - How hard did he hit you, on a scale of 1–10? How hard did you hit him back?
    - It's interesting that I have seen you let your friends hit you harder than that.
    - Defending yourself is okay in some situations, but *defense* means that you respond with enough strength to get the person to stop what they are doing. What you did went way beyond defense—you attacked him. Then you tried to justify your cruelty by calling it self-defense.
    - If he was hurting you, why didn't you tell an adult in charge?
  - If a youth justifies revenge by minimizing the issue and claiming, "*It was just a joke. We made up,*" helpful adult responses include:
    - In a joke, both people enjoy what is happening. In this situation, only you and your friends were laughing.

- The word for that is not "joking," it's "cruelty," and this is an unacceptable way for you to act.
- If a youth justifies revenge by jumping to conclusions and claiming, *"No one would have done anything,"* helpful adult responses include:
  - I have a thought about why you took matters into your own hands. I think a part of you likes being in charge/likes having others scared of you/likes causing others pain. You could have told an adult, but you chose not to take those steps because you wanted to be in charge/intimidate others/cause pain.
  - I need to make it very clear to you that that is not okay to justify your revenge by claiming that no one would have done anything.
  - The truth is that adults would have done something if they had been aware of the situation and you knew that. You didn't want them to intervene and so you chose to hurt her before anyone had the opportunity to stop you.
- Benignly confront the youth's various justifications, causing them to think twice about their self-deception and begin to feel a level of anxiety over the pain they have caused.
- The Insight goals of the Benign Confrontation intervention are to help the young person:
  - Recognize that they have been deceiving themselves through their justifications of harmful behavior.
  - Understand that they are paying too great of a price for their self-deception.
  - Accept that there are different, more acceptable ways they can get their needs met.

Stage 5: New Skills

Just as there was very little need for Drain Off in this intervention, there is rarely a need to teach new social-emotional skills *at this point in time.* While the young person for whom the Benign Confrontation intervention is appropriate can benefit from increasing their capacity for self-awareness and empathy, the New Skills stage is better used to create a bit of anxiety in the youth, leaving him with the nagging thought that he is too smart to trick himself into believing his cruelty is justified and that it's costing him a lot to maintain his guilt-free façade.

We compare this technique to the act of dropping a pebble into the young person's static pool of thought. Whereas the pool water had once been completely still due to the youth's entrenched justifications of his behavior, we seek to create ripples of a new pro-social awareness that fan out endlessly into the youth's consciousness, to the extent that even when he is not actively thinking about the problem incident, somewhere in the back of his mind is the nagging thought that he can no longer justify his cruelty. In the Benign Confrontation intervention, explicit social-emotional skill-building and rehearsal is replaced with creating new self-awareness and increasing the youth's regard for the feelings of others.

The adult's tasks in the New Skills stage are to:

- Drop a pebble of insight into his static pool of thought.
- Use silence purposefully to give the young person time to come face-to-face with the Insight.

Stage 6: Transfer of Learning

The last stage of LSCI prepares the young person to transition back into previous surroundings. It is likely that the young person, in whom you have created some feelings of anxiety and self-doubt, will be relieved to finish the conversation. At the same time, however, the experience should have been a respectful one, in which the youth felt respected as a person and gained a level of respect for you, given your calm ability to see through his excuses and justifications.

The adult's tasks in the Transfer of Learning stage are to:

- Determine a plan for restoration or restitution, as needed.
- Inform other adults of the outcome of the conversation. Alert them to the justifications used, so that they, too, can benignly confront the justifications if used in the future.
- Expect that you will have a similar conversation with this young person in the future. The Benign Confrontation is a powerful intervention that can bring about long-term behavioral changes in young people, but it is also an approach that requires repetition in order to the build trusting connections with the child that enable us to peel away entrenched defenses and instinctual justifications of behavior.

You now have a new way to understand young people who justify harmful behaviors and seem unmotivated to change. You are also newly equipped with stage-by-stage strategies to confront and change their self-defeating pattern of behavior. In the pages below, we return to Eric, the young boy we met at the beginning of the chapter. Play close attention to how the assistant principal, Mr. Byrd, skillfully connects with Eric during the early stages of the intervention, appealing to his narcissism by acknowledging his right to be upset along with his self-control, planning and strength. Yet, note that Mr. Byrd never wavers from his disapproval of Eric's brutal actions. Watch how the assistant principal uses the LSCI framework to benignly confront Eric, expose his self-deception, and guide the youth to question his pattern of aggressive behavior.

Example of LSCI Used to Challenge Unacceptable Behavior: A Benign Confrontation Intervention

"He got what he deserved."

Background

Eric is an overweight 14-year-old boy attending a middle school in a tough part of the inner city. He has had a weight problem most of his life and is very conscious of his inability to compete with his peers in sports or athletic activities. Since his pre-adolescent years, Eric has developed a low tolerance for heckling by other young people and has been known to retaliate with violence. He has a reputation for being a dangerous character, and most of the other young people stay out of his way.

The Incident

On a beautiful spring day, Mr. Brown, the physical education teacher, took the class outside for a game of softball. As he usually does, Mr. Brown selected two young people to serve as team captains. Each captain alternately selected one student at a time to form the two teams. As their names were called, the young people would join the captain who had selected them, and the growing groups loudly advised each captain who to select or not to select from the dwindling group. Eric hated gym to begin with, but he was further humiliated when Mr. Brown chose to select teams this way, as he was almost always the last one called. On this day, he again was the last to be selected and as he quietly walked over to join the team who was stuck with him, Mason remarked, "Now for sure we're going to lose with him on the team." Eric glared at Mason but said nothing. The game went on and each time Eric was up to bat, Mason would make another disparaging remark. Ultimately, Mason's prophecy came true and his team lost. As the group walked back to the gym, Eric overheard Mason comment to another student, "If it wasn't for that fat ass, we would have won."

When the dismissal bell rang, Eric made sure he was the first one out of the locker room. The young people poured out into the crowded hallway, and as Mason came through the door, Eric grabbed him by the front of his shirt and slammed him against the lockers. He then struck Mason a second time, throwing him off balance. As Mason fell to the floor, Eric began kicking him in the upper body. When Eric saw the school resource officers coming, he stepped away and put his arms in the air. "No need to get rough—I've got no fight with you. He's the one who started it." he said. As one officer attended to Mason, the other escorted Eric to the office where he was to meet with Mr. Byrd, the assistant principal. The following interview took place between Eric (E) and Mr. Byrd (T).

Stage 1: Drain Off (Practically Nonexistent)

T: Eric, let's start by telling me what happened.

E: What happened is that jackass got what he deserved. That's it. That's all.

T: You're saying that Mason deserved a beating? Can you explain that to me?

E: He thinks he can run his mouth like that, it's gonna cost him.

T: OK, you're going to have to help me out. What did he say that got you so angry?

E: He's talkin' about me, that's what.

Stage 2: Timeline

T: Where was he talking about you, in the hallway?

E: No, in gym.

T: Can you tell me what he was saying?

E: He was saying the team would lose because I'm no good. He was making all kinds of disrespectful remarks he wishes he hadn't made now.

T: Did Mr. Brown have the class divide up into teams?

E: Yeah, and Mason was telling everybody not to pick me on the team.

T: That must have been pretty hard for you to take. It's embarrassing to have that kind of attention called to you. It's understandable that you were angry about it. What did you do?

E: I just looked at him hard.

T: You didn't say anything, you just looked at him?

E: Yeah, but he saw me—he knew what that look meant.

T: What did the look mean?

E: It meant "Shut up or I'll kick your ass."

T: How do you know Mason understood that when you look at him it means "Shut up or I'll kick your ass?"

E: He knew—everybody around here knows that when I give them that look, they better keep quiet.

T: So, you have a reputation as a guy who will fight if he feels someone is disrespecting him.

E: That's right. I don't take no stuff from nobody.

T: So, Mason was making disrespectful remarks about you, and you gave him a look. He saw you. You believe he knew your look was a warning, and he kept on making comments?

E: That's right, so I busted him.

T: But you didn't bust him right then.

E: No, I waited until he came into the hall, then I jumped him.

T: Why did you wait until he came into the hall? Why didn't you bust him right when he was making comments?

E: See, that's what I have to do. I can't get around as good as Mason, so I have to wait 'til he comes to me.

T: I think I'm beginning to understand. Tell me if this is correct. You were in gym, Mr. Brown had the class divide into teams, and Mason was telling his captain not to pick you. That made you angry, so you gave him your look and figured that was a warning to him to stop. But he didn't stop. During the game, he made other remarks about you making the team lose. You were furious and decided that since Mason didn't heed your warning look, he deserved to be beaten up for disrespecting you. Since you can't get around as well as Mason, you waited in the hallway to jump him. Is that right?

E: Yeah, that's right. I warned him, he disrespected me, he's hurting.

Stage 3: Central Issue

T: You know, Eric, I'm kind of surprised that you didn't go off on Mason right there in gym. You could have found a way to get close enough to bust him, but you didn't. Instead, you gave him a look which you thought was a warning. A few months back, do you think you would have given him a look, or do you think you might have busted him right there?

E: I probably would have just busted him.

T: But this time you didn't; you showed some self-control. This time, you planned your revenge. Tell me about that.

Here, the interviewer is using the technique of appealing to Eric's narcissism. Without sanctioning Eric's specific behavior in any way, he is asking questions that allow Eric to provide details about how he planned the attack on Mason. Note (below) how the interviewer continues to ask clarifying questions that allow him to gather critical detail, while simultaneously resisting the counter-aggressive urge to pass immediate judgment on Eric's responses. This sets the stage for later in the intervention when Eric's meticulous planning can be benignly confronted.

E: I moved up to the door so I could be the first one out in the hall, then I waited for Mason to come out.

T: That was a well-thought out plan. That way you could be sure to grab him before he had a chance to run.

E: Yeah, that's right. I was making sure he was going to get what he had coming to him.

T: When he came out into the hall, did he see you?

E: Yeah, he saw me, but he didn't know I was going to kick his ass.

T: So, you took him by surprise; you didn't give him a chance to fight back.

E: No, I clocked him right away. That boy went down!

T: You jumped him and hit him hard—can you tell me where you hit him?

E: In the throat.

T: In the throat—how hard did you hit him?

E: I gave him a good shot—not as much as he deserved though.

T: So, you hit him hard enough to be sure to hurt him. What happened after you hit him?

E: He went down.

T: You mean he fell?

E: No, man, I dropped him. Boy was hurtin'!

T: So, he was in a lot of pain. What did you do after he went down?

E: I kicked him a few times, so he'll remember not to mess with me anymore.

T: So, while he was lying on the ground, you kicked him? Where did you kick him?

E: Wherever, I don't know.

T: In the face?

E: Yeah, maybe.

T: So according to your description, it was a pretty brutal attack and Mason never even had a chance to defend himself because you jumped him.

E: So, what? He attacked me first! I was settling the score.

Stage 4: Insight

T: There's no question that Mason should not have made disrespectful comments about you, Eric, and it's understandable that it would make you angry, but as I listen to your story, there are a few things I don't understand—maybe you can clarify them for me. You were in gym class and Mason made a negative remark about you; you looked at him to warn him, but he didn't seem to get it because he made several more remarks, is that right?

E: Yeah, he kept on even after I stared him down.

T: What Mason did was wrong. We have a rule here that says everyone has the right to be treated with respect and dignity, and Mason violated that rule. Did Mr. Brown hear him?

E: I don't know.

T: Well, Eric, here's the part I don't understand. If Mason violated a school rule, and the teachers are here to enforce the rules, why didn't you tell Mr. Brown about it?

E: (*Laughing*) Tell Mr. Brown? What for? He wouldn't have done anything.

T: How do you know he wouldn't have done anything?

E: Man, Mr. Brown likes those jock guys. He wouldn't have done one thing.

T: But how do you know? You never gave him the chance. How do you know that today he wouldn't have done something?

E: I just know.

Note the shift in the interview that is about to occur. In an effective Benign Confrontation, there is ample time for the adult to engage in dialogue with the young person, followed by a time where the adult calmly and directly challenges the young person about the unacceptable nature of their behavior. Notice how Eric's demeanor changes in response to the benign confrontation—from a surface defensiveness and arrogance to a much more thoughtful silence.

T: Well, Eric, I have an idea why you didn't tell Mr. Brown. You didn't tell him because you were concerned that he might do something to stop Mason. And if he did, you wouldn't have had any reason to beat him up. And what you wanted was a reason to make him hurt. In some ways, a part of you seemed to get some pleasure out of causing pain to Mason. You decided not to follow the rules of the school, and instead you followed the law of the street; get the guy when he doesn't expect it and do as much damage as you can before you're stopped.

E: (*Silent, becoming visibly uncomfortable*)

T: See, what you did, hitting Mason in the throat and kicking him in the face when he was down, was a cruel and brutal act. And you are sitting here telling me that it's OK because he made some comments about you. You are tricking yourself into believing you had a right to brutalize another person, and you don't. Think about this, Eric, you've been beaten on before. You know what it's like to be hurting—you don't like it, and you are telling me that it's OK for you to cause that kind of pain to others. As long as you keep fooling yourself into thinking you did nothing wrong, you'll find that you are the one who is paying a high price for the momentary pleasure of getting back at someone in a brutal way.

E: (*Silent*)

T: Have you thought about what the consequences of your actions today will be?

E: I don't care.

T: I just have to think that you are fooling yourself again, Eric. You might be expelled, and you might be facing assault charges in juvenile court. I know you've been working hard on some things and I know that's not what you want for yourself.

E: I don't care.

Stage 5: New Skills

T: Eric, it doesn't have to be this way. You have a lot on the ball. You're intelligent and creative. You have a whole lot going for you. I'm not saying you shouldn't get angry when someone says disrespectful things about you. But do you see how you create huge problems for yourself when you hurt others?

E: (*Silent*)

T: Your silence tells me that you're thinking about the choices you made. That's good, because you've shared your pattern of self-defeating behavior, Eric. Every time there is an incident in which you take the law of the streets into the classroom, we're going to remind you of this pattern and what it will cost you. We want to see you make choices that will make your life better, not worse. I want you to think about that. Just think.

E: (*Silent*)

Stage 6: Transfer of Learning

After a period of sitting together in silence, as a purposeful tactic to increase Eric's anxiety as he comes face-to-face with the cruelty of his behaviors, Mr. Byrd asks another staff person to remain with Eric while he privately discusses an appropriate course of action by the school. Mr. Byrd returns to the room, shares the plan with Eric, and remains with the student until his parent comes to the school for a conference and to take Eric home.

Mr. Byrd used this crisis as an opportunity to help Eric see his actions as brutality rather than bravado. If Mr. Byrd had simply administered the consequences without helping Eric gain some measure of insight, Eric would be adding the school administrators to the list of people who are devaluing him. This LSCI makes it troublesome for Eric to hold on to his comfort with causing pain to others, and that is the goal of the Benign Confrontation Intervention.

"I don't just have feelings; I am 'had by' my feelings."

14

THE REGULATE AND RESTORE INTERVENTION

Strengthening Self-Control

Young Person's Perception:

"When I'm upset, I do terrible things, and then I feel guilty and seek punishment."

Uses:

With young people who are burdened by anxiety, guilt, shame, inadequacy, or remorse about their own failures or unworthiness, and who seek out punishment as a way to try to relieve their overwhelming emotions.

Goals:

1. To strengthen their self-control by building up their self-concept.
2. To relieve some of their emotional burden by emphasizing their positive qualities such as fairness, kindness, friendship, or leadership potential.
3. To realize they can seek support and help from trustworthy adults to deal with intense emotions.

Focus:

Expand young person's self-control and confidence through abundant affirmations and reflections about existing socially desirable attributes. Developmentally, this goal requires a shift in the source of responsibility from adult to young person.

Young Person's New Insight:

"Even in upsetting situations or group pressure, I have the capacity to control myself. I can make mistakes without concluding that I am bad or worthless. I can seek help when I am feeling overwhelmed."

Assad

During math, ten-year-old Assad was working at a table with two other students. He became very angry and stormed out of the classroom. While in the hallway, Assad walked briskly, pounding on the cement block walls and muttering to himself. At the end of the hallway, he hit the wall, accidentally setting off the fire alarm. As the alarm rang, Assad immediately recognized what he had done and tried to fix the alarm so it would stop ringing. When he realized this was futile, he ran into an office and hid under the desk. He curled up in the fetal position, crying and hitting his head on the underside of the desk.

The Regulate and Restore intervention is used to help young people who become overwhelmed by feelings of anxiety, guilt, shame, and/or inadequacy. These intensely uncomfortable emotions are typically experienced at the wrong times and in the wrong proportions by these youth. In terms of time, young people experience intense guilt and remorse for an impulsive behavior *after the fact*, an emotionally destructive reaction that is not helpful to the young person in controlling future behavior. In terms of proportion, the youth's *overwhelming* feelings of shame and inadequacy frequently drive them to seek the punishment they believe they deserve, in a misguided effort to relieve themselves of uncomfortable emotions. Young people for whom the Regulate and Restore intervention is appropriate commonly make self-abusive, degrading comments such as:

- "I'm no good!"
- "It must have been my fault."
- "I wish I was dead."
- "Go ahead, hit me!"
- "I guess I'm just a loser."
- "I can't do anything right."
- "She'll never want to be my friend again."
- "It was a stupid picture." (after tearing up a drawing)

Initially the adult is sympathetic toward such young people since they are so distressed about the results of their behavior. The distraught youth promises to be good and to never do it again. They apologize profusely, write confessions, make new resolutions, and shed abundant tears. However, because of immature self-regulation skills, their good intentions are no match for their impulse-

These young people are easily stimulated, lack adequate self-control and experience burdensome guilt when they are caught in the Conflict Cycle.

driven behaviors. These young people don't deliberately defy or ignore rules; the problem is that they are easily stimulated, lack adequate self-control, are highly sensitive to what is happening around them, and experience burdensome guilt when they are caught in the Conflict Cycle.

After initial feelings of sympathy and compassion, adults may mistakenly conclude that these young people can control themselves if they want to. It is essential to remember that kids do well if they can. And if they aren't doing well, it is because they lack the skill—not the will—to do so (Greene, 2008). Truly, no child wakes up in the morning and says, *"How can I really mess up today? What should I do to bother my teacher and get myself in so much trouble that I lose all of my privileges? What do I need to do today to have a complete meltdown in front of everyone I know so that I can feel ashamed for the next few days?"* Young people who exhibit the Regulate and Restore pattern *want* to do well and they *want* to be in control of their behaviors, but they lack the self-regulation skills and self-concept strength to do so. The Regulate and Restore intervention gives adults the framework for how to help them.

> The outcome goal for these young people is to strengthen their self-control by restoring their sense of self-worth and self-concept.

The outcome goal for these young people is to strengthen their self-control by restoring their sense of self-worth and self-concept. When they have sufficient belief in their own capabilities and positive attributes, they are more able to maintain emotional regulation, control impulses, and put on the brakes *before* they react to stress with impulsive, unacceptable behavior.

Fritz Redl (1966) originally called this form of LSCI "Massaging Numb Values" to convey the point that these youth have internalized constructive values, but because of weak self-control skills, the values are not in use. According to Redl, unless they are reinforced and expanded, such values lie dormant or atrophy:

> No matter how close to psychopathic our children may sometimes look, we haven't found one of them yet who didn't have lots of potential areas of value appeal lying within him. . . . Admitting value sensitivity, just like admitting hunger for love, is quite face-losing for our youngsters. There are, however, in most youngsters some value areas that are more exempt from peer group shame than others. For instance, even at a time when our youngsters would rather be seen dead than overconforming and sweet, the appeal to certain codes of "fairness" within their fight-provocation ritual is quite acceptable by them. Thus, in order to ready the ground for "value arguments" altogether, the pulling out of issues of fairness or

similar values from the debris of their daily life events may pay off handsomely in the end. (p. 45)

Use the Regulate and Restore Intervention With Young People Who . . .

As we describe this self-defeating behavior, we share two distinct ways in which this pattern presents:

1. **The Impulsive Pattern**

   The youth act outs impulsively, then feels intense anxiety and remorse about their behavior. These young people tend to get stuck in cognitive traps such as magnification, all-or-nothing thinking, and emotional reasoning that exacerbate their emotional pain. They become so burdened by these uncomfortable feelings that they seek punishment to "cleanse" their intolerable remorse.

Avery

Avery carefully constructs an elaborate set out of Legos. When her younger brother runs into the room and knocks down her creation, Avery is furious! She punches her brother in the arm—hard!—and starts screaming, "I hate you! You ruin everything! You better rebuild the whole thing or I'm going to break all of your toys!" Avery is sent to her room by her parents to calm down. When her mother enters the room, Avery is lying on her bed crying. She looks at her mother and starts handing her all of her favorite stuffed animals while saying, "I'm in my room because I am bad. I am the worst sister in the whole world. I deserve to stay here all day. Please don't bring me any food. I don't deserve to eat. I should just starve to death. Take all of my stuffies—I don't deserve to have them anymore." Avery begins slapping herself in the face with one of her dolls.

2. **The Guilty Pattern**

   The youth is burdened by ongoing, entrenched feelings of guilt, shame and inadequacy. They assume responsibility for all that goes wrong in their life and seek punishment to atone for their perceived shortcomings. These youth often make self-abusive statements and may engage in self-injurious behaviors. Young people who present with this Guilty pattern also typically exhibit behaviors that push the limits of an adult's tolerance. Their actions, in fact, may initially resemble those of a youth caught in a Red Flag pattern, due to their intensity. The framework of LSCI, however, guides adults to Drain Off the emotional intensity and realize that beneath it lies guilt, shame, inadequacy, and self-loathing (rather than a displacement of angry feelings).

Jack

Jack has special reading instruction three times a week with his favorite teacher, Mrs. Beyer. Mrs. Beyer is patient and caring and tolerates Jack's hyperactivity better than any other adult in the school. There has been a new level of stress at home as Jack's mother has lost her job. During the last session, Mrs. Beyer was called out of the room for a moment and Jack stole $10 from her purse. The theft has gone undetected for two days and Jack's feelings of guilt are beginning to overwhelm him. When he is called to reading instruction today, he refuses to go. This is uncharacteristic of Jack. The adults, including Mrs. Beyer, are confused. When his classroom teacher repeats that he has to go to reading, Jack clings to his desk and screams.

Jack ends up in the principal's office, where he learns he is about to receive a detention. Jack does not protest and in fact suggests more than one day of detention. The principal recognizes that Jack seems to want the punishment. As the principal begins LSCI, Jack is nervous, but as he starts to talk and the Timeline unfolds, Jack finally confesses to the theft and then states repeatedly that he is a terrible person. The principal affirms him for showing the courage to take responsibility for his poor choice. Jack visibly relaxes as he plans his apology to Mrs. Beyer. The principal and Mrs. Beyer work on a plan for Jack to ask to talk with one of them when he is feeling stressed.

The Avery and Jack examples illustrate two distinct ways that young people present the Regulate and Restore pattern. The common goal of the intervention is to strengthen young people's self-control by recognizing and building on their existing positive attributes.

> The common goal of the intervention is to strengthen young people's self-control by recognizing and building on their existing positive attributes.

When selecting this outcome goal, it is important to avoid using it in a way that will reinforce unacceptable behavior. This is less likely to occur if you base your responses on your awareness of specific developmental anxieties and concerns (see Chapter 8), including:

1. A young person's level of development about who should take responsibility for control of behavior
2. The type of developmental anxiety with which the young person is struggling

3. The general level of values the young person currently uses and the possibility of challenging the young person to rise to the next level

How Trauma and Adverse Childhood Experiences Shape the Regulate and Restore Pattern

In Chapter 4, we shared that a young person's self-concept and personal belief systems are rooted in the experiences of their earliest years of life and continue to develop as they age. When a young person experiences chronic stress, when adults have been unsupportive, neglectful, or abusive, and when the child has felt powerless to improve conditions, the impact on their self-concept is profound and enduring. Have you ever heard a young child use very "adult" words to describe themselves? For example, when a four-year-old offers that she is the "bane of [her] mother's existence," we intuit that she has heard those words spoken by an adult and has internalized them, rather than assuming she came up with the pejorative phrase on her own. And when an adolescent says, "I wish I had never been born. I'm a drain on everyone around me," we have to wonder if that idea is organic or if they have heard similar messages so often in their past that they have come to own them as part of their personal belief system. The words adults speak to young people can have a lifelong impact. Peggy O'Mara (2000) explains, "The way we talk to our children becomes their inner voice."

> Young people for whom the Regulate and Restore approach is appropriate have internalized negative messages from influential adults and carry the weight of others' rejection and shaming in their self-concept.

Young people for whom the Regulate and Restore approach is appropriate have internalized negative messages from influential adults and carry the weight of others' rejection and shaming in their self-concept. They tend to view the world, and all of their interactions, through the lens of inadequacy, anxiety, shame, and guilt. These young people are chronically burdened by these feelings, which means that even on a good day, they tend to take responsibility for all that is wrong with life. On a bad day, following a mistake or an inappropriate behavior, they tend to become overwhelmed by their sense of worthlessness and consequently seek out the punishment they believe they deserve. In some cases, this punishment is self-inflicted; these are kids who use negative self-talk and engage in self-abusive behaviors. In other cases, they seek punishment from adults, whether by telling adults what penalty they deserve or by pushing adults to react angrily. In either case, as discussed in Chapter 4, seeking out the punishment they have come to expect from caregivers is a way of taking control of their life, putting themselves in charge of their pain, and making their world more orderly and predictable. For some young people, a cathartic release of emotional energy is experienced.

We know that traumatic stress and adverse childhood experiences create chronic activation of the limbic brain. The Regulate and Restore intervention helps adults recognize that young people who have internalized messages of guilt, shame, and inadequacy are living with a consistent level of anxiety and self-doubt. When these feelings are exacerbated by a stressful event, the young person may impulsively engage in inappropriate behavior, then become overwhelmed by a new wave of shame, guilt, and remorse. These intense feelings drive them to seek the punishment they believe they deserve. The ability to look beyond surface behaviors and recognize the pain underlying them gives adults the ability to address and change the root causes of the self-defeating pattern—thus paving the way for lasting change. Zero tolerance and rigid discipline procedures, in contrast, do nothing to accomplish this constructive goal.

The Adult's Tasks in a Regulate and Restore Intervention

The outcome goal of the Regulate and Restore intervention is to strengthen a young person's self-control by building their self-concept. This approach helps kids develop new beliefs about their self-worth and value that ultimately lead to more life-enhancing behaviors. By building and affirming a young person's positive qualities such as fairness, kindness, friendship, or leadership potential, we gradually lessen activity in the limbic brain and expand activity in the neocortex and teach them strategies for self-regulation. This enables youth to respond thoughtfully (rather than reacting impulsively) to stressful situations. In the pages below, we outline how the Regulate and Restore intervention accomplishes this stage-by-stage.

Sequence of a Regulate and Restore Intervention

Stage 1: Drain Off

The first task for adults in this intervention is to see through the smoke screen of emotionally reactive, often aggressive behavior. Remember, at first, the emotions expressed by young people in this pattern may mimic the explosiveness of a Red Flag crisis. As the adult provides support, however, underlying emotions of anxiety, guilt, shame, and inadequacy will surface. Self-degrading statements typically begin to be expressed by the young person. The adult may also pick up on indications that the child is seeking punishment.

The adult's tasks in the Drain Off stage are to:

- Actively attend to the young person, communicating that they are worthy of being heard and understood.
- Abundantly affirm and reflect on existing positive traits, such as empathy, kindness, fairness, and friendship.
- Maintain reassuring communication; the child should know that you are not angry with them but rather interested in helping them work through a problem. A helpful three-part message for a young person displaying intense guilt, shame, or remorse might sound like:

  - I can see that you are feeling really bad right now. Something very important must have happened. I don't know what is making you ask staff to punish you, but I'd really like to understand. I am here to help.

- Avoid any guilt-inducing statements. There will be ample time to discuss inappropriate behaviors later on, but during the Drain Off stage, a focus on problems will create further anxiety and shut down communication.
- Actively manage any counter-aggressive feelings that surface from mistakenly concluding that the child purposefully failed to control their behavior or is engaging in self-pity.
- Affirm the youth's willingness to share their story.

Stage 2: The Timeline

In this intervention, the Timeline is helpful in focusing the young person on details that bring out instances where they exhibited self-control and examples of their positive attributes, no matter how small these may be. (Beware: any strategy that creates more inadequacy, shame, remorse, or guilt in these young people will only complicate the problem.) Listen for and challenge cognitive traps and negative self-talk. In the Regulate and Restore pattern, young people tend to use magnification (e.g., "I am the worst sister in the world. I don't deserve to eat today"), all-or-nothing thinking (e.g., "Mrs. Beyer is never going to forgive me. She will always hate me"), and emotional reasoning (e.g., "I messed up again. I'm such a loser").

The adult's tasks in the Timeline stage are to:

- Highlight flickering signs of self-control and positive self-concept. When examples of constructive behavior and positive qualities become part of the LSCI discussion, decode to help young people begin to gain insight into why they succumb to behavior they know is not acceptable. Then connect this insight to the underlying positive values it represents (see

Chapter 6 for decoding strategies and Chapter 7 for a review of developing values).

- Listen for and explore the evidence surrounding cognitive traps, such as magnification, all-or-nothing thinking, and emotional reasoning. You will examine and challenge these further in the Insight stage.
- *With the Impulsive presentation:*

  - Focus on moments during the crisis situation where the young person used self-control. For example:

    - "Are you telling me that your brother had already knocked down your Lego tower twice this morning? And both times you told yourself that he was 'just a baby,' which helped you stay calm? I'm impressed!"

- *With the Guilty presentation:*

  - Affirm the young person's positive attributes. For example:

    - "You really care about Mrs. Beyer. You are the kind of kid that wants to do well and has a strong sense of honesty and fairness. When mistakes happen, it's really important to you to make up for them. It takes a tremendous amount of courage to own up to mistakes. I feel a lot of admiration for your honesty with the principal."

  - Begin to decode their self-talk, the cognitive traps in which they become stuck, and their desire for punishment. For example:

    - "I've noticed that you've called yourself a 'loser' twice already since we've been talking. You are really hard on yourself when you make a mistake. Maybe we can start to think about mistakes as opportunities to learn instead of as reasons to put ourselves down or think we deserve detentions. Talking about things, like we're doing now, is a great way to find helpful solutions."

Stage 3: Central Issue

With the Impulsive presentation:

The Central Issue in this presentation is that the young person acted out impulsively then became overwhelmed by guilt and remorse. The youth may seek punishment for their behavior.

The Central Issue in this presentation is that the young person acted out impulsively then became overwhelmed by guilt and remorse.

With the Guilty presentation:

The Central Issue in this presentation is that the young person has entrenched feelings of shame and inadequacy. They act out in ways to perpetuate this thinking and then seek punishment to relieve their anxiety.

> The Central Issue in this presentation is that the young person has entrenched feelings of shame and inadequacy.

With both presentations, the outcome goal is to strengthen self-control and build the youth's self-concept.

The adult's tasks in the Central Issue stage are to:

- Review the Timeline using the Conflict Cycle paradigm to highlight the self-defeating sequence of events, beliefs, thoughts, feelings, behaviors, and the reactions of others.
- Concisely state the Central Issue.
- Assess the youth's perceptions, thoughts, feelings, and motivations to change.
- Determine that the Regulate and Restore intervention is the most suited to the desired outcome and resolution of the crisis.
- Prepare the young person to consider that they have more self-control than they are giving themselves credit for and that mistakes in behavior do not equate to a person being "bad" or worthless.

Stage 4: Insight

With the Impulsive presentation, the adult's task in the Insight stage is to help the young person recognize that:

1. They have more self-control than they realize.

- To cultivate this insight, we want to highlight any good choices the young person made during the stressful situation and/or other times they exhibited self-control.
- E.g., "Your brother's Lego tower was right there near yours on the table. You could have knocked it down, just like he did to yours. You chose not to, however. You yelled at him and you threatened to break his toys—and we can talk more about that later on—but right now I'm focused on the self-control it took you in to resist getting revenge

right away. I'm impressed with how you held back. We can really build on that kind of self-control and good judgment."

2. Mistakes do not make them "bad" or worthless.

  • To encourage this change in self-concept, we use analogies to challenge their all-or-nothing thinking.
  • For example, a youth might have an "a-ha" moment when you point out that when she was nine years old, Beyoncé Knowles' all-girls group was cut from the television competition show *Star Search*. Beyoncé did not allow herself to become discouraged or to quit performing, however. Her group didn't accept the judgments of others about their ability. Beyoncé kept practicing and working hard and eventually became a multi-platinum, Grammy Award-winning recording artist and one of music's top-selling artists.
  • Young people diagnosed with ADHD might relate well to Michael Phelps, considered the greatest Olympic swimmer of all time. As a child, Phelps was diagnosed with ADHD. While many people assumed his mental health challenge would cause him to be too impulsive and unfocused to succeed, they neglected to consider that many people with ADHD have an incredible ability to hyperfocus on activities they love. By channeling his focus and energies, Phelps was able to win eight gold medals in a single Olympic Games and has 19 Olympic medals overall—15 of which are gold!
  • Or, Disney fans might relate to the fact that Walt Disney was fired by a newspaper editor for having a "lack of ideas." He went bankrupt several times before building Disneyland and is rumored to have been turned down by 302 different banks before he was given the financing to build his theme park.

With the Guilty presentation, the adult's task in the Insight stage is to help the young person see that:

1. They are weighed down by entrenched feelings of shame and inadequacy. Their negative self-talk only perpetuates their negative self-concept.

  • To cultivate this insight, we want to affirm existing positive qualities, characteristics, and successes.
  • E.g., "You have a really strong bond with Mrs. Beyer. She likes you and you like her. You work hard during your time with her and it shows! You've made so much progress in reading this year. When you

call yourself a loser or tell yourself that Mrs. Beyer will never forgive you, it makes it hard to remember all of the good things that have happened in your reading class with her this year. Let's make sure we don't throw away all of your good work, just because of this bad day."

2. Seeking punishment is not helpful or constructive.

   - To cultivate this insight, we want to affirm that guilt and anxiety can be helpful, but only when they are felt at the right time and in the right proportion to change behavior in positive ways. Seeking punishment is never helpful.
   - E.g., "I can see that you felt badly about taking her money. Looking back, you wish you hadn't done that. Guilt can be helpful when it leads us to make amends to someone or to right a wrong, but when guilt becomes overpowering and leads us to try to get punished, it's not helpful at all! In fact, it just makes things worse. Let's talk about how we can deal with feelings like guilt in more helpful ways, okay?"

Additional adult's tasks in the Insight stage are to:

- Help the young person begin to recognize their pattern of acting out impulsively or due to feelings of guilt, then feeling bad and seeking out punishment.
- Abundantly affirm the youth's good qualities, strong relationships, past successes, and the possibility of turning the problem into a learning opportunity.
- Challenge and change the young person's faulty thought patterns such as magnification, all-or-nothing thinking, and emotional reasoning.
- Help young people recognize that adults are available to help them cope when they are feeling overwhelmed or overcome by negative self-talk. Work with the youth to identify at least two trustworthy adults they could reach out to in future situations.
- The Insight goals of the Regulate and Restore intervention are to help the young person:

   - Strengthen their self-concept.
   - Increase their awareness that they have more self-control than they realized.
   - Accept the belief that "accidents happen" and that people can make mistakes and poor choices without judging themselves as bad or worthless.

- Acknowledge and affirm that the young person has learned something valuable about the role of guilt and the destructive nature of seeking punishment.

Stage 5: New Skills

The purpose of Stage 5 is to help both the impulsive and the guilty young person consider and practice the social-emotional skills needed to be successful in future stressful situations. The focus should be on using the existing positive qualities of the child (that have been abundantly affirmed throughout the intervention) as part of the plan to resolve the crisis. The adult should communicate their belief in the young person's ability to carry out a plan for success.

In his timeless reflection on this LSCI approach, Anthony Werner (1981) offered a major caution for adults using this intervention:

> Responding to this pupil's acting out behavior in punitive or moralistic ways does not help the pupil learn and grow but only creates additional problems. . . . He will either feel that he has "paid the price" and lose contact with his feelings of guilt and the desirable values behind them, or he will feel increased guilt and will act out more intensely. (p. 31)

Werner also described the particular qualities needed by adults to make this type of LSCI effective:

> The effective interviewer is one who is able to be supportive, compassionate, and empathetic. With these qualities and skill in LSCI, this interviewer can become an advocate for the child. He [or she] can help turn a specific problem incident into a valuable experience for the child. (p. 31)

The adult's tasks in the New Skills stage are:

- *For the Impulsive youth,* to discuss and practice self-regulation and impulse-control strategies such as:
  - Adding a "pause" before acting on a thought or feeling (e.g., Stop-Think-Act).
  - Challenging cognitive traps and negative self-talk.
  - Practicing mindfulness.
  - Using calming behaviors.

- *For the Guilty youth*, to discuss and practice self-regulation and self-esteem building strategies such as:

  - Challenging cognitive traps and negative self-talk.
  - Talking about, journaling, or otherwise putting feelings into words to activate the problem-solving part of the brain.
  - Identifying a trustworthy adult(s) in the setting with whom the youth can "check in" on a regular basis to prevent feelings of guilt, shame, or inadequacy from causing problem behaviors.

- Help the young person anticipate and plan for future stressful situations; discuss ways to recognize and check rising feelings.
- Rehearse new emotion management skills through role play and discussion.

Stage 6: Transfer of Learning

Use the final stage of LSCI to prepare the young person to transition successfully back into the classroom, group, or interpersonal situation. Since it is almost certain that emotions were heightened, when the young person transitions, be very mindful of helping the youth plan for dealing with people's reactions and any programmatic consequences upon their return. Stage 6 is important in all LSCI interventions, but it is especially critical to prepare young people whose self-concept remains tenuous and whose self-regulation skills are a work-in-progress. An intervention's lasting impact will be influenced by its immediate aftermath.

> An intervention's lasting impact will be influenced by its immediate aftermath.

The adult's tasks in the Transfer of Learning stage are to:

- Consolidate new insights and skills by summarizing the discussion and affirming the young person's participation.
- Discuss what has happened while the young person has been away from the group. Help them anticipate others' reactions when they rejoin the group and plan for how they can regulate their emotions, manage their impulses, and respond effectively.
- Encourage restorative practices to resolve issues involving adults and peers and rebuild relationships when necessary.
- Collaborate with others to designate an adult with whom the youth can consistently "check in."

Now that you have a thorough understanding of the adult's stage-by-stage tasks in the Regulate and Restore intervention, we return to Assad, the student we met at the beginning of the chapter. We give you the opportunity to "listen in" on the intervention and also to hear directly from the interviewer, who shares her thoughts on why she used specific techniques during the conversation. Note how the adult uses Drain Off skills to de-escalate Assad's intense emotional reaction to having set off the fire alarm and then skillfully challenges Assad's negative self-talk and cognitive traps. By highlighting the times where Assad showed self-control during the stressful situation and helping him understand that the mistake he made does not make him a bad person, the interviewer builds on Assad's existing self-regulation skills, helps him change negative self-talk, and guides him to Restore the damage done during the incident.

Example of LSCI Used to Build Skills That Strengthen Self-Control: A Regulate and Restore Intervention

"False Alarm"

Background Information

Assad is a ten-year-old with above-average intelligence but very poor social interaction skills. He is a frequent target of teasing in his classroom, where he is seen as the "nerd." He tries to be helpful by what he would call "sharing his knowledge" but what his peers would refer to as "butting in" and "knowing it all." He currently lives with his father, a recovering alcoholic, who has recently become very active in a religious community. There is an inordinate amount of pressure on Assad to be a "good" boy—pressure that Assad had already put on himself at a very young age, even before his father's sudden interest in being socially appropriate. Assad is generally a very good student and follows the rules, almost to the point of being compulsive. He has extreme difficulty accepting any form of constructive criticism and has a temper that explodes when he cannot meet his own high expectations.

The Incident

During math, Assad was working at a table with two other students. One of the students, William, is highly competitive in math. Assad finished first and offered to help William, an offer that was met with a very cruel response. Assad became very angry and screamed that he needed a "reset" and stormed out of the room. (Students can request a "reset" out of the room when they feel like they are going to lose control.)

While in the hallway, Assad walked briskly, pounding on the cement block walls and muttering to himself. At the end of the hallway, he hit the wall, accidentally setting off the fire alarm. (It was a new school and the alarm casing had not yet been installed to protect the button from being accidentally set off.) As the alarm rang, Assad immediately recognized what he had done and tried to fix the alarm so it would stop ringing. When he realized this was futile, he ran into my office and hid under the desk. I called the main office to tell them that it was a false alarm and the fire trucks should be diverted from coming. Unfortunately, the fire station was right next door, and the trucks were already on their way. The alarm was de-activated, and I (I) turned my attention to Assad (A), who was curled up in the fetal position, crying and hitting his head on the underside of the desk.

Stage 1: Drain Off

I: *(Gently gets down on the floor to sit next to Assad; remains quiet, with a soothing demeanor)*

A: *(Mumbling and hitting himself)* I'm so stupid. I never do anything right. I'm bad.

I: Sounds like you're feeling really bad about what happened and wish you could take it back.

A: *(Nods)* Now everyone will know how stupid I am. The other kids will hate me, the firemen will hate me, the whole town will hate me. It'll be on the news, and the whole country will hate me. It'll be on the internet and the whole world will hate me. I deserve to be put in jail or worse and have everyone hate me!

Notice Assad's magnification of the incident, a cognitive trap that makes it difficult for him to accurately view the impact of his actions.

I: You feel you did something so terrible that you deserve to be punished and that no punishment is going to be enough.

A: *(Looks at adult directly for the first time and speaks in a strong tone)* Even God won't be able to punish me enough for being so bad.

I believed that his change in body language indicated that I had connected with his feelings and we were ready to move into the Timeline stage.

Stage 2: Timeline

I: Assad, all I know right now is that the fire alarm went off and you feel you had something to do with it. Can you tell me what happened?

A: I did it. I hit it. It's all my fault.

I: It's great that you're being honest and accepting responsibility for your actions. (*Assad stops hitting his head*) So, you hit the fire alarm. How did that happen?

A: I just took my stupid hand and hit it.

I: Where were you?

A: In the hallway. My father is going to kill me.

I: You're worried about what your dad is going to say. We can talk about that in a minute, but first I need to find out what happened. Can you wait?

A: Yeah.

I: Who was in the hallway with you?

A: There were other people around, but no one was with me.

I: So, you were by yourself. Where were you going?

A: No place. I was taking a stupid voluntary.

I: A voluntary? You needed some alone time?

A: Yeah. I should be alone forever. Locked up so I can't do any more stupid things.

Even though I didn't have all the information yet, I decided that Assad was in desperate need of some intense affirmations. He was loaded with excessive guilt and was definitely beating himself up unmercifully.

I: Taking some alone time when we need it is a good decision.

A: Not good enough.

It is not unusual for students such as Assad to discount any affirming statements. Rather than continuing to reflect his rebuttals, I chose to ignore them and press on.

I: What happened to cause you to take a reset?

A: I was so mad I wanted to rip his head off. I shouldn't have been so mad.

I: Whose head?

A: William's.

I: You were angry with William. Tell me about it.

A: I was just trying to help him, and he called me names and I got mad.

I: Let's see if I've got this right. William called you names, and you got very angry. So angry you wanted to hurt him. But you didn't. Instead you made a good decision and asked for a reset and went into the hallway by yourself to cool down. While you were in the hallway, you hit the fire alarm. Have I got it right so far?

A: I can never do anything right!

I: You are feeling like you can never do anything right. That's very hard to handle, Assad. When you are feeling this way, what do you notice happening in your body?

A: (Looks confused)

I: Like, for me, when I am really, really mad, my face gets super red and I feel so hot that it's like I am burning up. Do you notice anything in your body?

A: Well, I don't feel hot but I do feel shaky!

I: You notice that you are shaky. Does that happen a lot when you are angry?

A: All of the time! It's like my muscles just get so tight that I shake. I hate that feeling. It's like I just need to do something or hit something just to get rid of that feeling!

I: Having your muscles tighten up is a really uncomfortable feeling. It's really good that you are noticing how your body responds when you are angry. That can actually help you learn to calm down before problems start to happen. (Pauses) I have a question. Did you hit the fire alarm on purpose or by accident? I mean, did you go out into the hallway and go right for the fire alarm?

A: No. I was hitting the walls with my fist, and it just happened.

I: So, it wasn't intentional. Were you surprised when the alarm went off?

A: Yes. I didn't even know I had hit it. I should've been more careful. I never even looked. I should've known it was there, and I shouldn't have been pounding the walls anyway.

Notice Assad's use of "should" statements, a cognitive trap that compromises his ability to view his behavior as a mistake.

Stage 3: Central Issue

Assad's excessive guilt and remorse, evidenced by his body language, self-deprecating statements, and cognitive traps of magnification, "should" statements, and all-or-nothing thinking were characteristic of his self-defeating behavior pattern. I selected the Regulate and Restore intervention strategy with two goals: helping Assad see that he has more self-control than he realizes and helping Assad recognize that he is not the worthless human being that he thinks he is. To accomplish this, we reviewed the Timeline again, and I highlighted all the good decisions that he was incapable of independently recognizing. I wrote down each good decision on a pad of paper.

I: You were trying to help William?

A: Yeah, I finished my math early and he wasn't done. So, I tried to help him. I should've just left him alone.

I: (*Writes down: Trying to help a fellow student*) But William didn't want your help and called you some names.

A: Yeah.

I: And that made you angry. Did you call him names back?

A: No. I wanted to, but I didn't.

I: And you said before, you wanted to hurt him physically, but you didn't. (*Writes down: Wanted to call names back and hurt William but didn't*) Instead, you made a good decision and decided to take a reset (*Writes down: Made a good decision to take a reset*)

A: Yeah, but I still hit the fire alarm!

I: It's hard for you to hear anything you might have done right when you are feeling so bad, isn't it?

A: (*Softly*) Yeah.

I: Let's go on. While you were in the hallway, you were hitting the walls. I have a question. All the time you were in the hallway, were there any other people there?

A: Yeah.

I: Did you hit them?

A: (*Looking shocked*) No, of course not.

I: Even though you were angry, you didn't hit a person.

A: No, I wouldn't hit anybody.

I: So, you just hit things that wouldn't get hurt. (*Writes down: Didn't harm others physically*)

A: Yes.

I: And in the hallway there are classroom doors. What did you do when you came to a door?

A: I skipped over it.

I: You mean you didn't hit the door?

A: No, I just pounded the walls.

I: Why didn't you pound on the doors?

A: I didn't want to bother the classes.

I: (*Writes down: Considerate of the other classes*)

A: (*Looks at the list; his whole body starts to relax*)

I: And when you got to the fire alarm, did you say to yourself, "Whoopee, hitting this will really be great"?

A: No. I didn't even know it was there!

I: Could you say that again?

A: I didn't even know it was there.

I: If you had known it was there, would you have hit it?

A: Of course not. You're not supposed to hit fire alarms when there is no fire.

I: So, what you are saying is that hitting the fire alarm was a mistake.

A: Yes. But I should have been looking.

I: It is difficult for you to believe it is OK to make a mistake, isn't it?

A: No, it's OK to make mistakes. But it's not OK for me!

I: And when you realized you hit the fire alarm by accident, did you go, "Wow, this will really get the joint hopping. I'm so glad I did it"?

A: No. I tried to fix it. I tried to shut it off, but it wouldn't shut off!

I: You mean to tell me that you realized you had made a mistake and you tried to make it right?

A: I guess so. Yes.

I: (*Writes down: Realized he made a mistake and tried to fix it immedi-ately*)

A: (*Smiling*) You know what, that alarm might even be defective. When I was trying to fix it, I noticed it said, "Pull for alarm." I didn't pull it; I hit it.

Stage 4: Insight

> I had two main goals for Assad. The first was to help him realize that he has more self-control than he realizes. The second was to address his irrational belief that he has to be perfect and that if he makes a mistake, he is a mistake. To accomplish the first goal, I folded the piece of paper on which I had been writing in half. On one side, at the top, I wrote, "Good Decisions." On the other side I wrote, "Mistakes."

I: Assad, earlier you said that you never do anything right. I wonder if you would read this list with me.

A: OK.

INTERVIEWER AND ASSAD:

- *Trying to help a fellow student.*
- *Wanted to call names back and hurt William but didn't.*
- *Made a good decision to take a voluntary.*
- *Didn't harm others physically.*
- *Considerate of the other classes.*
- *Realized he made a mistake and tried to fix it immediately.*
- *Honest and accepts responsibility for his actions.*

I: How many things are on this list?

A: Seven.

I: (*Turning the paper over*) Now how many things are on this list?

- *Hit the fire alarm by mistake.*

A: One.

I: Which is bigger: seven or one?

A: Seven.

I: Let's go back to your statement that you never do anything right. Does this evidence back that up?

A: (*Smiling*) Well, maybe I exaggerated a little.

I: Is it possible that when you make a mistake, you forget all the good decisions you have made and feel like just giving up?

A: Yeah.

Now that Assad had acknowledged that he did have the capacity for self-control and that he had made good decisions, we turned to his belief system regarding mistakes. I have found that sports analogies are particularly effective in helping students see that even the best players in a game are not even close to being perfect. Fortunately, Assad was a true baseball fan. I asked him to think of the greatest baseball player he knew. Then I asked him what that player's batting average was. It was around .300.

I: Let's see, a .300. That means that out of every 10 times at bat, he hits the ball about 3 times, right?

A: Yeah.

I: That means that he missed seven times?

A: I guess so.

I: Let me ask you a question. Do you think that he missed those balls on purpose?

A: No, of course not.

I: So, missing those balls was a mistake?

A: Yes.

I: Do you think he felt bad?

A: Probably.

I: Did he give up?

A: No.

I: Why didn't he just give up? I mean, he misses the ball more times than he hits it, after all.

A: Because he's good.

I: Even when he makes mistakes?

A: Yes.

I: And today you made a mistake, sort of like missing the ball. And when we count up all the good decisions you made, we got seven hits and one miss. You know what kind of batting average that would give you?

A: What?

I: About an .850.

A: Wow!

I: Assad, even the best ballplayers make mistakes and even the best kids make mistakes. The best ballplayers don't quit, they just keep on trying. Do you think you can keep on trying?

A: (*Smiling shyly*) I guess so.

Stage 5: New Skills

I: Assad, you have realized some really important things in this conversation! Let's write down some ideas for how you can remember all that you've learned so that you can put it into action next time you're in a stressful situation. Are you ready to make a plan?

A: Sure.

I: Great. So, should we start with ideas for putting your self-control and good decision-making skills into action or should we start with going a bit easier on yourself when you make a mistake?

A: Let's start with the good decisions part.

I: Okay. When you are feeling upset, what helps you calm down enough to make a good decision?

A: I don't know. I don't usually take time to calm down. I usually just do things that get me in trouble.

I: Assad, just realizing that about yourself—recognizing that you tend to act first and then think later—is one of the most important steps you could ever take toward changing that self-destructive habit. You've already done a lot of the hard work! Now, we can go straight to putting a plan in place. Let me ask you this: do you like watching videos online?

A: I'd watch YouTube all night long if my Dad let me. I even have my own channel!

I: Great, so if your Dad calls you when you are watching something and you don't want to miss any of the video but you don't want to ignore your Dad, what do you do?

A: I just press "pause."

I: That's right! You just press the "pause" button. Have you ever thought about trying that strategy in real life? You know, like when someone says something that makes you mad in a class, instead of responding angrily to them right away—and getting into trouble—you could imagine pressing "pause" on yourself. As soon as you start to notice that shaky feeling you get when your muscles get tight—that can be your signal to press the "pause" button immediately. Before opening your mouth or using your fists, you could give yourself time to think and make a better decision. We know from the list we made that you are definitely capable of making good decisions! Do you think that adding a "pause" between your feelings and your actions could help you make even more good decisions and save you from creating new problems for yourself?

A: Maybe.

I: Let's give it a try. I'm going to pretend to be a kid in your math class. I'll say things to try to get you upset and you practice pressing "pause" on yourself when you feel yourself about to do or say something that would get you in trouble. OK?

A: OK.

Assad and I practice a few different rounds of this back and forth dialogue to help him become more aware of the signs of angry feelings in his body (tightened fists, flushed face) and how to use a "pause" to regulate these uncomfortable feelings. We switch roles so that I can model effective calming strategies such as deep breathing and asking to get a drink of water. When Assad says he thinks he has the hang of the strategy, we move on.

I: We should also make a plan for what happens when you make mistakes. Instead of being so hard on yourself and doing things like calling yourself names and hitting yourself, what could you say to yourself after you make a mistake?

A: Well, if I press the "pause" button on time, I probably won't make any more mistakes, so I don't know if I need a plan for that.

I: Having the "pause" button in place will help prevent a lot of bad decisions, but you're still human, which means you'll still make mistakes and things will still go wrong. It happens to all of us,

Assad! The important thing to realize is that mistakes are just a part of life—they don't make us "bad" people.

A: Well, I guess I can just plan to tell myself that, then.

I: Tell yourself what?

A: That mistakes are a part of life and that they don't mean that I'm a bad person.

I: That's perfect, Assad! Short, sweet, and to the point! Easy to remember during a stressful situation! What would you think about writing that down?

A: What for?

I: Maybe you can keep it in a jacket pocket or in your desk and read it over anytime you start to get down on yourself. Having a written reminder can be really helpful when you are upset and can't come up with the words on your own.

A: Okay. I'll tape it to the inside of my binder, since I always have that with me in school.

I: Great idea!

Stage 6: Transfer of Learning

I felt that Assad's desire to change his behaviors was strong, but his actual ability to regulate impulses and "forgive" himself for making mistakes was still tenuous at best. I also knew that other students in the room, particularly William, were prone to teasing Assad when he returned from being in trouble. I felt it was imperative to prepare Assad for how his classmates might react when he returned to the classroom.

A: Do I have to go back to math? William is going to be there and he almost always gives me a hard time.

I: I have a thought. Instead of seeing this as a problem waiting to happen, let's look at this as an opportunity to practice your new skills. I'll pretend to be William and let's do another quick role play to practice how you can respond if he gives you a hard time. Ready?

A: Fine.

I: (*Pretending to be William*) Was that you that set off the fire alarm? I can't believe you didn't get arrested, man! You're probably going to have to pay a huge fine. Your dad is going to be so mad at you!

A: (*Calmly and with confidence*) I made a mistake, I accepted responsibility for it, and I am making reparations.

The word "reparations" was Assad's idea; he said it would probably confuse William, a thought that gave him much pleasure.

I: Wow—that's great. You said that with such confidence. If you use that tone of voice with others, they'll realize that they can't get you to lose control. They'll see how much self-control you really do have.

A: (*Smiles*)

I: There's one more thing, Assad. The fire chief is outside of my office and waiting to talk to you. Are you ready to have that conversation?

A: (*Looks afraid but remains composed*) Will you stay with me and help me explain about the mistakes and the "pause" button?

I: Of course.

Before going back to class, Assad spoke with the chief of the fire department, who had been waiting to see him. The chief was direct, yet understanding, and believed that Assad had set the alarm off by accident. He admonished him to be more careful in the future and they shook hands. I then asked Assad if he still was worried about his father's reaction. He asked if when I called him, I could share with him the good decisions as well as the mistake. I assured him that I would. He then went back to class and successfully completed the day.

Intervention Summary

When a young person is in their own "pit of despair," it is very difficult for the adult to avoid getting bogged down in intense feelings of counter-depression. These young people are so expert at discounting any positive statements that the interviewer often just wants to give up as well, which is exactly what the young person wants to do as well. When kids reject positive statements like Assad did, decoding their emotional message by saying something such as, "It's hard for you to hear nice things about yourself when you are feeling so bad" works.

The physical act of writing down good decisions is another helpful way of keeping positive attributes uppermost in the interviewer's mind while they are facing the young person's rebuttals. In essence, these rebuttals have no substance, while the positive written statements are concrete. Not only does writing help keep the interviewer focused, it also serves as concrete evidence for the young person. Written feedback is far more powerful than verbalizations because it can be seen, read and reread, and kept.

"I have to stop letting other people control my behaviors."

THE PEER MANIPULATION INTERVENTION

Exposing Peer Exploitation

Young Person's Perception:

False Friendship: "It's important to have a friend even if the friend gets me into trouble"

The Set Up: "I'm not going to let that kid tease me. I'm going to teach him a lesson!"

The Mastermind: "I can make this kid do anything I want. Watch me have some fun here."

Uses:

False Friendship: With young people who are socially isolated and rejected and become caught up in unhealthy friendships.

The Set Up: With young people who are unwittingly "set up" to act out by an exploitive peer.

The Mastermind: With the exploiting peer who finds satisfaction and enjoyment in controlling others and taking advantage of their vulnerabilities.

Goal:

False Friendship and the Set Up: To help a young person see that a peer is manipulating events and exploiting them.

The Mastermind: To benignly confront the behavior of the exploiting peer.

Focus:

Provide insight into reasons for the behavior of others; view social interactions from the perspective of motivations and behaviors of others. Developmentally, this goal requires considerable maturity on the young person's part, as the young person learns to understand how others think, feel, and behave.

Young Person's New Insight:

False Friendship: "A friend is someone who helps you solve problems and feel good rather than someone who gets you into trouble."

The Set Up: "I can make my own decisions; I don't need to 'take the bait' when someone is trying to get me in trouble."

The Mastermind: "I'm tricking myself into believing that it's okay to take advantage of others. It's wrong to hurt other people and that is reason enough to change my behavior."

False Friendship

Mrs. Rodriguez walks back in the classroom and sees Alex with a cell phone in his hand, which is a violation of school rules. When she asks him to give her the phone, she sees a text that has just been sent out to the whole eighth grade: "Kelsey is a fat whore." It is clear that Alex just sent the text, though it also seems likely that Leo had some involvement in the incident.

The Set Up

Eleven-year-old Carlos and nine-year-old Kahlil were working together at a table. Suddenly, Carlos started yelling, "I hate you Kahlil! He gave me the finger!" Kahlil began to shout back, "No I didn't! He's lying! You're a liar, Carlos!" Soon the boys were in a heated argument that disrupted the entire class and required immediate adult intervention.

Peer friendships are complicated relationships. Healthy friendships are based on mutual trust and respect, in which neither young person consciously exploits the feelings or resources of the other. Positive relationships and a sense of belonging are essential to a youth's self-esteem. Friendship means closeness, trust, sharing secrets, and providing emotional support. Peer friendship is an important source of psychological support for young people over nine years of age, and making and keeping friends is a major activity of adolescence. The primary issue of the Peer Manipulation intervention is the dynamic of peer vulnerability to the influence of unhealthy friendships at the hands of exploitive youngsters.

> The primary issue of the Peer Manipulation intervention is the dynamic of peer vulnerability to the influence of unhealthy friendships at the hands of exploitive youngsters.

The original name given by Fritz Redl to this form of LSCI was "Manipulation of the Boundaries of the Self." Redl said that the psychological boundaries of their personalities are so vulnerable to influence and manipulation by others that they are unable to form a confident or self-assertive presence. They have such a marginal sense of self-esteem and personal worthiness that they allow someone else to "pull their strings." It is easy to see how such young people fail to develop responsible, independently directed acceptable behavior. Redl (1966) vividly described this type of dynamic:

> From time to time one invariably runs into a child who exhibits a peculiar helplessness toward a process we like to refer to as group psychological suction. Quite vulnerable to even mild contagion sparks, he is often discovered by an exceptionally brilliant manipulator . . . and then he easily drifts into the pathetic role of the perennial "sucker." (p. 46)

Use the Peer Manipulation Intervention With Young People Who . . .

As we describe this self-defeating behavior, we share three distinct ways in which this pattern presents.

Pattern 1—The Dynamic of False Friendship

This pattern of self-defeating behavior involves socially isolated and rejected young people whose emotional needs make them vulnerable to the influence and control of exploitive peers. For these young people, the need for friendship and peer acceptance is so great that they seem willing to pay any psychological price to obtain it.

A *false friendship* develops when an exploitive young person recognizes a vulnerable young person's need to be accepted. Under the guise of friendship, they reach out to the socially isolated young person in a manipulative way by saying something like, "Come on over and have lunch with us," or "Hey, cool jacket!" The needy young person is so pleased by receiving interest from the more powerful peer that they readily accept any invitation or compliment. *However, the unstated contract of this new friendship is that it will last just as long as the vulnerable young person is willing to carry out the wishes of the exploitive young person.* Over time, the less socially savvy young person becomes a psychological puppet in the exploitive young person's game plan. The more powerful youth will get their new "friend" to carry their contraband, take responsibility for their misdeeds, or do their homework. They stay out of trouble while the vulnerable young person becomes their unwitting fall guy.

Doug

Doug is an unsophisticated 14-year-old loner. His best "friend" and idol is 16-year-old Russ, who is slick and streetwise. Wherever Russ happens to be, Doug can be found hanging around. One day, Russ brings a bag of marijuana to school and word gets around that he is selling it. Being streetwise and savvy, Russ is very tuned in to the environment and senses that things are getting hot. He already has a juvenile court record and doesn't want another offense, so he asks Doug to do him a favor: Would Doug hold the marijuana for him until after school? Doug is honored to be entrusted with the task. He willingly takes the bag and shoves it into his pocket.

When the principal calls Russ into his office on the basis of the rumor that he is selling drugs, Russ is happy to comply with the principal's request to empty his pockets. However, the principal knows Russ too well to be fooled by his "innocent act" and tells him that he is going to call the school resource officer to interview students because there is too much in question for the principal to be satisfied that Russ is not involved. Russ "breaks down" and tells the principal that he's got the wrong man. It's true that there is marijuana in the building, but he is not responsible. Doug is the one he's after. Russ is secretly gambling that Doug will take the rap for him in the spirit of "friendship."

The LSCI follows, after Doug has been brought to the office and the marijuana has been found in his pocket. The principal sees both boys together and begins the interview with Doug. Doug is sticking to a story that he found the marijuana on the way to school that morning, but the principal's careful structuring of the Timeline reveals so many inconsistencies in Doug's fabricated account that it becomes clear he is lying. At the point where it looks like the story is about to break down, Russ pipes up, telling Doug that he doesn't have to say anything to the principal and that he is better off shutting up and saving it for the school resource officer. Doug is scared, but he plays his loyal role, becoming defiant and refusing to answer any more questions. It is at this point that the principal reveals to Doug how he found out that he had the marijuana; Russ told him.

Doug is crushed and in disbelief. The principal goes on to point out how Russ is really no friend to Doug and will gladly cause him great trouble and pain if it saves his own skin. The truth is out, and Doug is hurt and ashamed. After dismissing Russ (temporarily), the principal does a second Timeline with Doug, and the truth comes out. The principal encourages Doug and tells him that he will help him out of the trouble he is in by speaking with the school resource officer and with the judge if necessary. A New Tools intervention is then used as a follow-up to help Doug understand that his intention to help a friend was positive, though his trust in Russ was misguided. Likewise, Doug would benefit from learning the social-emotional skills involved in finding healthy friendships. We sometimes refer to the Peer Manipulation intervention as a "gateway" because it opens the opportunity for follow-up interventions.

What happens to Russ? We answer this question below, as we explore the dynamic of the Mastermind in Pattern 3.

Pattern 2—The Dynamic of Being Set Up

This pattern of self-defeating behavior usually involves a bright, highly verbal passive-aggressive young person who enjoys dominating social interactions and controlling the behavior of others. The exploitive young person typically sets up the aggressive youth in two steps:

1. First, they find a way to trigger angry thoughts and feelings in an emotionally reactive peer, usually through teasing, mocking, or other public ridicule. They do this strategically, through subtle actions that they can deny, justify, or minimize. Likewise, they usually only instigate trouble when there is an adult nearby who can protect them when the volatile youth gets out of control.
2. Then, they meticulously create scenarios in which the volatile young person believes that they are being taken advantage of or disrespected. The "mastermind" continues to fuel the conflict until the emotionally reactive young person loses control and acts out. The exploitive peer watches, in satisfaction, as others carry out the behaviors that they have orchestrated.

What is fascinating about this dynamic is that the emotionally reactive youth is unaware of how they are being manipulated and controlled by their peer. The outcome, however, is predictable: the volatile youth takes the bait, lashes out, and ends up with disciplinary consequences. Meanwhile, the "mastermind" has been thoroughly entertained and remains consequence-free.

The outcome goal with young people who allow themselves to be set up by others is to expose the peer manipulation. Through the LSCI process, a caring adult helps a young person understand how they were exploited by a peer, how the peer gained power and pleasure by setting them up, and how they have lost out by being the one to get in trouble.

James and Ethan

Ten-year-olds James and Ethan are stuck in an antagonistic and manipulative peer relationship. James is extremely clever in getting Ethan to lose his temper and lash out in the classroom. On this particular day, James knows Ethan is having trouble completing an assignment. After a few minutes, James says in a loud voice, "I'm all done! The teacher gave me the easy job!" (James smiles and looks over to see Ethan's reaction.) This is enough to trigger an explosion from Ethan. He leaps out of his desk, throws his chair in James's direction, and shouts, "You're a dumb ass!" As the teacher moves in to avert further disaster, James says in her direction, "Ethan's really out of control; how can we work with all this noise?"

In the LSCI that followed between Ethan and his teacher, Ethan was able to recount the sequence of events. He also was able to describe alternative behaviors that are more acceptable ways to handle anger. The teacher recognized that Ethan was not aware of how he was set up and manipulated by James, despite several prior occasions in which Ethan had already lost control following James' incendiary remarks. So, the teacher chose the outcome goal of exposing James' exploitation and focused the LSCI on helping Ethan consider how his behavior resulted in his being in the time-out room, while James was still in the classroom, enjoying seeing Ethan in trouble. This was a new idea for Ethan!

And what about James in this situation? He would insist that he didn't "do" anything; after all, all he said was, "I'm all done! The teacher gave me the easy job!" and there's nothing wrong with that—is there? See below for how the Peer Manipulation intervention can be used to acknowledge and address James' role in the crisis.

Pattern 3—The Dynamic of the Mastermind

Let's return for a moment to Russ, the clever, passive-aggressive young man who formed a False Friendship with Doug in the Pattern 1 example. Last we saw, Russ was dismissed from the principal's office. Does this mean that he is off the hook for his clear exploitation of Doug? And what about James, the "innocent" bystander from the Pattern 2 example who "merely" announced that he had completed his work? The Benign Confrontation intervention, described in Chapter 13, is an ideal tool to address both Russ and James' instigating behaviors. It can—and should—be used to follow up both the False Friendship and the Set Up incidents described above to benignly confront the actions of Doug and James, the young men who masterminded their peers' misdeeds. The Peer Manipulation intervention is a "gateway" intervention that helps adults recognize dynamics of interpersonal exploitation and vulnerability to peer influence; the full range of LSCI interventions ensures that all of the destructive dynamics can be effectively addressed and that each involved young person can learn better ways to behave.

> The Peer Manipulation intervention is a "gateway" intervention that helps adults recognize dynamics of interpersonal exploitation and vulnerability to peer influence; the full range of LSCI interventions ensures that all of the destructive dynamics can be effectively addressed and that each involved young person can learn better ways to behave.

How Trauma and Adverse Childhood Experiences Shape the Peer Manipulation Pattern

In Peer Manipulation situations, we see the troubling interactions between one young person who *internalizes* stress and another who *externalizes* it. A youth who aims to control and exploit others is externalizing their pain; they believe their

wants and needs are primary and create a victim out of a vulnerable peer who desires their acceptance and friendship. The unwitting victim internalizes their feelings; they believe they are barely worthy of friendship or acceptance and are willing to do any-
thing to obtain it—even if it means being punished (which they believe they deserve any-
way). Without the intervention of an adult who is able to recognize this mutually destructive interpersonal dynamic, the youth may continue indefinitely in this pattern.

Without the intervention of an adult who is able to recognize this mutually destructive interpersonal dynamic, the youth may continue indefinitely in this pattern.

The Peer Manipulation intervention is unique in that the LSCI-trained adult works with both the young person who has been "pulling the strings" and with the youth who has inadvertently allowed themselves to be controlled like a puppet. The helping adult guides each young person to develop self-awareness and insight into their role in the conflict and to understand that by continuing to play this role, they are contributing to their own defeat.

The Adult's Tasks in a Peer Manipulation Intervention

In both the False Friendship and the Set Up subtypes of the Peer Manipulation intervention, the ultimate goal is to help young people develop more positive and constructive friendship skills. The specific outcome goals are defined as follows:

In both the False Friendship and the Set Up subtypes of the Peer Manipulation intervention, the ultimate goal is to help young people develop more positive and constructive friendship skills.

False Friendship: To demonstrate to a lonely, socially isolated youth that a real friend is someone who helps you and makes your life better—not worse. A friend does not exploit you for their own person gain but rather has your best interests at heart. Every person is worthy of real friendship.

The Set Up: To demonstrate to the volatile student that when they react aggressively to others' provocations, they are allowing others to control them.

The Mastermind: To demonstrate to the exploitive youth that adults are aware of their manipulative behavior and that it cannot continue. (This is almost always a Benign Confrontation intervention.)

The Peer Manipulation approach is versatile in its ability to address multiple angles of destructive peer dynamics. For this reason, it is used often in schools, groups, clubs, teams, and anywhere that youth interact. Because human nature has a tendency toward forming power imbalances (e.g., stronger vs. weaker, advantaged vs. disadvantaged), the Peer Manipulation is helpful in confronting the misuse of power and guiding youth to use their power in constructive, mutually beneficial ways. In the pages below, we outline how the Peer Manipulation intervention aims to accomplish this stage by stage.

Sequence of a Peer Manipulation Intervention

Stage 1: Drain Off

As in all LSCI interventions, the first priority in a Peer Manipulation intervention is for the adult to maintain safety and drain off the emotional intensity created during the crisis situation. Typical emotions displayed by young people during this stage include anger, frustration, confusion, and indignation. Once the limbic brain becomes more regulated, youth will be more capable of using language to explore and explain the sequence of troubling events. Since Peer Manipulation crises involve more than one young person, it may be tempting or seem expedient for the adult to begin the intervention with all of the youth together. There are times that this can work and times when it absolutely cannot; the adult should use their judgment to determine the intensity of each young person's emotions and whether or not de-escalation should be done separately.

The adult's tasks in the Drain Off stage are to:

- Actively attend to each young person, recognizing their needs and validating their feelings.
- Use plenty of affirmation, reflecting on the youth's willingness to calm down and to be part of a problem-solving conversation.
- Maintain reassuring communication, reminding each young person that you will help them find a fair resolution to the problem situation.
- Actively manage any counter-aggressive feelings that surface from past experiences of working with the youth and anticipating that another exploiting situation may have taken place.
- If youth have been separated during the Drain Off stage, and you believe that it would be productive to bring them together for the Timeline stage, they can be rejoined when Drain Off is completed and everyone is calm enough to engage in respectful conversation.

Stage 2: The Timeline

The foundation for a successful Peer Manipulation intervention depends upon a carefully constructed Timeline. By gathering detailed information about the incident, the adult should be able to discern exploitive behavior toward a victimized peer.

In a *False Friendship* situation, the adult will begin to realize that one of the young people has manipulated the behavior of another for their own personal gain. Though an adult may readily recognize this dynamic, the vulnerable young person will still be holding on to their belief in their "friend." In fact, the youth will almost always defend their "friend" initially, which is why the adult should refrain from openly casting the instigator in a negative light. The most effective way to expose the false friendship is by letting the vulnerable peer hear and see the evidence of exploitation themselves through the course of the Timeline. *For this reason, we recommend interviewing both young people together whenever possible.* (We acknowledge that this will not always be feasible since the adult may not know as they begin the intervention that this is a Peer Manipulation situation and/or conflicting schedules might make a joint intervention impossible. When details in the Timeline stage indicate a False Friendship dynamic, however, we advise that the adult make every attempt to bring both young people together.) The skilled LSCI practitioner should use the Timeline process to allow a young person to tell their story and witness firsthand their "friend" offering an alternative, blameless, self-serving version of the events.

> The most effective way to expose the false friendship is by letting the vulnerable peer hear and see the evidence of exploitation themselves through the course of the Timeline.

In the *Set Up* dynamic, the adult will realize through the Timeline that an impulsive, emotionally reactive youth has been controlled by a socially savvy, exploitive peer. When conducting this type of Peer Manipulation intervention, it is best to separate the young people and conduct each interview separately. Our main focus in the Set Up intervention is to help the emotionally reactive peer understand how they gave up their control to someone else and was set up to get in trouble.

> Our main focus in the Set Up intervention is to help the emotionally reactive peer understand how they gave up their control to someone else and was set up to get in trouble.

The behavior of the *Mastermind* will also come to light during the Timeline stage. In most instances, the Benign Confrontation intervention will be most helpful to use as a follow-up intervention with the exploiting young person. During the Timeline stage, the adult should be using key skills such as appealing to the young person's narcissism once they have begun to recognize the exploitive behavior.

For all subtypes, the adult's tasks in the Timeline stage are to:

- Work backward in time to a point before the stressful event occurred. Then, move forward discovering how each young person perceived, thought, felt, acted, and reacted to the stressful incident.

- If you are interviewing more than one young person at a time, use care to ask about each person's perspectives on the event. Do not allow one youth to speak for, intimidate, or silence the other.
- Recognize any cognitive traps, defense mechanisms, and/or basic justifications that youth are using as they describe the stressful incident.
- Ask questions to establish the relationship between the young people present in the interview: Are they friends? How do they know each other? What do they do together? Explore the concept of mutual friendship to determine if there is a power imbalance in the relationship.

Stage 3: Central Issue

False Friendship

- The Central Issue is that a socially isolated young person has become part of an unhealthy friendship with a peer that he doesn't realize is exploiting him.

The Set Up

- The Central Issue is that an impulsive, emotionally reactive young person is manipulated by an exploiting peer and acts out, not realizing he was set up.

The Mastermind

- The Central Issue is that a bright, socially savvy young person is exploiting a peer for their own needs or enjoyment.

In all types of the Peer Manipulation intervention, the outcome goal is to expose the peer exploitation.

The adult's tasks in the Central Issue stage are to:

- Review the Timeline using the Conflict Cycle paradigm to highlight the self-defeating sequence of events, beliefs, thoughts, feelings, behaviors, and the reactions of others.
- Concisely state the Central Issue.
- Assess the youth's perceptions, thoughts, feelings, and motivations to change.
- Determine that the Peer Manipulation intervention is the most suited to the desired outcome and resolution of the crisis.

- Prepare the young person to consider that they have become involved in an unhealthy peer relationship.

Stage 4: Insight

False Friendship

- In this subtype, the task of the Insight stage is to help the socially isolated young person realize that they have become entangled in an unhealthy relationship with a peer who is taking advantage of or exploiting them in some way. Whenever possible, both the vulnerable student and the exploitive one should be interviewed together. The adult's goal is to have the vulnerable young person see for themselves how their "friend" has exploited them.
- For the vulnerable youth, the adult might ask:
    - Is a friend someone who helps you out of trouble or gets you into trouble?
    - Do you really want to spend your time with people who are willing to put you in jeopardy just to cover for themselves?
- For the exploitive youth, the adults might ask:
    - Why did you ask him to do it instead of doing it yourself?
    - I have a thought about that. I think you didn't do it yourself because you knew there was a good chance you'd get caught and you didn't want to get in trouble. To avoid problems for yourself, you asked him to do it instead.
- Once the false friendship has been exposed, be sensitive to the sense of loss that the vulnerable young person may be experiencing. In their mind, a significant friend—no matter that it was an abusive relationship or a false friendship—has been lost. For young people with histories of broken relationships, loss, and social isolation, this may be quite painful.
- An important task of the False Friendship intervention is to abundantly affirm the young person's new insight along with their capacity to make and maintain new, more positive friendships. This is often an ideal time for a New Tools intervention.

The Set Up

- In this subtype, the task of the Insight stage is to help the impulsive, emotionally reactive young person realize that by reacting to others' provocations, they are giving up control over their own behaviors and allowing others to manipulate them. In this intervention, the adult should interview the reactive youth without the manipulator present, to expose the details of the set up.

- Use concrete analogies in this intervention to help the impulsive young person truly understand the dynamics that were created by the manipulative peer. For example, talk about:

  - Their role as the marionette puppet, while their peer has been pulling their strings and controlling their actions.
  - Their role as the video game character who keeps crashing into walls because their peer has a firm grip on the game controller.
  - Their role as the light bulb that keeps getting turned on and off by their peer who controls the light switch.

The Mastermind
- The task of the Insight stage in this subtype is identical to the tasks outlined in the Benign Confrontation (Chapter 13).

Additional adult tasks in the Insight stage are to:

- Help the socially isolated young person recognize their pattern of becoming entangled in unhealthy friendships. Affirm their good intentions of being a friend while helping them realize that they are worthy of finding friends who help them feel good about themselves.
- Help the impulsive, emotionally reactive young person recognize their pattern of giving up their controls to others. Affirm any occasions in which they have shown control over their anger.
- Challenge and change the Mastermind's basic justifications for exploiting others.
- The Insight goals of the Peer Manipulation intervention are to help the young person:

  - *False Friendship:* Understand what it means to have a positive friendship.
  - *The Set Up:* Avoid attempts by exploitive peers to control their actions.
  - *The Mastermind:* Acknowledge and change exploitive behaviors.

- Acknowledge and affirm that the young person has learned something valuable about the nature of friendships, interpersonal relationships, and the way they allow themselves to be influenced by others.

Stage 5: New Skills

For both the socially isolated and the impulsive, emotionally reactive youth for whom the Peer Manipulation intervention is designed, Stage 5 is an invaluable opportunity for adults to provide guidance and coaching in social-emotional skills. In the *False Friendship*, young people benefit from exploring ideas for making and maintaining healthy friendships. Because these young people have such limited skills and experience with peers, it is helpful to emphasize that "to have a friend, you have to be a friend" and to role play specific friendship-building skills.

In the *Set Up*, kids benefit from learning new self-awareness and self-control skills to recognize and resist others' attempts at manipulation and provocation. Both types of youth benefit from adult reassurance that new social-emotional skills are within their reach and will help them be more successful.

The adult's tasks in the New Skills stage are to:

- Teach and practice the social-emotional skill(s) the young person needs to engage in healthy interpersonal relationships.
- Consider following a False Friendship interview with a New Tools for the socially isolated youth and with a Benign Confrontation for the exploitive "Mastermind."
- Consider following a Set Up interview with a Regulate and Restore intervention if the impulsive, emotionally reactive youth shows signs of intense guilt and remorse after their outburst.
- Continue on with the thread of using analogies to help the Set Up victim develop new skills to resist being controlled by others. For example, if you have used the puppet analogy, help the child imagine that in response to provocation, they simply untie the strings that others are pulling. Or, using the video game analogy, suggest that kids imagine themselves removing the batteries from the game controller so that it no longer has power over their character.

Stage 6: Transfer of Learning

The last stage of LSCI should be used to prepare the young person for a transition back into the ongoing activity or interpersonal situation. Help the young person anticipate and plan for how they will calmly respond to peers, adults, and any programmatic consequences.

The adult's tasks in the Transfer of Learning stage are to:

- Summarize the conversation with an emphasis on the new insights developed by the young person.
- Affirm the young person's competence for carrying out the plan for success.
- Plan for what the young person will do when they return and how others may react as they rejoin the group.

- Inform other staff of the plan. Ask them to support the young person upon their return and to affirm when the new social-emotional skills are used.
- Encourage restorative practices to resolve issues involving adults and peers.

Now you have a thorough and comprehensive understanding of the adult's stage-by-stage tasks in both forms of the Peer Manipulation intervention. Below, we share examples of actual LSCI conversations—first a False Friendship, then a Set Up—so that you can see firsthand how the process works.

Example of LSCI Used to Expose Peer Exploitation: False Friendship

"With a friend like you, who needs an enemy?"

Background Information

Leo is a socially sophisticated and charismatic 13-year-old middle school student. He has the reputation of being clever and good with his words. Adults often tell him that he'll make a great attorney or politician someday, as he is always trying to make a case for something or convince others to do things his way. Whenever there is a problem in the class, Leo seems to be at the center of it, though he almost always manages to talk his way out of trouble. Alex is a socially awkward, insecure 13-year-old classmate of Leo's. He follows school rules faithfully and is quiet but kind to everyone. They live on the same street and Alex has looked up to Leo ever since they were in the same preschool class. Leo is never outwardly mean to Alex, though over the years he has frequently taken advantage of Alex's admiration and desire to be his friend. In Leo's mind, this behavior is justified because he "lets" Alex hang out with him after school sometimes and keeps other kids from making fun of him.

The Incident

While the teacher is out of the classroom, Leo grabs Alex's cell phone out of his backpack. Alex tells Leo to give it back since the school has strict rules against phones being out during class. Leo laughs and hands it back to Alex, saying, "Fine, then you send the text about Kelsey!" Alex looks at Leo with confusion then listens as Leo instructs him what to type. Alex types, "Kelsey is a fat whore." After Leo confirms that he has spelled everything correctly, Alex presses "Send."

When Mrs. Rodriguez returns to the room, she sees the phone in Alex's hand. She immediately tells Alex to hand her the phone, which is standard procedure whenever a teacher sees a cell phone out during a class. Mrs. Rodriguez takes the phone, glances at the screen, and sees the text that Alex has just sent out to the entire eighth grade group chat. She is immediately outraged and appalled. After getting the rest of her students on task and asking the instructional support teacher to monitor the class, she asks Alex and Leo to step out into the hallway with her. Knowing the personalities of both boys, she chooses to do LSCI with them together since she suspects that Leo may have instigated this event.

This LSCI shows how the teacher (T) managed the topic of exploitation with both the victim (A) and the mastermind (L) present.

Stage 1: Drain Off

T: Wow—this phone is nicer than the one I have! Whose is this?

A: *(Nervously)* It's mine.

T: Is this the newest model?

A: Yeah.

T: I bet you were happy to get this! Was it a present?

A: *(Visibly relaxing)* Yeah, I just got it last week for my birthday.

T: Nice! Happy belated birthday!

A: Thanks.

Stage 2: Timeline

T: When did you first bring this new phone to school?

A: Today.

T: Where do you keep it?

A: *(Looking relaxed and enjoying the discussion)* In my backpack.

T: Did you have it in your backpack when you walked into my class?

A: Yeah, I had it there all day.

T: Who had you shown it to so far?

A: No one.

T: What? *(Showing surprise)* You mean you had this awesome new phone in your backpack all day and you didn't show it to anyone? Is that true?

A: Yeah.

T: That's amazing. I'm very impressed. You must have excellent self-control! Most kids who had a phone like that would have shown it to everyone. Most kids wouldn't be able to keep it in their backpack all day.

A: Well, the school rule is that we can't have it out during classes, so I was just following the rules.

T: You followed the rule all day—that's impressive, Alex. But then, something must have made you decide to break the school rules because when I walked in to the room, you had the phone out and were texting.

A: Well, Leo really wanted to see it so he kind of took it from my backpack. But he gave it back as soon as I asked him to, so he was really following the rules too.

T: I'm sure you were glad to get it back. So, what happened next?

A: Leo asked me to send out a funny text to make kids laugh.

T: I assume that you are friends then. Are you good friends or are you just friendly in this class?

A: We are good friends.

T: Is that true for you, Leo?

L: Yeah, we're friends.

T: I see. So, as a friend, you took Alex's phone out of his bag even though you know that was putting him at risk of having his brand-new phone confiscated?

L: Well I didn't know you'd be back so soon. It's not like I meant to get caught or anything.

T: Right, of course not. Thank you for being so honest. Then what happened after Leo took your phone, Alex?

A: Well, he said he had a funny idea for a text that would make the kids laugh, but when I told him to give me back my phone, he did. He told me that if I was so freaked out about my phone, that I could just send the text. Then he said that people would think I said the funny thing.

T: That must have been very tempting for you. A popular kid like Leo gives you the chance to get everyone's attention by texting something funny.

A: I told Leo I'd better not send the text, though, because my mom says not to use the eighth grade group chat.

T: What did Leo say?

Stage 3: Central Issue

A: He said if I didn't want to, Antonio would send it. He said that everyone would think Antonio was hilarious.

T: Let me guess, Alex. You decided to go along with Leo's idea to make other kids laugh.

A: (*Nods*)

T: Did you come up with the words for the text?

A: Leo had the idea. He told me what to type.

T: Do you remember what you were thinking about the words when you were typing?

A: (*Looks very nervous and starts swinging feet*) No, not really.

T: Looking at you, Alex, you seem upset and worried about this problem.

A: A little. (*Clearly upset*) I wasn't sure what I should do but then when I saw you come back in the room, I freaked out and just hit "Send" so that I could put the phone back in my backpack and not get caught.

T: A part of you knew that what you were doing was wrong and you didn't want to get caught.

A: I mean, but Leo said it was just a joke, so maybe it wasn't really a big deal.

T: What I don't understand, Leo, is why you asked Alex to send the text instead of doing it yourself? You had already taken his phone out of his backpack and it sounds like you had the idea for the joke.

L: Well, Alex is my friend and he told me to give the phone back, so I did. I thought he'd want to make the kids laugh.

T: I see, but help me understand why you told Alex to send the text or you would tell Antonio to do it.

L: Well, I didn't think Alex would be dumb enough to actually send it.

T: Oh, you didn't think Alex would do it! So, you were testing him?

L: Yeah, it was just for fun.

T: That's right. You were having fun because you are a very smart person! You knew that the guy who sent a text like this one would be in trouble. Since you didn't send it, we can all agree that you are very smart. Alex, if Leo is very smart for not sending a text like this, what does that make you?

A: (*Deep silence*) Dumb!

Stage 4: Insight

T: I'm going to tell you what I've heard so far, just to make sure that I have all of the facts correct. You can let me know if I missed anything, okay?

L & A: (*Nod*)

T: So, Alex, your friend Leo takes your new phone out of your backpack without permission, even though he knows school policy is that the phone will be confiscated if a teacher sees it out during class. When you ask for the phone, he gives it back to you but then tells you what you should text in the group chat. You told him you didn't want to do it because you're not supposed to use the group chat, but you did it anyway because Leo said he'd get Antonio to do it if you wouldn't. You wanted to make the kids laugh, so you felt torn. You panicked and pressed "Send" when I walked in the room. Now, Leo says he didn't think you'd be dumb enough to do that. . . . (*Long silence*) . . . Alex, let me ask you an important question. Is a friend someone who helps you or hurts you? Is he someone who gets you into trouble or someone who helps you stay out of trouble? Think about it. Remember, Leo is a very smart guy.

A: (*Looks uncertainly at the teacher while Leo is looking anxious*) I'm not sure . . .

T: Alex, it is important to have friends, and I want you to have friends. But you need friends you can trust, not friends who take advantage of you.

A: (*Silence*)

T: I know what kinds of friends I want. Maybe it is different with you. Maybe you enjoy him taking your stuff and getting you to do his dirty work. If so, you are free to continue, but don't trick yourself into believing you have a good and trustworthy friend. It's your choice.

A: Leo does get me into trouble. Even my mother doesn't want me to hang out with him anymore.

T: Alex, let me ask you something else. When Leo was telling you to text the words, "Kelsey is a fat whore," did you think those words were funny or did you think they were cruel?

A: Well, I'm not really sure what a "whore" is, but I knew that "fat" was kind of not good. I didn't really think about it that much, though, because you came back in the room and I just wanted to put my phone away.

T: Thank you for being honest, Alex. You're telling me that you are smart enough to know that it's not good to call someone "fat" and that you shouldn't have your phone out during the school day. In other words, you are smart enough to make good choices no matter what other kids tell you to do.

A: (*Nods*)

At this point, I felt confident that Alex had gained a new insight about the way that Leo had exploited their friendship and used him to hurt Kelsey. I wanted to complete the rest of the intervention without Leo present, however, knowing that from this point forward, Leo's presence could hinder Alex's ability to talk about a plan for success. I instructed Leo to return to the main classroom and begin his work, letting him know that I would follow up after class was over.

T: (*To Alex*) You have a difficult situation to think about, but it sounds as if you have a new idea about friends. It is important to have friends, but they need to have your back, not let you get in trouble for the things they tell you to do.

A: Yeah, Leo can get me into trouble.

Stage 5: New Skills

T: You've got a good insight there. How should this change what you do around Leo?

A: Well . . . maybe I ought to stay away from him.

T: That's an idea. I'm thinking we need to go deeper, though, since you and Leo live on the same street and you are in a lot of classes together. It'll be hard to stay away from each other. What can you do when you are around Leo and he does something like telling you to send a cruel text?

A: I'll tell him I won't do it.

T: Great plan! Sometimes things like that are easier said than done. Let's practice a little so that you know what tone of voice to use to let Leo know that you are serious and how to use eye contact to tell him that he can't talk you into doing something that you know is wrong.

Alex and I spent a few minutes role-playing various scenarios in which I pretended to be Leo and Alex had to resist my creative attempts to convince, pressure, and dare him to break the rules. Then, we switched places and Alex pretended to be Leo. I wanted to demonstrate effective skills for resisting peer manipulation and asserting myself.

Stage 6: Transfer of Learning

T: It's not easy to change things up in a long-standing friendship, Alex, but it sounds like you have the right ideas! Tomorrow, we can talk about it some more and perhaps think about some other kids in the grade that might be better friends to you, OK?

A: OK. What's going to happen to Leo now? I don't want him to be mad at me or to send texts to other people about me.

T: I am going to follow up with Leo after class. I will be clear with him that what happened today has to do with *his* actions. We'll talk about school rules regarding social media and texting. Your job, for now, is to keep your focus on what you and I talked about—making good choices for yourself and resisting pressure from others. Can you do that?

A: (*Nods*)

You probably recognize the need for a second, follow-up LSCI with Leo, with a different therapeutic goal—to benignly confront him about his unacceptable behavior (see Chapter 13). Our objective in conducting a Benign Confrontation with Leo will be to show him that he used Alex to hurt Kelsey. If he continues to treat his "friends" this way, he will soon find himself without them.

You also may have noticed that the teacher selected Alex's exploitation and need for friendship as the central issue, rather than the incident itself. In this LSCI, Alex was able to understand the dynamics of his relationship with Leo and how he is being influenced and used by this false friend. Alex will need additional assistance in follow-up LSCIs to learn new social skills for making and keeping friends. Social communication instruction, along with other social-emotional learning, will all be helpful to Alex.

The success of this LSCI was in large part due to the interest the teacher showed in the relationship between the boys and the care with which each detail of the situation was brought out. The initial focus on the phone reduced defensiveness and made it possible to move the young men freely into a discussion about the sequence of events. By bringing out the small details as she worked through this LSCI, the teacher was able to show Alex the facts. The Timeline, developed through questions about "Where? When? What?" and "Who?" provided these facts without the teacher having to make accusations that would have heightened the boys' defensiveness and made this LSCI more difficult.

Example of LSCI Used to Expose Peer Exploitation: The Set Up

"He gave me the finger!"

Background

Carlos is an 11-year-old boy of below average intelligence who is diagnosed with attention deficit hyperactivity disorder (ADHD). He has been in our program for 3.5 years. He is highly distractible and unable to ignore the smallest of distractions in the classroom. He is also extremely impulsive and frequently pokes at, pushes, or kicks young people walking past or near him. To complicate things further for him, Carlos has many tics, including sticking out his tongue, sticking up his middle finger, dropping his jaw, smelling his fingers, shaking his fingers, and repeatedly saying "Huh?" Carlos typically overreacts to situations by yelling out, swearing, and/or becoming physically aggressive.

Kahlil is a nine-year-old boy of average intelligence who is also diagnosed with ADHD. He is new to our program and has only been in the classroom for four weeks. He does well academically but has difficulty with peer relationships. Kahlil has frequently been observed mimicking other young people and making rude comments to them. He also intentionally gets in other young people's personal space and makes sexual gestures to distract them. Kahlil typically knows everyone else's business and frequently tattles on other young people even when the situation doesn't involve him. He is often subtle with his actions but usually gets a big reaction from other young people in the classroom.

The Incident

Carlos and Kahlil were working together at a table in front of the classroom with a teaching assistant and one other young person. There were three other groups being run simultaneously by two other teaching assistants and myself. When the third young person in Carlos (C) and Kahlil's (K) group refused to work and began distracting by repeatedly tapping his pencil on the table, the teaching assistant left the table briefly to escort the young person to a divider area. Suddenly, Carlos was yelling, "I hate you, Kahlil! He gave me the finger!" Kahlil began to shout back, "No I didn't! He's lying! You're a liar, Carlos!" Soon the boys were in a heated argument. The teaching assistant (TA) immediately returned to the table and attempted to find out what happened.

TA: What's going on over here?

C: Kahlil gave me the finger!

K: No, I didn't! I was just minding my own business, working.

C: He's lying! He stuck his middle finger up at me!

K: (*Half smiling*) I have a tic too, you know.

C: He's making fun of me! Shut up! (*He pounds on the table*)

K: What? I didn't do anything.

C: *Yes, you did!*

The teaching assistant directed Carlos to a divider area to get himself together, but he was so angry by this point that he ran to the divider and attempted to tip it over. He was then directed to open-door time-out, which made him even more furious. Carlos threw his shoes at the staff and began to punch and kick the walls in time-out, swearing. Then he began to cry hysterically.

Stage 1: Drain Off

It took Carlos about ten minutes to settle down to the point where he could sit against the back wall of the calm down space. I let him know that I was glad to see he was working on getting calm and that as soon as he was ready, I would like to hear him tell me about what happened.

Stage 2: The Timeline

T: You did a great job getting yourself calm and ready to talk. Can you tell me what happened?

C: Kahlil was teasing me.

T: What did he do to tease you?

C: He gave me the finger.

T: OK. Let's start at the beginning. Where were you and Kahlil when this happened?

C: In the Makerspace with Miss Margaret.

T: OK, so you went to Makerspace with Miss Margaret and what happened?

C: Kahlil gave me the finger.

T: Did anything happen before Kahlil gave you the finger?

C: No. She took Keith to the divider area.

T: Let me see if I understand this. You went to Makerspace, and I assume that Keith began to have some difficulties and had to leave the group.

C: Yes.

T: Was anyone else in the group having trouble at this time?

C: No.

T: OK, so when Miss Margaret walked Keith to the divider area, Kahlil gave you the finger?

C: Yeah. He told me to look under the table and when I did, he stuck his middle finger up at me.

T: How did you feel when Kahlil stuck his middle finger up at you?

C: Mad! He's not my friend anymore. He said he has a tic, but he's lying. He made fun of me because I have a tic, but I can't help it.

T: I understand you being upset with Kahlil when he teased you about something you have very little control over. When you got angry for Kahlil giving you the finger, what did you do?

C: I yelled at him and kicked his chair.

T: And when you yelled at Kahlil and kicked his chair, what happened to you?

C: I had to use time-out.

At this point, I chose to draw the Conflict Cycle for Carlos to help him see what happened. He usually benefits from concrete examples and visual aids. We discussed how the incident triggered angry feelings and how Carlos reacted physically to those feelings. As a result, Carlos had to use time-out.

T: While you were using the calm down area, what was Kahlil doing?

C: Sitting at the table.

T: So, Kahlil got to stay with the group?

C: Yeah. It's not fair.

Stage 3: The Central Issue

T: Carlos, you have given me a lot of information here and really helped me understand so much more about what happened. I want to try to put it in my own words to make sure I heard you correctly. Is that all right with you?

C: Okay.

I saw this crisis as a Peer Manipulation, Set Up situation. The goals of a Set Up intervention are to help Carlos realize that he had been manipulated by Kahlil and that while he had to use time-out, Kahlil was able to stay in the group.

T: Great, thanks. So, you and Kahlil were sitting at the same group of tables in Makerspace. You were both on task and doing your work, which is terrific. Were you upset about anything at that point?

C: No, I was fine. I was in a good mood. Makerspace is my favorite class.

T: OK, so everything was fine. But then things changed.

C: Right. Kahlil started the whole thing.

T: So, if I have this right, you told me that Keith was having some problems, so the teaching assistant went with him over to the divider. That left just you and Kahlil together in your group. That was when Kahlil told you to look under the desks?

C: Right. For no reason.

T: And what did you think at that moment about why he wanted you to look *under* the desk instead of just showing you *at* the desks, since the two of you were alone in your group.

C: I don't know. I didn't really think about it. I just did what he told me to do. He's always telling me what to do.

T: Oh, so this isn't the first time Kahlil has tried to get you to do something?

C: No, he is always trying to get me to do stuff.

T: I see. Are you and Kahlil usually friends? Do you joke around with each other and get each other to do stuff?

C: No, it's not like that. We're not friends. He tries to get me to do stuff and then makes fun of me.

T: Oh! So, you are telling me that when he tells you to do stuff like looking under the table, you know he's not being friendly.

C: Exactly.

T: That makes me wonder, Carlos. If you are sort of used to Kahlil trying to get you to do stuff and then making fun of you, what made you agree to look under the table today?

C: I don't know. I didn't really think about it. I just did it.

T: You didn't really think about it. You just did it. I get that. Sometimes we all act quickly without really thinking.

C: I do that all of the time.

T: How does that usually work out for you?

C: Sometimes it's OK. A lot of the time, I end up getting in trouble.

T: How did it work out today?

C: Really badly.

T: You know, Carlos. I think you are right. That's a really important thing you just said. When you listen to what people like Kahlil tell you to do without thinking first, it can end up really badly for you. You are really on to something here, Carlos. So, today when Kahlil told you to look under the table, you did it without really thinking, and you saw that he was giving you the finger. That made you really, really angry. You yelled at him and kicked his chair. When the teaching assistant asked you to go to the divider area, that made you even more furious, which is when you tried to knock down the divider. Is that accurate?

C: Yeah.

T: OK, thank you Carlos for being so patient and so thoughtful about what happened. I think I have a new understanding about what happened.

Stage 4: The Insight

T: There is still one thing I am wondering about, though. If Kahlil was swearing at you or teasing you, who should get in trouble?

C: He should.

T: One would think so, but who actually got in trouble?

C: I did.

T: Yes, so what happens when you react to Kahlil's behavior?

C: I get in trouble.

T: And how about Kahlil?

C: Sometimes he gets in trouble but not as much as I do.

T: I'm wondering about something. Do you think it's possible that Kahlil enjoys getting you to act out so that you get in trouble?

C: Yes.

T: I want you to think about something. You and Kahlil are like a fire-cracker and a match. Which one of you has the ability to make the other explode?

C: I saw fireworks on the Fourth of July.

T: Oh, yeah?

C: Yeah, they were loud, but I wasn't afraid of them.

T: You are brave. I want you to think of those fireworks for a minute. I want you to picture you and Kahlil, one as the fireworks and one as the match to set off those fireworks. Which one of you is able to set the other off?

C: Well, he set me off today.

T: That's right. He was like a match. He did something to you to make you explode like fireworks. When you react to him, you get in trouble and he usually gets to stay with the group.

Stage 5: New Skills

T: I think we need to come up with some ways to help you deal with Kahlil without exploding.

C: I could just ignore him.

T: That's a good idea, but sometimes it's very difficult to ignore somebody when they are trying to get you in trouble. If you're having trouble ignoring Kahlil, what else can you do?

C: I can ask to move my seat or go get a drink.

T: Great! Physically removing yourself from the situation is a terrific idea!

C: I can also just tell a teacher without overreacting so that Kahlil gets in trouble.

T: That's right.

Stage 6: Transfer of Learning

T: What do you think Kahlil might do or say when you return to class?

C: He might still tease me.

T: How will you handle that?

C: I'll just ignore him.

T: Do you think you will be able to do that?

C: Yes, because I don't want to get in trouble again. He should get in trouble.

T: That's right. Remember that you can ask to go for a walk or get a drink.

C: I will.

T: Great! I'm really proud of you that we could talk about this problem
      and come up with some better ways of dealing with it in the future.

Intervention Summary

Carlos rejoined the class and the rest of the day went smoothly. Carlos does not always react so calmly. Due to his high level of impulsivity, these types of situations will probably continue to be a struggle for him. However, he seems to be more aware of the fact that sometimes other young people attempt to set him up and he has begun to make better decisions in terms of his own behavior more often now.

Following Carlos's interview, I took Kahlil aside and did a Benign Confrontation intervention with him. The situation detailed in this article highlights the cleverness Kahlil—a trait common in the youth who typically do the "setting up" of volatile youth. Kahlil only set Carlos up when the adult was away from the area and he did it under the desk to avoid detection. At first, Kahlil denied any wrongdoing and insisted he was the innocent victim. Eventually, he seemed more willing to see his role in the conflict and admitted that he likes to see Carlos "go off" because it's "funny." A couple days later, Kahlil attempted to set Carlos up again, and I was so pleased to hear Carlos tell Kahlil, "I'm just going to ignore you. You're just trying to get me in trouble."

PART 3

ADDITIONAL APPLICATIONS OF LSCI SKILLS

As you've read the Intervention chapters and realized how comprehensive LSCI's approach is in addressing the most common patterns of self-defeating behavior among school-aged children and adolescents, it may have occurred to you that LSCI skills could also work with fully grown adults, with young children, with your own children—and more! If so, *you'd be right!* We dare assert that the brain-based, trauma-informed, relationship-building skills of LSCI are *universally applicable* and that our six-stage framework lends itself easily to multiple populations, all across the world.

In Part 3 of our book, we share with you how the skills of LSCI can be applied in professional settings with adult colleagues and through supervision, coaching, and ongoing training of LSCI skills (Chapter 16). In Chapter 17, we share an excerpt from our book *The Angry Smile: Effective Strategies to Manage Passive-Aggressive Behavior at Home, at School, in Relationships, in the Workplace & Online* to show you how LSCI skills are used to confront and change passive-aggressive behavior. Then, we describe how to adapt the LSCI process for use with children in the home (Chapter 18) and in early childhood education and special education settings for youth with developmental challenges (Chapter 19). Chapter 20 features sample sections from our eight-session *LSCI Group Curriculum for Children & Youth*, an SEL group curriculum that builds self-awareness and self-regulation in young people while building an understanding of the dynamics of conflict and self-defeating behaviors. Lastly, in Chapter 21, we describe the implementation of LSCI in three different settings in Belgium over the course of the last 20 years.

Before you go, be sure to check out the appendices, in which we share examples of forms and assessments that have been developed by LSCI Master Trainers to document the use of LSCI for data collection, assess before and after learning, rate LSCI skills, and help young people successfully transition back to their classrooms and programs after an LSCI intervention is complete.

"I earned my LSCI certification. Now what?"

MAKING IT WORK

Implementing LSCI into Daily Practices and Supporting Staff in Mastering Intervention Skills

T he choice to bring LSCI into your organization or school is a choice to accept a trauma-informed belief system that is infused into the program at all levels. The cornerstone of this philosophy is the notion that change begins with the adult. It is our responsibility to establish a safe, predictable environment that reduces the likelihood of triggers that tap into children's unresolved trauma issues. It is our duty to create trusting relationships with young people by responding to pain-based behavior with calm understanding rather than adrenaline-fueled punishment.

> The choice to bring LSCI into your organization or school is a choice to accept a trauma-informed belief system that is infused into the program at all levels.

Anyone who has worked with challenging young people knows that these tasks are more challenging than they sound. We are actually asking ourselves to repress our own lower-brain survival instincts and engage in higher-order thinking at a time of intense stress. To accomplish this requires a support system for adults. We, too, need an environment in which we can feel safe talking about our emotions and sharing our experiences with others. That level of support is available only when the entire system, from administration to direct care staff, is trained in the fundamentals of trauma-informed care and is accepting of the fact that it will take work to bring the program into alignment with those principles.

LSCI certification is a rigorous training that pays off for years to come. Once you have made this investment in the highest level of professional training for your staff, we want to help you be successful integrating LSCI skills into daily professional practices and supporting your newly certified staff to develop mastery over their new set of skills. In this chapter, we first provide a set of how-to guidelines from the LSCI Institute's Master and Senior Trainers, based on their experiences successfully implementing LSCI in their programs and schools. Then, we share with you a unique and highly effective way to apply the LSCI process to adult staff who inadvertently fuel conflict cycles and/or who feel hesitant to use their newly minted LSCI skills with young people during problem situations.

Guidelines for Implementing LSCI into Programs and Practices: Best Practice Tips from Trainers

Tip 1: Be Strategic in Your Rollout of LSCI Training

When selecting staff to attend LSCI certification training, it is helpful to keep these guidelines in mind:

1. **Build Strong and Supportive Teams**

   While some school districts or organizations are tempted to enroll two to three staff members from each school or program in initial training sessions, we find that it is more helpful to train a core group from each school or program so that they can support each other in learning and practice after the certification is complete.

2. **Identify Role Models**

   Rather than sending staff members who "need LSCI the most" (because they tend to be reactive, hot-tempered, or easily baited into Conflict Cycles with kids) to your first few certification trainings, prioritize sending your positive role models and those most likely to influence others in constructive ways. These natural leaders will return from certification training with confidence, ready to talk about LSCI, demonstrate their new skills, and help encourage others on the team to learn and apply the skills of LSCI.

3. **Make LSCI Part of On-Boarding**

   Pressley Ridge is a national training site for the LSCI Institute and has been hosting LSCI trainings for its staff since 1990. Having observed the impact of several different training roll-out strategies over the years, learning development coordinator for West Virginia and Virginia Jim Natural recommends that staff receive LSCI training upon being hired.

   > It is far easier to instill good habits in staff than it is to undo harmful ones.

   "Give people the skills they need to do their jobs," he urges. "Don't wait until someone 'proves they will stay' before you invest in them."

It is far easier to instill good habits in staff than it is to undo harmful ones. Natural explains that when new staff are "brought into the LSCI fold right away," they are shown how to see a young person's problem behavior through a trauma-informed lens and taught how to respond in ways that bring about meaningful growth and change.

4. Include Leadership in LSCI Training

Encourage administrators to attend training whenever possible. Even if their daily interactions tend to be with other adults rather than with young people, having decision-makers understand, support, and endorse LSCI is key to its long-term success.

5. Present LSCI Training as an Opportunity—Not an Obligation

When it comes to professional development and training, there are generally three kinds of participants:

1. Vacationers—those who envision the training day(s) as a pleasant opportunity to daydream, scroll social media, and otherwise multi-task.
2. Prisoners—those who pessimistically anticipate that training will be a waste of their time and resent the imposition before it even begins.
3. Learners—those who optimistically anticipate that training will offer helpful insights and skills and come to training with minds open, ready to soak up new knowledge.

Whether you have vacationers, prisoners, or learners, *all* professionals want to have a clear understanding of "what's in it for them" when it comes to training. *Before registering a staff person for training*, educate them about LSCI, letting them know that it is an invaluable professional opportunity to learn how to:

- Build more positive and enjoyable relationships with young people
- Disengage from endless cycles of conflict
- Prevent crisis situations from spiraling out of control
- De-escalate problem situations
- Reduce disruptions and time off task
- Become trauma-informed
- Better understand the causes of problem behavior
- Use a consistent verbal framework for processing stressful incidents
- Positively impact kids' lives
- Show professionals they are valued
- Offer professional development hours (e.g., CEUs, DOE service hours), compensation (e.g., don't ask staff to give up a free weekend or

summer vacation time to attend training without pay), or promotion opportunities (e.g., a staff person must be certified in LSCI in order to be eligible for advancement) for LSCI certification.

The good news is that once participants take LSCI training, they tend to eagerly encourage others to take LSCI training as well! Word of mouth has always been on LSCI's side because once people have the set of skills and see how effective they are in building positive relationships and changing unwanted behaviors, they naturally want their colleagues and teammates to jump on board. The more LSCI becomes embedded into your school or organizational culture, the better it works!

> **The more LSCI becomes embedded into your school or organizational culture, the better it works!**

Tip 2: Build LSCI Into Your Culture

> **When leaders are clear about how they want each professional to interact with each youth, LSCI grows from a one-time training program to a consistent cultural norm.**

The Society for Human Resources Management (SHRM) says that an organization's culture defines the proper way to behave while at work and consists of shared beliefs and values that shape employee perceptions, understanding, and behaviors. When leaders are clear about how they want each professional to interact with each youth, LSCI grows from a one-time training program to a consistent cultural norm. Consider these elements that LSCI Trainers say have helped their sites make LSCI both a skill set and a mindset:

1. **LSCI Beliefs and Values Are Operationalized**

   Marcus Martin (2020), an LSCI Trainer at a private academic special education school, says "[LSCI is] so ingrained in our culture that when new staff come in, they almost have no choice; they look around and see that this is the way everyone talks to and interacts with kids." Indeed, LSCI is a shaper of a school or program's culture because its beliefs and values are easily translated into daily practices and ways of thinking. When professionals use LSCI skills with young people, they are making the decision to approach them with a trauma-informed curiosity about their perceptions, thoughts, and feelings. They are changing their way of thinking from *"Why does she act that way"* to *"What happened in her life to lead her to make that choice?"* They are choosing to genuinely connect with a child and use verbal de-escalation strategies to help the young person become more emotionally regulated. They are aiming to turn down the heat on a stressful situation and keep it from escalating into a restraint. They are conveying their belief that people in stress deserve to be heard and understood. They are looking beyond surface behavior to uncover the central issue of a crisis, which, in turn, enables youth to gain new insight into their behaviors. They are teachers of new skills, advocates for success, and long-term supporters of kids who develop resilience through the presence of a consistent, nurturing adult.

Organizations in which LSCI is implemented most successfully are those in which top leadership understands and endorses LSCI as a standard way of operationalizing organizational beliefs and values.

2. **Leadership Sets the Tone**

Organizations in which LSCI is implemented most successfully are those in which top leadership understands and endorses LSCI as a standard way of operationalizing organizational beliefs and values. Martin (2020) says that "leaders set the tone" at his school, providing constant support, answering questions, helping out with tough behaviors, and promoting the use of trauma-informed interventions. "[Our supervisor] believes in us and [communicates that] what we are doing will make a positive impact. She asks the staff for input, asks what things are going well, and helps with things we can improve upon. Along with all of this, our entire staff gets frequent LSCI refresher trainings so we always have our skill set sharpened and prepared to handle any situation."

3. **Teams Speak (and Understand) the LSCI Language**

When you first started to read this book, attend training, or hear people talk about LSCI, you probably wondered about all of the novel terms, such as *Drain Off, Timeline, Conflict Cycle*, and *Benign Confrontation*. Just as spoken language is a powerful transmitter of a nation's culture, LSCI terminology is an important shorthand that connects staff and helps them quickly understand each other, even when there is no time for a full conversation. For example, if a teacher completes a successful Red Flag intervention with a student and needs to run to a meeting before filling in a colleague on the plan for success, they can still communicate a great deal of meaning simply by saying, "This was a Red Flag; I'll follow up with you in an hour." This simple use of LSCI language communicates a complex amount of information about the sources of a young person's stress, their new insights, the social-emotional skills that were likely discussed, and the basics of their plan for success.

Those who have completed LSCI training and can "speak the language" have an effective, efficient, and nuanced way to communicate. This mutual understanding, in turn, builds trust among staff members. The more staff who are "fluent" in the language, the more effective the communication and teamwork.

Further, Senior Trainer Serena Bridges (personal communication, June 2, 2020) says that LSCI gives staff language to explain the "why" behind behavior. Bridges explains that the language of LSCI "created empathy within our staff because they could put a name (e.g., Reality Check, Peer Manipulation) to what was happening. It took the mystery out of behavior."

4. **Create Space and Time for LSCI**

Can LSCI be conducted in a noisy hallway, crowded cafeteria, or bustling outdoor recreation area? Yes. Any experienced LSCI practitioner will tell you that "crisis doesn't happen by appointment" and that we've all had to make do with the time, space, and place we are given. But when a program intentionally creates calming, quiet places and spaces for a young person to become more emotionally regulated and to process a stressful event with a trusted adult, it shows its commitment to making LSCI (and other trauma-informed interventions) successful.

Do all LSCI interventions have to take place in the "regulation room" in order to be effective? No. The success of an LSCI intervention depends far more on the connection between the adult and child than the physical space. But when a program makes a space(s) available, they are making a powerful statement about their prioritization of kids' emotional well-being.

5. **LSCI Fosters a Safer, More Collaborative Culture**

LSCI takes professional teams from a place where they feel unprepared to manage difficult situations to one in which they are confident about what to say, when to listen, and how to respond. Because LSCI unites team members through their understanding of children and a consistent framework for how to verbally process problem situations, staff grow in their trust of one another.

> LSCI takes professional teams from a place where they feel unprepared to manage difficult situations to one in which they are confident about what to say, when to listen, and how to respond.

One LSCI participant says that training in LSCI helped her team become "more collaborative." She explained that prior to being trained in LSCI, her staff's unspoken way of approaching problems was to have whatever staff was present "deal with it" and move on, but that this was only a band-aid approach that kicked the can down the road for the next adult who was present at the next stressful moment. "When we started using LSCI," she said, "we started working through problems together. We talk about the things that have happened in kids' lives and how those things affect the way the kids perceive us as helpers. We started to be more compassionate and really listening to kids. Most of all, though, we started to trust each other more."

In her program, Bridges (2020) notes that "after using LSCI for so long, there is an unspoken agreement between staff and students that we aren't going to put 'hands on.' It's so rare to [use a physical restraint] that students trust us more. There is less of a 'defensive' mentality on both sides. Kids aren't scared of staff, therefore they use our staff as a tool to help them sort through their problems. When we do see aggressive behavior, it's often with new students who haven't had time to build trust with staff."

6. **Learning and Professional Growth Are Supported**
   Working with young people is challenging. Working with challenging young people is *incredibly* challenging. The skills of LSCI are up to the incredibly complex task of reaching and teaching challenging young people. But just as a surgeon must perform hundreds of a specific type of operation in order to become completely competent at the procedure, so must an LSCI-trained staff person apply the skills of LSCI in real-life situations dozens of times in order to become fully adept. What's more, true mastery of the skills of LSCI requires that a staff person have the opportunity to debrief interventions with colleagues, consult with more experienced staff about challenging moments during an LSCI, feel supported by supervisors even when they inadvertently fuel a conflict that they were meant to de-escalate, and generally feel affirmed in their earnest efforts to use LSCI to engage young people. Organizations and schools that have implemented LSCI most successfully into their culture are those that fully support staff in their professional development by consistently discussing how interventions were carried out, using mistakes as coaching moments, eliminating fear of blame, and valuing vulnerability as adults try their hand at applying newly acquired professional skills.

Tip 3: Help Staff Maintain and Master LSCI Skills

The advanced skills of LSCI are best maintained through regular practice, consultation with colleagues, self-reflection, and ongoing supervision. LSCI Trainers recommend these practices as helpful follow-ups to LSCI certification training:

1. Use *daily* documentation and communication tools such as the *Interviewing Skills Checklist*, *Reentry Checklist*, and *Plan for Success* (see Appendix B) to consistently keep LSCI skills on the minds of staff.

2. Support recently LSCI-certified trained staff by keeping their new skills fresh. Hold *weekly* LSCI consultations during which newly trained staff can discuss challenging real-life scenarios with fellow LSCI practitioners.

3. Use the One-Hour Review Sessions (available through the LSCI.org website) during *monthly* or *quarterly* staff meetings to review the foundational skills and interventions of LSCI.

4. Schedule *monthly* video-conferencing calls to bring together staff from throughout your organization to discuss specific uses of LSCI, successes, challenges, skills, interventions, and innovations. Consider partnering with other LSCI-certified schools and organizations to broaden perspectives and gain additional insights.

5. Hold live LSCI Refresher trainings *annually*.

6. Make use of the online LSCI Refresher training (Level 2). There is a one-time fee for participants to access the course; after that, their access to the 19 video-based modules will never expire.

7. Use the eight-session LSCI Group Curriculum (see Chapter 20) with kids. This SEL program teaches young people to recognize patterns of self-defeating behaviors, bringing them into greater alignment with adults when it comes to identifying central issues and developing new insights.

8. Call upon the expertise of tenured LSCI Senior Trainers. Stay connected with your original LSCI Trainer for ongoing consultations either in person or by video-conferencing, phone, and e-mail. With our network of certified Trainers around the world, the LSCI Institute can provide valuable support at any time.

9. Select "coaches" from each of the schools/programs/departments in your organization who have LSCI-certified staff. Empower these coaches to oversee the maintenance and integrity of the LSCI model at their respective site. It is helpful to have an LSCI Trainer meet with these coaches initially (and then as needed) to establish expectations, discuss ongoing training and review activities they can use with their staff, develop data collection forms, schedule dates for future coaches' meetings, etc. The feedback from individual coaches has proven to be very effective in keeping LSCI strong in an organization following certification training.

10. Certify LSCI Senior Trainers in your own organization. Our network of Senior Trainers are hand-selected from the professional staff of our international training sites as well as qualified professionals from the fields of education, psychology, social work, counseling, child and youth care work, and related fields. Visit www.lsci.org to learn more about the requirements and process to become a certified Senior Trainer and a training site for the LSCI Institute.

In the second half of the chapter, we share with you a unique way that supervisors, mentors, and colleagues can create cultures in which the use of LSCI is encouraged and supported among adult staff.

The Double Struggle Intervention: Supporting Staff in Their Use of LSCI Skills

In LSCI terms, a *Double Struggle* is a problem situation that begins within an adult staff person. The struggle is between what that adult knows they *should* do and their internal conflict that makes it difficult for them to carry out this professional responsibility. Sometimes, the internal conflict is expressed as counter-aggressive behavior toward a young person but other times it is expressed through inaction, as when an adult lacks the confidence or will to apply their LSCI skills. The resulting struggle finds the adult either engaged in a power struggle with the youth or withdrawing from him/her, both of which can lead to an escalation of a problem situation.

> The Double Struggle intervention is a way that supervisors, mentors, and even colleagues can apply LSCI skills to adults who inadvertently fuel conflict or miss opportunities to effectively engage young people.

The Double Struggle intervention is a way that supervisors, mentors, and even colleagues can apply LSCI skills to adults who inadvertently fuel conflict or miss opportunities to effectively engage young people. In the pages below, we introduce the Double Struggle intervention to you and show you how to apply it, much like you would any of the interventions described in Part 2 of this book.

Adult's Perceptions:
1. "I'm not going to take his abuse! If he wants to challenge me, I'm ready!"
2. "I'm in charge here. She'll follow my rules or she's out!"
3. "That's the last straw! I'm done with her."
4. "I knew it would be him again!"

Uses:
With adults who inadvertently fuel conflict or miss opportunities to effectively engage young people for any of the following reasons:
1. They become caught in a Conflict Cycle.
2. They hold rigid and unrealistic expectations regarding normal developmental behaviors.

3. They lack an understanding of how the brain responds to stressful situations.
4. They are caught prejudging a young person's reaction to stress and fail to realize that the young person is doing the best they can in the moment.
5. They lack confidence and/or experience in carrying out the skills of LSCI and need additional support from supervisors and mentors.
6. They are caught in a bad mood.

Focus:

- To benignly confront the adult by using the Conflict Cycle to help them gain insight into their role in perpetuating conflict.
- To use the Conflict Cycle to help adults understand how their perceptions, thoughts, and feelings affect their willingness to apply LSCI skills.

Goals:

1. To use the Conflict Cycle as a way of understanding the dynamics between adults and kids during a stressful incident.
2. To acknowledge the adult's good intentions in dealing with a problem situation and to encourage their use of the LSCI process.
3. To support the adult with affirming statements (rather than blame) and to provide additional training to build their confidence and skill in using LSCI.
4. To share information about the young person or the incident that the adult may not have had at the time of the crisis, thus helping the adult accept a new and more accurate perception of the incident.
5. To review the importance of using the diagnostic stages of LSCI in a stressful situation in order to help a youth feel regulated and understood and to determine what about the problem is most important to the youth.
6. To facilitate reconciliation and problem resolution.

Adult's New Insights:

"Now I understand the situation from the young person's point of view and I recognize how I contributed to the problem."

"Now I can see the value of using LSCI to help youth process stressful situations."

"Now I feel more supported in my own learning and professional development."

In Chapter 3, we shared with you the legend of the US Naval ship versus the lighthouse. Anyone who works with challenging youth has felt like the captain at some point. Many of us were raised to respect authority and we expect young persons to do the same. This expectation is a social norm that many young people can live up to. However, in every group there are those young persons who struggle to meet traditional expectations. In particular, youth who have experienced trauma at the hands of adults do not automatically show respect based on age or position of authority. Rather, they develop maladaptive ways of interacting that tend to be self-defeating. There are also kids who experience warm and well-supported childhoods that still exhibit impulsive, disrespectful, defiant behavior due to a chronic mental health challenge or specific stressful incident.

Adults who rely on authority rather than relationship as their primary management style are quickly left feeling frustrated, helpless, and incompetent in their work with challenging youth. These adults can be easily baited into Conflict Cycles and ultimately develop a strong dislike for individual young persons. Unfortunately, rather than perceiving these kids as youth in need of support and guidance, they think of them as troublemakers who deserve punishment and need to be removed from the group. Adults who are not trained in LSCI or not yet competent at managing the behaviors of challenging kids tend to fall back on the only tactics they know: (1) proclamation of authority, (2) referral for discipline by someone else, and/or (3) complete disengagement from the youth, leaving them to their own devices.

The parallel is interesting. Challenging kids are challenging because they possess a rigid and limited range of relationship skills. They know only a few responses to stressful situations, and these responses tend to escalate problems rather than bring them to resolution. *The same is true of some adults.* Without training and skilled support in applying the skills of LSCI, well-meaning adults tend to fuel Conflict Cycles rather than breaking them. The adage applies: *If the only tool you have is a hammer, everything looks like a nail.*

No one enjoys feeling incompetent, so it is understandable that adults can become outraged by the predicaments they find themselves in with challenging youth. We can help our colleagues become more competent in applying LSCI skills through the Double Struggle intervention. The Double Struggle is a highly effective approach that helps supervisors and mentors reinforce their staff's understanding of conflict and support a staff person's ability to successfully engage challenging kids. In the Double Struggle, the Conflict Cycle paradigm is used to subtly suggest how a well-intentioned adult intervention may have inadvertently escalated a problem situation. Through a discreet dialogue, we help staff understand that *the problems young people cause are not the causes of their problems.*

The Interviewer's Task

Working with challenging children and adolescents is a daunting task. When staff are routinely confronted with young people's stresses and conflicts, it is not surprising that their own psychological armor wears thin. Adults may experience real anger toward a young person along with anger at themselves for "taking the bait." This anger coincides with feelings of embarrassment and incompetence.

When we choose to benignly confront staff who contribute to a young person's crisis, we must be mindful of the adult's need to protect self-esteem and save face. Defenses will be up; tact and skill are required to disarm them. Remember that our goal is to help the staff person take a fresh view of the situation. At the onset of the Double Struggle intervention, the adult may believe that the young person is fully responsible for the incident and may feel "righteously indignant" about justifying their own actions. At the close of the intervention, we hope the adult will gain insight into how their good intentions went awry and they ended up fueling the crisis. If the interviewer is successful, the adult will arrive at this insight feeling respected, non-defensive, and willing to think about the young person with a depth of understanding that was not present before.

In the pages that follow, we share two real-life examples of how the Double Struggle intervention was used with adult staff to help them increase their self-awareness, improve their confidence in using LSCI, and build their overall effectiveness in working with challenging young people.

Example 1: *What Are You Looking At?*

Tom lives with his mother, older brother, and sister in a rural area. Life at home is turbulent, and issues of money, privacy, and alcoholism are ever-present. From his elementary school years, Tom's teachers have characterized him as defiant and challenging. When he began middle school two years ago, he was diagnosed with attention deficit hyperactivity disorder (ADHD) and oppositional defiant disorder (ODD). Now age 14, Tom is a student in Ms. Keller's homeroom. He has made progress this year with Ms. Keller's help, but he still distrusts adults. Only those who take the time to get to know him and pass his "tests of tolerance" can recognize that Tom is struggling to overcome many pressures and obstacles. The demands of school are formidable, and he is trying to be successful given the hand life has dealt him.

On Monday morning, Tom was having a particularly difficult time. He appeared distracted and Ms. Keller was unsuccessful in getting him started on his work. He seemed absorbed in his own thoughts. While the rest of the group was completing work, Ms. Keller asked Tom to come with her to a quiet room that is accessible from the classroom and has a separate door which opens into the hallway. In the quiet room, Ms. Keller began a Timeline, and Tom disclosed that he had been thinking about his sister's girlfriend, who had been killed in an automobile accident about ten days ago. The story was in the news, but Ms. Keller didn't realize until today how well Tom had known the girl or how much a part of his life she had been. Just as the discussion reached its most sensitive moment, Mr. Riley, Tom's art teacher, passed the quiet room door as he walked down the hall. Mr. Riley doesn't have much patience for Tom and when he saw him talking with Ms. Keller, he immediately concluded that Tom must have been causing problems in class. He stopped outside the door and stared at Tom through the window. The following exchanges occurred among Ms. Keller (K), Mr. Riley (R), and Tom (T).

T: (*Loud enough to be heard through the door*) What are you looking at?!

R: (*Opening the door*) You don't talk to me like that!

T: Get out of here!

R: You can't tell me where I can be in this school.

T: Get out! I'm talking to Ms. Keller!

R: That's exactly what I expect from you! You have no respect for yourself or anyone else! I'll let Mrs. Andersen [the school principal] know your mother will need a phone call.

T: Who cares? My mom doesn't care about Mrs. Anderson or you!

K: It's OK, Mr. Riley; I can handle it. Tom, please.

R: You may be able to handle it, Ms. Keller, but I won't take that kind of disrespect from any young person, much less this loser! I don't want him in my class today, and we'll have to talk about whether he should even come back to this school.

K: OK, I'll keep him with me today. Let's you and I talk later.

R: It's a waste of time.

K: I'll get back to you.

R: (*Shaking his head and looking at Tom, Mr. Riley leaves the room*)

At that point, Ms. Keller used Drain Off skills to de-escalate Tom's intense feelings about Mr. Riley. She returned to the subject of Tom's grief and conducted a Red Flag *Tap In* intervention to help Tom understand that he was displacing the anger he felt about his friend's death to Mr. Riley. She helped him understand that the feelings he was having, though unpleasant, were a normal, expected response to a tragedy. She told him she would be available if he wanted to talk further. Feeling more grounded, Tom returned to class, where Ms. Keller helped him get started on his work. She then arranged to see Mr. Riley later in the day. The following dialogue ensued.

Stage 1: Drain Off

к: (*Mr. Riley enters the conference room where Ms. Keller has been waiting for him*) Hey, thanks for coming.

R: I'm here, but it's a waste of my time and yours.

к: Well, that was quite an encounter this morning.

R: Yes, it was, and I'm sick and tired of his garbage behavior! He can't get away with talking to me that way!

к: Tom needs to think before he speaks; that's one of the many issues we're working on right now.

R: Well, I think you're being way too easy on him. If he doesn't have consequences, you might as well tell him it's OK to do it. Everybody else has to follow the rules; why not him?

к: It doesn't make his behavior OK, but he is a very troubled young man. He's really struggling—you know what he has to live with. And there's something else you need to know to put what happened into perspective.

R: All I know is that you let him get away with murder, and then you get upset when I put my foot down.

Stage 2: Timeline

к: Listen, I agree that he has to have limits. I am constantly setting limits for him in class, and he has been more accepting of them in last couple of months. He's making real progress in his classes too. But you need to know what was going on this morning that set off the conflict between you two. When Tom arrives in the morning, he's usually loud and talkative. No question about it, everybody knows when Tom is here. But today he was unusually quiet and withdrawn. It was obvious that something was wrong, so I asked him to come to the quiet room to talk. As it turns out, the girl who was killed in that accident a week and a half ago was a good friend of his sister. Tom saw her almost every day, and he considered her practically a member of the family. She was one of the few people in his life that he felt really liked him; she enjoyed his sense of humor and, to use his words, she treated him "like he was somebody."

R: That's too bad, but it doesn't give him the right to be disrespectful to teachers and carry on the way he does.

K: I agree that he does need learn how to talk to adults; he won't get anywhere in life if he continues to be defiant and rude. Part of what's going on is that he is hurt and angry, and he doesn't know what to do with those feelings. Any little thing can be a trigger; that's what happened this morning. The anger wasn't about you—it was an expression of his anger about the death of his friend.

R: So, I'm supposed to walk on eggshells with him because he's having problems?

K: No, I'm asking you to recognize that there's more to Tom's outburst than meets the eye. Tom was wrong today, no question. He made the first mistake, saying to you, "What are you looking at?" You didn't start this conflict, he did.

R: That's right; it never would have happened if he hadn't opened his mouth.

K: When you stopped and looked at him through the window, he was right in the middle of telling me this about the death of his friend. He was choked up and it was hard for him to speak. When he saw you stop, he knew you believed he was in the quiet room because he had been a behavior problem. That thought triggered his anger, and he showed it by making that remark.

R: So, what was I supposed to do?

K: Now, in this situation, you couldn't possibly have known what was going on, so I have to give you the benefit of the doubt. You didn't start it, but you did keep it going. You responded to his surface behavior and you gave in to your immediate impulse—a threat of punishment. Tom doesn't need any more punishment.

R: What, it's my fault that he talked to me that way?

Stage 3: Central Issue

K: What I'm saying is that you allowed yourself to be drawn into a Conflict Cycle. Each time Tom made a disrespectful remark, you countered it. The effect was to keep the cycle going until you threatened him with a call home and called him a loser. He already believes he's a loser; that's the self-concept we're all working to change. What he does, though, is he baits adults into these conflicts where we end up accidentally reinforcing his idea of himself as a loser.

R: You know, I'm not out to get him, but we can't tolerate that kind of behavior. It's not good for us and it's not good for him, no matter what's going on at home.

K: I don't mean to suggest that you are against him; if I thought that I wouldn't be here now. I'm bringing this to you because I do believe you want to see Tom succeed; I believe you want the best for him.

R: So how do you handle it when he starts mouthing off like that?

Stage 4: Insight

K: The first thing I do is tell myself to stay calm, and then I observe how he tries to make me angry. As soon as he begins to say or do something designed to draw me into a conflict, I point out to him that it appears he is trying to make me fight with him. I decode the behavior for him. For example, last week he came in and erased the morning assignment from the board. My first impulse was to lecture him, but instead I said to him, "Tom, when you come in here and the first thing you do is something you know is going to upset me, that tells me something is upsetting you, too."

R: What did he say to that?

K: He didn't say anything. He went to his desk and sat down. I said to him, "I'm going to put the assignment back up on the board, and then I'll check in with you." He still didn't say anything, but he stayed at his desk. After I finished rewriting the assignment, I went over to him and asked, "What's bothering you today?" He said, "Nothing." I told him I wanted to see him during the morning break. He answered, "Maybe." As it turned out, he did talk to me during break, and he apologized for erasing the board. We discussed what else he could do when he came into school with a lot on his mind, and he agreed to check in with me. He was OK for the rest of the day. I think he just needed to know that I recognized his stress and that I cared about him.

R: Once again, no consequences!

Stage 5: New Skills

K: There were consequences; I talked to him and he apologized. What you mean is that there was no punishment. I decided that since he apologized, and the apology appeared genuine, I would let it go at that. That's not to say he never has to pay the price for poor choices; I've taken away points for some things and he has had to sit out of a few fun activities. In this case, though, adding a punishment wouldn't have helped teach him anything.

R: I'm not so sure I agree. Anyway, he might get by with that in your class, but not out in the real world. How long do you think it would be before we had mass chaos if we all excused a blatant act like that? The kids are all watching to see who's in charge.

K: If something like that happened, and you were in a position in which you had to set a limit, you might send Tom to me instead of to the office. The other kids would see that he had a consequence, having to leave class, and maybe you and I could discuss it with him together. After all, what's the goal here? If he could be convinced that we're in his corner, the defiance will begin to fade. Every time we fight with him, he comes away believing we're all against him and he hasn't got a chance. What do you say we give that a try?

Stage 6: Transfer of Learning

R: I've got to tell you; I don't like the idea of spoon-feeding kids who don't follow the rules. It really goes against my grain. If I try this and it doesn't work, we'll be talking.

K: If you don't allow yourself to be drawn into a Conflict Cycle, things will get better between you and Tom. The kid's life is complicated—he has a lot of emotional baggage. Usually, the real source of his stress is not school or teachers—it's all the other issues happening at home. We have to teach him a better outlet for his stress than taking it out on us, and that means gaining his trust.

R: Well, you can't win an argument with him anyway, so why get into one? You better know, though, that this is going to eat up a lot of my time and I'm not happy about that.

K: It'll be worth it, because you'll be one of the few that makes a difference in a life that needs a lot of kindness.

R: OK, you're doing a good selling job; I'll give it a shot.

K: Thanks. See you tomorrow.

Ms. Keller may have made a significant contribution to Tom's chances of success in Mr. Riley's class. Like many teachers, Mr. Riley was not trained to work with challenging young people. They made him angry and threatened his position of authority in the classroom. It is also true that, like Mr. Riley, most teachers want to see young persons succeed and are willing to try new approaches if they are supported. The type of support and follow-up demonstrated in this situation by Ms. Keller is critical in supporting adult staff as they practice and master LSCI skills.

Example 2: *Mrs. Borland, "The Big, Fat Know-It-All!"*

Mrs. Borland is a math teacher who has been teaching seventh grade in the middle school staff for five years. She is seen as a tough, no-nonsense teacher with high expectations for behavior and academic performance in her class. As might be expected, that approach results in problems with some students. Mrs. Borland has sent more students out of her classroom and made more discipline referrals than any other teacher in the school. She has been trained in LSCI but struggles to use the skills and strategies when confronted with student performance that does not conform to her expectations. The principal and assistant principal have talked with Mrs. Borland about her reactiveness, but she dismisses their concerns as micro-managing. She also complains that they don't support her because, as she says, "those kids don't get any consequences and they're right back in my class the next day." Mrs. Borland does not believe that LSCI pertains to the problems she experiences with students; her belief is that the students that she sends out of her classroom are just undisciplined and disrespectful.

One of Mrs. Borland's students, David, is a bright seventh grade student who is inconsistent in both his academic and behavioral performance. David maintains a passing grade, but Mrs. Borland believes he is capable of doing much better if he would just "buckle down." Mrs. Borland is especially frustrated with David because of his inconsistency and his recent negative changes. Before she sends David to the office Mrs. Borland usually tells him, in front of the other students, how disappointed she is in him. On this particular day, Mrs. Borland's direction to David to leave the classroom came with some harsher words than usual. David responded with some disrespectful words of his own, then slammed the classroom door.

On this occasion, Mrs. Borland followed David to the hallway and yelled, "This time, I'll make sure that you don't come back to my class—or any class—tomorrow." David responded saying, "I don't want to be in your class tomorrow or any other day. You're a big, fat know-it-all, but you don't know anything about me!" Mrs. Borland yelled back at David, "I know everything I need to know about you! You're lazy and disrespectful and I'm not going to put up with it anymore!"

The commotion in the hallway was loud enough to be heard by others, including Mr. Watson, a science teacher who also had David as a student. He stepped in, and in a quiet voice suggested that Mrs. Borland and David's conversation take place in a different location. Mrs. Borland said there was no need for conversation and that David just needed to go to the office and she would follow up later to make sure that this time, David is suspended.

Mr. Watson offered to walk David to the office as soon as he could get someone to cover his classroom. Soon, they walked toward the office and stopped in a courtyard along the way to calm down and talk for a bit. David was past his anger and was now trying to hold back tears. After Mr. Watson helped him feel more regulated, he asked David to talk about what happened in math class. David said school is hard these days and math class "is the worst!" Mr. Watson said that he noticed that school seemed to be harder for him recently. David said that Mr. Watson and other teachers aren't as hard on him, so he doesn't get in trouble in their classes.

Mr. Watson allowed David to talk about changes that have happened in his family over the past year and how hard they have been for him. First, his grandfather died suddenly and that was hard because David used to spend a lot of time with him. Then, David's parents got a divorce after fighting all the time since he could remember. He hadn't seen his father for two months. And now, his mom's new boyfriend had just moved in to the house. David explained that "this guy comes in with *his* rules and *his* punishments." While his mom's boyfriend, Todd, hasn't hit him "yet," he has threatened to do so when his mother wasn't around. Todd also tells David that he hopes that soon he'll be able to "ship your ass out to go live with your worthless father." Mr. Watson acknowledges how hard that must be for David and tells him that with all that stress in his life, it's no wonder that school is harder for him now. David thanks him and tells him that he's the first person he's been able to talk to about "all this stuff."

Mr. Watson takes David to the office, where he can sit quietly and continue to become more grounded. Then, he arranged time to talk with Mrs. Borland after school. When Mr. Watson entered Mrs. Borland's room, she was sitting at her desk. As soon as he brought up what happened earlier with David, Mrs. Borland got out of her seat and began to pace, saying, "I've had enough of that kid and don't need to talk about it anymore."

Stage 1: Drain Off

MR. W: I can see you're still really upset about what happened.

MRS. B: (*In a loud, agitated voice*) Yes, I'm upset. I can't allow him to disrespect me like that. He's the worst of the bunch and he's worse now than before!

MR. W: This seems like it is really important to you. You got upset again as soon as our conversation started.

MRS. B: You'd be upset too if you had to put up with his crap. And the administration doesn't support me. They'll just send him back tomorrow. That's disrespectful too!

MR. W: Well, I appreciate your willingness to talk with me about this. I hope I can understand what's going on for you and, hopefully, be helpful in some way.

MRS. B: (*In a quieter voice, as she goes back to sit down*) So far, you're the only one that seems interested in me.

MR. W: That's interesting—David said something like that to me just a while ago. We know that listening is always helpful.

Stage 2: Timeline

MR. W: I know this has been going on for a while with David. For now, can we just talk about what happened today?

MRS. B: Today was worse because he took it to a whole other level with his language and slamming the door.

MR. W: So, today was different for you and David?

MRS. B: What do you mean, for me?

MR. W: Well, this was the first time I can remember hearing you yelling at any student in the hallway like that.

MRS. B: Yeah, I guess that's true. But today I had a good reason to do that!

MR. W: You're saying that today was different, so let's start at the beginning. Did David come in to class on time and take his seat as expected?

MRS. B: He came in with some other kids. They were laughing, but he had a sourpuss look on his face and slumped down in his seat.

MR. W: Sounds like the kids came in at the same time, but David wasn't really with them.

MRS. B: That's about right.

MR. W: What happened next?

MRS. B: I told them to get out their homework. I like to walk around the room and have each of them hand their homework to me rather than just put it on a pile. I want them to know I think it's important.

Also, I can see right away if it's done and if it looks like they put in the proper time and attention. I grade all of it and make comments. I don't just collect it and check it off like lots of other teachers—if they even give homework at all.

MR. W: It does seem like you let the students know you think that homework is an important part of their learning. Did David hand his homework to you today?

MRS. B: He did, and I could see that it wasn't done very well. It was sloppy and incomplete, so I said it looked like he did it on the bus on the way to school. Then he smart-mouthed me and said, "So what? I did it, didn't I?"

MR. W: Did you respond to that?

MRS. B: Of course I did! I told him that it looks like the same effort I see from him regularly these days.

MR. W: Since you were walking around collecting homework it seems like all the other students could hear that too. Did David do or say anything after that?

MRS. B: I'm sure the other students heard it and I don't have a problem making an example of someone who falls below my standards. That's when David yelled that I should be glad he did the "stupid homework" at all. Well, that was it! That's when I sent him out of my classroom and he mumbled something under his breath and slammed the door.

MR. W: OK, so all of that happened pretty quickly after class started. I can see how that would be upsetting to you. You mentioned something about things being worse now than before. Can you say more about that, like when it started getting worse, and how?

MRS. B: Here's the problem, he can do the work. At the beginning of the school year, he did well and didn't give me any trouble. He was a quiet kid who just did his work. I told him a lot that I thought he could do better if he just tried harder. I don't know what got into him. Then, when I started sending him to the office, the administrators would send him back and tell me I should use that LSCI stuff. That's their job. I'm just supposed to teach math!

Stage 3: Central Issue

MR. W: Let me see if I understand what you're telling me. David is a student who you see as capable enough to pass your math class.

You've been a little frustrated with him because you think he could do even better if he tried. Then, in the past few months, things have gotten worse with the quality of his work and his behavior in your class. When you've sent him to the office for discipline, the administrators tell you to try to work with him differently and they send him back to your class. All that makes you more frustrated and leaves you feeling unsupported.

MRS. B: That's right. I don't like being disrespected.

MR. W: Yes, I can hear that too.

Stage 4: Insight

MR. W: On those days when you're feeling disrespected or when something happens like with David earlier today, does it affect you? I mean, can you just walk back in to the classroom and everything is fine?

MRS. B: Do you mean can I still do my job?

MR. W: What I mean is, when you are upset about something, can you do your job in a way that meets your own high expectations?

MRS. B: I'm not a machine. Nobody can be at their best all the time.

MR. W: Yes, that's what I mean. So, when we're upset and off balance about something, it makes a difference in how we perform. Do you agree?

MRS. B: Yes, but what does that have to do with David and the way he is every day now?

MR. W: When we're upset and it gets in our way, we know there are things we can do to get through it and move past it. We're adults and we have experience being successful like that. How would it be if the things that upset us were really big and happened every day?

MRS. B: Are you saying that's what's going on with David?

MR. W: Yes. When I talked with him before we went to the office, he told me about some serious things that have been going on in his family over the past year and how, for him, it's worse now than ever. Remember when our LSCI Trainer Ms. Shepard told us about that script from Nicholas Long? *"The problems kids cause are not the causes of their problems."* That really stuck with me.

MRS. B: I really don't remember that but when you say it now, it makes a lot of sense. What am I supposed to do about it though? I can't fix those problems for him.

MR. W: No, you can't fix those problems. None of us can. What kind of things can we do here though?

MRS. B: I'm not sure what I can do, but I can see that I'm probably making things worse. I'm so worried about my high standards and being respected that it didn't occur to me that he might be hurting.

MR. W: That's a really good start—just being aware of what's going on with another person in our interactions.

MRS. B: But what can I do?

MR. W: Let's talk about that a little bit. First, I want to say thank you for talking with me about this and for being willing to be so open-minded about your approach and David's struggles. I also want to let you know that this conversation that is working so well for us was really just using the process we learned in LSCI training. What got in your way with David is that you were looking for things to work in the way you believed they should and he has been seeing things very differently because of what's been going on in his life. In LSCI terms, we could call that a Reality Check problem.

MRS. B: I guess I should have paid more attention in that training. I just kept thinking that that's what counselors and administrators should be doing and didn't think through how it could help me as a math teacher.

MR. W: Your priority is to teach math to your students. That's correct. You may not have time to do all of this all the time. Just making the time to listen and to understand things from a student's perspective is extremely helpful. Do what you can to connect with students and de-escalate conflicts, and then ask for help from others who may be able to have more time to engage one-on-one with a student like David.

MRS. B: So, send him for help instead of punishment?

MR. W: That's the idea.

Stage 5: New Skills

MR. W: Let's just think a minute about what's next. What kind of things can we do for a student who, as you said about David, can do better but is struggling at school because of things going on at home?

MRS. B: I could cut him some slack on his homework, maybe. I could spend a little time with him in class to see if he's understanding the work.

MR. W: Those seem like really good ideas.

MRS. B: I could also see if there was time in our day where I could give him some extra help. Maybe just finding some common ground would help us to be less hostile toward each other.

Stage 6: Transfer of Learning

MR. W: Thanks again for being so willing to talk with me about this, Mrs. Borland. What would you like to do to move forward?

MRS. B: The first thing I want to do is go to the office before I leave today to talk with the administrators about this. I know David will be in school tomorrow and I'll try to make time to talk with him before class starts so I can apologize and talk with him about how I can try to not make things worse for him. Thanks for helping me see things more clearly and understand what's been happening right in front of me all this time.

MR. W: I'm really glad we could do this, and I'll look forward to talking with you again.

Chapter Summary and Further Training

More than 80% of classroom problems are caused by 10% of students who challenge or undermine teacher authority. These students are skilled in frustrating adults and pushing the emotional buttons of even the most competent teachers.

Many teachers, like Mr. Riley and Mrs. Borland, become irritated by the behavior of select, challenging students like Tom and David. This is understandable; teachers are human, and their emotional brains are trigged by the same perceived threats that kids experience. Few teachers are trained to understand and acknowledge these normal brain-based reactions and counter-aggressive feelings. It's not a problem to feel anger toward a student during a stressful situation, but it is a problem to stay angry with a student. When a conflict develops, teachers are less likely to perceive accurately or reason coherently when lingering hostilities have activated their limbic brain. *Though competent teachers rarely initiate conflicts with students, they often keep them alive though their unintended, counter-productive reactions.*

In addition to the Double Struggle intervention, the LSCI Institute offers the *Turning Down the Heat* training program to assist professionals in more fully understanding and managing their emotional reactions to young people. This one-day course identifies common reasons that teachers become counter-aggressive with select students and offers specific, highly practical skills to manage conflict in the classroom. Unlike most professional development opportunities, Turning Down the Heat is about *you* and not your students; it leads to powerful insights that will change the way you think and behave when you are angry. More information about the Turning Down the Heat training program for staff is available on the LSCI Institute website (www.lsci.org).

"I'm fine.
Whatever."

17 THE ANGRY SMILE
Confronting and Changing Passive-Aggressive Behavior

As we worked to identify and change the most common patterns of self-defeating behavior exhibited by young people, a seventh pattern began to clearly emerge. Similar in some respects to the Benign Confrontation and Peer Exploitation patterns, but distinct enough to need its own targeted approach, we developed a variation on LSCI's six-stage process to confront and change passive-aggressive behavior.

In the pages below, we include excerpts from the LSCI Institute's book *The Angry Smile: Effective Strategies to Manage Passive Aggression at Home, at School, in Relationships, in the Workplace & Online* to help you learn more about changing this additional pattern of self-defeating behavior.

What Is Passive-Aggressive Behavior?

Call it *hostile cooperation*, *sugarcoated hostility*, or *compliant defiance*. Call it all of the above. Along with these synonymous phrases, the term *passive-aggressive behavior* is an oxymoron. Passive aggression does not alternate between passive behavior and aggressive behavior, but rather combines them simultaneously into one behavior that is both confounding and frustrating to others.

> Passive-aggressive behavior is a deliberate and masked way of expressing covert feelings of anger.

Passive-aggressive behavior is a deliberate and masked way of expressing covert feelings of anger. Passive aggression involves a variety of behaviors designed to get back at another person without the other recognizing the underlying anger. In the long run, passive aggression is even more destructive to interpersonal relationships than is aggression, and over time, all relationships with a person who is passive-aggressive will become confusing, discouraging, and dysfunctional.

Passive aggression is motivated by a person's fear of expressing anger directly. The passive-aggressive person believes life will only get worse if other people know of his anger, so he expresses anger indirectly. For example:

- The passive-aggressive teenager might veil anger by smiling and saying, "Hey, Dad, no problem about not letting me use the car tonight. It's no big deal. I'll call Cindy and see if she'll go out with me another Saturday night." On the inside, however, the teen is seething with anger. He decides to hide his father's car keys so that no one has use of the car.
- The passive-aggressive spouse who doesn't want to be bothered with household chores might conceal her anger by saying, "I'll do it in a minute," but then wait so long to complete the chores that her frustrated spouse does them for her. Her response, when confronted, is feigned shock along the lines of, "I didn't know you wanted me to get it done immediately."

What Does Passive-Aggressive Behavior Look Like?

The passive-aggressive person derives genuine secondary pleasure out of frustrating others. For this reason, we call this pattern of behavior "the angry smile." Regardless of the term used, people who are passive-aggressive often:

- Deny or repress feelings of anger
- Send hidden, coded, and confused messages when frustrated. Brief deflecting responses such as "I'm fine" and "Whatever" are commonly used when someone asks them if they are upset
- Withdraw and sulk
- Use the silent treatment
- Create minor but chronic irritation in others
- Are overtly cooperative but covertly uncooperative
- Procrastinate or carry out tasks inefficiently
- Can be evasive and secretive
- Use email, texting, social media, and other forms of technology to avoid direct communication
- Project angry feelings on others
- Cast themselves into the role of victim of an overtly angry person
- Are quietly manipulative and controlling
- Cause others to swallow their anger and eventually blow up

- Make endless promises to change
- Create a feeling in others of being on an emotional roller coaster

How Is Passive-Aggressive Behavior Confronted and Changed?

Over the years, participants in LSCI Institute trainings have been fascinated by the passive-aggressive personality type and challenged by the various levels at which the behavior is displayed at home, in school, in close adult relationships, at work, and via technology. Those on the receiving end of passive-aggressive behavior know what it means to "catch" someone's hidden hostility and react in ways that fuel a Passive-Aggressive Conflict Cycle. They also know that in order to effectively manage and alter this pattern of behavior, they will need to be equipped with skills to recognize it early on, avoid the natural human tendency to mirror the behavior, and carefully expose the passive-aggressive expression of anger. To accomplish these complex tasks, we adapt the LSCI skill of Benign Confrontation for use in changing passive aggression.

Benignly Confronting Passive-Aggressive Behavior

Benign Confrontation is the only technique that is successful in changing the behavior of passive-aggressive persons. At its core, it works by identifying underlying anger. While a passive-aggressive person directs their cunning and effort into hiding anger and getting others to express it through their out-of-control reactions, Benign Confrontation helps put the responsibility for the thoughts, feelings, and behaviors squarely back in the hands of the passive-aggressive person.

While Benign Confrontation has a powerful impact on the passive-aggressive individual, it is equally influential as a tool for an adult dealing with a passive-aggressive child, student, spouse, friend, or coworker. Instead of getting caught up in frustrating arguments, endless conflict cycles, and relationship-damaging wars of words, the step-by-step process of Benign Confrontation gives the adult a framework for conflict navigation and hidden anger management. What's more, Benign Confrontation allows an adult to maintain control of their emotions because of the adult's increased awareness of the dynamics taking place.

The step-by-step approach helps the adult recall—even in the heat of the moment—where he or she is in the process with a passive-aggressive person and

> Instead of getting caught up in frustrating arguments, endless conflict cycles, and relationship-damaging wars of words, the step-by-step process of Benign Confrontation gives the adult a framework for conflict navigation and hidden anger management.

where to go next. The following is an outline of the steps of Benign Confrontation, as adapted for use with passive-aggressive behavior.

Sarah: "Put the Cards in the Box, Please"

The Incident

Sarah is an intelligent 12-year-old who attends an alternative school. She is described as "delightful" whenever she is in control of an activity. When she feels she does not have control over a situation, however, her behaviors become manipulative and passive-aggressive.

In this situation, Sarah was involved in a writing lesson. She was asked by her teacher to stop her activity and put the cards from her writing lesson in a box so they could begin her math lesson. The box was right in front of Sarah. Sarah didn't respond to the teacher's first directive, so the teacher asked again. Sarah didn't respond to the second, third, or fourth requests, either. Each time the teacher spoke the request, her voice rose by a few decibels. By the fifth request, the teacher was aware that Sarah heard her but was being silently oppositional. The teacher simultaneously gave herself this message: "This is a reasonable request and this girl is not going to win. There's no way I'm going to back down. She will put the cards in the box!" Already, the Passive-Aggressive Conflict Cycle was in full swing.

Sarah was clearly angry on the inside but smiled and looked pleasantly confused on the outside. She kept this up for the next ten minutes without saying a word. The teacher began mirroring Sarah's behavior. She was angry on the inside but being sweet on the outside by repeating, "Please, put the cards in the box! You can put the cards away."

Finally, the teacher lost her cool. She stood up and yelled out, "Put the cards away, right now, Sarah, or else you will spend your entire lunch period doing it and I will be calling your parents." The other students turned around in shock, trying to figure out why their teacher was so red in the face and harsh with Sarah. Sarah, playing up the role of victim, responded innocently, "Geez, OK. I'm doing it. I was just trying to finish my writing like you wanted me to. I didn't know you would get so mad all of a sudden."

The teacher felt ashamed of her outburst.

Benign Confrontation provides the teacher with a framework for responding effectively to passive aggression. The following section describes a step-by-step framework for how the teacher could have avoided this counter–passive-aggressive outburst:

Step 1: Recognize the Warning Signs of Passive-Aggressive Behavior

In this first step, the teacher should recognize Sarah's silent opposition passive aggression. Sarah appears to not hear the request, but smiles.

Step 2: Refuse to Engage in the Passive-Aggressive Conflict Cycle

In this step, the teacher should strive to control her mounting angry feelings toward Sarah. After the second request to put the cards away, the teacher should have identified Sarah's behavior as passive-aggressive and said to herself, "Sarah is being passive-aggressive, but I will not mirror her feelings or behaviors."

Step 3: Affirm the Anger

In Step 3, the teacher should share with Sarah her thoughts about the girl's underlying anger. The teacher should say calmly:

> "Sarah, let's stop. I have a thought I want to share with you. I asked you to put away the cards, and you pretended not to hear me. I know I speak clearly, and other students can hear me easily. What I have to figure out is why, at this particular time, you are choosing not to hear me and follow my reasonable request."

If Sarah does not respond, the teacher should continue:

> "My guess is that a part of you may be upset with me. You probably would prefer to continue to write than to do math right now. If so, let's talk about your feelings instead of pretending you don't hear me.
>
> Sarah, the difficulty we are having right now is not about the cards. We can forget about the cards for now. What is happening between us right now is important. I think see a pattern of behavior you use when you are angry. Perhaps, when I ask you to do something you don't want to do, you act as if you don't hear me. Sarah, you are a smart student. What do you think about this situation?"

Step 4: Manage the Denial

After this Benign Confrontation, which exposes Sarah's hidden anger, Sarah's first response is likely to be either to refuse to talk or to deny it. At this time, the teacher should back off and not persist. The scenario would likely play out in the following way:

SARAH: (*Refuses to discuss the incident*)

TEACHER: It is difficult to talk about personal issues, but I want you to think about it.

SARAH: There is no problem here. I don't know what you're talking about. I'm not the one who is angry.

> TEACHER: I'm glad you believe this is not a problem. In other words, if I ask you to do something like put the cards away, you will be willing to do it?
>
> SARAH: Duh.

The teacher would choose to ignore this snarky and disrespectful final comment from Sarah, knowing that it was spoken with the passive-aggressive intent to elicit another angry reaction. The self-aware teacher knows that the best way to change Sarah's behavior is to maintain control of her own responses, thus proving to Sarah that her passive-aggressive efforts are ineffective. Adults who get caught up in the moment, thinking they need to "show that kid who is in control" by responding punitively to side comments such as Sarah's, have usually already been ensnared in a Conflict Cycle.

> Adults who get caught up in the moment, thinking they need to "show that kid who is in control" have usually already been ensnared in a Conflict Cycle.

To keep the conversation on track, the teacher should repeat the direction to Sarah to put the cards in the box. A new level of insight will have developed between Sarah and her teacher. This process of Benign Confrontation will change the way Sarah and her teacher think about each other in the future. Sarah's passive-aggressive behavior is no longer a secret and effective technique of getting back at the adults in her life.

Step 5: Revisit the Thought

Each time the teacher identifies a clear example of Sarah's passive-aggressive behavior, she should use Benign Confrontation to identify Sarah's underlying anger. The day after the cards-in-the-box-incident, Sarah nods her head at the teacher that she will clean up her art supplies, but she continues to paint long after the request is made. The teacher should revisit the thought from the previous day by saying the following:

> "Sarah, I have a thought about what is happening here right now. Remember yesterday when I shared that I thought you were angry over our writing lesson ending and having to begin math? Your not cleaning up your paint today reminds me of yesterday's situation, and I am wondering if this is your way of letting me know that you are angry again. What do you think?"

Step 6: Identify Areas of Competence

Though the moments immediately following a Benign Confrontation should be reserved for some calculated, intentional silence in which the passive-aggressive person is left to consider the thoughts shared by the adult, there should be a follow-up time in which the adult works to build the relationship with Sarah. By identifying genuine areas of competence in Sarah, the teacher will show that although the passive-aggressive behavior is not functional in the relationship, the relationship itself is worthwhile.

In this scenario, because the teacher is aware that Sarah is "delightful" when she is in control of a situation, it might be to her advantage to give Sarah control over specific tasks in the classroom. The more Sarah can feel powerful in constructive ways, the less she may need to control through destructive passive aggression. The following are examples of areas of competence for Sarah:

- Making her the "class timekeeper," whose job it is to alert the teacher when an allotted amount of time for an activity or lesson has passed
- Putting her in charge of collecting the card boxes when reading is over
- Giving her a daily lesson checklist so that she can mark off each subject as she completes it

The specific competency area is not as important as the sheer act of reaching out to Sarah as a means of shrinking her hostility and increasing her motivation to relate on a new, more emotionally honest level.

The LSCI Institute offers online and live training workshops based on *The Angry Smile* to help those professionals and parents living and working with people who exhibit passive-aggressive behaviors. To learn more about how people develop passive-aggressive behaviors, the five increasingly pathological levels at which passive aggression is displayed, the passive-aggressive conflict cycle, eight strategies for managing our own emotional responses to the behavior, additional examples of benign confrontation, or general information about the book and training programs, please visit us at www.lsci.org.

"I can understand why you were feeling so upset when you got home."

18 PARENTING THE CHALLENGING CHILD
Adapting LSCI Skills for Use at Home

After almost thirty years of helping professionals work with some of the most challenging children and adolescents, the LSCI Institute has adapted its brain-based, trauma-informed, relationship-building approach to the unique needs of parents and caregivers. *Parenting the Challenging Child: The 4-Step Way to Turn Problem Situations Into Learning Opportunities* provides straightforward, practical strategies that shed light on how simple changes in the way parents interact with their kids during stressful moments can significantly improve the parent-child relationship.

Parenting the Challenging Child teaches fundamental LSCI skills and focuses on the six patterns of self-defeating behavior described here in this book. It uses an abbreviated four-step framework for processing stressful situations within the family and challenges parents and caregivers to recognize that while they can't always control their child's behaviors, they can absolutely control the way they *respond* to those behaviors. The parent's approach is the decisive element. Instead of waiting and hoping for a young person to change their ways, *Parenting the Challenging Child* empowers readers to modify their own approach to kids' behaviors, which, in turn, brings about meaningful, long-term improvements in relationships and behaviors.

Throughout the book and training, we share dozens of real-life examples and situations to shed light on how the LSCI approach works. One of the examples we share at the very beginning of the book helps readers consider what happens when LSCI is *not* used—what happens when a parent misses an opportunity to use a school-based problem as a skill-building experience:

The Situation

Just as Dylan arrived home from school, his mother was hanging up the phone from a conversation with his classroom teacher. The mother was feeling furious after hearing about Dylan's reported refusal to participate in science class. When Dylan walked in the front door, his mother grabbed his cell phone from his hand and told him he was grounded for two weeks. She yelled at him for having the nerve to reach into his teacher's desk drawer, before sending him to his room.

What Dylan's mother did not know—and failed to ask about—was that just before science, a classmate had taken Dylan's science project out of his backpack and hidden it under the teacher's desk. The whole class laughed and taunted Dylan as he searched the room to find it. He was humiliated. When his teacher saw him rummaging about the classroom, she yelled at him in front of everyone and refused to listen to his explanation of why he was out of his seat in the first place.

As discussed in Chapter 3 of this book, there are three possible outcomes to any parent-child conflict.

Parent-Child Relationship Unchanged

In families, an adult's immediate reaction to a problem situation with a child is often punishment. Many parents have a go-to set of "consequences" they use with their kids. For many young people, however, these rote punishments have little effect on changing behavior because they address only the symptoms, and not the perceptions, thoughts, and feelings that underlie the behavior. As a result, nothing really changes except that the likelihood of future problems increases.

> *In the example above, Dylan's mother responded angrily to her son—yelling at him, taking his cell phone, grounding him, and sending him to his room. While these may be routine consequences for misbehavior in Dylan's family, they fail to teach Dylan any of the skills he needs to prevent the problem from happening again. What's more, the mother has no insight or understanding into why her son behaved this way in the first place. An opportunity for mutual understanding between the parent and child was completely missed.*

Parent-Child Relationship Damaged

As parents, we have a lot on our plates on a daily basis. From our own busy and stress-filled lives to managing the inevitable highs and lows of a young person's day, we are often quick to speak and slow to listen. When a problem arises, our instinct is to quickly solve it. While efficiency is often valued in our fast-paced lives, whenever we address a surface behavior without understanding its cause, we run the risk of making matters worse.

Sometimes, our spontaneous reactions even cause pain to the very people we are trying to help. In our hurry or frustration, we may unintentionally humiliate, degrade, or belittle our loved ones. Over time, resentment builds and our children begin to feel rejected. This alienation breeds mistrust and practically guarantees that conflicts will continue.

By rushing to judgment in the example above, Dylan's mother ran the risk of causing real damage to her relationship with her son. Dylan is a young man who already had the experience of being humiliated by his peers that day in school and felt disregarded by his teacher when he tried to explain his situation. By quickly punishing him and failing to first find out his side of the story, the mother became the third source of alienation and rejection her son experienced that day and likely confirmed his belief that others are cruel and untrustworthy.

Parent-Child Relationship Improved

When we address kids' misbehaviors (e.g., disrespect, yelling, cursing, rule-breaking) but fail to understand what is *causing* those behaviors, we make problems worse. *Parenting the Challenging Child* teaches practical strategies to take readers past rigid discipline and toward a more effective way to relate to their children. The LSCI approach helps parents and children build better relationships, based on mutual understanding and genuine trust, which leads to lasting changes in perceptions, thoughts, feelings, and behaviors.

Had the mother been equipped with LSCI knowledge and skills, she could have handled the situation in a far more positive way. Rather than rushing to punish Dylan, she would have used a specific set of Drain Off and Timeline skills to find out Dylan's side of the story, then based on this information, could have helped him understand where things went wrong and what to do differently in future situations to prevent a similar problem. Through the LSCI process, Dylan's trust in his mother and knowledge of how to handle peer manipulation would both have increased.

Parenting the Challenging Child also teaches readers how to use a consistent four-step verbal framework to address and change a child's self-defeating pattern of behavior. In the pages below, we share with you an excerpt from the book. You will no doubt recognize the pattern being addressed as the Red Flag. Note how the father uses Drain Off and Timeline skills to identify the son's displacement and teach his child alternative ways to cope with anger.

The Incident

Ray is a nine-year-old boy who is small for his age and intimidated by older, bigger kids. On the school bus, a teenager named Nate repeatedly threatens Ray and humiliates him in front of the other kids. One afternoon, Nate took the math homework that Ray had just completed, tore it into shreds, then threw it out of the bus window. Ray felt helpless. He didn't know how he could keep his property safe around Nate. On top of that, he was furious that none of his friends stepped in to help. Ray arrived home feeling defeated, embarrassed, and angry. When his father asked him to get started on his homework, Ray refused to open his backpack, swore at his dad, kicked the kitchen table, and yelled, "Why won't you just leave me alone already?"

To Ray's father, his son's response seemed to come completely out of the blue. *"All I did,"* the father insisted to his wife later that evening, *"was ask Ray to start his homework—same as I do every other day when he gets home. You would have thought I asked him to scrub the floors with a toothbrush with that reaction!"*

Indeed, it happens more often than any parent would like that a seemingly minor or routine request is met with a major emotional response or meltdown. While brain science explains that it is natural for adults who are on the receiving end of a child's anger to react emotionally, it is just as certain that "catching" the young person's anger, as if it were a contagious disease, only worsens the situation and damages the parent-child relationship.

Instead of mirroring your child's anger and escalating the problem, bear in mind that *nothing comes from nothing.* This four-word mantra, followed by its three-word counterpart, *look beyond behavior,* is a powerful and effective reminder to parents and caregivers everywhere that a child's surface behavior (e.g., swearing, kicking, yelling) is not always directly related to an immediate stress (e.g., a request to start homework) but rather may be due to other experiences and unresolved feelings (e.g., Ray's mistreatment at the hands of Nate).

Whenever a young person's reaction seems out of proportion with the situation at hand, LSCI guides parents and caregivers to recognize the very real possibility that there's more to the situation than meets the eye. In the pages that follow, we offer you an example of what an LSCI intervention between Ray and his father could sound like, including useful phrases for Drain Off, effective Timeline questions, helpful ways to understand the dynamic of displacement, and social-emotional skills for positive anger management.

Stage 1: Drain Off

RAY: (*Yelling, pacing around the room, head down*) Why won't you just leave me alone already?

DAD: (*In a calm, lowered voice*) I can see that you are really worked up and upset right now.

RAY: (*Silent, looks at father*)

DAD: Let's just sit here together for a few minutes and see if we can work this out. Would you like some cold water to drink?

RAY: (*Shakes his head "no" to the water, but sits down at the kitchen table*)

DAD: (*Sits at the table with Ray*) Thanks for sitting with me. I know it's hard to come home from a long day at school and then have parents start talking about homework right away. I apologize if I made you feel pressured.

RAY: I don't feel pressured! I'm mad! I hate math! I hate the bus! I hate everyone!

DAD: The fact that you were willing to sit here with me, even when you are feeling so mad and so much hate, shows me that despite it all, you are trying to get back in control and willing to work things out. I'm really impressed. It's not easy to sit and talk when your whole body is filled with anger.

RAY: I've never even done anything to Nate, but he keeps picking on me every single day. And no one does anything about it. The bus driver doesn't care, and the other kids just watch him do whatever he wants to me. I'm going to get in so much trouble tomorrow in math! (*Begins to cry*)

DAD: (*Puts his hand gently on his son's shoulder and makes eye contact*) That's a lot to handle. I'm starting to understand why you are so upset. I'd like to know more details so that we can try to work things out. Can you start from the beginning and tell me how this started?

RAY: (*Shrugs his shoulders; looks defeated, yet grateful for his father's quiet reassurance*)

Stage 2: The Timeline

DAD: What happened in math today that made you think you're going to be in trouble?

RAY: Nothing happened in math. Math was fine. But it's going to be terrible tomorrow. I'm going to get in a ton of trouble and it's all Nate's fault but no one will believe me.

DAD: It's a terrible feeling to think that you won't be believed. I want to hear the truth about what happened. To start with, who is Nate?

RAY: He's a tenth grader, and he's such a jerk! He picks on me for no reason, and he always gets away with it. I hate him.

DAD: It sounds like this problem isn't about math as much as it is about Nate. What happened with Nate today?

RAY: It's not just today. It's every single day with that kid!

DAD: Having to deal with a difficult kid every single day can be so hard.

RAY: It is! It's so hard!

DAD: What has been going on with him?

RAY: He makes fun of me every day on the bus. He pushes me out of my seat. He takes my stuff. He calls me names. Yesterday, he stole my headphones and wouldn't give them back the whole ride. Today, he grabbed my math homework, ripped it up, then threw it out the window. It took me the whole ride to get the homework done and now it's completely gone. I'm going to get in so much trouble tomorrow.

DAD: Wow—that's a lot! Let me just make sure I have all of this straight. So, this tenth grader named Nate has been picking on you for a while now. He's been calling you names, pushing you, and taking your stuff. Today, he took your math homework and ripped it up. Then, he threw it out the window. You're worried that you're going to get in trouble tomorrow in math for not having your homework. I can definitely understand why you were feeling so upset when you got home!

RAY: I hate him so much. He never leaves me alone.

DAD: Dealing with an older kid who is pushing you around and messing with your things would be hard for anyone to handle. I'm really sorry that this has been happening to you for so long. I'm also really glad that you are telling me about it because now that I know, I can help you figure out what to do about it. Is there anything else I need to know about your day or what's been going on with Nate?

RAY: That's pretty much it. Happens every day.

Stage 3: Understand the Problem

DAD: Okay. So, let's think about what happened today. You're dealing with a really mean kid on the bus ride home every day. Today was an especially bad day because he destroyed the math homework that you worked hard on and you won't have anything to turn in tomorrow in class. You are worried that you are going to get in trouble.

RAY: Yep.

DAD: So really, there are a few problems happening all at once. There's dealing with Nate, and there's dealing with your math teacher tomorrow.

RAY: Right—and it's not even my fault!

DAD: Things are feeling out of your control between this bigger kid that takes your stuff and your math teacher who might be angry that you don't have your homework.

RAY: Exactly! What am I supposed to do?

DAD: That's a good question. And I can help you figure out a good answer for what to do about Nate and how to talk to your math teacher about what's happened to your homework.

RAY: Thank you. Maybe you could talk to my bus driver and email my teacher?

DAD: I can definitely help you with both of those situations. But before we get to those things, there's one more problem from today that I think is important for us to work out. Do you know what it is?

RAY: (Looks confused)

DAD: We need to talk about what happened between you and me—and the kitchen table. (Dad smiles)

RAY: I was just so mad!

DAD: You swore at me and kicked the table.

RAY: I know. I'm sorry about that.

DAD: Thank you for apologizing. That shows a lot of maturity on your part. Now that you've told me about your day, I understand that you weren't really angry at me. Your anger has to do with someone else.

RAY: Yeah—Nate!

DAD: Right. You were angry with Nate, and that is completely understandable. You felt like you couldn't do anything about your anger when you were on the bus, so instead, who got your anger?

RAY: You did. The kitchen table did.

DAD: That's right. Can you think of any other times when this kind of thing has happened? When you've been angry at one person and taken it out on someone else?

RAY: It happened two days ago after I got mad at Nate for making fun of me on the bus in the morning. When I got to school, I called my friend the same names that Nate called me. He got so mad that he told the teacher and I lost recess.

DAD: Ray, listen closely. I understand why you have been feeling angry lately. What Nate has been doing to you is wrong and you have every right to be upset about it. I will help you figure out what to do about Nate. But even before we do that, we need to do something about the fact that when you take your anger out on friends at school or family at home, you create a whole new set of problems.

RAY: I never thought about it like that.

DAD: And the worst part about it is that the people you are taking your anger out on are exactly the people you need to have on your side when you are dealing with people like Nate. Does that make sense?

RAY: Yeah. After I teased my friend in school, he hasn't talked to me since.

DAD: That's the problem with taking anger out on people who don't deserve it. We create new problems in addition to our old ones and push away the people who could help us.

RAY: (*Nods in understanding, then says defensively*) I hate Nate.

Stage 4: New Skills

DAD: So, what can you do to turn around this problem of taking your anger out on the wrong people?

RAY: Well, I could take it out on the right person instead! I could punch Nate next time he messes with me. Or steal his homework. Or take his whole backpack and throw it out the bus window.

DAD: I understand that that might feel good in the moment. But the problem is that getting revenge also causes new problems. If you punch Nate or throw his backpack out the window, you sink to his level and risk getting yourself in a lot of trouble. I promise that we're going to talk about Nate and about your math homework, but first, let's settle the issue of taking out your anger on the people who are actually on your side. What do you think you can do about this?

RAY: I have no idea.

DAD: Well, let me tell you what works for me. When I get really mad at someone, it helps me to get a cold drink of water to cool down my insides. Then, I usually need to just walk away from the situation for at least ten minutes. I like to be by myself to just calm my brain—maybe listen to music or take a walk if it's nice outside. When I feel completely calm, it helps to try to talk to someone about the problem.

RAY: I do like to listen to music. And drawing really helps me calm down.

DAD: Those are both great ideas.

RAY: But I'm never going to be able to talk to Nate about how I feel. He'll just make fun of me more.

DAD: You're probably right. Telling Nate how you feel probably won't do a whole lot of good because he doesn't sound like a trustworthy person who would be willing to listen to you. Can you think of any people who are trustworthy who would listen and try to help you out?

RAY: You?

DAD: Absolutely. I'll listen to you and try to help you any day. Is there anyone at school you can talk to if Nate bothers you in the morning?

RAY: Mrs. McIntyre is pretty nice. She usually has time to talk.

DAD: That sounds like a good option. Would it be helpful if I called Mrs. McIntyre and told her a bit about what's been going on with Nate? Maybe together we can make a plan for how to deal with him.

RAY: You can call her but I don't want Nate to know that I said anything. He'll call me a tattletale and things will get even worse.

DAD: How about if you, me and Mrs. McIntyre all sit down together to talk about what's been happening and come up with a plan to deal with Nate that doesn't end up making things worse for you?

RAY: That would be great! (*Pauses*) What about my math homework?

DAD: What do you think we should do?

RAY: Maybe I can try to talk to my teacher before class and explain what happened. If he can give me another handout with the problems, I can get the assignment done.

DAD: I think that sounds like a solid plan. How are you feeling now?

RAY: Better. A little nervous about Nate still, but I feel better having a plan and having you on my side to help.

LSCI Parenting Skills in Practice

Ray's dad systematically guided his son through this conversation and turned a problem situation into a skill-building opportunity. Notice that the father and son carried on a two-way dialogue all the way through the process; at no time did Ray's father lecture, threaten, or dominate the conversation. The four-step LSCI process works precisely because it is a back-and-forth dialogue that allows a young person to feel heard, understood, and valued. What's more, because the young person is involved in understanding his problem and suggesting solutions, they gain invaluable problem-solving experience.

> The four-step LSCI process works precisely because it is a back-and-forth dialogue that allows a young person to feel heard, understood, and valued.

After using Drain Off skills to reduce the intensity of Ray's anger, the father used Timeline skills to help his son tell his story and begin to make sense of the problem. Because of his careful building of a Timeline, Ray's father was able to realize that his son's anger at Nate had been displaced onto him. With this new knowledge, the father could then help his son understand what went wrong and how to more effectively manage anger in future situations so that potential helpers are not pushed away.

Parenting is an incredibly demanding and difficult responsibility. Just when we think we have our child figured out, they grow and change and do something that takes us by complete surprise. That's why LSCI is so powerful; it gives us a framework for understanding what's going on in a child's brain (no matter what may be coming out of their mouths!) and offers us a system for responding in way that builds a more positive relationship while teaching more effective behaviors.

The LSCI Institute offers online and live training workshops based on *Parenting the Challenging Child* to help parents improve their relationships with their kids and, in turn, help their kids make genuine and lasting behavioral improvements. For more information about the book and training programs, please visit us at www .lsci.org.

First, we talk about it.
Then we fix it.
Then we smile.

19

LSCI WITH YOUNG OR DEVELOPMENTALLY DELAYED YOUTH

This problem-solving "recipe" was contributed by a five-year-old boy named Sam. In its simplicity, there is the essence of adapting the LSCI process for working with children who are very young or who are developmentally delayed. Sam's recipe begins with "we," signaling recognition that conflict resolution is the combined effort of two people—the child and the adult. The adult provides support, security, understanding, and guidance. The child must go beyond the stress of the moment to participate actively in the problem's resolution by putting language to emotion.

"Talk" describes the process of converting behavioral expressions of intolerable emotions into a coherent, verbal form. Without talk, we have no way to transform a problem situation into a learning opportunity and or to create a sense of calm.

"Fix It" is a statement of naïve faith in adult omnipotence. Adults know that there is no quick fix. Yet, young children have a need to believe that when something is wrong, somebody (an adult) can fix it. This is an indication of the pre-existential phase of development described in Chapter 8. In an abbreviated LSCI, the point of "fixing it" is to communicate that adults and children can work together to deal with problem situations. Knowledge of developmental skills and developmental anxieties (see Chapter 8) is essential for an adult as they make a determination as to whether to use a full LSCI or to abbreviate it to meet the needs of young children and developmentally delayed youth.

> Knowledge of developmental skills and developmental anxieties is essential for an adult as they make a determination as to whether to use a full LSCI or to abbreviate it to meet the needs of young children and developmentally delayed youth.

"Smile" touches every child's need for optimism and confidence for the future. Things must get better! While this may appear forced to some adults, it is essential that young children be sensitized to more positive feelings. Remember that while negative feelings evoked the crisis, "fixing it" should result in positive feelings and a sense of satisfaction (Wood, 2015, p. 35). Lasting change happens when a young person generally believes that better things are to come. Our adult responsibility is to provide the process whereby this happens and negative feelings are replaced with feelings of success, pleasure, self-confidence, security, and trust. For young children, the time immediately following the selection of a new behavior holds promise for successfully sensitizing them to their feelings of relief at crisis resolution and pleasure in the results of a new, successful behavior. This learning provides the foundation for future motivation, teaching that changes in behavior can produce desired responses from others. This is what Sam's "smile" ingredient is all about. At the end of this chapter, we include the abbreviated LSCI used with Sam when this recipe emerged.

The Abbreviated LSCI

To resolve a problem situation, a young child must struggle through a series of difficult understandings that are essentially the same as the ones addressed in a full LSCI with older kids, though in a more simplistic form. The same six LSCI steps we have described throughout this book are distilled into three general steps for the very young or youth with developmental delays:

1. Talking about the incident and the issue
2. Developing a solution by selecting a new behavior
3. Enhancing self-esteem

Here are the three parts of the abbreviated LSCI and the learning processes that are tapped during each part:

"TALK Phase" (Includes LSCI Stages 1, 2, and 3)

- Draining off intense feelings so that perceptions of reality dominate behavior.
- Using words (instead of behavior) to describe the events and actions of self and others.
- Ordering the events into a sequence that conveys what came first, next, and last.
- Discriminating between relevant information and elements that confuse or cloud the incident.

"FIX-IT Phase" (Includes LSCI Stages 4 and 5)

- Understanding that something can be done to make the situation better.
- Learning a new behavior to make it better.
- Stating the new behavior in words.
- Wanting to try the new way of behaving.
- Rehearsing the new behavior.

"SMILE Phase" (LSCI Stage 6)

- Acknowledging that better feelings have resulted from the problem resolution.
- Practicing the expression of these new feelings to carry them over into the next activity and the future.

Even in this abbreviated form, the essential LSCI elements are present. The streamlined process provides a structure to move a child forward developmentally, from a marginal ability to manage behavior toward full participation in talking about a crisis, agreeing on its resolution, and taking on personal responsibility.

How to Tell Whether a Young Person Needs an Abbreviated LSCI

Young children in crisis, or those of any age who are developmentally delayed, usually do not understand the source of their psychological pain, even though they feel it acutely. They do not possess sufficient impulse control to curtail the expression of intolerable feelings through unacceptable behavior. They do not understand the Conflict Cycle (Chapter 5) and may fail to connect their behavior to the responses of others. Their own needs are paramount and when thwarted in their attempts to gratify personal needs, they express outrage. In a child three or four years of age, this behavior is normal (although still unpleasant for adults). Their lack of skills is expected, and adults often see it as their role to teach new behaviors. In a school-aged child, however, behavioral expectations are increased and adults become more prone to using punishment to deal with unwanted behaviors than they are to teach new skills. Yet, as you know from reading this book, these are exactly the young people who, due to age, trauma, or developmental delay, need a teaching approach the most. In the simplest terms: teaching builds needed skills; punishment does not.

Teaching builds skills; punishment does not.

Young people who are developmentally unprepared to benefit from a full LSCI may have difficulty relating bits and pieces of an incident to a central issue. Their sequencing of events may be faulty and they may tend to focus on only one particular aspect of an incident (usually the part that has evoked the greatest emotional response). Their receptive verbal skills are limited and they often fail to fully comprehend the meaning of the words used by adults. Their expressive verbal skills may limit their ability to communicate feelings in words. They struggle to connect feelings to behavior. Their memory can be fragmented and they may need assistance to reconstruct basic sequences of events.

In their social and emotional development, young people who would benefit from the abbreviated LSCI are driven by their own needs, and their concern about others is seldom present. Fairness is viewed as something that benefits themselves only. They want adults and other children to agree with them, and they will go to extremes for adult attention and support. When you recognize a youth like this, who is developmentally unprepared for a full LSCI, consider using the abbreviated form to manage the crisis at hand.

Developmental Objectives for an Abbreviated LSCI

Many developmental objectives can be worked on while doing an abbreviated LSCI (Wood, Quirk, & Swindle, 2007, p. 154). Here are examples of such objectives that we have used with young children during abbreviated LSCI:

Behavioral Objectives

- To recall routine
- To show awareness of expected behavior through actions
- To tell about expected behavior using words
- To refrain from inappropriate behavior when other children have behaved inappropriately
- To explain why an event occurred (cause and effect)
- To tell about different ways to behave

Social Communication Objectives

- To use simple words to answer an adult's question
- To use words to describe events
- To use words to describe characteristics and behavior of self and others
- To show feelings appropriately through words and actions
- To make positive statements about self
- To participate and talk with others

Socialization Objectives

- To seek adults spontaneously
- To initiate appropriate behavior toward another child

- To interact appropriately with other children in play
- To cooperate with other children in group activities
- To share and take turns
- To imitate appropriate behavior of other children
- To label events with simple values

Pre-Academic Objectives

- To identify details in objects and people
- To tell a story sequence
- To use concepts of "same" and "different"
- To distinguish between opposites
- To categorize things that have the same characteristics
- To give reasons "why"
- To listen to a story with comprehension of what happened
- To learn rules of play and participation

If you already use a developmental approach to working with young children, you will have recognized these objectives as major milestones of development. They are essential skills for youth to master in the process of normal social and emotional growth. When you use the abbreviated LSCI with a child who lacks these developmental skills, the process becomes a strategy for teaching specific readiness skills in preparation for future participation in full LSCI.

You also may have recognized the connection between these developmental skills and the specific therapeutic goals of LSCI described in the preceding chapters. As you teach specific developmental skills in the abbreviated LSCI, you also are able to provide for several of these therapeutic goals:

- To organize reality (see Chapter 11)
- To teach new social-emotional skills (see Chapter 12)
- To improve self-regulation (necessary in most LSCI situations)

What Happens in an Abbreviated LSCI

Young children, and older youth who are developmentally delayed, typically respond to problem situations with emotions flooding their behavior. When this occurs, they generally display noticeably regressed behavior. You may see this in meltdowns, temper tantrums, screaming, crying, sobbing, kicking, spitting, biting, thumb-sucking, rolling around on the floor, waves of profanity or other "shock" words, or running away. When such signs of regression are evident, Surface Management (described in Chapter 9) is necessary before attempting to use LSCI. We look for indications that the child has calmed down physically before attempting any talk. Many well-meaning adults choose to ignore a child in this condition, using phrases such as "I'm waiting for you to get it together" or assigning the youngster to "take a time out." Neither approach is particularly productive if children lack developmental skills to calm themselves without help. To be left alone may increase confusion in children who have a fragile grasp of reality or it may increase resentment and anger in children who struggle with anxiety about abandonment (see Chapter 8).

> This is a time to show understanding, support, and your availability to help solve the problem.

It is important for a child to settle down before you begin LSCI, but ignoring or extended periods of waiting are not usually the best ways to get their attention and readiness to begin. This is a time to show understanding, support, and your availability to help solve the problem. Be specific and concrete in your suggestions for ways to calm down and show readiness:

- *I can tell you're ready to talk when you breathe slowly*
- *When you shout, I can't hear you. Let's talk softly so we can take care of this problem.*
- *We're going to figure out what to do together. I'll help you. When you can sit up quietly in the chair, I'll know you are ready.*

"TALK Phase"

When a child shows any change from regressed behavior, try to shift the communication mode to words. A sympathetic question that requires only a "yes" or "no" response often helps get the process started.

- *Are you feeling better now?*
- *Did someone hurt you (your feelings)?*
- *Do you want to solve this problem?*
- *Something has upset you; let's talk about it.*

When asked, "What happened?" children typically respond with:

- *I don't know.*
- *It's his fault!*
- *I didn't do it!*
- *I don't care!*

It is not unusual for young children to begin to talk and then cycle back to emotional flooding again. When this occurs, just repeat the expectation that they can show you they are ready to talk by a specific behavior. *Caution: don't use a time refer-ence such as counting 1, 2, 3 or demand a specific quiet behavior for a sustained period.* These expectations can become stressors in themselves, and young children may lose the drift of the incident as they concentrate on the performance you demand.

> Simple, direct questions are suitable for young children who have some verbal ability to respond, even if it is with limited words or phrases.

Simple, direct questions are suitable for young children who have some verbal ability to respond, even if it is with limited words or phrases. If they can coherently describe simple experiences at times when there is no crisis, they should be able to benefit from answering your questions. They may emphasize one aspect of the event to exclusion of others. However, the important point is that the child is sharing perceptions with you. The session may be short and a full investigation may not be appropriate. But the exchange teaches the child that you listen and value what the child has to say.

For children who are not ready to share information openly with an adult, putting the talk time into the form of a story narration that parallels the incident can be very effective. This is a useful alternative when a child cannot tolerate or accept painful reality because of too much mental or emotional confusion, guilt, difficulty comprehending the incident, or poor reality testing.

Begin with a standard story opener like, "This reminds me of a story about . . . Ask questions to obtain the child's input and use this to construct the story, touching on the important points of the real incident. Join your words to the child's perceptions, however limited or strange the perception may be. By dealing in a fantasy mode, some children are better able to "hear" and accept the problem and to consider alternate behaviors required to resolve the incident. Bring closure during the make-believe part of the story, weaving the storyline around the hero or heroine going to a private place to talk about problem-solving ("fixing it") with an adult. End the story with a return to reality and the real situation. When this strategy is used, children are usually able to transfer the make-believe solution to the real incident and to rephrase the change needed in their own behavior.

Creative art materials provide excellent alternatives for communicating during the abbreviated LSCI. Drawing materials, chalk, music and rhythm, puppets, dolls, and stuffed animals stimulate certain children who have no use for other avenues of communication. The adult must structure the activity so that the child is given sufficient content and direction to explore the incident. The material should already be familiar and preferred by the child. Many young children will communicate through art, reliving or expanding on a stressful event. This is an excellent opportunity for teaching children to symbolize a critical event and then to use words to describe what they have created and experienced (Williams & Wood, 2010, pp. 1–2). These media also provide opportunity for the adult to structure an appropriate resolution using verbal and nonverbal channels, such as solutions through creative play, pictures, pantomime, or role play.

FIX-IT Phase

In the section above, the emphasis is on communicating about the problem situation and the child's feelings and behaviors connected with it. With children, talking itself is a part of the process of problem resolution because they are learning to use words to solve problems instead of acting out through unacceptable behavior. The actual Fix-It phase may be fairly brief, with the solution almost always being generated by the adult. This should not be surprising to you, if you recall from Chapter 8 that young children are almost always in a pre-existential phase of development where they look to adults for authority and resolutions to problems. Remember, it is not until about eight or nine years old that children enter the existential crisis phase of development where they begin to see themselves as having responsibility for problem-solving.

> With children, talking itself is a part of the process of problem resolution because they are learning to use words to solve problems instead of acting out through unacceptable behavior.

With any of the strategies described above in the Talk phase, the adult structures the resolution and reentry process. Children feel relief when they are assisted in finding a solution to their problem situation. At their stage of development, young children must rely on adults for resolution and new alternative behaviors. If you tend to think that children are old enough to solve a problem of their own making, remind yourself that if they knew how to handle things in a better way, they probably would do so. Almost all children want good things to happen to themselves.

Most abbreviated LSCIs focus on the therapeutic goals of organizing reality or teaching new social-emotional skills. Keep these goals in mind as you move to close down an abbreviated LSCI. These goals, in the Fix-It phase, form the ideas that you and the child will use to solve the problem, change behavior, and relieve intolerable feelings. If a child is primarily disorganized or in fragile touch with reality, clearly the therapeutic goal is to organize reality, and constructing a sequential Timeline of events may be the first achievement. Solutions should be in keeping with ways to assist the child in staying organized by learning to observe what happens with others, staying in touch with events, and reporting them to the teacher.

With young children who are in touch with reality, are aware of what happened, and are receptive to new, more successful ways to behave, the therapeutic goal of teaching new social-emotional skills and behaviors is appropriate. This goal might include such behavior choices as learning to signal the teacher when problems seem to be creeping into an event or actively seeking the teacher for help. Other solutions include planning, with the child, ways for the teacher to restructure or redesign an activity so that the child has the opportunity to demonstrate more successful behaviors.

It is essential that the Fix-It phase includes an attempt by the child to state or restate the selected solution to the problem situation. Most children who are receptive to the abbreviated LSCI can describe simple behavior alternatives such as:

It is essential that the Fix-It phase includes an attempt by the child to state or restate the selected solution to the problem situation.

- Tell the teacher
- Listen to the teacher
- Follow directions
- Share
- Ignore him
- Tell him to stop it
- Wait for my turn
- Find another toy to play with
- Use words to let teacher know
- Be friends by . . .

Learning to do and say these sorts of things seldom comes spontaneously. Because of their stage of development, young children need help from adults to articulate and achieve the alternative behavior. They seldom can successfully implement new alternatives without initial massive support from an adult.

At the end of the Fix-It phase, structure the resolution and the child's reentry into the classroom or ongoing activity carefully with the child so that it is clearly understood how and when the child will need to use the new behavior. Children must be reassured that adults will help with the resolution and reentry. Here are several statements used by adults to convey this idea of ongoing support:

- *We can handle this together now.*
- *You can do it really well now. I'm sure of that!*
- *When you go back, remember just how well you did it here. It will work again.*
- *Each time this trouble comes up again, remember that you know how to handle it now!*

A problem situation is resolved (fixed) when children are sufficiently aware of the behavior required of them that they can:

1. Restate the solution
2. Demonstrate it with an action

SMILE Phase

The smile itself is not the requirement for this last phase of the modified LSCI; it only serves as a symbol for feelings of pleasure in accomplishment. Each child who goes through an abbreviated LSCI with you should have a sense of relief and accomplishment at the end, with the knowledge that he or she had a problem and has solved it!

Find numerous ways to recognize the new behavior as the child tries it out. Smiles, approving looks, a high five, and positive words convey a genuine interest in the child's new behavior and provide social reinforcement in a warm and meaningful manner. *Remember that an abbreviated LSCI is only as effective as the quality of the follow-up the child experiences.*

> Helping children to have a sense of accomplishment and to be aware of their own feelings of relief and pleasure in resolving a problem is a fundamental premise for every LSCI.

Helping children to have a sense of accomplishment and to be aware of their own feelings of relief and pleasure in resolving a problem is a fundamental premise for every LSCI. Too often, a child may resolve a crisis (fix it) but not be fully aware of feelings of satisfaction or accomplishment. Creating awareness of a satisfying outcome is the essential purpose of the Smile phase. Self-regulation of behavior includes the ability to control and direct the emotions that fuel behavior. Before children can learn to regulate emotional behavior, they have to have an awareness of their feelings, especially a sense of accomplishment or control when they have fixed a problem. While no child is too young to begin to learn this lesson, the form this instruction takes must be suited to the age and developmental stage of the youth. For young children, traditional preschool education instructs in the meaning of feeling words such as happy, sad, scared, or mad. In this way, preschool teachers begin to teach words for these feelings and their behavioral expressions. But long before young children are ready to use these basic feeling words, they have been decoding their parents' facial expressions and body language. Infant researchers tell us that an infant's smile and the parent's response are the foundations for the infant's first intrapersonal relationship.

In the example that follows, you will see that Sam's smile at the resolution of his crisis is a symbol of his new feeling of elation that he has learned a new skill—how to solve a problem. We want Sam to be aware of the sense of pleasure he is actually experiencing over this new mastery. Sam actually grinned as he marched back to his classroom to tell the others about how to solve a problem. If you watch carefully, almost every young student with whom you use LSCI successfully will show some smile, distinctly or fleetingly, as he or she completes the LSCI and returns to the activity. When the adult using an abbreviated LSCI reciprocates with a similar sign of sharing in the student's pleasure, the mutuality of the moment is solidified. A relationship is strengthened and offers a bridge to future exchanges.

There are many other ways to complete this part of the abbreviated LSCI where the child is assisted in getting in touch with positive, pleasurable feelings. Some teachers use an interactive model, such as "Let's shake!" As they do so, they smile to themselves. Children automatically respond with similar behavior. They accompany this response with words that reflect well-being and pleasure for the satisfactory end of the crisis. Still others provide proximity in a sense of psychological closeness that conveys support and caring, accompanied by affirming words. In all these strategies, the intent is to obtain similar verbal statements of well-being and pleasure from the child.

You may be asking, *Why go through all this time and effort after you have resolved the crisis and developed a new, alternative behavior for the child?* This emphasis on the resulting feelings as a last phase of the abbreviated LSCI is essential in creating lasting behavior change and social-emotional growth. Because young children are often unaware that the quality of their feelings has changed during LSCI, adults must provide a way to create awareness of these positive changes.

Example of an Abbreviated LSCI: The Saga of the Yellow Towel

Five-year-old Sam walks into the daycare center sobbing his heart out. His mother leaves after a quick explanation that Sam wants a yellow towel for the swimming trip today but she has no yellow towel to give him. Sam's teacher tries to console him and redirect his attention to his beautiful blue towel. The strategy doesn't work. Sam's sobs increase and tears flowed down his cheeks. He is in an emotional spiral that quickly turns into a tantrum. Between gasps, sobs, and tears, Sam blurts out, "*But . . . I want . . . a yellow towel! I have to have it!*" More sobs and another outburst follow. The teacher tries another strategy, reminding Sam of the fun they will have at the pool and reflecting on Sam's previous accomplishments and swimming. "We're going to have a really good time at the pool today, Sam. Last time you were the one to jump in and swim to the other side. Remember that? Everyone clapped when you got to the other side." Sam responds with another flood of tears interspersed with, "I can't go without a yellow towel!" Sam's teacher then tries the reality approach, "Well, Sam, I guess you'll just have to use a blue towel if you want to go swimming today."

With that, Sam disintegrates into uncontrollable sobbing and insisting, "I don't want to go swimming!" By now, Sam's emotional state is having a contagious effect on the other children. They stop their play, staring at Sam and the teacher. Thumbs go into mouths and tears well in children's eyes. One child pushes another. A blanket of unhappiness sweeps through the room. It is time to reverse the rapid disintegration of the emotional climate in the classroom. A break is needed in the Conflict Cycle occurring with the interactions between Sam and his teacher. The teacher, finally recognizing this need to divert Sam from emotionally driven behavior to a rational, problem-solving mode, chooses to use abbreviated LSCI with Sam. As the teacher begins, she knows that the first step is to get Sam to talk without breaking down into emotional flooding.

TALK Phase

TEACHER:	Do you know we can do something about this problem?
SAM:	(*Shakes head to indicate no, but sobbing slows and he glances at the teacher*)
TEACHER:	Sam, let's do something about this problem. Let's talk about a yellow towel, with words not tears.
SAM:	(*Looks again at teacher, with some interest; then breaks down again sobbing*)
TEACHER:	We can fix things if we talk about it . . . with words not tears.
SAM:	(*Sobs continue but less intensely*)
TEACHER:	I can tell your words are wanting to come out and are waiting for you to put away your tears.
SAM:	(*Sobs end*)
TEACHER:	Good work! Now we can figure out a way to fix things so you will feel better.
SAM:	(*Sobs begin again*)
TEACHER:	Tell me in words, Sam, not tears.
SAM:	(*Haltingly*) I have to have a yellow towel to go swimming! (*Tears begin again but teacher interrupts*)
TEACHER:	Use words, Sam, to tell me about it.
SAM:	I need a yellow towel.

Teacher begins helping Sam recall events and organize reality.

TEACHER: Did you pack your towel in your bag before you went to bed last night?

SAM: Yes, but it wasn't a yellow towel. I didn't like it!

TEACHER: What color was the towel you packed?

SAM: Blue, but I don't like blue.

TEACHER: You like yellow. I can understand that. It is your favorite color, right?

SAM: Yes! And I am not going swimming.

TEACHER: Did you take a bath before you went to bed last night?

SAM: Yes.

TEACHER: Think about last night. Can you remember the color of the towel you used?

SAM: No . . . but it wasn't yellow. I hated it!

TEACHER: Could it have been this blue towel?

SAM: No! It was white. I hate that blue towel!

TEACHER: So, let's see what you did when you got up this morning. Your mom brought you to school?

SAM: Yes.

TEACHER: And did she fix breakfast for you before you left?

SAM: Yes.

TEACHER: What did you have?

SAM: Cereal and raisins.

TEACHER: Sounds delicious. Your mother really takes care of you, giving you a good breakfast like that.

SAM: (Nods and looks directly at teacher)

           Teacher notes Sam's responsiveness to the idea of being cared for.

TEACHER: So, your mom took care of you this morning. She fixed you a delicious breakfast and then helped you pack your bag for swimming trip today?

SAM: (Looking guarded now) Yes, but I told her I didn't want that towel.

           Observes that Sam has demonstrated all of the processes at work in the Talk phase, so she begins to look for resolutions.

TEACHER:	Where do children get towels?
SAM:	(*Silence, but looks at teacher hopefully*)
TEACHER:	To get a towel, we have to know where the towels are kept.
SAM:	(*Nods agreement*)
TEACHER:	Now, what I hear you saying is that you like yellow towels and you do not have one today. Is that right?
SAM:	Yes! I want a yellow towel.

FIX-IT Phase

TEACHER:	To get any color of a towel, we have to first find the place where towels are kept.
SAM:	Right! (*Leans toward teacher and conveys interest in the idea*)
TEACHER:	Do you know, we keep towels here at school for children who sometimes forget their towels?
	Teacher knows there are no yellow towels at school, but she also knows that Sam is not yet emotionally ready to hear the full facts.
SAM:	(*Shakes head*) I don't know where the towels are.
TEACHER:	Can you think where they may be in this building?
SAM:	(*Now very interested*) Maybe in the office?
TEACHER:	If not there, where else should we look?
SAM:	Maybe in the supply room? Maybe in the bathroom?
TEACHER:	Good ideas on how to fix this problem, Sam!
SAM:	(*Beaming*) Let's go look!
	Sam and teacher go to the places he has suggested. The last stop is the supply room where the school keeps a few clean towels on hand for emergencies.
TEACHER:	Sam, look what we found!
SAM:	The towels . . . we found the towels!
TEACHER:	Right! Let's look at them.
	They go through the stack of towels, naming the colors as they go, blue, green, pink . . .

TEACHER:	What funny color is this, Sam? (*Singles out a grey yellow towel that had once been white*)
SAM:	(*Dubiously*) I don't know.
TEACHER:	Some people may call it white, but I wouldn't, would you?
SAM:	No, that's not white.
TEACHER:	Then, what color is it?
SAM:	I don't know.
TEACHER:	Some people call this color cream or beige.
SAM:	(*Listening but looking disappointed*)
TEACHER:	Do you know how people make this color called beige?
SAM:	(*Shakes head but looks interested*)
TEACHER:	You mix white and yellow to make beige. So, we have found a towel that is made of white and yellow.
SAM:	But I want a yellow towel.
TEACHER:	Now we have found a towel made with yellow and white; so you have fixed the problem of no yellow towel! Now you can go swimming with us!
	Sam's love of swimming overcomes his resistance. He reluctantly takes the towel, clutches it to his chest, and starts back to the classroom.
TEACHER:	When your friends tell you what color towels they have, what will you tell them about your towel?
SAM:	(*Thinks about question, looking confused again*)
TEACHER:	How many colors are in your towel?
SAM:	Two! My towel is two colors!
TEACHER:	That's right. Your towel is a special color made of two colors. That's something they will be interested in. Before we came down here to hunt for towels, we had a problem. Do you remember?
SAM:	(*Nods*)
TEACHER:	What did we do about it?
SAM:	We found the towels.
TEACHER:	And before that?

SAM: We talked about it.

TEACHER: That's right! We talked about it, and then we fixed the problem! Now there is something else we need to do, so you will feel good.

SAM: (*Clutching the towel; impatient now to rejoin the group for swimming*) I want to go swimming!

TEACHER: Before we go back, let's see how you can tell the other children about fixing a problem. When you have a problem, what do you do first?

SAM: Talk!

TEACHER: Right. Then what do you do?

SAM: Find the towels.

TEACHER: That's it! How did you fix the problem?

SAM: My towel is white and yellow. (*Grinning happily*)

Sam has accomplished the processes involved in the Fix-It phase and has stated the solution in his own limited way.

SMILE Phase

TEACHER: And after children fix a problem, they feel better! I can see that you really feel better now because you're smiling.

Teacher begins final phase, sensitizing Sam to a new feeling and giving him practice that will carry over into the next activity.

SAM: (*Thinks about it and gives teacher another faint smile*)

TEACHER: What will you tell the others about how they will feel when they fix a problem?

SAM: Smile!

TEACHER: Sam, you have learned something important today that the other children in the group will want to hear about: how to take care of a problem. Everyone has problems, but not everyone knows how to fix them.

As Sam and the teacher returned to the room, the other children come over to him with great interest. They also had been caught up in Sam's emotional outbursts.

TEACHER: (*To other children*) What do you do if there is a problem? Sam had a problem and now he knows what to do. Sam, tell them the three steps you use to take care of a problem.

SAM: (*With pride and eagerness*) First, we talk about it. Then, we fix it. Then, we smile!

Summary

Children and youth of every age can be caught in Conflict Cycles, resulting in crisis. We have used the abbreviated LSCI with children as young as four years of age, as long as they have the prerequisite skills to participate. They must be able to listen and attend mentally, have some verbal skills for sharing information, understand meanings and words, understand that there has been an incident, and trust that the adult is a helping person.

But solving one crisis is not the end in itself! Life presents one crisis after another, and the solution to one crisis does not necessarily free the child from having another, and another, and another. The important point is to teach young people ways to deal with crisis that are within their capacity to use. When they try new behaviors with successful and pleasurable results, the motivation is laid for retaining the new behavior to avoid future Conflict Cycles that bring unpleasant reactions from others.

Having nearly worked your way through to the end of this book, we hope you have developed a perspective about crisis as occurring when young people are not able to regulate their own feelings and behavior in ways that bring about the results they desire from others. We hope you have an understanding of LSCI, and its abbreviated form, as a process you can use for supporting children and youth in stressful situations.

We also hope that you view your roles and responsibilities during LSCI as changing to adjust to the particular problem, behaviors, anxieties, and developmental needs of each young person. The roles and messages you will be required to deliver are complex. The variations are endless. Sometimes you will have to be an adult authority who enforces the rules, brings order, and mediates justice. At other times you will be the benevolent nurturer, the teacher, the sympathetic supporter. Sometimes, you will protect a youth from situations that are too overwhelming for them to handle; at other times, you will back off from a central role to allow experience—the great teacher—to teach the hard way. In all of this, the adult remains the source of support, affirming belief in the child—whatever their age, behavior, or problem.

"Now, we are speaking the same language."

20 USING LSCI AS A SOCIAL-EMOTIONAL LEARNING PROGRAM FOR CHILDREN AND ADOLESCENTS

What Is Social-Emotional Learning?

Social-emotional learning (SEL) refers to the process through which young people develop skills to monitor thoughts, manage emotions, show empathy, establish positive relationships, solve problems, resolve conflict, and make responsible decisions. By its very nature, LSCI not only is a verbal intervention strategy but also offers effective SEL programming to children and adolescents.

> LSCI not only is a verbal intervention strategy but also offers effective SEL programming to children and adolescents.

According to the Collaborative for Academic, Social, and Emotional Learning (CASEL, 2019), students participating in SEL programs showed improved classroom behavior, an increased ability to manage stress and depression, and better attitudes about themselves, others, and schools. A landmark study involving more than 97,000 students from kindergarten through high school showed that conduct problems, emotional distress, and drug use were all significantly lower for students exposed to SEL programs and that the positive impact of SEL programming can endure for up to 18 years (Taylor et al., 2017).

Why Teach LSCI Concepts to Young People?

Because effective SEL programming drives such important outcomes for young people, the LSCI Institute developed an eight-session SEL curriculum to bring the basic concepts of LSCI to kids. Unlike our certification course for adults, the Group Curriculum does not teach intervention skills, but rather helps kids learn about the dynamics of conflict, recognize patterns of self-defeating behaviors, and develop problem-solving practical skills capacities. The LSCI Group Curriculum gives young people a foundation in LSCI concepts that improves their ability to recognize and grasp important insights from LSCI interventions. In essence, it gives adults and kids a common language to talk about stressful situations. In the pages below, we provide you with an overview of the curriculum itself along with two sample chapters:

> The LSCI Group Curriculum gives adults and kids a common language to talk about stressful situations.

Program Purpose

The *LSCI Skills for Kids* curriculum is a helpful tool for professionals trying to integrate the five core SEL competencies (self-awareness, self-management, social awareness, relationship skills, and responsible decision-making) into their classrooms, programs, and therapeutic milieus.

Time Frame

Each of the eight lessons is designed to be completed in a 40- to 50-minute period, though the activities and discussions are flexible enough to adapt to the available time frame, group membership, individual needs, and the mood of the day (among other variables)!

Group Size

Because each session is built largely around group activities and discussions, the ideal group size is eight to ten kids per adult facilitator. Whenever possible, enough adults should be present to allow each participant the chance to feel heard and understood and to be sure that all concerns, questions, and issues that are raised receive due attention.

Group Membership

Who benefits from LSCI skills? Is SEL just for the kids who exhibit challenging behaviors? *Any* child can benefit from the *LSCI Skills for Kids* group experience because, as author Carrie Goldman (2012) points out in her book *Bullied*, getting through life requires all people to manage social dynamics. Human beings are called upon to use social-emotional skills every day of their life, at all ages, throughout the lifespan. It only makes sense for educational and therapeutic settings, whose goal it is to develop productive citizens, to provide explicit instruction in these skills.

Group Age and Ability

The discussions and activities in this curriculum are designed to be used across a large span of ages and abilities. There will likely be instances in which certain individuals are able to move quickly through concepts while others may need more focus and explanation. Since this is designed as a group experience, the facilitator(s) is called upon to use their skill to make the material meaningful for all.

To assist with this task, the Facilitator's Guide provides suggestions on how to adjust the material for different ages/abilities. Also, there are two versions of the Participant's Handbook: a Kid's Version for young children or those with less ability to write and/or deeply process the material and a Youth Version for those who can take limited notes and process the material more readily.

Facilitator Qualifications

The *LSCI Skills for Kids* curriculum is written as a step-by-step facilitation guide so that *any adult with professional training in working with challenging children and youth* may lead the group. Those who have completed the LSCI certification course will have the added benefit of a thorough understanding of specific LSCI terms and concepts.

SESSION ONE—
INTRODUCTION TO LIFE SPACE CRISIS INTERVENTION

Supplies Needed:

❑ One copy of the group handbook for each participant

❑ Prepared labels for icebreaker activity

❑ Candy for icebreaker activity

❑ Flipchart paper

❑ Markers

Welcome to the Group

Icebreaker Activity: The Candy Caper

- Briefly summarize LSCI training, letting kids know that LSCI is a certification course that trains adults in skills for building helpful relationships with kids. (More information about LSCI will be provided later in this session.)
- Let the kids know that when adult teachers/staff attend LSCI training, they work in groups with other staff in order to learn from each other, just as the kids will do in this group.
- One of the fun ways that adults organize their groups is by playing a simple game, which we will use to begin this first group session.
- See attached for activity instructions. *(Not included in this sample chapter)*
- Even in groups where kids know each other well, it is important to allow for an "icebreaking" period each session where they can get out of school/class/placement/treatment mode and into group mode.
- The intention is to lay the foundation for a trusting, safe atmosphere in which the kids will get to know, trust, and help each other in all new ways. Starting sessions in this fun, humorous way is one way to build the right atmosphere for a successful group experience.

Group Ground Rules

- Group leader should use flipchart paper and markers (or some other visible way) to have the group brainstorm ground rules.
- Examples of helpful group ground rules are things like:

- Kids maintain the confidentiality of what is shared in the group.
- Kids respect each other and what fellow group members share in the group.
- Don't talk while others are talking.

- In establishing group ground rules, it is most effective to have kids come up with the majority of the rules.

  - Usually, kids generate very good rules. Adults should only intervene if a rule is completely off-base.
  - Intervene by asking other group members what they think about the rule or, in a non-judgmental way, talk about why the rule might not work well in the group.
  - If important rules are omitted by the kids, adults should add them at the end of the brainstorming.

Introduction to Life Space Crisis Intervention

- Explain that LSCI stands for Life Space Crisis Intervention.
- LSCI is a process for helping adults and kids communicate effectively with each other when the kids are experiencing problems or stressful situations.
- LSCI is a way for adults and kids to better understand each other by talking through problems, including:

  - What led up to the problem(s).
  - If the problem is a pattern for the kid (in other words, if it is something that seems to happen again and again).
  - How the kid can understand the pattern and keep it from continuing to cause trouble in his life.

- LSCI is also a process that helps kids build strong and trusting relationships with helpful adults.
- If applicable, explain the LSCI training process for staff in your organization.

  - (E.g., "All adults who work with kids in this school become certified in Life Space Crisis Intervention within their first two years of working here.")
  - Having all staff trained means that staff will approach kids in consistent ways and kids should be able to count on staff to help them through the LSCI process, to better understand their problems and to change self-destructive patterns.

Purpose of Kids' LSCI Groups

- Just as adults need to know and understand common patterns of self-defeating behavior in kids, kids should learn to recognize common ways that they cause problems for themselves.
- Learning about LSCI will help kids prevent problems for themselves by recognizing and stopping problems before they start.
- Let kids know that this group will run for the next eight weeks.
- Preview of what we'll be learning:

  - Use attached scenarios to offer examples of self-defeating behavior patterns.
  - Have kids identify "what's going on" in each scenario and offer any personal examples.

Conclusion

- **Scavenger hunt**: On page 2 of the group handbook, participants have an "LSCI scavenger hunt." This hunt can be used throughout the eight-week curriculum as a way to emphasize for participants some of the highlights of the material and add in a little fun as participants are challenged to "hunt" for the answers to key questions. Group leaders may add a small incentive to any participant who completes the hunt.
- Summary of group purpose and group rules.
- Preview of next week.

To illustrate the types of self-defeating patterns of behavior we will be learning about in this LSCI group.

NOTE to Facilitator and Participants: some of these scenarios may be used again during the later weeks of the group. Make note of how the participants respond to the scenarios in this initial session versus how they respond to them in later weeks when they have learned more about LSCI and self-defeating behavior patterns.

Scenario #1

Ray is a nine-year-old boy who is small for his age and fearful of older/bigger kids. On the school bus, a teenage boy named Chris has been threatening him and humiliating him in front of his peers. This particular morning, Chris takes Ray's math homework and rips it into shreds. Ray feels like there is nothing he can do to defend himself. He arrives at school feeling weak, miserable, abused, ashamed, and angry. When his first period teacher asks the class to open their textbooks, Ray refuses to open his book, swears at the teacher, kicks his desk over, and lies down on the floor.

Scenario #2

Ms. Johnson tells the class to walk in line to the gym. Sean, who is first in line, sets a pace so fast that no one can keep up with him. When Ms. Johnson removes him as the line leader, he is angry and non-compliant and insists that he wasn't doing anything wrong. In reality, Sean knew exactly what was expected of him as the line leader and was testing Ms. Johnson's limits.

Scenario #3

Russell wants to be friends with the other kids on the unit, but he always feels like he doesn't quite fit in. One afternoon, he steals money from the staff office and gives it to one of the most popular kids on the unit in order to try to gain acceptance and seem "cool."

Scenario #4

A person is arrested for stealing several bicycles from around his neighborhood. When questioned by the police, he says that he only took bikes that were not locked up. He never broke any locks or took bikes from inside anyone's house. Therefore, he says that what he did was not illegal.

Scenario #5

Chris is a nine-year-old resident of a group home, who sometimes has trouble with wetting the bed. Even though doctors tell him that his problem is normal, whenever it happens, Chris feels very ashamed of himself. One morning, he wakes up and his bed is wet. Chris takes all of his bed sheets and wet clothes and throws them in the trash. Then, he begins to empty his closet and dresser and throw all of his dry clothing in the trash can also. Finally, he begins hitting the wall and even punches a hole right through the drywall. When his counselor hears the noise and asks him what he is doing, Chris replies, "I'm so stupid. I hate myself. I don't deserve to have nice things."

Scenario #6

Johnny and Lenny are working together at a table. While their teacher is distracted, Lenny prompts Johnny to look under the table, then sticks his middle finger up at Johnny, knowing that it will make him feel tricked and upset. As predicted, Johnny starts yelling, "I hate you, Lenny!" Lenny shouts back, "No I didn't! He's lying! You're a liar, Johnny!" Soon the boys are in a heated argument that disrupts the entire class.

SESSION SEVEN—
FRIENDSHIP SKILLS AND ASSERTIVENESS

Welcome
- Remind kids that next week will be our last week of group.
- Check in on the Challenge Logs from last week.

  - How did the Challenge Log increase your focus on solutions instead of on challenges?
  - Does anyone want to share an example of a time this week that you took control of a challenge instead of letting a challenge take control of you?

Icebreaker: Famous Pairs
- See attached for several "famous pairs." *(Not included in this sample chapter)*
- Before group, the facilitator should give each participant a slip of paper that has one member of a famous pair.
- The challenge for participants is to walk around the room and find the other participant who has their pair.
- For example, one person may have the words "Peanut Butter" on their slip of paper and their task is to find the person with the word "Jelly" on their slip.
- Once each pair has been found, group members should exchange ideas on what it takes to be a good friend to someone else.

False Friendship: What Is a Friend?
- One of the most important things in the world for a child or teenager is to have friends. In childhood and adolescence, friends are a source of fun, learning, and support.
- However, as most of us know, some friendships can be dangerous and destructive.
- Ask clients to take two minutes to write down in their handbook as many things that they look for in a friend as possible.
- Once clients have written this down, make a group list, writing kids' answers down where everyone can see them.
- Next, challenge kids to think about things they would want to AVOID in a friend.

- For example, if a friend was always nice "to their face" but talked about them behind their backs, would they want to hold on to that person as a friend?
  - Why or why not?

- Kids should call out their answers and leader should write down a group list for all to see.
- Once the two lists are done, leader may want to make some comparisons between the two lists—emphasizing positive qualities to look for in friends versus qualities to avoid.
- Lastly, ask the group why they think that sometimes kids make friends with the "wrong" people.
- Allow for discussion and encourage kids to talk about things like peer pressure, fitting in, intimidation, etc.
- It can be very helpful for kids to hear that their peers have the same anxieties and insecurities about making and keeping friends.

Activity: I-Messages and Assertiveness

- Begin by asking if anyone knows how to define "assertiveness."
- Define "assertiveness" as a style of communication in which a *person directly expresses his thoughts, feelings, or needs without being offensive or violating the rights of someone else.*
- Assertiveness is an ideal style of communication that allows both persons in a conversation to feel good about the outcome.
- Assertiveness is kind of "in the middle" between being passive (not standing up for yourself, letting others walk all over you, not expressing your true thoughts, feelings, or needs) and being aggressive (being demanding, pushy, stepping all over someone else just to get what you want, or even being physically aggressive to get what you want).
- *For younger participants:* Simple definitions of *assertiveness* and *passive* behavior are provided in their handbook. Both advanced and younger participants have blank space to fill in characteristics of *aggressive* people.
- A good way to practice assertive behavior is to use I-messages.

  - I-messages are a positive form of communication that assert the speaker's feelings about an event or behavior without calling the other person names, accusing them, or being aggressive in any way.
  - Though I-messages can take many forms, the following template can be helpful for kids first practicing this style of positive communication:

I feel *(feeling)* _____

when *(describe behavior* _____

I want *(describe desired behavior)* _____

I don't want *(describe behavior to be discontinued)* _____

Example: I feel angry when you grab the ball out of my hands. I want you to wait for me to pass it. I don't want you to take it without asking.

- This template is provided in both versions of the handbook.

- Use two to three of these quick scenarios to challenge kids to:

    a. Identify if the initial response was aggressive or passive
    b. Come up with an I-message to respond assertively to the situation.

Scenarios:

1. (Aggressive): Joe is playing basketball. Jason comes up and snatches the ball from Joe. Joe runs after him and throws a punch, knocks him down, and grabs the ball. What is a more *assertive* way that Joe could have handled the situation?
2. (Passive): Kerry and Rebecca got into a fight because Kerry told everyone Rebecca was ugly. Rebecca didn't talk to Kerry. She just hoped the problem would go away. What is a more *assertive* way that Rebecca could have handled the situation?
3. (Passive) Kelly was jumping rope in the gym. Tina came up to her and took the jump rope away. Kelly said, "That's OK, you can take it," and walked away. What is a more *assertive* way that Kelly could have handled the situation?
4. (Aggressive) Tim gets in front of Mike in the dining hall line. Mike calls him an "asshole," first under his breath and then loud enough for everyone to hear. What is a more *assertive* way that Mike could have handled the situation?

Small Group Role Plays

- Using the pairs from the icebreaker game, assign participants to come up with at least two examples from their life—one in which someone behaved in a passive way and one in which a person behaved aggressively.
- Selecting either the passive or the aggressive scenario, the pairs should prepare a two-minute role play to act out in front of the group.

- The group should identify if the role play is demonstrating aggressive or passive behavior.
- After correctly identifying either aggressive or passive behavior, a volunteer should offer an assertive response as an alternative.
- Briefly discuss, as a large group, the likely consequences of the aggressive or passive response versus the assertive response if this scenario were to occur in real life.
- Be sure each pair gets to act out at least one of their role plays.
- If time permits, group facilitator can add additional practice role plays. Set up one participant volunteer to behave aggressively and give a second volunteer the chance to respond assertively on-the-spot.
- Ask kids if they can relate this discussion about communication styles to the discussion about friendships. Encourage them to talk about things like:

  - People who behave aggressively are typically the type of "friends" you want to avoid.
  - If someone is pressuring you to do something, either by violence, by intimidation, or other aggressive means, this should be a signal to you to that this person is not a true friend.
  - Sometimes people respond in a passive way when someone else is being aggressive. It's not fair to take advantage of passive people, just because you know they won't fight back.
  - If you see someone being bullied, is there something you can do about it?
  - What do you do when you are bullied?
  - Being assertive can be a challenge. It requires you to think about your response, rather than to just react quickly. You have to choose your words carefully. What are the rewards of taking the time to act assertively?
  - How does acting assertively help you make and keep friends?
  - How does acting assertively help you from falling into the traps of peer pressure?

Journaling

- Topic for Advanced Participants:

  - *Use this space to journal about the friendships in your life. Do you have friends who are fun to be around and supportive of you? Do you have friends who try to walk all over you? Do you ever find yourself being ag-*

gressive toward your friends? How can acting assertively help you make and keep friends?

- Topic for Younger Participants:

  - *Use this space to draw a picture of a good friend in your life. What do you like to do together? How do you show each other support and friendship?*

Conclusion

- Summarize the group session, validating the kids' participation and sharing their ideas.
- Preview next session agenda.
- Remind kids that next week will be our last group session.

The *LSCI Skills for Kids* program is a helpful tool for professionals trying to integrate SEL skills into their work with kids through easy-to-use, engaging group activities. For more information, please visit us at www.lsci.org.

"Thanks to LSCI training, I am not only a better professional, but I can become a better parent and human being."

21

IMPLEMENTING LSCI TRAINING IN BELGIUM

LSCI "Returns" to Europe

As you learned in the first chapter of this book, the roots of LSI came from Europe. In this final chapter, we share with you the implementation of LSCI in three different settings in Flanders (the Dutch-speaking part of Belgium), over the course of the last 20 years. Throughout LSCI's development and evolution in schools and treatment settings around the world, LSCI has remained well-matched for the theoretical background of education and youth care professionals in Flanders. In the pages that follow, you will hear from three distinguished professionals and LSCI Master Trainers from the Flemish community:

1. Franky D'Oosterlinck, PhD, director of the Orthopedagogical Center for Children, describes how LSCI fits into integrative orthopedagogical practice and how his team worked to create a high-quality environment (D'Oosterlinck et al., 2008) for education and treatment.
2. Wim Hanssens, social worker and vice director of Don Bosco Groenveld, tells the story of the implementation of LSCI in a secondary school for vocational education and special education for children with autism.
3. Bram Soenen, PhD, campus director of De Zande, a forensic residential center for young offenders, describes the early start of LSCI in Flemish community institutions a decade ago and how it has evolved into a pillar of the Flemish policy on residential forensic care and treatment.

Creating a High-Quality Environment for Children With Emotional and Behavioral Disorders

By Franky D'Oosterlinck

For 20 years, LSCI has been one of the applied methods in the orthopedagogical center Nieuwe Vaart (OC NV) in Ghent. OC NV welcomes children between the ages of 5 and 14 years old with behavioral and emotional disorders. The children receive special education combined with daycare and treatment. Most of the children live at home with their parents. In order to handle conflict and crises in a methodical and theoretically grounded way, leaders searched for a useful system that could be properly implemented. In this article, we highlight the most important elements we learned from LSCI. We are keen to share the insights we cherish to offer the children a quality environment and a therapeutic setting.

How LSCI Changed Our Organization's Culture and Practices

In 2002, LSCI Master Trainer Mark Freado and I visited LSCI Founder Dr. Nicholas Long. We discussed the results of the research we conducted in Belgium to measure the effects of the LSCI method in residential groups. One of our first findings was that the number of psychosomatic complaints by the youth actually increased. Although we were a bit embarrassed by this result, Dr. Long had a different interpretation. He stated that this may be good news, indicating that the children and youngsters were starting to be willing to talk about their pain. We were establishing a relationship of trust, he explained. Children were slowly letting us into their private reality.

When we asked team members how LSCI changed the operation of the organization, they repeatedly noted that we are now talking less *about* kids and more *with* kids. We listen to their stories, how they are experiencing life and how they are surviving:

9-Year-Old

A: I miss my teacher. He isn't at school because his wife gave birth to a baby boy.

T: Yes, your teacher became a father. Have you seen the baby yet?

A: Yeah, sure, what an ugly one!

T: I would be careful with such statements. Daddies and moms find their children beautiful most of the time.

A: Nobody thinks I am pretty. I don't know my father and my mother tells me I look like my dad.

Often youth offer direct and intense messages. Listening in a non-judgmental way helps adults respond neutrally to the emotional and sometimes shattered messages. In this way, we radiate serenity, we act as role models, and we help regulate the child's emotions. Sometimes the children or youngsters show magnificent insights.

12-Year-Old

B: I often argue with my mom when I return home from school.

T: What is the fight about?

B: I often try to do things my way. I want play on the computer or I want to eat sweets.

T: Do you ask for candy?

B: Sometimes I just take the box and eat it all.

T: Do you always eat everything or do you sometimes leave some?

B: Sometimes I leave some, when I think about my mom. I know she likes to eat sweets a lot, then I want to leave it for my mom and I can quit eating. I argue even more with my father. He's very strict with me. Last week, I was ten minutes late. My watch was lagging and now I can't use my phone for one week. My father is a trainer of a sports team and he thinks that I will only learn with hard discipline and punishment.

T: What do you think your father wants to teach you?

B: To come home on time?

T: Does he tell you that?

B: No, he says he can't trust me.

T: When will he trust you?

B: When I show responsibility.

The behavior of children and youngsters is sometimes violent and aggressive. It can paralyze and embarrass educators, teachers, and parents. As adults, we experience success if we see the child searching for words during a crisis in order to express his message in a verbal way. To calm down a child, to initiate a conversation, and to establish dialogue are important processes. Even though we realize we didn't fundamentally alter the child's life with one conversation, we made good use of the moment and strengthened our relationship. A relationship is created

A relationship is created as a collection of many thin threads that are woven together, especially during difficult moments.

as a collection of many thin threads that are woven together, especially during difficult moments.

Since the use of LSCI began, the whole team has been drinking coffee in the morning at the playground. Together, we welcome the children. This morning routine gives us the opportunity to work on our staff-child relationships. We also capture more easily the emotions the children bring in from home, and we take the time to talk about them. This not only builds positive relationships but also serves to prevent potentially explosive emotions from escalating early in the day.

In addition to the positive experiences in the program, our staff discovered during the research process that the number of conflicts in the living group where LSCI was implemented diminished. Children performed better at school and their social skills improved. The interesting thing about the LSCI method is that it is masterfully applied in practice and has been further developed over time. Today we see that Redl, Wineman, Long, Fecser, and so many others developed a method that reflects recent scientific findings in neurology, traumatology, and emotion regulation.

The implementation process and the development of LSCI in a center require courage and engagement from all team members. To discuss openly what the behavior of a child stirs up in you and what it does to you, to present a critical event to a team, to speak to a team member about the course of a conflict—these all require team members to leave themselves vulnerable and to express their feelings without fear of judgment. Searching together for the most appropriate response to a child's behavior, looking for the lever that moves the child's strength, is only possible when there is safety and trust in the group. The fascinating thing about this work, about the LSCI method, is that it is never finished. There are always new problems to think about and work on.

Applying LSCI Skills to Parenting

Everyone working with vulnerable children knows that the child's parents want to protect them. Often, parents experience many stressors in their own lives. Some have experienced negative and sometimes traumatic events. As a result, they don't always have the necessary self-regulation, communication, or problem-solving skills.

At our center, six family counselors who work intensively with parents are always prepared to discuss reports from parents with educators and teachers. It often takes years of intense investment to teach the family system how to deal with parenting stress in an appropriate way. We notice that our counselors often need to invest a large period of time building trust with families. Only after a trusting relationship is established are they are allowed to intervene in the family system and talk with the family members about their problems. Often, the Conflict Cycle™ is used as a way for parents to understand stress. Many parents are eagerly interested in LSCI methods. They, too, recognize that listening, feeling in control of their emotions, and communicating effectively promote better interactions with their child, even though the problems they face are severe. One mother participated in an LSCI training. She stated that any parent who has a child with behavioral problems should have access to this training. It could help ensure that children are less quickly placed out of home if parents and care providers become better attuned to children.

> Any parent who has a child with behavioral problems should have access to this training.

For the past ten years we have held a three-day meeting with parents of children who receive daycare and go to school in OC NV. We start these sessions by listening to the stories of the parents. They may introduce a moment when they were struggling with their child. Then, we introduce a relevant concept. In the evening, parents go home with a plan to try out some of the ideas they have learned. The last day is scheduled a few weeks later than the first two days. On that day, parents talk about how it went. Parents find it helpful to be able to share challenging situations with each other without being judged as a "bad" parent. Of course, they also share experiences of their own life that partially define how they take care of their children. During these days, parents mainly learn to listen to their children again. They often think that listening carefully to their child's story means that they seem to agree with the child's behavior and accept it, as if they are giving in. It's a big step to acknowledge the child's perception and from there to find out together whether they made the right choices.

Staff Certification in LSCI

Finally, we would like to add that our research shows that children appreciate educators who are competent in the use of LSCI. Children and young people indicate that educators must be able to listen carefully, show understanding, and offer acceptance. They should be clear, honest, authentic, and fair.

All employees of OC NV are trained in LSCI. They are part of a group of approximately 7,000 LSCI-trained educators, teachers, and social workers in Flanders. In addition to our educators, the technicians at the OC NV are also trained in LSCI. Last year, one of our 12-year-old students was allowed to participate in woodwork once a week to help regulate the stress he experienced from going to school. Henri, a technician trained in LSCI, worked with the student to make a bird cage. Then, for the student's birthday, Henri gave him a lovebird. The youth's mother said that this project meant much more to her son than school life itself. A lifelong memory and friendship arose.

LSCI is propagated and maintained from our center both internally and externally by Senior Trainers Eline Spriet and Katrien Sel, and by Master Trainer Gerrit De Moor. These Trainers inspire many people through their fascinating stories, in which they testify to their own insight and practice in combination with their excellent knowledge of the methodology. The translated LSCI book has already been reprinted 17 times. In the words of LSCI Master Trainer Mark Freado: "If we all help one child or young person every year to create more possibilities in his future by LSCI conversations, then we all contribute to a better future." LSCI is and remains a basic method that inspires every day to take small actions that make a difference.

Walk the Talk

By Wim Hanssens

In 2007, our secondary vocational school experienced exponential growth in terms of students. We also noticed a remarkable increase in the number of students in need of psychosocial support. Today, data suggests that for 69% of our students psychosocial care in the school is indispensible. In 2007, however, we did not have an adequate approach to the needs of these young students. This resulted in an increase in transgressive and challenging behavior.

What started in 2007 as a search for an intervention method to effectively support our students resulted in refinement of our educational project, now translated into the Circle of Courage® and into a project where LSCI forms the methodological framework to guide people in general, and youngsters in particular. Today, the implementation of LSCI and the Circle of Courage in the school is a fact and is supported by all the employees and students. Moreover, school employees and students find it an integral element in our teaching and daily interactions. However, this transition and the implementation of LSCI and COC were not obvious. In this article, I offer insight in the trajectory and the elements that were crucial to this transition.

Four Conditions That Enabled the Implementation of LSCI

There are four important conditions that enabled the implementation of LSCI :

1. **Intrinsic motivation:** In 2007, after a series of rigorous exercises to discover the roots of the problems, it became evident that as a team, we did not have professional know-how and expertise in dealing with the steep rise in students with care needs in the school. This then manifested itself as an increase in the frequency and intensity of transgressive behavior among students and an increase in absenteeism among teachers. This observation and the feeling of powerlessness led to a great openness toward a new work method.

2. **Strong leadership:** In such a turbulent period, a ship needs a captain with vision. The management team adhered to a number of basic but clear foundational principles:

    a. No repressive policy toward young people with transgressive behavior

    b. Exclusion/expulsion of young people from the school can never be the first solution to a problem

    c. Focus on increasing the competency of the in-house team instead of outsourcing

    d. Adoption of a dialogue style toward students and colleagues

3. **Open communication:** Always involve and inform all employees about every single step in the transition process. By doing so, both the final goal and the path toward it remain visible at all times.

4. **Team-oriented approach:** The challenge we faced at the time was structural, and therefore we had to work as a school team. We opened up to critically asking "What is our problem?" rather than "What is your problem?" This shift in perspective made our connection strong during the process. The actual implementation and transition took place via eight clear steps, described next.

> We opened up to critically asking "What is our problem?" rather than "What is your problem?"

Eight Steps in the Implementation and Transition to LSCI

1. **Vision Development: Which Methodology to Choose?**

   In our search for a methodology to deal with transgressive behavior, we were introduced to Life Space Crisis Intervention by Dr. Franky D'Oosterlinck. During those first meetings it became clear that LSCI had important potential for us:

   - *Verbal methodology*: Don Bosco's project stands for dialogue in education. The fact that LSCI gives us tools to engage in dialogue with children, even during a crisis situation, and that we do not fall back on the principle of 'carrots and sticks,' is due to our foundational values in our organization.
   - *Proven effectiveness of the methodology*: LSCI is a concrete, clear, and structured methodology with many years of history. The effectiveness of the methodology has been substantiated scientifically.
   - *Translation* of the LSCI intervention methodology within Don Bosco's existing education project. The education project of Don Bosco has a

few concrete tools; however, they are more like declarations of intent. LSCI, on the other hand, provides us with a variety of concrete tools to act methodically, consistently, and in a structured way, and at the same time matches the expectations described in the education project of Don Bosco. LSCI tools strengthen the vision of the Don Bosco project and allow us to bridge from intention to concrete actions.

> LSCI tools strengthen the vision of the Don Bosco project and allow us to bridge from intention to concrete actions.

- *Blending* of Don Bosco's four educational goals with the values of the Circle of Courage. Don Bosco stated that a school cannot be solely a place for learning, but should also be a home, a playground, and a place for spirituality. Only then, according to Don Bosco, is integrated education possible. The Circle of Courage not only offers a translation, but is also a roadmap to achieve the education goals. According to the Circle of Courage, Belonging, Mastery, Independence, and Generosity are universal needs of every human being. Today, LSCI as a methodology and the Circle of Courage as a framework of values are included in our vision and mission statement and in documents such as the school regulations.

2. Communication

From the start of the implementation process, we were aware of the importance of open communication, consultation, participation, and respect for the pace of the team members. The goal we were working toward became clear relatively fast. The path toward it, however, had to be mapped out step by step. A steering committee, in which all parts of the organization were represented, formed the core group that would monitor and supervise this transition. This delegation was also responsible for the informal and formal communication to all employees.

3. Training/Education

Today, our LSCI team consists of over 90 colleagues. Not every employee could immediately be trained in LSCI. Initially we chose to put together and train a 'crisis team' for our school. This team consisted of the internal social workers, the members of the management-team, and an employee of the administration. This crisis team functioned as a safety net for students and teachers and served both a preventive and an intervention function. The work and attitude of the crisis team strongly contributed to the sense of safety and well-being of students and colleagues. As a result of this positive evolution, we also saw a rapid increase in support for the further implementation of LSCI and COC. We continued to train the employees and today, 80% of the employees are certified and three LSCI Senior Trainers are connected to our school. We yearly train many professionals in Flanders.

4. Infrastructure

Our school building is more than the sum of classrooms and practice rooms. To give the LSCI methodology every opportunity, one should invest in both people and infrastructure. We designate meeting rooms, spaces for conversation, and spaces where students can relax, unload, and take time out. LSCI is highly visible on our campus.

In general: the school invests substantially in creating a pleasant and attractive school infrastructure where young people can feel welcome. The continued investment in attractive infrastructure is undeniably conducive to the well-being of students and staff. People feel welcomed!

5. Coaching and Support

The basis for continued implementation of LSCI starts with regular clarification of the methodology and the framework of values; that is why constant training is so important. In addition, there is the conscious coaching of colleagues, especially in difficult situations. This gives us the opportunity to live up to the richness of the framework and the methodology. Students and colleagues can count on unconditional support. For example, restorative conversations are very important. Every student or colleague can ask for support in the preparation of these important conversations. We do believe in a restorative spirit!

6. Daily Practice

It is our conviction that the extent to which such a project is supported by employees and students strongly depends on the extent to which it is presented and experienced in an authentic way. Nothing is more deadly for a project than the inconsistent living of a framework of values, both among colleagues and toward students.

The strength of the implementation also lies to a large extent in the translation into daily life and the consistent application of each component. To this end, a clear step-by-step plan was drawn up for students and colleagues. In addition, there are, of course, the formal consultation moments with staff members during student counseling sessions, during class councils, and in conversations with parents and third parties.

7. **Cooperation With Third Parties**

A school is not an island and standing still is going backward. This is why it is extremely important to keep a clear vision and an open mind to the future. Internally, we draw up annual surveys for students and colleagues. But external organizations also visit our schools very often and from their interest, new partnerships grow. We banish complacency and continue to improve our approach where necessary. In addition, we work intensively with Create, the national training site for LSCI, and we are a member of the European Federation EFeCT. These and other collaborations are certainly a helping factor in keeping alive not only the methodology, but also the spirit behind LSCI.

8. **Passing On and Sharing With Partners Inside and Outside Education**

As a result of the transition from the previous sanctioning policy to a care policy and the pronounced positive results in terms of well-being and learning quality, interest grew among external organizations, the city of Leuven, the province, the University of Leuven, and the Ministry of Education. Today, we organize at least four training sessions in LSCI every year with our three senior trainers, and we are welcomed as speakers at many professional development days.

Final Thoughts

We look back with satisfaction and gratitude on the process of implementing LSCI. This is primarily due to the shift from the previous sanctioning policy to a care policy in which the well-being of employees and students is central. It is striking that, by taking into account universal needs, as described in the Circle of Courage and by using LSCI as an intervention method, the self-regulating capacity and resilience of young people and of colleagues are growing spectacularly. We, both students and adults, discover the importance of expressing our feelings, instead of suppressing them, which ultimately results in transgressive behavior.

"Thanks to the LSCI training, I am not only a better professional, but I can become a better parent and human being. LSCI should be a compulsory part of teacher training in Belgium."

The work is never finished, but we are hopeful.

A teacher and pedagogue put it as follows when she received her LSCI certificate: "Thanks to the LSCI training, I am not only a better professional, but I can become a better parent and human being. LSCI should be a compulsory part of teacher training in Belgium."

LSCI in the Flemish Community Institutions for Young Offenders

By Bram Soenen

In Flanders, most of the youth care is sponsored by private organizations. An exception to this is closed youth care, which is organized by the government itself in three community institutions (De Zande, De Grubbe, and De Kempen) and one Flemish detention center (De Wijngaard). These institutions have a total capacity of approximately 350 adolescents. Although youth are placed in the community institutions for delinquent behavior, the institutions are part of the Flemish youth care and not the justice system. In 2019, a new decree on youth delinquency was approved by the Flemish parliament. This new decree greatly impacted the goals and programs in community institutions by focusing on forensic themes such as restorative justice and reducing the risk of recidivism.

Evolutions That Led to LSCI

The initial implementation of LSCI in the community institutions took place around 2010. This period was characterized by several evolutions that resulted in the need for new approaches to dealing with challenging youth behavior. These evolutions paved the way to start with LSCI in the community institutions.

Population Shifts

A first evolution was a shift in target population. We noticed that youth with more complex problems and care needs were placed in the community institutions. This shift expressed itself not only in an increase of frequency and intensity of challenging behavior, but also in a greater unpredictability of student behavior. Staff felt they needed more skills to set up treatment plans for these youth, and the search for appropriate care became more urgent.

At the same time, we noticed a shift from a primarily group-oriented approach to an approach with more attention on the individual youngster. Along with activities for the whole living group, more and more individual activities were organized. Action points in the treatment plans of the youth evolved from action points concerning functioning in the living group to action points concerning knowledge or skills the youth needed in his own trajectory.

Pedagogical Shifts

A second evolution involved newly developing ideas within the pedagogical framework, especially considering how to respond to challenging behavior. In the past, challenging behavior was often approached from a merely behavioral point of view, with elements such as control and punishment. More and more, a strength-based approach found entrance, with attention to dialogue, needs behind behavior, youth's own choices and responsibility, and the idea of learning by acting together. Therefore, it is no coincidence that concepts such as restorative justice and experiential learning gained a foothold.

Enhancing Safety Awareness

The direct motives to start with LSCI were some specific incidents in the living groups in which youths' behavior endangered the safety of youth and staff. It was decided to implement LSCI with the aim of enhancing staff's safety awareness. Although the pedagogical and therapeutic climate was changing at that time, LSCI was situated rather in a safety discourse and only to a lesser extent in a pedagogical or therapeutic discourse.

The government then decided to free the budget for all staff of community institutions to attend the LSCI certification training. LSCI Trainers Franky D'Oosterlinck and Benny Leesen were asked to offer training, which was mandatory for all teachers, group workers, social workers, and therapists. This full training process took several years to roll out because of the large group of staff members. Despite all the trainings, it initially proved difficult to implement LSCI in daily practice, presumably because the goal of LSCI (to help children and youth in crisis) did not accord with the initial purpose of implementation (to enhance safety awareness of staff members).

Refocusing and Restarting

Some years later, the foundation had been laid, but the use of LSCI was diluted. At the beginning of 2019, we as the team of directors of De Zande, decided to restart the implementation of LSCI. Staff members still need the skills and understanding to cope with challenging youth behaviors, and as a team of directors, we strongly believe that LSCI can provide these skills. In an attempt to establish a more profound implementation and the effective use of LSCI in daily practice, we asked a group of staff members to develop a plan for this restart. Because of my own experience with LSCI I was part of this project group.

Within this current implementation plan, we focus on clarifying why we use LSCI (vision), on enhancing training competencies of our own staff, on intensive coaching, and on an integrative approach and anchoring in the programs. As such, LSCI is a now part of the community institutions' general policy on dealing with challenging behavior.

Theoretical Integration

A first step was aligning the vision of LSCI with the vision and objective of the community institutions. We wrote a new position statement on LSCI in our institution in which the primary safety discourse was left behind and replaced by a pedagogic and therapeutic discourse. This vision clarifies how conflicts are a part of daily life in the community institutions. We prefer to look at conflicts as learning opportunities and believe that LSCI can provide the necessary tools for our staff members.

Further, it is the mission of the of the Flemish community institutions to reduce the risk of recidivism as well as to enhance juveniles' well-being. In doing so, the community institutions have chosen an integrated implementation of the Risk-Need-Responsivity (RNR) model (Andrews & Bonta) and the Good Lives Model (GLM, Ward). Because we wanted to know whether the theoretical background of LSCI is compatible with our forensic mission, a theoretical fit between RNR and GLM and LSCI was sought and found. The relational component of LSCI and its positive impact on living climate can be seen as a responsivity factor from the RNR model (Andrews & Bonta). Further, use of incidents in the here and now (life space) helps to focus on the relevant criminogenic needs, as described by Andrews and Bonta, and primary goods, as described by Ward. It was concluded that LSCI should be seen as part of a broader entity of methodological action in forensic residential care.

In addition to this theoretical integration with our forensic models, we do not look upon LSCI as separated from our other methods and frameworks in daily practice. We strongly believe, for example, that LSCI can contribute to fulfilling basic human needs such as those identified in the Circle of Courage. Further, we use LSCI together with methods that help us in setting limits to disruptive behavior. LSCI can also facilitate the use of restorative justice. By integrating LSCI with other methods in our institutions, we have made LSCI a standard component of our forensic-orthopedagogical program.

> By integrating LSCI with other methods in our institutions, we have made LSCI a standard component of our forensic-orthopedagogical program.

Certification of Senior Trainers

Subsequently, we decided to let all staff members attend the LSCI certification training. Those who had already attended the training in the past could decide for themselves whether they wanted to attend the training a second time. Because we wanted to have our own LSCI Senior Trainers, staff members could also become candidates to be trained as Senior Trainers. A group of about ten candidates was selected and thoroughly prepared for this task. Although they all already had some years of experience with LSCI, they also had to go through the certification training again. Afterward, and in cooperation with Franky D'Oosterlinck, we provided them a four-day training in which LSCI was presented combined or integrated with other methods or models (contextual work, restorative work, Circle of Courage, psychophysical work), and with the integrative orthopedagogical theory (Broekaert) as the overarching framework. Further, the candidate-trainers used cases from their own practice to discuss the integration of LSCI in the individual treatment plans of the youngsters. The final step in this pathway was the "train the trainer" session of the LSCI Institute.

Supporting and Ongoing Coaching of LSCI-Certified Professionals

Along with certification training and refreshers, we also invest in supporting staff members in their use of LSCI. We are aware of the fact that LSCI can generate resistance for some colleagues. We want to give wide attention to coaching and supervision in order to attune the vision of the community institution, the vision of LSCI, and the vision of each team and each individual colleague, and to strengthen staff belief in their own skills. Through daily practice, our Senior Trainers and other staff members support each other by giving tips and tricks in approaching challenging behavior in general and use of LSCI specifically. Structural supervision moments are used to discuss cases more in depth and to link LSCI to the individual treatment plan of the youngster.

LSCI is a pillar of the program in the Flemish community institutions for young offenders.

Where Are We Now?

Although the implementation of methods such as LSCI is never finished, today we can state that LSCI is a pillar of the program in the Flemish community institutions for young offenders. The continuous interplay of development and explanation of vision, integrating LSCI in the broader methodical action, staff training, coaching and competence development, and the explicit choice of the government agency facilitates the further implementation of LSCI.

APPENDIX A

A Comparison of Traditional Accommodations and Accommodations Using the Lens for Adverse Childhood Experiences (ACEs)

What Do You Need?

Many of our students who need emotional support and resources do not have an IEP or 504 or a team of educators and staff available who consistently meet their social and emotional health needs each day! These students often come to school in a survival brain state and they are plagued by the adversities that have accumulated throughout the days, weeks, months, or years. This template is created collaboratively to support all students who come to school with significant Adverse Childhood Experiences. These supports and resources are for our children and youth who carry in pain-based behaviors, needing accommodations and possible modifications during the school day regarding their environments and schoolwork. These supports will address the critical needs of attachment and regulation. Often, as students move to different classrooms and environments, we are not consistent in providing a routine of two or three practices that students can implement to calm and regulate while building relationships with adults or other students throughout the school day.

What Can We Do to Make It Better?

We are not adding more work to what we are already doing; we are intentionally and transparently handling this child or adolescent with care and understanding that pain-based behaviors show up in disrespectful, defiant, or shut down ways and that these accommodations can occur naturally through our procedures, routines, transitions, morning bell work, and meetings!

How Can I Help?

We know that many of our roughest and most dysregulated students do not have these accommodations with accompanying accountability . . . or if they do, they are not consistently available and monitored! As a district, school, department, classroom, or grade level, we need to create these accommodations so they are consistently dispersed, discussed, and implemented each day.

Why?

If our social and emotional learning outcomes, programs, and competencies are to be reflective of the current brain research addressing the severe life disruptions/ trauma that are occurring in our student populations across the country, we need to address specific areas of brain development with regard to acquiring these competencies. Brain development is complex, and even today, we know very little about how individual regions of the brain work collectively through neuronal connections and projections. We do know, however, that human brains are not complete at birth, but, by design, continue to develop throughout a person's life. This development is intimately impacted by experiences. Because our students spend over 13,000 hours in school during their K-12 span, educators have the opportunity and the obligation to address social and emotional skills and competencies through creating the accommodations and adjustments needed for emotional, social, and cognitive well-being.

School Accommodations

Traditional Accommodations	Accommodations Using ACEs Lens
1. Seating at the front of the class	1. A seat where I feel safe and secure
2. Graph paper to line up math problems	2. Two adults in the building I can trust and a place to walk when I begin to feel triggered
3. Multiplication table or use of calculator	3. A personalized routine of three practices that I can implement when I begin to feel anxious, angry, or negative in any way (getting a sip of water, five deep breaths, drawing or creating with an art form for a couple of minutes)
4. Repetition and explanation of directions when needed	4. Access to sensory area or table in our classroom for patterned repetitive activities used to calm me down
5. Pre-printed classroom notes from the teachers	5. A personalized set of my accommodations given to all who work with me to allow me to de-escalate and calm down and become ready to learn

6. Occupational therapy every Wednesday	6. Meeting with my resiliency team each week (two or three individuals at school I trust)
7. Math one-on-one tutoring twice a week during study hall	7. One-on-one scheduled time with my pre-arranged mentor with whom I meet regularly as a check-in and who I can go see to help me co-regulate as needed

Test Accommodations

Traditional Accommodations	Accommodations Using ACEs Lens
1. Extended time on tests and quizzes	1. Extended time to regulate as needed and academic accommodations when I am dysregulated
2. Quiet testing room with small group setting	2. Quiet area for me to use when I need to regulate my nervous system—routine of three options (taking my pulse, drawing or writing in my journal, working in another classroom)

My Goals

Traditional Goals	Goals Using ACEs Lens
1. Improve my mental math skills	1. Lessen the number of times I need to use the resiliency team and the amygdala reset area
2. Get better at asking for help when needed	2. To learn to regulate with an adult before I reach the tipping point
3. Join a school club or activity	3. Create a journal of my ups and downs to track my progress

Note. From "Accommodations through an ACE's lens," by L. Desautels, 2019, *Revelations in Education* (http://revelationsineducation.com/wp-content/uploads/2020/02/%C2%A9Accommodations -Through-an-ACEs-lens-.pdf). © 2019 by Lori Desautels. Adapted with permission.

APPENDIX B

Full-size, printable checklists and forms are available.

www.proedsoftware.com/lsci/

CHECKLIST FOR RATING YOUR LSCI SKILLS

LIFE SPACE CRISIS
INTERVENTION

Name of Staff Person: _____   Name of Youth: _____

Start and End Time of LSCI: _____   Date: _____/_____/_____

Part One

Check the type of Reclaiming intervention selected by the Interviewer:

☐ Red Flag intervention

☐ Reality Check intervention

☐ New Tools intervention

☐ Benign Confrontation intervention

☐ Regulate and Restore intervention

☐ Peer Manipulation intervention

Check the steps the Interviewer used during the LSCI:

☐ Drain Off of emotional intensity

☐ Develop an accurate Timeline

☐ Define the Central Issue and select the most appropriate LSCI intervention

☐ Assist the youth in gaining Insight into self-defeating behavior patterns

☐ Develop a plan and practice New Skills

☐ Assist with Transfer of Learning and transition to ongoing activity

Part Two

From the following list, rate the skills the Interviewer used effectively during the LSCI:

1   Almost never
2   Sometimes
3   Often
4   Most always

NON-VERBAL BODY LANGUAGE				
Conveys support and alliance through body posture:	1	2	3	4
Uses eye contact or the opposite as needed to provide "space":	1	2	3	4
Varies voice quality and volume as needed:	1	2	3	4
Maintains physical proximity or distance as needed:	1	2	3	4

RELATIONSHIP SKILLS				
Engages in active listening:	1	2	3	4
Communicates respect for students:	1	2	3	4
Conveys confidence and optimism:	1	2	3	4
Avoids value judgments:	1	2	3	4
Avoids counter-aggression:	1	2	3	4

VERBAL STYLE				
Uses concrete words for clarity:	1	2	3	4
Decodes and affirms accurately:	1	2	3	4
Uses imagery to motivate:	1	2	3	4
Maximizes youth talk:	1	2	3	4
Uses a Timeline to help youth organize events:	1	2	3	4
Assists youth in seeing cause-and-effect relationships:	1	2	3	4
Uses "I-messages" vs. "You-messages"	1	2	3	4

LSCI INTERVIEWING SKILLS CHECKLIST

LIFE SPACE CRISIS
INTERVENTION

QUALITY OF INTERVENTION RATING TOOL

Rating Scale:
0 = Skill was not evident/used   1 = Skill was observed during intervention

1. DRAIN OFF OR DE-ESCALATION

	Rating
Reassurance: *"I am here to help. We're going to work this out."*	0 1
Decoding: *"I can see that you're upset . . ."* (name the feeling and validate)	0 1
Validation: *". . . and not for nothing. Something important must have happened."*	0 1
Affirmation: *"I like the way you're using words. You used to use your fists. That shows progress."*	0 1
Attending: *Show by your words, voice tones, and posture that you care and want to help.*	0 1

Remember: Do not begin the Timeline until the youth has begun to calm down.

2. TIMELINE

	Rating
Ask Questions: *Use the Conflict Cycle to find out the sequence of events.*	
• *"Help me understand what happened . . . Where? When? Who else? . . . etc."*	0 1
• *"What were you saying to yourself at the time?"*	0 1
• *"How did you feel . . .?"* (scaling 1–10)	0 1
• *"What did you do?"*	0 1
• *"What did others (adults/peers) do?"*	0 1
• *"What happened next?"*	0 1
• *"How were you feeling this morning?"* (check for Red Flags)	0 1
• *"Has this happened before?"* (look for a pattern)	0 1
Active Listening:	0 1
• Elaboration: *"Tell me more about . . ."*	0 1
• Neutral phrases to encourage talking: *"Uh-huh . . . I see . . . Oh?"*	0 1
• Paraphrase: *Repeat what was said in your own words.*	0 1
• Clarification: *"What do you mean by 'messing' with you?"*	0 1
• Summarizing: *"Let me see if I have it straight . . ."* (then repeat what you heard)	0 1
• Affirming: *Frequently give positive statements.* "Thank you for speaking with me." "You are doing a good job of remembering what happened."	0 1
Pursuit of Clues: *Listen for unusual comments. "You had to get up at 2 a.m.?"*	0 1
Drain Off Skills: *If the youth becomes dysregulated, utilize Drain Off skills.*	0 1

Remember: Really listen. Ask questions to discover the youth's point of view. Don't ask "Why?" Avoid trying
to solve the problem. Learn about the issue from the youth's point of view.

© 2021 by PRO-ED, Inc.   #40003

3. CENTRAL ISSUE

	Rating
Determine if this is one of the six LSCI self-defeating patterns of behavior and whether or not to move forward into a full LSCI. If appropriate to continue, identify which of the LSCI interventions (patterns) seems to be occurring for this youth. The Central Issue is your "a-ha" moment—your realization of the pattern. During the Insight stage, you will begin to help the youth to see the pattern.	0 1
State the Central Issue in age-appropriate language. Use the information from the Timeline to make it concrete for the young person. This is the beginning of the shift from your understanding of the self-defeating pattern to helping them realize the self-defeating pattern.	0 1

4. INSIGHT

	Rating
Selected LSCI Is Carried Out.	
Review the Timeline using the Socratic method of questioning and examples from the youth's experience to help them gain insight:	0 1
• Ask questions that will lead the youth to understanding.	
• Ask questions so that the youth will gain a new perspective.	
• Ask questions about other similar incidents, helping the youth to see the pattern. "Could it be possible?"	
• Ask questions that will lead the youth to an understanding of how this behavior is affecting their life.	
If the youth is not able to accept the Insight, plant the seed for future interventions ("It is just something to think about . . ."), move to New Skills. If the youth accepts the Insight (i.e., sees or considers the self-defeating pattern), move to New Skills.	0 1

Remember: Do NOT lecture or moralize. LEAD the youth to Insight by asking questions (except in New
Tools intervention) and using concrete examples.

5. NEW SKILLS

	Rating
Develop a personal plan with new social emotional skills or new practical strategies based on Insight.	0 1
• Brainstorm potential solutions.	
• Discuss pros and cons of each solution.	
• Ask the youth which solution they want to use. Which option is most likely to help?	
Teach the social-emotional skills or strategies in a developmentally appropriate manner.	0 1
Role-play/rehearse the new social-emotional skills in a few contexts. If the youth suggests something that you think will not be successful, one strategy might be to say, "OK, if you do that, let's follow that through—what would happen next?"	0 1
Discuss consequences of behavior (suspension, restitution, loss of privileges, etc.).	0 1

Remember: Rehearse so that the youth will be successful with the new skill.

6. TRANSFER OF LEARNING

	Rating
Discuss current activity and how peers/staff may react to the youth's return.	0 1
Role-play the youth's reentry and Plan for Success for use in current activity/class.	0 1
Share the reentry and Plan for Success with key staff; discuss ways to help the youth with the plan.	0 1

Remember: Rehearse so the youth will be successful returning to the ongoing activity.

Note. From *LSCI Certification Course Participant's Manual* by N. Long, F. Fecser, and S. Whitson, 2017. © 2007 by Carol Dawson.
Adapted with permission.

© 2021 by PRO-ED, Inc.   #40003

LSCI
TRACKING AND FIDELITY FORM

LIFE SPACE CRISIS
INTERVENTION

Date: _____ / _____ / _____   Youth Name: _____   Setting or Location: _____

Staff Name: _____   Staff Position: _____

Time Began: _____   Time Ended: _____   Total LSCI Time: _____

Intensity of Incident: Stage of Escalating Behavior When LSCI Began
(1 = low; 5 = high) 1 2 3 4 5 □ Regulated □ Agitated □ Accelerated □ Peak □ De-escalated □ Recovery □ Regulated

LSCI TYPES, STAGES, AND OUTCOMES	
DIAGNOSTIC STAGES	**RECLAIMING STAGES**
1. DRAIN OFF	**4. INSIGHT**
□ Validated youth's feelings	□ Identified self-defeating pattern of behavior
□ Used "I-Messages"	□ Youth gained new Insight
□ Used attending, reassuring, validating, affirming, and decoding	Indicate Which Reclaiming Intervention to Address Self-Defeating Pattern
□ Avoided the Conflict Cycle	□ Red Flag □ Reality Check □ New Tools
Outcomes for Drain Off Intervention	□ Peer Manipulation □ Benign Confrontation
□ Youth has calmed down	□ Regulate and Restore
□ Safety was established or no longer a concern	Outcomes for Insight-Oriented Intervention
	□ Youth ___hears, ___accepts, ___articulates the self-defeating pattern (In)
2. TIMELINE	**5. NEW SKILLS**
□ Used interviewing skills to hear the youth's story	□ Pro-social skills were identified
□ Youth indicated that they felt understood	□ Self-regulation skills were identified
□ Used core listening skills to discover the youth's point of view	□ Self-monitoring skills were identified
□ Validated the youth's perception of the situation/crisis	□ Practice/role-playing was done to illustrate these skills
3. CENTRAL ISSUE	**6. TRANSFER OF LEARNING**
□ Identified how the youth perceives, thinks, feels, and behaves during a crisis	□ Staff consulted with each other to understand and address the youth's self-defeating behavior
□ Determined that a short-term intervention was sufficient	□ Staff adjusted behavioral plans/guidance forms/etc. in order to track the pattern
□ Determined that the Central Issue would be best managed by using one of six LSCIs	□ New skills training will be addressed by the treatment team/classroom team
Outcomes for Diagnostic Intervention	
□ Youth understands why this crisis happened and their role (Issue)	
□ Adult establishes the Central Issue or self-defeating pattern (CI)	

Stage of Escalating Behavior When LSCI Ended

□ Regulated □ Agitated □ Accelerated □ Peak □ De-escalated □ Recovery □ Regulated

Comments (optional): *(continue on back of page if necessary)*

Name of Person Completing LSCI and Documentation: _____

LSCI REFLECTION FORM

LIFE SPACE CRISIS
INTERVENTION

Student: _____   LSCI Facilitator: _____   Date: _____/_____/_____

Location of Incident Prompting LSCI _____   Duration of LSCI: _____

1. Student's emotional level on arrival was:

☐ *Regulated and calm* (body and voice are relaxed; is communicating effectively using words; is emotionally well-regulated)

☐ *Agitated or defensive* (body rigid or hyper-energized; easily angers; resistant to verbal communication; may manifest as externalized or internalized behaviors)

☐ *Escalated* (in a sustained highly emotional state; unavailable to verbal support or mediation)

☐ *Highly escalated/unsafe* (may be unsafe to self or others; may require physical containment)

2. Student was able to:

☐ *Drain Off* emotions and settle down; begin to use words to describe what happened (is generally "regulated" per definition above)

☐ Describe (*Timeline*) his/her perspective of the sequence of events: ☐ prior to ☐ leading up to ☐ during the incident (Check (✔) which achieved)

☐ Connect words to feelings. Named feelings:

_____

☐ Identify stressors (i.e., stress triggers both distal and proximal) that may have impacted thoughts, emotions, actions/behaviors:

_____

_____

☐ Demonstrate *Insight* that the result of the incident (or pattern) may be self-defeating or goal-defeating

---

☐ Identify and practice a strategy or a *New Skill* that addresses the LSCI *Central Issue*:

    ☐ **Red Flag** (identify and deal with the real source of stress)

    ☐ **Reality Check** (see a different perspective or new way to understand the sequence of events)

    ☐ **New Tools** (learn a new social-emotional solution)

    ☐ **Benign Confrontation** (foster value of social responsibility)

    ☐ **Regulate and Restore** (nurture self-regulation skills)

    ☐ **Peer Manipulation** (find positive friendships; avoid exploitation)

☐ Identify and practice a stress reduction or stress management strategy to help regain better self-control:

_____

☐ Demonstrate readiness to reenter class (or activity) through engaged behavior, evidence of effective emotional regulation.

3. Anything teacher needs to know:

4. If needed, identify plan to contact home (behavioral support, administrator, community support):

LSCI REENTRY GUIDELINES

Student: _____   LSCI Facilitator: _____

Date: _____/_____/_____

Staff Roles and Responsibilities

When youth returns, *act in ways that will increase the likelihood that reentry will be successful:*

- ☐ Let go of emotions that may make successful reentry less likely.
- ☐ Sincerely welcome youth back (be glad to see him/her).
- ☐ Validate youth perspective.
- ☐ Model responsibility/accountability. *If appropriate, model ownership for your own part in a conflict.*
- ☐ Share your perspective with the LSCI facilitator when he/she checks in with you.

Check (✓) if recommended:

- ☐ Complete an LSCI Tracking and Fidelity form
- ☐ Contact parent: promote partnership
- ☐ Other: _____

LSCI Facilitator Roles and Responsibilities

- ☐ Developed Plan for Success with youth.
- ☐ Followed up with youth after their initial return to class:
  - • Will provide affirmation for successful reentry.
  - • Will check on implementation of youth role in plan.
    - • Will validate youth concerns.
    - • Will promote positive relationship.
- ☐ Followed up with staff:
  - • Will *seek first to understand:* Get staff perspective.
    - • Will check on staff role in Plan for Success.
    - • Will promote partnership.

Check (✓) if to do:

- ☐ Contact parent: promote partnership
- ☐ Contact key school/program personnel
- ☐ Contact community support
- ☐ Other: _____

Youth Roles and Responsibilities

Check (✓) if completed:

- ☐ Identified a plan to restore relationships and classroom/group belonging (as needed).
- ☐ Considered:
  - ☐ Do I need to speak with staff/peer to resolve a conflict? Who? _____
    When? _____
  - ☐ Do I need to practice what to say?
  - ☐ Is there work (e.g., school work) I need to get done?
  - ☐ Is there anything else to take care of before returning?

- ☐ Practiced Plan for Success.

LIFE SPACE CRISIS INTERVENTION
COURSE SURVEY

PRE / POST (CIRCLE ONE)

Name: _____

School/Organization: _____ Date: ____/____/____

Please circle the number that currently rates your ability in the following areas:

1. I am aware of how positive relationships between adults and youth foster positive outcomes.

1	2	3	4
Strongly Disagree	Disagree	Agree	Strongly Agree

2. I have knowledge of how a young person's brain typically responds to stressful situations.

1	2	3	4
Strongly Disagree	Disagree	Agree	Strongly Agree

3. I can identify the elements of a young person's psychological world and describe how they relate to behavior.

1	2	3	4
Strongly Disagree	Disagree	Agree	Strongly Agree

4. I can identify the elements of a Conflict Cycle.

1	2	3	4
Strongly Disagree	Disagree	Agree	Strongly Agree

5. I am able to de-escalate a youth experiencing distress.

1	2	3	4
Strongly Disagree	Disagree	Agree	Strongly Agree

6. I am able to identify the specific triggers to the problem behavior by talking to the youth.

1	2	3	4
Strongly Disagree	Disagree	Agree	Strongly Agree

7. I am able to help a youth reflect upon his/her behavior and understand the underlying reason for the problem behavior.

1	2	3	4
Strongly Disagree	Disagree	Agree	Strongly Agree

8. I am able to help a youth select a replacement behavior that meets the same need as the problem behavior and teach/rehearse until the youth is comfortable using the new skill.

1	2	3	4
Strongly Disagree	Disagree	Agree	Strongly Agree

9. I am able to share the plan for a replacement behavior with key staff so that we can all help the youth learn to cope with similar situations.

1	2	3	4
Strongly Disagree	Disagree	Agree	Strongly Agree

10. There are fewer crisis incidents due to my ability to respond to young people in distress.

1	2	3	4
Strongly Disagree	Disagree	Agree	Strongly Agree

11. I am confident in my abilities to respond to young people in distress in an effective and efficient manner.

1	2	3	4
Strongly Disagree	Disagree	Agree	Strongly Agree

LSCI PLAN FOR SUCCESS

Instructions: Staff and youth complete this form together to plan for positive outcomes following a stressful situation.

Date: _____/_____/_____   Youth Name: _____ Staff Name: _____

1. What happened?

2. What did I learn from the situation?

3. What solutions were agreed upon?

4. What are the benefits for me of this solution?

5. What new skills have I practiced?

6. Who or what was hurt?

© 2021 by PRO-ED, Inc.   #40003

---

7. What do I need to do to make things right?

8. Do I need to apologize to anyone? If so, to whom and why?

9. Are there any consequences as a result of what happened? How will I show responsibility?

10. What will I do when something like this happens again in the future?

11. Who are two people I can go to for help when I feel upset or triggered?

12. What are three strategies I can use to calm myself down when I begin to feel upset?

13. What are some likely things that may happen when I return? How can I respond in an effective way?

© 2021 by PRO-ED, Inc.   #40003

REFERENCES

Acharya, S., & Shukla, S. (2012). Mirror neurons: Enigma of the metaphysical modular brain. *Journal of Natural Science, Biology, and Medicine, 3*(2), 118–124. https://doi.org/10.4103/0976-9668.101878

Baars, B., & Gage, N. (2010). *Cognition, brain, and consciousness: Introduction to cognitive neuroscience* (2nd ed.). Elsevier, Ltd.

Beck, M. (2008). He gave me the finger! A manipulation of body boundaries intervention. *Reclaiming Children and Youth, 17*(3), 54–57.

Canadian Mental Health Association. (2019, October 17). *The importance of human connection.* CMHA National. https://cmha.ca/blogs/the-importance-of-human-connection

Center on the Developing Child, Harvard University. (2020). *Resilience.* Center on the Developing Child. https://developingchild.harvard.edu/science/key-concepts/resilience

Centers for Disease Control & Prevention. (2020, April 3). *Preventing adverse childhood experiences.* CDC. https://www.cdc.gov/violenceprevention/childabuseandneglect/aces/fastfact.html

Cherry, K. (2019, October 31). *Differences between implicit and explicit long-term memory.* VeryWell Mind. https://www.verywellmind.com/implicit-and-explicit-memory-2795346

Dawson, C. A. (2001). *Crisis intervention training and support for school staff of junior high school special education students with emotional disturbance* [Practicum II report, Nova Southeastern University]. ERIC Documentation Reproduction Service No. ED 477 212.

Dawson, C. A., & McBride, A. (2014). Experiences and beliefs activity. In *Fundamentals of behavior support: Tier 1 strategies from life space crisis intervention.* New York City Department of Education Special Education Office.

Desautels, L. (2016, March 31). Contagious emotions and responding to stress, *Scholarship and Professional Work – Education, 94.* https://digitalcommons.butler.edu/coe_papers/94

Desautels, L. (2019). *A comparison of traditional accommodations and accommodations using the lens of adverse childhood experiences (ACEs) as well as adverse community environments.* Revelations in Education. http://revelationsineducation.com/resource-comparison-of-traditional-accommodations-and-accommodations-using-the-lens-for-adverse-childhood-experiences

D'Oosterlinck, F., & Broekaert, E. (2003). Integrating school-based and therapeutic conflict management models in schools. *Journal of School Health, 73*(6), 222–225.

D'Oosterlinck, F., Goethals, I., Broekaert, E., Schuyten, G., & De Maeyer, J. (2008). Implementation and effect of life space crisis intervention in special schools with residential treatment for students with emotional and behavioral disorders (EBD). *Psychiatric Quarterly, 79*(1), 65–79.

Ehmke, R. (n.d.). *What is PSTD?* Child Mind Institute. https://childmind.org/article/what-is-ptsd

Forbes, H. T. (2012). *Help for Billy: A beyond consequences approach to helping challenging children in the classroom.* Beyond Consequences Institute, LLC.

Freado, M. (2007). I can't hold it in forever: Connecting with a youth in pain. *Reclaiming Children and Youth, 15*(4), 229–233.

Freado, M. (2014). The three part message [MOOC lecture]. In *Level 2: LSCI refresher course.* Life Space Crisis Intervention. https://www.lsci.org/modules/stage-1-drain-off/

Freeman, J. (2015). Developing social skills and relationships. *Reclaiming Children and Youth, 23*(4), 48–51.

Freeman, J., & Garfat, T. (2014). Being, interpreting, doing: A framework for organizing the characteristics of a relational child and youth care approach. *Child & Youth Care Online, 179,* 23–27.

Frye, R. E. (2018). Social skills deficits in autism spectrum disorder: Potential biological origins and progress in developing therapeutic agents. *CNS Drugs, 32*(8), 713–734. https://doi.org/10.1007/s40263-018-0556-y

Garfat, T., & Fulcher, L. C. (2012). Characteristics of a relational child and youth care approach. In T. Garfat & L. C. Fulcher (Eds.), *Child and youth care in practice* (pp. 5–24). Pretext.

Ginnot, H. (1993). *Teacher and child: A book for parents and teachers.* Scribner. (Original work published 1972)

Goldman, C. (2012). *Bullied: What every parent, teacher, and kid needs to know about ending the cycle of fear.* Harper One.

Greene, R. (2008). *Lost at school: Why our kids with behavioral challenges are falling through the cracks and how we can help them.* Scribner.

Hanson, R. (2020). *Confronting the negativity bias.* Rick Hanson. https://www.rickhanson.net/how-your-brain-makes-you-easily-intimidated/

Hewitt, M. B., & Long, N. (1999). False alarm: A massaging numb values intervention. *Reclaiming Children and Youth, 8*(2), 112–116.

Kessler, R. C., McLaughlin, K. A., Green, J. G., Gruber, M. J., Sampson, N. A., Zaslavsky, A. M., Aguilar-Gaxiola, S., Alhamzawi, A. O., Alonso, J., Angermeyer, M., Benjet, C., Bromet, E., Chatterji, S., de Girolamo, G., Demyttenaere, K., Fayyad, J., Florescu, S., Gal, G., Gureje, O., . . . Williams, D. R. (2010). Childhood adversities and adult psychopathology in the WHO World Mental Health Surveys. *The British Journal of Psychiatry, 197*(5), 378–385. https://doi.org/10.1192/bjp.bp.110.080499.

King, J. A. (2020, March 28). *COVID-19: Our brains, our bodies, our trauma.* Medium. https://medium.com/@jak292/covid-19-our-brains-our-bodies-our-trauma-8ece7779cc9b

Lieberman, M. D. (2014). *Social: Why our brains are wired to connect.* Broadway Books.

Long, N., Long, J., & Whitson S. (2016). *The angry smile: Effective strategies to manage passive-aggressive behavior at home, at school, in relationships, in the workplace and online.* The LSCI Institute.

Mann, E., & Muscott, H. (2014). Effective listening skills. In *Life space crisis intervention certification course trainer's manual.* Life Space Crisis Intervention.

Mayo Clinic Staff. (2017, November 18). *Narcissistic personality disorder.* Mayo Clinic. https://www.mayoclinic.org/diseases-conditions/narcissistic-personality-disorder/symptoms-causes/syc-20366662

McBride, A., & Dawson, C. A. (2014). Personal plan for button pushing activity. In *Fundamentals of behavior support: Tier 1 strategies from life space crisis intervention.* New York City Department of Education Special Education Office.

Nawrocki, M. (2018). *Thanks for chucking that at the wall instead of at me: Teaching at-risk children and youth.* Brush Education, Inc.

O'Mara, Peggy (2000). *Natural family living: The Mothering Magazine guide to parenting.* Pocket Books.

Perry, B. (2020, March 26). *State-dependent brain functioning: Neurosequential network stress & trauma series* [Video]. YouTube. https://www.youtube.com/watch?v=PZg1dlskBLA&feature=youtu.be

Perry, B., & Szalavitz, M. (2017). *The boy who was raised as a dog and other stories from a child psychiatrist's notebook: What traumatized children can teach us about loss, love, and healing.* Basic Books.

Porges, S. (2015, December 9). *Polyvagal theory and how trauma impacts the body* [Video]. YouTube. https://www.youtube.com/watch?v=iAqiiOy4IyQ

Redl, F. (1959). The concept of a therapeutic milieu. *American Journal of Orthopsychiatry, 29*(b), 721–736.

Redl, F. (1966). *When we deal with children.* The Free Press.

Stuart, C. (2013). *Foundations of child and youth care* (2nd ed.). Kendall Hunt.

Taylor, R. D., Oberle, E., Durlak, J. A., & Weissberg, R. P. (2017). Promoting positive youth development through school-based social and emotional learning interventions: A meta-analysis of follow-up effects. *Society for Research in Child Development, 88*(4), 1156–1171. https://srcd.onlinelibrary.wiley.com/doi/full/10.1111/cdev.12864

Thompson, R., Flaherty, E. G., English, D. J., Litrownik, A. J., Dubowitz, H., Kotch, J. B., & Runyan, D. K. (2015). Trajectories of adverse childhood experiences and self-reported health at age 18. *Academic Pediatrics, 15*(5), 503–509. https://doi.org/10.1016/j.acap.2014.09.010.

US Department of Health and Human Services, Administration for Children and Families, Children's Bureau, Child Welfare Information Gateway. (n.d.). *Adverse childhood experiences (ACEs).* https://www.childwelfare.gov/topics/preventing/overview/framework/aces

van der Kolk, B. (2002). *In terror's grip: Healing the ravages of trauma.* Cerebrum.

van der Kolk, B. (2014). *The body keeps the score: Brain, mind and body in the healing of trauma.* Penguin Books.

Wachtel, T., & McCold, P. (2004, August 5). *From restorative justice to restorative practices: Expanding the paradigm* [Paper presentation]. IIRP's Fifth International Conference on Conferencing, Circles and other Restorative Practices, Vancouver, British Columbia, Canada. https://www.iirp.edu/news/from-restorative-justice-to-restorative-practices-expanding-the-paradigm

Werner, A. (1981). Massaging numb values interview. *Pointer, 25*(2), 29–31.

Walker, B., & Muscott, H. (2020). *How features of LSCI fit within the multitiered model.* The LSCI Institute. https://www.lsci.org/learn-more/pbis-lsci

Whitson, S. (2019). *Parenting the challenging child: The 4-step way to turn problem situations into learning opportunities.* The LSCI Institute.

Williams, G., & Wood, M. (2010). *Developmental art therapy in the classroom* (2nd ed.). Developmental Therapy Institute.

Wood, M. M., Quirk, C. A., & Swindle, F. L. (2007). *Teaching responsible behavior: Developmental therapy-developmental teaching for troubled children and adolescents* (4th ed.). PRO-ED.

Wood, M. M. (1996). Vibes, values, and virtues. *Reclaiming Children and Youth* (5)3, 17.

Wood, M. M. (2015). The heritage of psychoeducation with troubled students. *Reclaiming Children and Youth, 24*(1), 33–37.

INDEX